CLIMBING
the LADDER
of SUCCESS

DAVID —
TO YOUR SUCCESS!

CLIMBING
the LADDER
of SUCCESS

---

19 valuable lessons

for increasing your performance and your results

DOUGLAS SMITH

TRAFFORD

Printed in Victoria, Canada.

Note for Librarians: a cataloguing record for this book that includes Dewey Classification and US Library of Congress numbers is available from the National Library of Canada. The complete cataloguing record can be obtained from the National Library's online database at:
www.nlc-bnc.ca/amicus/index-e.html
ISBN 1-4120-2066-2

TRAFFORD

This book was published on-demand in cooperation with Trafford Publishing.
On-demand publishing is a unique process and service of making a book available for retail sale to the public taking advantage of on-demand manufacturing and Internet marketing. On-demand publishing includes promotions, retail sales, manufacturing, order fulfilment, accounting and collecting royalties on behalf of the author.

Suite 6E, 2333 Government St., Victoria, B.C. V8T 4P4, CANADA
Phone   250-383-6864   Toll-free   1-888-232-4444 (Canada & US)
Fax   250-383-6804   E-mail   sales@trafford.com
Web site www.trafford.com   TRAFFORD PUBLISHING IS A DIVISION OF TRAFFORD HOLDINGS LTD.
Trafford Catalogue #03-2645   www.trafford.com/robots/03-2645.html
10   9   8   7   6   5   4   3   2

For my wife Kirsten,
who has helped me climb my own ladder of success.

— Contents —

Introduction — 9

19 valuable lessons

1 Climb a Ladder One Step at a Time — 13

2 Turn Your Time into Money — 17

3 Create More Opportunities to Sell — 23

4 Relationships Are Built on Trust — 27

5 Speed up the Process — 33

6 Knowledge Is Money — 41

7 Keep Flying High! — 49

8 Managing Your Money Wisely — 55

9 Find a Mentor — 63

10 Play More Offense — 69

11 Learn to Let Go — 77

12 Spend Your Money Where You Make It — 83

13 Preparation Pays Off — 89

14 Don't Be a Part-Time Originator — 95

15 Satisfied Customers Are not Enough — 99

16 Put Your Ideas into Action — 105

17 Move up to the Next Level — 111

18 Start Thinking like a Superstar — 117

19 It's All About Commitment — 125

— Introduction —

Have you ever wondered why some mortgage loan originators are more successful in their business than others? Why is it that some turn out to be high performers while others are just average?

I have spent the last twenty years of my life immersed in all aspects of the mortgage industry: retail lending, sales management, training, marketing, coaching, and consulting. I have had the good fortune to meet and work with hundreds of extremely successful loan officers. I have also had the opportunity to know just as many who were mediocre, or who simply didn't make it.

When I first got into this business I searched for a road map or guide showing how to do this business right. I figured that someone, over the home financing industry's one hundred year history, had sat down to write *The Mortgage Origination Manual to Success*. That manual didn't exist. I realized that if I wanted to be successful in loan origination I had to figure it out on my own or watch what successful people were doing, and then try to emulate them.

This approach presents a problem for originators who don't have the luxury of a successful mentor. They are forced to fly by the seat of their pants and hope to someday find someone to help show the way. The latter is what this book is all about.

This book is a collection of nineteen lessons in success. It contains the highlights of what I have learned during the past twenty years in mortgage origination. It's the kind of book you can read a little at a time or all at once. Its lessons are timeless. It's a perfect book for any mortgage loan originator who is looking for answers, ideas, and the right formula to make it in this business. It's a book for you.

The title of this book, *Climbing the Ladder of Success*, is quite deliberate. The word *Climbing* infers that rewards and success in this business (or any business for that matter) do not come easily. It takes work, effort, and determination to reach new heights of personal achievement. The metaphor of a *ladder* suggests career advancements in levels, one step at a time. No loan originator, no matter how talented, scales the ladder of success in one giant leap. Some, however, scale it more quickly than others. Finally, *success* is what almost everyone strives for in this business. We all define success a bit differently; for some, success is measured in income, for others in production volume, loan units, or company awards. In whatever way you define success in your business, you must define it. It is difficult, if not impossible, to achieve success in your mortgage lending career if you are not sure what success really means to you.

As you read through the nineteen lessons for success in this book, you'll discover that each lesson is simple, practical, and relevant to every loan originator at any stage of his or her career. You won't find any high-altitude strategies or theories in these pages. It's all brass tacks–straightforward and real world. It's nineteen pieces of tangible advice combined with hundreds of tactical ideas that you can put to use tomorrow morning. It's how I've taught thousands of originators to be successful. It's how I want to teach you, too. More than anything else, it's my desire to help you achieve the level of success in this business that you are willing to work for. Let the lessons begin!

"You cannot push anyone up a ladder unless he is willing to climb himself."

— *Andrew Carnegie*

— Lesson 1 —

Climb a Ladder One Step at a Time

Picture for a moment, a ladder–a tall one. That ladder represents your career in the mortgage business. The bottom rung symbolizes your first step, taking a job as a loan originator. The top rung is the pinnacle of a highly successful and profitable career. The higher you climb, the greater the risk and the greater the reward. Each step means added success and along with that, added commitment. The question is: *How high do you want to climb?*

So, you say you want to be on top . . . or as close to the top as you can get. You're enticed by the money, the recognition, and the personal gratification of being one of the best in the business. That's terrific! Now ask yourself: *Am I willing to do what it will take to get there?* Those people at the top of the ladder of success in our business didn't arrive there overnight, or as the result of dumb luck. It took them time, dedication, hard work, and passion to climb each step. Perhaps the biggest reason there are so many mediocre performers in the mortgage industry is not so much that they don't know what to do, they simply aren't willing to do it. Talk to those on top. You'll learn that most successful originators share a similar story: In climbing the ranks of the mortgage business, just like climbing a ladder, the steps are laid out for you. You just have to be willing to grab hold and climb.

Not everyone can be a superstar in this business. For that matter, not everyone wants to be a superstar. I once spoke with a loan originator who averaged $15,000,000 to $20,000,000 in production a year. He was completely happy. He had worked to climb his personal ladder of success to a certain level and enjoyed all that he'd achieved. While I had no doubt he could produce and earn more, he really didn't want to. "I know I could do fifty million a year," he told me. "But I also realize what that means in terms of hard work and sacrifice. That's great for some, but not me. I'm happy with my success."

Perhaps you too are satisfied with where you are in your climb to the top. As long as it provides you with the income you want and it contributes to your company's results, good for you. But if on the other hand, you are not as high on the ladder of success as you aspire to be, you must ask yourself: *Am I willing to do what it will take to get there?*

What are your reactions to the following ten questions?

1   Am I willing to work more hours than I do now?
2   Am I willing to work some Saturdays and Sundays?
3   Am I willing to invest as much as 5% to 10% of my yearly income in personal marketing?
4   Am I willing to maintain a customer database and contact my borrower clients and prospects throughout the year?
5   Am I willing to take more risks and try new and different things?
6   Am I willing to embrace new technology and adapt it to my way of doing business?
7   Am I willing to build a detailed business plan every year and follow it with discipline?
8   Am I willing to hire support staff and pay their salaries out of my pocket?

9 Am I willing to read books, attend seminars, study loan products and train hard to become a master of my trade?

10 Am I willing to hire a personal coach or mentor to help me run my business?

Some pretty serious questions, right? Note that they don't ask, *can* you do these things. You *could* do every one if you wanted to. They ask, are you *willing* to do them. Each one of these steps is a rung on the ladder to success. Climbing them is how super-successful mortgage originators got to the top. How you answer these ten questions will show your real desire to make the climb.

Start today by deciding what you want out of your career. Do you want to earn $50,000 a year? You'll have to be willing to do certain things. Maybe $100,000? To do that, you must be willing to do more than you would to make $50,000. Some might say they want to achieve an income of $500,000, or even as much as $1,000,000. Great! You know it can be done, because other originators are doing it right now. But I guarantee that they are working a lot harder and are much more invested in their careers than those making $50,000 or $100,000. Each step up the ladder of success requires more of you in every way.

The message is simple: *As your desire for greater success grows, so does the price you must be willing to pay to achieve that success.* With that in mind, let's do a little exercise.

1 **Write down what you produced in total loan volume last year.** Under that number, make a list of the key things you did to achieve that result. These might include sales activities, marketing, client retention strategies, learning initiatives, your work schedule and more. This project may take you twenty or thirty minutes, but it's important to start here.

2 **Next, write down your production goal for this year.** Is this more than what you originated last year? Good! Now, list what you plan to do differently than you did last year. Remember the old saying: *If you always do what you've always done, you will always get what you've always got.* Some loan originators repeat the same activities each year and wonder why they aren't producing more business. To get more, you have to do more . . . Period.

3 **Finally, write down your dream production goal.** Envision the absolute best you'd like to achieve at the height of your career. What do you think you'll have to do to get there? What major steps must you be prepared to take? Are you willing to take those steps? Describe what your business would look like at that production level. How many hours would you be working? How many people would be on staff? How much marketing would that volume require? If you are not sure, talk to people already at that level of success. Discover what they are doing. Chances are, you'll be doing the same.

We all climb our own ladder of success, and we all reach different heights in our careers. Ask yourself: *How high do I really want to go?* Then, set a long-term plan to get there. Break down that plan into a series of steps or activities (rungs on your ladder) and get started on your first step tomorrow morning, no matter how small that step might be. Don't worry about looking up that tall ladder and thinking of all that's ahead of you. Just look at the next step, grab hold, and take it. You are now officially on your way. Even a journey of a thousand miles begins with a single step.

— Lesson 2 —

Turn Your Time into Money

How do you spend your time? That's a tough question for many mortgage originators to answer accurately. In a typical week, you may put in 40, 50, 60 hours or even more. Within those hours of work are hundreds of activities–some productive, some not.

One of the biggest challenges mortgage originators face each day is how to properly plan and organize their time. Ask yourself the following questions:

- ▸ Do I often feel I don't have enough hours in the day?
- ▸ Am I constantly playing catch-up?
- ▸ Do I have trouble getting out of the office?
- ▸ Am I frequently doing someone else's job for them?
- ▸ Do I try to take on too much at once?
- ▸ Am I still unclear of where my time should really be spent?

Answering yes to any or all of the above questions places you in the same category as most mortgage originators. The daily challenge of job organization and time management is a simple fact of life. No one will ever completely master it.

But there are some loan originators who manage their time better than others. How do they do it?

High performing loan originators understand that having a clear picture of where they want to go, a good road map for how to get there, and the discipline to take control of their time is *essential* to long-term success. They have developed good work habits and routines that keep their hours and activities productive and profitable. For these successful people, time truly is money.

Suppose you work 50 weeks a year and put in an average of 50 hours a week. That equates to 2,500 hours of work a year. If you're on track to earn $100,000 this year, your time is worth $40 an hour. Are you earning what you're worth? Are the tasks that occupy your time most days at least $40-an-hour tasks?

Much is said about the topic of time management. But, technically, you can't manage time. You cannot change it, add to it, speed it up, or slow it down. A common mistake some originators make is to try to organize time with various systems. What they fail to realize is that although a system can help organize activities, the key is to make those activities productive. Poor time management habits combined with a lack of discipline can rob valuable hours each week and thousands in yearly income. So how can you become more productive? Simply by spending more of your time in more productive activities every day.

Try the following exercise. Take out a clean sheet of paper and divide it into two columns. Label one column HIGH PRODUCTIVITY and the other column LOW PRODUCTIVITY. Write down on the high productivity list the activities that you feel are the most profitable use of your time as a mortgage originator. This list might include:

▸ Taking loan applications
▸ Making sales calls on quality referral clients
▸ Following up on leads and pre-qualification prospects
▸ Personal marketing

- ▸ Community events and sponsorships
- ▸ Pipeline management and file review
- ▸ Group presentations
- ▸ Booking new referral client appointments

You may end up with ten to twenty business activities in which you are highly productive. (Really! Put the book down and do this now. It's an interesting exercise!)

Now, compile a list of low productivity, low profit activities. Include things that occupy your time but do little to drive your production and income goals. This list might include:

- ▸ Personal errands and phone calls
- ▸ Dealing with high maintenance or low volume real estate agents
- ▸ Processing loans and chasing down loan conditions
- ▸ Office gossip and chitchat
- ▸ Delivering packets and papers around town
- ▸ Driving long distances to visit remote clients
- ▸ Faxing, copying, scanning, filing and paperwork

This list will contain work-related activities that occupy your time on a regular basis but do little to make you money. Think of all the stuff you do each day and write it all down.

Now, stare at the two lists for a moment. Glance back and forth. Where do you spend the bulk of your day? How much of your time is spent on the HIGH PRODUCTIVITY side and how much on the LOW PRODUCTIVITY side? Is a typical day filled with non-revenue-producing tasks that eat up valuable time? Is what you do every hour worth your personal hourly wage?

If this exercise was an eye-opener, then perhaps you wish to do something about it. The first step is to believe that you can. Many originators can simply change their work habits and become much more productive and profitable. The key is not to work more hours; the key is to do more *productive activities* in the hours you already work.

Your optimum goal is to achieve a 70% productivity level. That means that 70% of your average day would be invested in high productivity activities, leaving 30% for everything else. (It would be impossible to become a total productivity machine and be productive 100% of the time. There are always other things we must do.) As an example, in a ten-hour work day, seven hours of your day (70%) would be invested in productive activities, leaving three hours a day (30%) for anything on the LOW PRODUCTIVITY list. You can do this! Here are five suggestions to get you there:

1 Eliminate or delegate absolutely everything on your LOW PRODUCTIVITY list that you possibly can. If it doesn't need to be done, or if you can get (or pay) someone else to do it, move these activities out of your world . . . fast! They are blocking your chances for success.

2 Review the HIGH PRODUCTIVITY list and ask yourself which activities on the list you are most serious about spending your time doing. Perhaps you want to make more sales calls or expand your database marketing. Pick one or two activities and commit yourself to making more time for these moneymaking activities. This alone will squeeze out some of the less productive ones.

3 Leave your comfort zone. The reason many loan originators spend so much time processing paperwork, filing, faxing and delivering packets is to keep them from doing the things they are afraid to do, such as sales calls, presentations and setting appointments. While busywork can fill up your day, it's time to admit that you aren't making money by doing it. To illustrate: A $100,000 a year originator earns $40 an hour. If he spends most of his time processing, then he's a $40-an-hour loan processor! Does that make sense?

4 **Schedule highly productive activities on your calendar as you would schedule appointments.** Schedule time each week for sales visits, client meetings, getting out your newsletter, prospect follow-up and so on. Plan to do the important things first and leave whatever time is left for everything else. Do your productive activities first.

5 **When you draft your to-do list every morning, give it a once-over to see what kind of day you're about to have.** Are the next ten hours filled with productive activities or junk? Remember that 70% of your list should be full of productive activities. If you don't like what you see, change the list before you get started with your day. Plan to do the things you want and need to do.

More importantly, understand that as a commissioned salesperson your time is your most valuable commodity. Every day you are trading your time and talent for money. I don't know about you, but if I'm going to work hard today, I want to be productive and make the most money I possibly can.

— Lesson 3 —

Create More Opportunities to Sell

No matter how you dress it up, the business of loan origination is a business of selling. You compete with other lenders for a consumer's choice in which mortgage company to borrow money from. You make your best presentation and use your personal sales skills to convince your prospect that you have the best solution. If you win, you're rewarded with a loan and a commission. If you lose, you get nothing. That's selling. That's our business.

Selling has always been a numbers game. Suppose you average ten customer encounters a week, such as rate shoppers, Realtors with buyers looking for financing, phone calls from ads, etc. Of those ten encounters, let's say you can turn two into loan applications, or a 20% conversion rate. (Others either don't qualify, aren't ready to commit, or go somewhere else.) You decide that two loans a week is not enough production to reach your personal goals. You must net at least twice as many loans to get where you want to be. How are you going to make that happen?

There are two ways to look at this situation. First, ask yourself if you're losing deals because of how you handle the opportunities you have. Try these example questions:

- ▸ Am I saying the right things to prospects?
- ▸ Do I take time to build a comfortable rapport with people?
- ▸ Can I sell my company's capabilities strongly enough?
- ▸ Do I ask the right questions?
- ▸ Am I really listening to what they need?
- ▸ Can I explain my products clearly?
- ▸ Am I asking for the business?

If these questions trouble you, maybe you are converting only two out of ten opportunities because you need to enhance your selling skills. Some loan originators believe they can't do the volume they want because they don't have the right products or their rates are too high. Sometimes that's true, but most of the time we lose business to a competitor who uses superior selling skills to present a client with a better solution. To illustrate this, look at your own company. How many originators does it employ? Although all of you have the same products, pricing and delivery system, others in your company will originate more loans than you will this week. Why? Could it be because they can sell better than you can? Think about that.

The second way to obtain the number of applications you want each week is to increase the number of opportunities you have to compete for business. Even if your conversion rate is only 20%, increasing your number of customer encounters each week from ten to twenty, would yield your goal of four loan applications. Remember that sales is a numbers game. You can quickly increase your sales by increasing your opportunities to sell.

Many loan originators write a minimal amount of business each week because they initiate a minimal number of contacts. They don't advertise, they make few sales calls, they have a small number of referral clients, and they don't leverage their existing customer base for referrals. By contrast, high performers secure more business by simply creating more opportunities to sell.

Observe these practices of successful loan originators:

- ▸ Make frequent sales visits to key referral clients
- ▸ Maintain marketing and advertising activities
- ▸ Hand out business cards to every person encountered
- ▸ Stay involved in community activities
- ▸ Attend real estate and builder events
- ▸ Take advantage of rate shopping calls-ins
- ▸ Mine personal databases with frequent mailers
- ▸ Follow up on leads and prospects diligently
- ▸ Always think about finding new business

All of these activities create multiple opportunities every month, week, and day to attract new prospects. Like you, even top producers don't convert every prospect. Some will tell you they lose out on as much as 80% of the leads they receive. The point is that their personal marketing and outreach efforts work to create dozens of opportunities for them each week. Even if they convert just 20% of those opportunities, they still write five to ten loans a week (and that's some pretty good production).

Want to try a great experiment? Next week, keep a record of the number of sales opportunities you create. Note where you were and what you did to create that opportunity. What may surprise you is that the reason your loan production is off your goal is directly related to your having a limited number of sales opportunities to begin with. If you only create four or five encounters a week, how can you expect to write ten loan applications? It won't happen.

Set a goal during the next few weeks to create more opportunities for yourself. This may involve increased sales visits, making presentations, hosting an event, mailing letters, running an ad, telemarketing, and anything else that will put you face-to-face with business prospects. Momentum creates energy. Activity breeds activity. Before long you'll notice your phone rings more as a result of your new marketing efforts. More production means another step up your ladder of success.

— Lesson 4 —

Relationships Are Built on Trust

At a recent mortgage industry event I had the opportunity to facilitate one of those "superstar" discussion panels. We had three of the area's top producing loan originators up front to discuss what makes them so successful.

One of my favorite questions asked by a new loan originator in the audience was this: "What's the one thing you feel separates you from every other loan officer out there?" Pretty good question. Interestingly, all three superstars replied with a similar answer:

Superstar 1: "I promise only what I know I can deliver, and I keep my promises."

Superstar 2: "I am sincere in my dealings with my customers. People see me as their friend in the business. They count on me."

Superstar 3: "I built my business on trust. People know they can trust me to get the job done."

The superstar panel went on to say that fancy marketing ideas were nice, and having many products was OK, but those weren't what differentiated them. What made them different (and as their mega-volume numbers would suggest, better) is that they all had been successful in establishing the *trust factor* with their borrowers and referral clients. That trust factor, they felt, was far more powerful than anything a competitor could do to try to steal their business away.

Want more proof? That afternoon the event featured an invited guest panel of four top real estate agents talking about mortgage lenders and what it takes to earn their business. The agents shared their experiences candidly and fielded questions from the audience on their views about referral relationships with loan officers. I asked the question, "Who is your favorite loan officer and why?" Here are the four agent's answers as to why:

Agent 1: "My loan officer takes care of my clients. She can be counted on to deliver a great experience. She has never let me down."

Agent 2: "My favorite originator is someone I know I can trust. If he says he can make a deal work, he can make the deal work. If he says it won't work, I know it won't work. He's very open and honest."

Agent 3: "When I recommend my lender, I don't have to worry about my buyers having a good experience. I know they will. The loan officer I use can be trusted to get the loan closed right and on time."

Agent 4: "My loan officer treats my clients with the same care and respect I do. I get rave reviews about him. People love him. That's a positive reflection on me. If I put my reputation on the line with a referral, that person has to be good."

Do you see a common thread running through these testimonials? It isn't so much what they said as what they didn't say. At no time did the top producing originators or real estate agents mention pricing or products. Not one superstar loan officer said, "I am successful because of my low rates." Not one real estate agent said she selected her favorite lender, "Because he had the most loan products to offer." The common denominator for success, from both perspectives, was trust. The message is simple: *People in our business do business with people they trust.*

Now, if this is true, why do so many loan originators spend the bulk of their time selling product and price to their referral clients? Perhaps it's because they have to. Loan officers who don't have a strong *trust platform* are forced to regress into selling the commodities of product and price. They have nothing else to offer. "Here's my rate sheet!" they exclaim. "We've also got a lot of great programs. Do you have any borrowers to give me today?" No wonder they get the door slammed in their face.

Real estate agents, or any referral partners for that matter, want to refer a loan originator whom they have confidence in. Look at it this way: If you were a successful real estate agent, builder, CPA, financial planner or developer, and someone asked you to recommend a lender, would you refer an originator based on their cheapest price or most loan programs? My guess is that your criteria would be the same trust factors that those professionals use every day. It's a decision of who you trust to get the job done right.

If you're looking to strengthen your sales approach with referral clients based on a platform of trust, here are some good ideas to consider:

1 **Sell yourself first and foremost.** Essentially, the referral client isn't buying your product. He or she is buying you. Make sure your sales presentation contains strong, compelling reasons why the client can trust *you* to get the job done right. If the client doesn't trust *you*, then your product and price won't make a difference.

2 **Do business from a core of ethics, not deception.** Only untalented, unskilled, unscrupulous originators practice deceptive tactics to get business. Why? Because they have nothing else to sell. Trust isn't an important issue in their lives, and they assume it isn't important to their clients either. As in western movies and mortgage origination, the good guys always win in the end.

3 **Give clients the straight scoop up front.** Tell your referral partners openly and honestly what you can and cannot do for them. Never over-promise. Never set closing dates and deadlines you know your backshop can't meet. Realtors often complain about lenders who renege on promises. Make the decision you are not going to be one of those lenders. Build a reputation for reliability.

4 **If you mess up, take the heat.** Nobody's perfect. Even the best originators drop the ball from time to time. When something goes wrong and it's your fault, be big enough to tell the client: "I made a mistake. It wasn't intentional and I apologize. Let me make it up to you." People appreciate when others are upfront about their errors.

5 **Listen and learn.** Referral clients trust lenders who listen to their needs and interests. Make sure you take the time during your

customer encounters to learn what is important to your referral partners and borrowers. Trust starts with rapport, and rapport starts with your willingness to listen.

6 **Trust takes time.** Don't expect a real estate agent or other referral partner to recommend you after a fifteen-minute visit. It's probably not going to happen. That first referral is going to come through several visits and contacts, once you demonstrate to the agent your sincere desire to help her with a sales transaction. The mere act of coming back again and again shows her you're serious about what you do and that you're willing to work hard to prove it.

7 **Put the client's best interest first.** Let's be honest: You are in this business to write loans and make money. But at what cost? Would you put a borrower into a program he doesn't need? Would you gouge a customer for an extra discount point just because you know you can? Can you feel good about yourself by lying to a Realtor? The golden rule is still alive and well: Treat others as you would want to be treated. This advice will never, ever fail you.

Think about the people you trust to take care of you. Do you trust your dentist with your teeth? Do you trust your stylist with your hair and your drycleaner with your suits? Now think about this: If a friend asked you for the name of a good dentist, stylist, or drycleaner, would you suggest yours? If the answer is yes, it's not because of their prices. It's because you know your friend will be treated well and enjoy a great experience. When it comes to earning referrals, the trust factor is more powerful than we can ever imagine.

— Lesson 5 —

Speed up the Process

Back when I was in college, a good friend of mine landed a great summer job. He was hired as an intern at Lear Corporation, assigned to assemble, package and ship those little automobile turn switches/windshield wiper controls for cars. Larry was paid in the age-old fashion of piecework. The more turn signals he correctly assembled and shipped, the more money he made. It didn't matter if he worked fifteen hours a week or fifty; he was paid according to his output. It also didn't matter if it took him five minutes or an hour to finish each little control; he was paid for what he actually produced.

In many ways, you have the same job as Larry. You are paid on your production output. As a loan originator, you assemble, package and ship mortgage loans. It doesn't matter if you work fifteen hours a week or fifty, or if you spend two hours on a file or twenty. You are paid piecework for every loan you complete. That being understood, you should ask yourself this question: *How can I produce more loans in less time to make more money?*

It's fascinating to meet and talk with high performers in this business. There are many amazing men and women in loan origination that produce thirty, fifty, even one hundred loans a month! What's their secret? Like Larry, they understand the idea of piecework. While other originators hover over their files and baby-sit each document, superstars are busy operating their system of assembling, packaging, and shipping loans smoothly and quickly. By spending minimal time on each loan, they have the capacity to generate more and more production. That's not really a secret; it's just a smart way to run a business.

Is that where you'd like to be? Here are ten ideas that will take you there:

1 **Improve your quality.** Like an assembly line, the better the quality of the product you put into the system, the better the quality of the output. Some originators clog their pipelines with marginal and low-quality loan applications that require intense effort and time. Instead of investing two or three hours on a file, they pour in ten to twenty hours trying to make a bad loan work. They can't get out and originate more loans because they have too many problem loans that are stuck. What's even worse, their fallout ratio of applications to closings is poor, creating frustration and anxiety. Remember that it's not your job to repair a consumer's credit problems or financial situation. Your job is to assemble, package and ship quality mortgage loans. The higher the quality of the loan, the less work you will have to do, the less paper you will need, and the more likely the deal will close. Improving the type of borrowers and referral clients you work with will improve the quality of the product you are assembling. That means more time to produce more loans. And that means you will make more money.

2 **Prep the borrower up front.** It can be tempting to rush out the door whenever a new loan application opportunity shows itself. Don't! Wasting time with unprepared or unqualified borrowers is

very costly. What do high-producing originators do? Their first step is to get the borrower on the phone, introduce themselves, establish a great working rapport, and prepare the client in advance before an application is submitted. Requesting that the borrower gather his or her W-2s, bank statements, pay stubs and tax returns allows you to:

▸ See if the borrower is genuinely interested and ready to proceed, and

▸ Save you time and energy in chasing around VODs, VOEs, and other types of paperwork. If it's in compliance with your company guidelines, you might also get a verbal authorization to pull a credit report to discover ahead of time any issues you will want to discuss with the client. Properly preparing your borrowers up front will mean a faster loan application interview, less paperwork, a ready-buyer, a faster approval and a speedy closing. Isn't that what everyone wants?

3 **Offer application options.** In today's origination world, there are five ways people can apply for a mortgage loan. They can meet you face-to-face, they can apply over the telephone, through the mail, by fax or online. Give your borrowers all of these options. While some originators say you have to meet with everyone in person to establish a relationship, I know dozens of top producers who have actually never met the hundreds of satisfied clients who frequently refer their friends. Certainly, if you have a nervous first-time home-buyer with many questions you'll want to meet face-to-face. But a busy corporate executive refinancing for the second time? Ask her to visit your web site, or send the application by mail! Think about this: driving to someone's home or a real estate office, taking a full appli-

cation and driving back may take two to three hours out of your day. That's time you could spend setting up another loan. Look for ways to streamline your business by carefully exploring how you do your business. Loan applications are a big part of that. Be persistent in this.

4 Submit complete loan applications. If you've been in this business for a few years, you have no doubt been lectured time and again about this. Applications turned in with items missing, such as credit card numbers, bank account numbers, previous addresses and upfront paperwork slows down the entire approval process. High volume loan originators make certain that everything they are responsible for is complete before the handoff to processing. This allows them to quickly move on to another opportunity. Loan originators that submit spotty files and incomplete application forms are haunted with a string of requests from their processors for the items they should have secured in the first place. As they say: *If you don't take the time to do it right the first time, you'll have to spend time doing it again.*

5 Lock it in. Here's a controversial idea: If the borrower likes today's rate, ask if they would like to lock it in. When your borrower is floating the rate, he is likely to call you every day to ask where the rates are, costing you time, and take his loan to another lender who offers a lower rate before closing, costing you money. With that in mind, doesn't it make sense to try to lock in more borrowers? I hear horror stories from loan originators every month about loans (especially refinance loans) that fell out because borrowers were not fully committed. One originator I spoke with said he expected to close

$2,000,000 the previous month, and only funded about $700,000 because the rest had "floated away" when rates went up just half a point.

Maybe locking more loans in is a sound strategy for you, too. Ask yourself how many rate check calls you take a week from your floating pipeline. Ask yourself how many loans fell out the previous month that you might have saved had the borrowers been locked in and committed. If the numbers trouble you, start advising more clients to lock in by saying, "Mr. Jones, rates today are very attractive. They could come down more or just as easily go right back up. If you think the rate today is good and are ready to move forward, we should lock in that rate to protect this transaction. What do you think?"

6 **Educate clients on what happens next.** Constant status calls from borrowers interrupt your workflow, your time management and your ability to generate the next loan. It also might be a telltale sign that you need to communicate better with your borrowers from the get-go. Consider developing a one-page *What Happens Next* flyer that clearly lists the steps in the loan approval process for your borrowers. Explain likely time frames so expectations are clear. Say to the borrower after the loan application: "We're off to a good start here. If we need anything else, we will call you. If you don't hear from us, that's good news. This chart will give you a good idea of what happens next." Speeding up your process requires you to remove roadblocks and time consuming activities. Status calls consume time; time is money.

7 **Follow a checkpoint system.** We say that every loan is

different, but they're not. It's the borrowers that are different. In most cases, the loans you originate flow through the system with the same process: application, processing, approval, closing and funding. Why not create a step-by-step checkpoint system for every file? Design a file cover page displaying the ten to twenty key steps in the transaction and check them off as they're completed. That way you'll be able to see the progress on every file without opening the folder and thumbing through all the paperwork. If a file is lagging behind you'll discover where the holdup is and head off possible closing delays before they happen.

8 Deliver proactive status to your referral clients. Just as it's time consuming to answer status calls from borrowers, so is it to handle the same calls from your Realtors and other referral clients. One successful loan originator I know who deals with around twenty transactions a month gets almost no status calls from her real estate agents. Why? Every Monday morning she comes into the office early and meets with her loan processor to review the pipeline. Once she knows the status of every deal, she places brief voicemail messages with her agents informing them of where each loan is in the process. This takes little time, no cost, and is seen by her loyal agents as a great value-added service. On top of all of that, she has virtually eliminated unwanted status calls from agents. Pretty clever! You might consider a similar system with email or fax status updates, if it would work better for you. Just make sure your system is saving you time each week, not costing you more.

9 Give deadlines. Top producers in this business maintain a sense of urgency in everything they do, and that includes putting a loan

together. They are professionally persistent in dealing with their borrowers about items needed to get an application to closing. The best
way to create this sense of urgency is to assign time frames to your
requests. Instead of telling a borrower, "I still need your tax returns,"
you might instead say, "Mr. Jones, it looks like we have what we need
to move your application forward except for one thing. I have not yet
received your tax returns. If I can get these by Wednesday, I can submit your application for a decision this week. Can I get them by
Wednesday?" The same approach works with return phone calls. Don't
say to someone, "Call me back". Consider saying, "I will be in my
office the remainder of the day and I need to speak with you. When
you have three minutes this afternoon, please call me at . . ." The
bottom line is to keep the file moving forward.

10 **Hold file review meetings.** Sometimes loans get stuck in
the system because they get abandoned. How many times have you
had a loan scheduled for closing and the appraisal hasn't been
ordered yet or the survey isn't completed? A weekly file review meeting with your loan processor and/or backshop support staff can prevent these nightmares. Consider scheduling a standard meeting (for
example, every Monday at 9:00 A.M.) to review each loan in your
pipeline and where it is in the process. A one-hour investment of your
time once a week can save you hours of firefighting time and frustration throughout the month. It will also help strengthen your relationship with your support team.

If I could suggest one more idea here, it would be to keep your fingers out of the
machine. If you have a competent processor and office support team, get out of
the way and let them do their jobs. Too many loan originators slow down their

assembly line process by getting too involved in the daily details of their loan files. This results in duplication, repetitive status conversations and misunderstandings about whose responsibility is it to do what. As Teddy Roosevelt once said: "The secret to being a good leader or manager is to hire great people and then get out of their way and let them do their jobs." The same is true with your mortgage business.

— Lesson 6 —

Knowledge Is Money

We have all heard that knowledge is power. In the mortgage business, knowledge is more than power . . . knowledge is money, and I am about to prove it. Answer the following statements as TRUE or FALSE:

1 Originators with a strong knowledge of their loan programs and guidelines are more successful than originators with very little knowledge of their programs.

2 Originators with a strong knowledge of real estate and how homes are bought, sold, and financed are more successful than originators with very little knowledge of the real estate industry.

3 Originators with a strong knowledge of their market, local trends, the local economy and its peculiarities are more successful than originators who know very little about what's happening in their market.

4 Originators with a strong knowledge of sales, marketing, branding, and self-promotion are more successful than originators who know little about selling and marketing themselves.

5 Originators with a strong knowledge of their referral partners' business plans, needs and goals are more successful in building strong relationships than originators who know very little about their referral partners.

It is clear that the obvious answer to all these statements is a resounding TRUE. As you grow your working knowledge of your products, the real estate business, your market, selling strategies and your business partners, you also increase your likelihood of success, and in the end, your chances of making more money. A key common denominator among top producers is a thorough knowledge of their business. It's not an overnight process, but rather a steady accumulation of knowledge as the months and years go by.

By comparison to other professions, loan origination is a highly compensated position. I know hundreds of mortgage loan officers that earn six-figure incomes. I have met several whose tax returns show over a million dollars. This is just as much as (or more than) professionals like physicians, attorneys, financial planners, and engineers. Think about the training and continual learning required of these fields of work. It is no secret that to rise to success in any endeavor, you must become a professional at what you do. To do that, you must become a student of your profession.

Do doctors, attorneys and engineers spend all day reading? Certainly not. But they do make time during the course of a week or month to brush up on news and changes affecting them and their business. The same can be said for successful mortgage originators. A little time and effort invested in the pursuit of knowledge will not only keep you current, but also pay huge dividends in new business opportunities, new prospects, and self-confidence. In short, when you know what you're talking about, others know it too.

So if knowledge is money, increasing your knowledge will help you increase your chances of making more money. How do you do this?

Here are some great ideas that can work for you:

1 **Know your products.** While most originators in business today have hundreds of financing options available to them, most originators are fluent in only about three to five programs. This limited knowledge also limits their lending opportunities. Consider these guidelines to help you expand your knowledge of loan products:

   ▸ Set a personal goal to learn one new loan program a month. Copy the product description and take it with you to lunch, to the dentist office, and anywhere else you may find a few minutes to read and review it.

   ▸ Ask a successful originator in your company to lunch one day and ask her about the types of programs she uses to develop new business.

   ▸ Sit with an underwriter, a wholesale rep, or your secondary marketing expert and talk about their opinions of great but underused mortgage programs you should be selling.

   ▸ Plan to promote a *Loan Program of the Month* campaign and create a series of flyers highlighting a new home financing option for your real estate agents or other referral partners. Publish a new flyer every month.

   ▸ When new programs come out, don't just pile the information up on the corner of your desk. Take ten minutes the next morning over coffee to review the product to see if it has merit. Imagine adding just one new product every couple of months to your mix. In only one year, that would be six new products, and that's probably twice as many as you know right now!

2 **Know the real estate industry.** We are as much in the business of real estate as we are in the business of mortgages. With that in mind, make attempts to learn more about the real estate business. For example:

▸ Attend a class on real estate. Many are offered through your local Association of Realtors.
▸ Take an evening class at your local college or university on real estate law, real estate finance or real estate principles and practices. (Guess who also attends these classes: Realtors!)
▸ Read a good book on real estate from your library or bookstore.
▸ Join your local Association of Realtors or Women's Counsel of Realtors as an affiliate member and attend the workshops, lunches and events to stay in tune with what's happening in your real estate market.
▸ Get your state license as a Realtor. The prep course, books, and exam will teach you a lot about how the business works from the inside out.

3 **Know your market.** Every city and town has its unique features, and you need to know what's going on in yours to be successful. That knowledge gives you a competitive advantage and makes

you look informed with your clients. Consider the following activities:

▸ Join your local chamber of commerce and attend the monthly meetings, breakfasts, and luncheons to learn what is new and upcoming in your market.

▸ Read the real estate section of your Saturday and Sunday newspaper from front to back. Know what's selling, where people are buying, and what areas of town are hot for new construction.

▸ Get out and drive around. Take mental notes of new subdivisions, thruways, schools, malls and shopping centers being built. Some of the best originators I know can speak confidently about every aspect of their communities. That impresses real estate agents, builders, and borrowers.

▸ Subscribe to your local community weekly newspaper and read the articles about current events and happenings close to home.

▸ Take a real estate agent to lunch one day and open up a discussion about what he sees going on around town. High producing, active Realtors can offer a wealth of local information.

4 Know sales techniques. As a commissioned sales professional, it pays to learn as much as you can about the art of selling. Combining this knowledge with good product knowledge, good real estate knowledge and good market knowledge makes you an eminent force. Ideas for increasing your knowledge of sales, marketing, and personal promotion follow:

- Attend a seminar or workshop on sales or marketing. Many are offered through your local MBA or NAMB, mortgage insurance companies, local universities, and independent trainers and speakers.
- Buy a good book on sales or marketing and implement at least three good ideas you learned.
- Join an area leads club or networking group (BNI, etc.). The meetings are full of self-employed, entrepreneurial types (like you) who share their success stories on how they prospect for business. Their ideas will likely work for you too.
- Shadow a talented loan originator in your company on sales calls, office presentations, and other client activities. They can teach you much about great sales presentations and how to convert more prospects and leads into loans and relationships.
- Learn from successful salespeople outside of our industry. When you are a customer buying a new car, shopping for clothes or any other purchase, learn from the salesperson working with you. What do they do well? What don't they do well? You can learn as much from their skills as from their mistakes.

5 **Know your referral partners.** Perhaps you have Realtors, builders, CPAs, attorneys, and other referral clients sending you leads. But are they really your business *partners*? Do you know their plans, goals and needs well enough to create the rapport to take that relationship to new levels? Consider the following:

▶ Begin to compile a list of personal information gleaned from each encounter. Slowly learn things like birthdays, spouse's name, children's names, hometown, hobbies and favorite sports teams.

▶ Hold a one-on-one discovery session with your key business partners and probe into their wants, needs, likes and dislikes when it come to home financing and working with lenders. Ask how you can better serve their needs.

▶ Each January, schedule beginning-of-the-year goal-setting and partnership strategy sessions to find out about your referral clients' goals and plans for the year. Suggest ways you can help them reach these goals.

▶ Most professionals in business today (Realtors, attorneys, etc.) publish a website with loads of great information about their background, business philosophies and areas of expertise. Visit these sites. Make an effort to learn more about the people you rely on for your business.

▶ Spend some social time with your referral partners. What a client reveals to you on the golf course, at a ball game, or over dinner can help you understand him better as a person and as a client.

There are twenty-five ideas listed in this lesson. Maybe you are already doing some of them. Maybe you need to do more. Select two or three and get started on broadening the scope of your knowledge. Become a well-rounded and well-informed mortgage professional. There are so many ways to differentiate yourself in your local mortgage market. Being regarded as one of the brightest and best will quickly set you apart from the crowd. It's just a smart thing to do.

— Lesson 7 —

Keep Flying High

A motivational poster I once saw proclaimed, *Your attitude affects your altitude.* It displayed a majestic eagle soaring in the sky high above a mountain range. It made me realize that this wasn't just a pretty picture, but a strong message. How you think about your career, how you feel about your job, how you look at your chances for success, all impact your attitude, and ultimately, how high you will soar.

Have you ever noticed that top performing originators who are making money and having fun are those with the positive outlooks, excited attitudes, and the highest productivity? By contrast, you have likely observed that low to moderate producers have gloomy dispositions and are usually complaining about their programs, fighting with their processors, griping about rates and hanging around the office making excuses. Do top producers have a great attitude because they are successful, or are they successful because they have a great attitude? It's the chicken or the egg question. I wonder which comes first?

Let's face it, people want to work with people who have positive attitudes. This includes your borrowers, peers, support staff and especially your referral clients. We'd all like to think of ourselves as positive, upbeat professionals. Are you? Ask yourself these questions:

1. Does my boss see me as an enthusiastic, can-do person?
2. If someone that knew me well were asked to describe my characteristics, would they use words like *dynamic, upbeat* and *fun*?
3. When I walk into a real estate office, do faces light up or turn away?
4. How many times so far this year has someone said to me, "I admire your attitude."
5. Do I start out each working day with a high degree of emotional energy and excitement?

If the answer is yes to these questions, then keep soaring! Your positive attitude will create positive results. Even if things aren't going so well right now, a positive attitude will get you turned around a whole lot faster than a negative one. If you answered no more than yes to these questions, then it's time for a little attitude adjustment coaching. We all need some help with our attitudes now and then. Perhaps one or more of the following suggestions would apply to you:

1. **Lose the losers.** We are all affected by our environment. If you spend most of your day hanging out with loser loan originators with little business and loser clients who have no referrals to send you, break free! Their negative outlook can be the cause of your negative attitude. Hang out with the winners. Make sales calls and visits on highly productive referral clients and interact daily with top performing originators. You may like your old buddies and comfortable clients, but it's time to realize that they're squashing your chances for success. As the old saying goes, It's hard to soar like an eagle when you're surrounded by turkeys.

2 Move on. Sales is about rejection. Accept that. Even the best loan originators get doors slammed in their face, and prospects that say no every day. Take your hits, learn from them, brush yourself off and move on. Dwelling on your defeats only makes you feel defeated, and your attitude can't afford to feel that way. A baseball player that strikes out comes back again and again until he gets a hit. When you're rejected, say, "Oh well, not everyone's going to say yes. Who's up next?" As the legendary football coach Vince Lombardi once said, "It's not whether you get knocked down, it's whether you get up."

3 Look for silver linings. Let's suppose you talk with ten prospects this week. In the end, you secure two loan opportunities and lose eight. You can either walk away from this experience thinking you're a failure or a success. Some will say, "I can't take this rejection! I lost eight deals this week!" Those with a positive attitude will look back and say: "I had a great week! I talked with ten prospects, landed two deals, and made $2,000. If I can do that every week, I'll make $100,000 this year. All right!" Remember that when you focus on failure, you see failure; when you focus on success, you find even more success.

4 Use perpetual motion. Loan originators that are active seem to stay active. When you hustle to make sales calls, follow up on hot leads, take clients to breakfast, and mail out stacks of letters every week, you create momentum in your daily routine. This momentum feeds off itself to create more excitement and energy. Actions create a domino effect. When you have a lot going on in your business world, you feel productive, you feel like you're making headway, and you feel good. Originators that sit around all day reading and shuffling paperwork lose momentum. They wonder if they're moving forward with their business and career. This leads to depression and loss of enthusiasm. Stay in motion!

5 **Keep your focus.** The best loan originators are focused individuals. They know what they want in their careers, and they know what they must do every day to get it. When we lose focus, we start to second-guess our future and ourselves. This leads to a waste of our great talent. Think about it. Why did you take this job? You took this job to originate loans, put people into homes, and make good money. Everything else in your job, every day, comes second. Get focused! Get your objectives and priorities in order. Get out there and originate!

6 **Let rejection motivate you.** Can rejection make you more motivated? Absolutely! Remember when you were a kid playing games and sports with your friends? When your opponent scored a point on you, didn't that strengthen your resolve to play harder and score back? Use that same competitive spirit to your advantage in sales. When one prospect turns you down, be determined to get the next to say yes. When one real estate agent blows off your lunch appointment, respond immediately by phoning another to take his place. When you lose a rate shopper to the competition, work harder to save the next one. Don't get mad, get even.

7 **Reward your success.** When things are going well and you're on a roll, celebrate your success. Did you just make two productive sales calls? Good for you! Now take yourself out to a nice lunch. Did you close a record fifteen loans last month? Go to your favorite store and get fitted for a new suit. Were you able to push a tough loan

through to approval? Reflect on the hard work you did and congratulate yourself for your extra effort with a new pair of shoes. Celebration and reward encourages you to want to celebrate more. Don't think this is corny. Top producing salespeople do it all the time.

8 **Keep smiling.** No matter how difficult things get, keep smiling. When you walk into work every day, wear your professional best. And that includes a warm, genuine smile. You'll naturally attract others to you (unless you haven't smiled in so long you scare them). Say hello to your colleagues every day. Say hi to your boss. Smile and say thanks to people who are helping to you build your business. When the day is done, wander the office and say goodnight to everyone and wish them a nice evening. Go home and kiss your kids, pet your dog or hug your cat. You'll be amazed not only at how you make them feel, but how good it will make you feel too!

9 **Count your blessings.** When tough times overwhelm you, step back for a moment and reflect on the positive things in your life. At the very least, you have a job, a car, a place to live, and you have clothes to wear. That puts you ahead of millions of others less fortunate. Maybe you also have a supportive spouse, a hard-working team behind you, a quality company to work for, and good clients who call you with their referrals. Not bad, huh? In tough times, take a *life inventory* of what's going right in your world, and you'll see your attitude change for the better.

We can't control everything that happens in our lives. But we can control how we respond. Every morning when you wake up you have two choices. You can choose to be positive or negative. You can choose to fly high or lie low. The choice you make dictates what kind of day you're likely to have, and most importantly, what kind of career you're going to have as you climb your ladder of success. Starting tomorrow morning, the choice is yours. What will it be?

— Lesson 8 —

Manage Your Money Wisely

Mortgage loan originators lend tens of millions of dollars each year. We are comfortable dealing with big money and helping clients make the largest and most important financial decision of their lives. But some originators face a personal challenge in managing their own money. It's one thing for a loan officer to lend $2,000,000 a month. It's another to manage wisely the $10,000 a month he makes.

First, let me say that I'm not a financial advisor. But after two decades in the mortgage industry, working with thousands of loan officers, I have met many who manage their incomes and success quite well . . . and many who do not. My purpose in this lesson is to make seven simple suggestions on how to manage the lucrative income you work hard to make as a professional originator and how to avoid some common pitfalls of money mismanagement so many commissioned salespeople seem to trip into.

I Live within your means. There's no doubt you'd look great behind the wheel of that new Lexus or BMW. And with the money you're now making, maybe you can afford it. But how are you going to feel about a $600 car payment if the market turns south and you're making less than you do now? The same can be said for expensive houses, boats, jewelry, and clothes. Every day as mortgage originators, we are amazed at borrowers we meet who are stretched to the max trying to support a lifestyle far beyond what they can comfortably afford. Make it your goal not to become one of them.

Consider applying the guidelines we have used in the mortgage business for years: the old 28/36 rule. Your house payment should not exceed 28% of your gross monthly income, and all of your monthly debt obligations should not exceed 36%. As an example, if you are making $10,000 a month, your house payment should be at or below $2,800 and the total of your monthly obligations should be at or below $3,600. It should also be mentioned that in times of inflated loan volume due to extra refinance business, you should base your budget on your normal *purchase* loan business volume and income. Remember that strong purchase loan volume sustains itself at a more stable level than the fickle refinance activity, which can shut off without warning. Many originators either don't understand this fact, or try to ignore it. That's why when a refinance wave is over, the classified ads of your local newspaper are littered with nice cars, boats, and houses up for sale by loan officers in your town who can no longer afford them.

2 **Reinvest in your business.** I have always believed in and coached loan originators to the *5% rule*. Essentially, you should reinvest at least 5% of your gross income back into your business in ways that can generate more business. Using our earlier example, a $10,000 monthly income means setting aside $500 for marketing,

gifts and advertising for the next month. This money goes into your marketing budget to be spent for things like newspaper ads, personal brochures, sponsorships, seminars, closing gifts and other means of client loyalty recognition and new business generation.

The best and easiest way to do this is to set up a separate ledger or bank checking account to manage your incoming investments, outgoing expenses and sales activities. Each time you get your monthly paycheck, deposit 5% of your income into this account. As you withdraw funds, make a note on the checkbook entry ledger line as to what the money is for, such as *Homes & Land* ad. This will give you a running total of the money you have available throughout the year and where that money is being reinvested. Putting a nickel back into your business for every dollar you earn will pay big dividends in more opportunities and phone calls month after month.

3 **Originate higher-profit loans.** With very few exceptions, loan officers are compensated on the dollar amount of the loans they originate. That means the higher the loan amount, the more money they make. As you have likely discovered, it takes no more work or time to originate a $300,000 loan than a $60,000 loan. Yet the originator who closes the $300,000 loan will earn five times more than his colleague closing a $60,000 loan. With that in mind (banking on the assumption that you want to earn as much money as you can in this business), why not write more $300,000 loans?

Clearly, every market is different and average sales prices and loan amounts vary. There are originators in small markets who produce ten to twelve loans a month and close only a little over $1,000,000 in volume. Other originators in higher priced markets can close $1,000,000 with just two transactions. But look at it this way:

even if you raise your average loan amount this year by 20% (in this example, from $60,000 to $72,000), you have rewarded yourself with a 20% pay increase. Not bad! While you may not have $300,000 loan opportunities where you live, I'm sure there's an opportunity to go up 20%. Work to push your average loan amounts to the limit in your market.

4 **Pay for performance.** Perhaps you have an assistant or support team you are responsible for. Are they being compensated on loan production volume like you are? Is their income tied to your success? Do they have a strong financial incentive to see that loans are closed, clients are happy and business is growing? The answers to these questions should be yes.

I once worked with a bank-owned mortgage company that paid their originators a straight salary with a small—a very small—stipend for volume. I was asked to come in and motivate the group to produce more business. The bottom line is that the training didn't work—not because what I taught them wasn't effective—it didn't work because the originators saw no financial reward for producing more business. If you pay your assistant or personal loan processor a set salary, the same could be happening to you. To them, more loans are not more money, just more work.

In talking with top producers across the country, I've discovered that more and more are compensating their support staff on a percentage of their overall team volume. For example, instead of paying an assistant a flat $3,000 a month, the assistant earns one basis point of total volume closed. (For an originator averaging $3,000,000 a month, that's $3,000 in incentive income.) As the originator's business grows, the assistant earns more money. When more loans come through the door, the assistant doesn't think, *Oh no! More work!* He thinks, *All right! More money!* Should business take a downturn, the originator isn't locked into an assistant's high salary, and both will work hard to get things moving again because both have a vested interest in the bottom line. It makes sense.

5 **Save for the valleys.** Anyone in this business for more than a few years knows that there are dramatic peaks and valleys in housing demand, interest rates, and the resulting mortgage loan production. I know loan officers who went from earning $40,000 one year to $140,000 the next and back down to $40,000 after that. As my first boss taught me: "It's a roller coaster business. Expect a lot of ups and downs and twists and turns." Boy, was he right.

   Everyone has their own savings goals they shoot for. Part of your personal savings plan should not just be for the kid's college and your retirement; it should also be for the potential slow times in your career. If I were to dish out advice here, I would recommend socking away 5% to 10% of your earnings as a comfortable pad in case you meet with hard times. To stay with our example, let's consider that a $10,000 monthly paycheck means squirreling away $500 to $1,000 in a rainy day fund. Who knows what can happen? In the 1970s, rates moved in a range of 7% to 10%. In the late 1980s, they jumped to 17%. As of this writing, rates now trend around 6%. What would happen to your business if interest rates started rising tomorrow and reached 15% to 16%? If it happened before, it can happen again. Be prepared in case it does.

6 **Grow your business every year.** Some originators are content with the level of volume and income they have. While in

some ways I think that's terrific, in other ways I think it's dangerous. Here are two reasons why: First, inflation goes up every year, sometimes by 5% or more. This makes each dollar you earn less and less valuable because the cost of living is on a constant rise. (I don't know about you, but I'm paying more today for electricity, cable TV, gasoline and airplane tickets than I did last year.) Second, your needs are changing. What was OK for you five years ago is no longer acceptable. Your standards increase for the quality of food you eat, the furniture you buy and the vacations you take. Along with that the price tags increase to meet those standards.

A loan officer happy with $2,000,000 in volume and $10,000 in monthly income will find a way to stay at that level. While he may feel that he is keeping afloat, he is actually sinking under a rising cost of living. If you are looking for a benchmark, your goal should be to grow your income by a minimum of 10% a year, not only to keep up, but also to stay ahead. To accomplish this, you'll have to grow your production volume at the same pace. So, an originator averaging $2,000,000 a month this year should look at $2,200,000 a month next year, $2,420,000 the year after that, and so on. While many grow at a more accelerated rate, 10% should be the minimum.

7 Spend your money on those who help you make it. I am happy to report that most mortgage originators I know live by this rule. They recognize that without the help and support of their families and support team, they would not be capable of running a strong and profitable business, or earn such a great income. When you find ways to allow the people important to you to share in your success they want to see you succeed even more. This may include but not be limited to, a fantastic family vacation, a new backyard spa, and a special birthday gift for your processor. It's nice to spend the hard-earned money you make on yourself as a means to celebrate your success. But when you spend it on others, the rewards are even richer.

One originator I know purchased a small vacation condominium about four hours from her home. One weekend every month she takes her husband and kids to their cozy family get-away to enjoy quality time together. Another originator told me his loan processor mentioned to him she wanted to join a popular health club that was just across the street from their office, but found the membership fee was too high. So what did he do? To say thanks for her hard work, he walked across the street, wrote a check for $500, and bought the membership for her as a gift.

If you're like most successful mortgage loan originators, you enjoy the luxury of a great income for your hard work. If you're new in the business of loan origination and do well, you'll soon be making more money than you ever have in your entire life. Enjoy it, but manage it wisely.

— Lesson 9 —

Find a Mentor

In the mortgage business, as in most businesses, knowledge, information, and skills are passed down from person to person. We learn from our managers, we learn from our support team, and we learn from seasoned producers who have gone before us and found a pathway to success. Most originators pick up what they learn in this business through painful trial and error. Others have found a better, faster and more structured road to success. They found a mentor to show them the way.

A mentor is a personal teacher, trainer, or coach. The concept of mentoring is as old as humanity, but very much in vogue these days because it's easy to implement, it can be very inexpensive, and most importantly, it pays off. Below are the four levels of mentoring in our business and how each works:

I   **The Model Mentor** The first type of mentor is a *model mentor*. A model mentor is another loan originator, typically in your company or branch office, whom you admire. Your model mentor is extremely successful; she exudes the traits and characteristics you'd like to emulate. You pattern your actions after her. You watch her to learn how things should be done. The model mentor also becomes your guide through tough times. When other originators around you are struggling, she seems to be consistently writing business. You observe her activities and strategies and mimic what she is doing. By simply following the habits and practices of your model mentor, you teach yourself the right way things should be done.

The best thing about having a model mentor is that she does not even have to know about it. Being a model mentor requires no specific time or resource commitment. The downside to having a model mentor is that she isn't actually dedicated to developing you. She is simply a role model you watch at arm's length and try to copy. Is there someone that you work closely with who could become your model mentor? If so, leverage this fantastic opportunity. Learn the right way to originate from an experienced pro who has gone before you and figured it out.

2   **The Peer Mentor** The second type of mentor is a *peer mentor*. A peer mentor is another loan originator who takes you under his wing to support you for a brief period of time. This person is usually a solid producer inside your office or company who can work closely with you, testing ideas, sharing best practices, answering technical questions, and helping you maintain focus and motivation. Some companies have peer mentor programs for new hires. Experienced loan officers are assigned to rookies as peer mentors to show them the ropes anywhere from the first few months of employment to up to one year.

The advantage of a peer mentor is that he is there for you when you need him. Peer mentors are also familiar with your company's unique systems and procedures. The disadvantage of this arrangement is that it can be difficult vying for your peer mentor's time as a personal resource for an extended period. Peer mentors have their own business to worry about. Finding someone to be your peer mentor that truly wants to help you grow and stay with you for up to six months or a year is critical.

Ask around at your company to see if others have interest in starting a peer mentor program. You may be surprised at the positive response you get.

3 **The Coach Mentor** The third kind of mentor is called a *coach mentor*. This is becoming the most popular type of mentor arrangement. With many very busy managers and top producers focused on their own pipelines, there's not a lot of time available to help others. Thus, more and more originators today are hiring coach mentors to educate them on the best practices of the business. A coach mentor, often a seasoned veteran or industry sales trainer, is a paid teacher who serves as your personal trainer and coach. The coach mentor provides ongoing counseling via assessments, personal meetings, one-on-one telephone conferences, emails and other distance learning methods. Coach mentors can cost from $100 to over $1000 a month, depending on the specific coaching program and the talent of the person you hire.

A coach mentor program typically lasts from six months to one year and is renewable indefinitely based on the student's interest. Your coach mentor will share valuable strategies and techniques he has learned, both as an originator and through his exposure to perhaps hundreds of other successful loan officers around the country. He gives you the benefit of an unbiased expert in matters such as whom to target for business, where marketing dollars are best invested, how to hire and work with a personal assistant, and effective cutting-edge techniques for growing your business. Most loan officers who've hired coach mentors will tell you they received ten times in added income what they'd paid for coaching. If this sounds like something that entices you, check around the industry and investigate the resources out there. You'll find some good ones.

4   **The Apprentice Mentor** The fourth and final level of mentoring is the *apprentice mentor*. In an apprentice relationship, you create a partnership with a mentor in your company who will agree to develop your skills and your business in return for personal compensation. I have met several loan officers that are doing this. Here is one example:

Being new to loan origination, Kathy approached Jason, a high producer in her office, and asked him to teach her the business. For one year, Jason would be there to help Kathy—to counsel her, train her, answer her questions, take her out on sales calls, and invest a specific number of scheduled hours each week to teach her the loan origination business. In return for this commitment, Kathy would pay Jason ten basis points of all loans she closed for that twelve-month period. So, if Kathy were to close $10,000,000 that year, Jason would earn a $10,000 fee as her mentor. The more Kathy would produce, the more Jason would earn.

As Kathy's apprentice mentor, Jason would have a strong vested interest in her success. Kathy, as the apprentice, would have demanding expectations of her mentor since she'd be paying him a part of her own commission for the training and coaching she'd receive. Sound far-fetched? Kathy isn't the only one who's done this. Dozens of future superstars in the mortgage business are now operating under apprentice mentor relationships. Perhaps you could be too.

Superstar sports athletes all have mentors. Future superstar mortgage originators should be no different. Whether with a model mentor, peer mentor, coach mentor, or apprentice mentor, learn this business the smart way. Find a mentor to help you climb your ladder of success.

— Lesson 10 —

Play More Offense

Over the past twenty years I have experienced four refinance waves. These are the boom years when rates drop steadily and create an influx of phone calls and refinance opportunities for rate, payment, and term reduction loans. For the most part, a refinance wave year is a *defensive* year for mortgage origination. A steady stream of inbound refinance activity keeps many loan originators reacting and responding to heavy consumer demand. Sales calls, marketing, prospecting, and other *offensive* business outreach activities are put on hold. Hey, why market yourself to find business when you can barely handle what's already coming in, right?

When the refinance wave is over it's a different story. As incoming refinance business drops back down to a normal cash-out and debt consolidation of 10% to 20% refinance level, the focus shifts back to generating purchase volume to fill the huge void left behind. The problem is, after a refinance wave is over, too many originators struggle to get moving. Too many originators are still playing defense.

It's a well known fact that a sports team can score more points playing on offense than on defense. The halftime stats during a football game typically reveal that the team with the greater time of possession on offense is in the lead on the scoreboard. The same trend holds true for our business. The loan originators who spend more time on offense put more points on the board (applications and closings) than those originators playing mostly defense, simply reacting to things as they happen.

I hope it's OK if I continue with a sports analogy for this lesson. Before doing so, let me identify what I mean by offense and defense. Offensive plays include the following:

▸ Sales calls to referral clients
▸ Presentations to borrowers
▸ Phone calls for appointments
▸ Client lunches
▸ Advertising in newspapers and magazines
▸ Networking in your market
▸ Attending community events
▸ Sponsorships
▸ Prospecting for new business
▸ Mailers to past clients
▸ Serving on industry committees
▸ Following up on leads
▸ Other activities that create new relationships and loan opportunities

Defensive plays in our business include the following:

▸ Waiting for the phone to ring
▸ Processing your own loans
▸ Chasing down conditions

- ▸ Putting out fires
- ▸ Reacting to others' demands
- ▸ Answering loan status calls
- ▸ Administrative and internal office tasks
- ▸ Other activities that take place behind the scenes

I am not advocating that you spend all your time playing offense. Certain things have to be done, and you must make the time to do them. Nonetheless, I am suggesting that you may be spending far too much of your valuable time each day in a defensive position. As a result, your pipeline and your paycheck are both nowhere near as big as they could be. Playing too much defense hurts you and your chances for greater success. If this sounds all too real to you, it may be time to do something about it. Here's a great little experiment:

1 Write down how many hours, on average, you've been working in a typical week. Be honest and accurate.

2 Think about the list of offensive plays shown here. Write down how many total hours you spend each week playing on offense. Be realistic.

3 Divide list two's hours by list one's to get the percentage of time you are now actually playing on offense.

Let's stop for a moment and see where you are. For example, if you work fifty hours a week and you determined that you spend only about eight hours on offense, that's 16% on offense and 84% on defense. Does that sound right to you? Can you grow your current production levels with that kind of game plan? Could a football team score many points if they spent more than 80% of the game on defense? Certainly not. Let's continue our experiment:

4 Set an offensive goal for yourself. How many hours a week would you like to be playing on offense? Write that number down.

5 Compare your current number of offensive hours to your goal number.

6 Write down specifically the changes you'll have to make to get yourself where you want to be.

You may, for example, be working eight hours a week on offense and you'd like to take that to sixteen, doubling the time you spend in sales and marketing efforts. Ask yourself, *What is holding me back? Why am I not spending more time on offense?* The answer may be one of the following:

1 You have call reluctance. You really don't want to sell, therefore, you find other less intimidating, defensive activities to occupy your time and keep you off the streets.

2 You're too close to your loans. You've become too intimate with your files and spend an extraordinary amount of time over-processing loans and chasing down paperwork. This keeps you on the defense most of the time.

3 You're disorganized. The reason you play so much defense is because playing offense takes strategies and game plans. Without strategies and weekly planning, you end up reacting and firefighting all week long. You plan to get out, but your lack of focus and personal organization keep you in.

4 **You don't have an adequate support staff.** Because the people or skills aren't available at your branch or company, you work too many defensive hours doing things a sales *support* staff could be doing.

5 **You're making excuses.** You're trying to convince yourself that you want to be on the offense, but the reasons you can't do it are _____ (fill in the blank).

If you're serious about playing more offense, you'll have to clearly identify the barriers keeping you on defense. If one or more of these barriers are yours, consider the ideas below:

1 **Battle call reluctance.** You may be new to the business and sales call prospecting intimidates you. Or, you may be more experienced and have pulled yourself off the streets for a long time. Fear not. You can overcome call reluctance. But to do it, you have to take action. Get on the phone and call several referral clients and prospects every Monday morning and try to set up visits and appointments—lots of them. You'll keep those dates because someone is expecting you. Set a goal of two, five or ten appointments a week. Get out of the office and in the field where the loans are. Your confidence will increase with newly generated business and your call reluctance will go away fast. Trust me, this works!

2 **Let go of your loans.** A former boss once told me, "You only get paid on a loan once." He was right. Spend your time on what you were hired to do: originate! Leave the processing, underwriting and closing to processors, underwriters and closers. Bring in a complete

loan application, document your conversation, get the initial paper-work up front, hand off the loan to your talented sales support staff and go out and get another one. Isn't that what $50,000,000 pro-ducers do?

3 **Getting organized to sell.** Offensive activities like prospect-ing, marketing, sales visits, follow-up and networking shouldn't be the last thing you do every day, but the first thing. Reverse your mindset of, *I'll just go in the office and take care of a bunch of things, and if I get time I'll try to get out,* to a mindset of, *I need to start out the day with great sales and marketing activities for the first few hours, and when I'm done, I'll go into the office and take care of the other things.* When you make offensive activities a prior-ity and do them first, they will get done.

4 **Foster a talented support staff.** If someone on your staff is new and needs help and training, invest the time and the money to get him help and training—now. If your backshop support is swamped and can't meet your turnaround deadlines, hire more back-shop support—now. If you have people on your team that aren't team players or don't possess the desire to do their job skillfully, replace them—now. Trying to play more offense when your support team can't handle the defense is a formula for disaster. Take care of the problem—now!

5 **Stop making excuses.** While you say you can't find time to get out and make sales calls, other loan originators *are* out making sales calls. While you claim that marketing and advertising don't work, other loan originators *are* responding to phone calls and inquiries from their marketing and advertising. While you claim that there is simply no business out there right now, other loan originators *are* out of the office, taking that business away from you. If hundreds of other loan originators are out there playing offense, that means you can too. Excuses are for sissies.

Get excited about the fact that this will be a more offensive year for you and your business. Set a goal for how much time you want to play on offense each week. Stick to that goal. You'll have more fun, you'll get more done, and you'll put a lot more points on the board at the end of each month.

— Lesson 11 —

Learn to Let Go

Almost every top performing loan originator I know had a major breakthrough point in his career. For some, it came with the landing of a top referral client or a new source of business. For others, it was a move to a new company with great tools and resources to support their potential. But for most top performers, the pivotal moment of success was less obvious. It came the day they finally learned to let go.

What keeps us from moving forward are the things that hold us back, the old saying goes. Do you feel you have the ability and desire to take your business to a new level of success? To do so, you just might have to let go of what's keeping you from that leap forward. How else do you think high producers generate forty, fifty, even one hundred loans a month? Doesn't that sound enticing? If you ever hope to get there, it may be time for you to let go of whatever is holding you back. Let's look at what that something might be.

1 Let go of the process. We'll start with the big one. What holds the majority of originators back from producing higher volumes of loans is that they can't let go of the paperwork and the process. They baby-sit their files, hover over their loan processors, and become engulfed in every little detail of the mortgage transaction. Some of today's superstars once did the same. But they learned how to delegate, how to trust people and how to focus on what they were hired to do: create new loans.

You may have to do the same. If you have good support people, leave them alone and let them do their jobs. If you don't have a good backshop processing and underwriting team, talk with your boss about ideas and suggestions to get them up to speed. If you work for a company that can't or won't support your high volume sales efforts, resign and join one that will. It's nearly impossible to both originate and process a big volume of business by yourself. You have to let go of one to master the other. If you don't, it will forever hold you back.

2 **Let go of old habits.** As the business changes, successful originators must change with it. Some found that their breakthrough point came when they learned to let go of the old way of doing things in favor of the new way. This meant learning new technology, tapping into timesaving loan origination software systems and alternative documentation loan applications. While some old school loan officers still insist on meeting with every one of their borrowers, high volume producers are writing twice as many loans every month via online loan applications, telephone interviews and mail-away do-it-yourself loan kits. While some old school originators are chasing down VODs and VOEs, high volume producers ask the borrower for bank statements and pay stubs to move the loans through the system faster.

Do you have old habits holding you back? Are you still trying to originate the same way you did five or ten years ago? While you may be comfortable in your old habits, they are keeping you from growing your business and your income. Let go.

3 Let go of low volume agents. Just as partnerships with high volume real estate agents can skyrocket your career, relationships with low volume agents can hold you down on the ground. There's hardly a top producing originator out there who hasn't had to fire a low volume Realtor by breaking free and moving on. Low volume agents can strain your time, your resources, and your sanity. Regardless of how nice they are or how much they welcome your visits, business relationships with low volume agents who send you one referral every three months are hardly worth the effort.

Look at it this way: if there are one thousand real estate agents in your marketplace and 20% of those are writing the lion's share of the business (the old 80/20 rule), that's a pool of two hundred agents to fish out the five to ten you actually need to be working with. There's no excuse for dealing with the other eight hundred. They just don't have enough business to refer you. If you're working with any of the low volume agents in your community, identify who they are and let them go.

4 Let go of poor quality business. You're only paid for what closes, so take in loans that you're sure will close. That seems like simple advice, but it's often ignored. When we get started in the mortgage business, we're hungry. Hungry loan officers will take in any loan just to have a loan to work on. As we move up in our careers, we can afford to be more choosy. We must learn to let go of the bad deals as quickly as we smell them going bad. Time invested in poor quality loans rob us of time we need to prospect for good quality loans. Today, hundreds of originators are saddled with lousy loans, challenged clients, and worthless paper pipelines that will never close. If you want to be respected in your market as a quality mortgage loan officer, you should search for and produce quality mortgage business. Let the rest go.

5 Let go of the money. Top producing mortgage originators make a lot of money. They spend a lot of money as well. I know one loan officer who invests $5,000 a month in database farming. I know another who takes all of her Realtors on a cruise every year. There are originators who sponsor little league teams, run ads in the newspaper, buy leads lists, hire personal coaches, and fly across the country to attend personal development seminars. All this, they figure, costs them nothing. Why? Because they had a breakthrough at some point in their careers. They discovered that to make a lot of money in this business you have to spend a little first on your business. They also learned that those investments, with the revenue of just one or two loans a month, pay for themselves many times over. To validate this, talk with a successful originator in your company or city. Ask about the money he spends to run his $50,000,000 to $100,000,000-a-year business. It's amazing what you'll learn.

6 Let go of low expectations. Big producers think big. When you set your sights on originating ten loans a month, you create the motivation and systems to achieve that. When you set your sights on fifty loans a month, the motivation and systems look quite different. Learn to dismiss small thinking. You will aspire to achieve the level of success you think you are capable of achieving. Ask yourself, *What am I capable of? If I put my mind to it and my heart and soul in it, where could my business take me?*

Top producers continue to raise their expectations as they reach each level of success. Why? It's because they have high expectations of themselves. In the beginning, they dream of a $1,000,000 month. Once that's been reached, they think about $2,000,000. When they earn $100,000 a year, rather than being content, they ask, *How do I get to $250,000?* Follow in their footsteps. Start thinking about big numbers and big goals. Believe that it's possible because others in this industry have shown you so. Develop the plan and the timeline that will take you there. When you let go of low expectations for yourself, you grab on to larger ones. Reach up.

What's holding you back? Is it old habits? Is it poor quality clients or old-fashioned systems? To move up your ladder of success, you may have to learn to let some things go. Make a list of what those things are. Then, one at a time, let them go.

— Lesson 12 —

Spend Your Money Where You Make It

With all the new laws and regulations affecting our industry, I would like to propose a new law of my own. I will call it *The Client Reinvestment Act*. This law will apply to all commissioned mortgage loan officers and will read as follows: All mortgage originators will, from time to time, reinvest the revenue received from one loan back into their clients as a means of creating referral opportunities, customer loyalty and goodwill.

What do you think? For most successful originators, this law will have little or no impact. They already follow the principles of investing in their customers. Without any hesitation, some originators spend anywhere from 5% to 10% of their personal income each month in database mining, closing gifts and other forms of marketing. It's the rest that will take issue with my new law. Many loan officers are so preoccupied with working from one deal to the next and hounding real estate agents for possible leads, that they haven't stopped to think about what this idea could mean to them. It could mean more repeat business, a continuing stream of referrals, stronger client loyalty, and a whole lot less prospecting. It may even open their eyes to a completely new and enjoyable way of originating loans.

Maybe the concept of legally forcing loan officers to spend money on their business is a little much. But you must admit the idea has merit. For example, let's suppose the commission income you generate on an average loan transaction is $800. (I realize that many of you earn more or less than $800 per transaction. But let's use that number as an example to show just how far the profits on a single loan can go to generate many more.)

Here are seven suggestions. While there are hundreds of ways to reinvest in your customers and referral clients, these may give you a jump start finding creative ways to spend 800 bucks. In all examples, I have accurately estimated the total cost of the activity to show that a little money can really go a long, long way.

I **Magnetic Business Cards** Visit your local Office Depot (or similar office store) and purchase a one hundred pack of peel-and-stick magnetic business card backings. Attach one of your cards to each. Mail the card with a special letter to the last one hundred clients to whom you provided a loan. Mention that you wanted them to have your name and number as handy as the front of their refrigerator for any questions or needs on mortgage financing. Remember to thank them for selecting you as their lender for life. The cost of this activity including one hundred magnets, business cards, letters, and postage is $90.

2 **Halloween Haunted RV** Arrange to rent a large recreational vehicle at your nearest RV dealer for a day. (They rent these by the day or week.) Decorate the RV with fun, attractive Halloween décor and have lots of goodies to eat and drink. Send out a fax announcement beforehand to your real estate offices, builder's model homes,

title companies, and other referral clients that the Haunted RV is making a call at their office on October 31. Ask your office staff to dress in costume, load up, and take off! Spend the day stopping at your clients' places of business and invite them to come out to the RV to take a break, meet the staff, and celebrate the Halloween holiday. The cost of the RV rental, mileage charge, gas, refreshments, and decorations is about $400.

3 **Thanksgiving Cards** Get the latest catalogue from a high quality business greeting card company (Greenwoods, Brookhallow, In Touch Today, etc.) and order enough cards to send to every closed customer this year, along with every referral client you dealt with. Imprint a special message of thanks from you for their business. Since so few people send Thanksgiving cards, your gesture will really be noticed. The cost of three hundred, high quality, custom-printed cards, envelopes and postage is $620.

4 **Breakfast of Champions** Arrange to rent a banquet room at a local high profile country club or exclusive hotel. Send out one hundred personal invitations to the area's top real estate professionals asking them to join you and their peers at the Breakfast of Champions event. Feature a well-known keynote speaker who would be willing to lend his or her time to your function. This could be a well-loved sports coach in the community, a former president of the Board of Realtors, a city mayor, etc. (You'd be surprised how easy it is.) Host a first-class event at a stunning location with a beautiful breakfast and an honored guest speaker. Collect business cards for a door prize raffle and make plans to follow up one-on-one with everyone that attended your event. The cost of the room rental, breakfast, invita-

tions, and a door prize (assuming fifty people actually RSVP and attend) is just under $800.

5 Blockbuster Letter Compile the names of the last twenty-five customers you financed. Draft a letter thanking them for their trust in you. Drive to your nearest Blockbuster video store and purchase twenty-five $5 gift cards (they look like little credit cards). Insert the gift cards with a letter that thanks your customers for selecting you, plants seeds for referrals and closes with the sentence, *One night this month, relax in your beautiful home and enjoy a movie on me!* The cost of this promotion including the letter, postage, and twenty-five gift cards is $145.

6 Traveling Massage Make arrangements to hire a masseuse for a day. Send out faxes and emails to two or three of your preferred Realtor offices (or other referral clients) saying, *I take the stress out of home financing. Next Tuesday a personal masseuse and I will be visiting your office offering free stress relief gifts and a complimentary five-minute massage. Look for us!* Purchase about fifty stress balls or novelty mood rings or both from the local dollar store as gimmick gifts. You'll make a positive impression, and enjoy a day in your clients' offices while making friends and having fun. The cost of the masseuse and fifty novelty gifts is about $550.

7 Apartment Mailers Stop by your local hardware store and ask to purchase one hundred uncut keys. (They charge about $1 to $2 to cut a duplicate house key, but will sell you uncut keys for around $0.50 each if you bargain to buy a hundred of them. I have done this.) Draft a letter to people living in apartments with the message,

I have the key to your new home. I can get you there! Insert your shiny silver key into the fold of the letter and mail them out to one hundred apartment addresses. The cost of this entire project is $150.

This list could go on and on, but you get the idea. By reinvesting the revenue from a single loan you can do so much. And the best part is that if each activity ends up generating just two or more loan opportunities, your investment didn't cost you a thing. The activity actually paid for itself and generated a profit.

Consider beginning this new concept next month and continue it throughout the year. Brainstorm some fun and high-impact ways to thank customers for their loyalty and generate referrals. They say that in sales the best place to look for new business is with those you have already done business with, and it's true. Current and past customers are goldmines just waiting for you. It might cost you a little money to start digging, but the financial rewards when you hit the mother lode make it all worthwhile.

— Lesson 13 —

Preparation Pays Off

Have you ever watched a professional golfer before he takes a shot? The golfer will survey the layout in front of him, select the right club, take a few practice swings, set up his stance, look forward again, place the correct grip on the club, relax, and hit the ball. Professional golfers know the importance of preparation. Just a moment or two of preparation increases their chances of making a great shot.

Professional salespeople in our business think the same way, and that's why preparation is an important part of their routine. Whether it's taking a loan application, calling to schedule an appointment with a real estate agent, making a sales visit to a builder client, delivering a group presentation, or just starting off another productive day, the pros know that preparation pays off. Just a few minutes of prep time can mean the difference between success and failure. Successful golfers know this. Successful salespeople do too.

If the first step is to understand the importance of preparation, the second step is know how to prepare. How do you get both yourself and a borrower ready for a loan application appointment? Here are some great examples:

I Taking a New Loan Application Let's say you have an application appointment coming in today for a face-to-face visit. Fifteen minutes before the scheduled appointment time, you should stop everything you're doing and prepare according to a checklist similar to this:

▸ Get out a clean application form.
▸ Get copies of any disclosures and forms needed.
▸ Insert any information already discovered into the application form.
▸ Alert your receptionist of your appointment and the customer's name.
▸ Straighten up your office.
▸ Update your telephone voicemail to say you are in session with a client for the next hour.
▸ Make a quick trip to the restroom to check your professional image.
▸ Be ready to greet your customer with a smile as he or she arrives.

While all this seems elementary, so many loan originators start application appointments late and unprepared. They appear disorganized and scatterbrained to their customers as they apologize for running late, rushing around for the proper forms they need. In doing so, they waste their customers' valuable time simply because they were not prepared in advance for the application interview. Customers notice when you're properly prepared for them. They notice especially when you are not.

2 **Calling a Realtor for an Appointment** Suppose you've identified a high quality Realtor you'd like to meet. Today, it's nearly impossible to visit a real estate office and ask to see a top producer. You need an appointment. Your chances of getting that appointment are as good as the phone call you make to request one. Before picking up that phone, make sure you do the following:

> ▸ Visit the agent's web site to discover an interesting piece of information to break the ice.
> ▸ Script out on paper what you want to say.
> ▸ Pick up your phone and call your own number to recite your script on your voicemail.
> ▸ Call your voicemail, listen to the message you just left and evaluate it for content and enthusiasm.
> ▸ Make necessary changes to your script.
> ▸ Put a smile on your face.
> ▸ Stand up straight, pick up the phone and make the call with confidence.

Your chances of getting an appointment with a real estate agent increase when your request is clear and strong. Appointments lead to meetings, meetings lead to relationships, relationships lead to referrals, and referrals lead to loans. This simple phone call could be the gateway to a profitable new business partner. Prepare to do it right.

3 **Making a Sales Visit to a Builder Referral Client** Let's imagine you have a good relationship with a builder. Your goal is to keep that relationship alive with frequent visits and personal contacts. It's been a couple of weeks since you've seen him and

you've called ahead to learn if he'll be in his office and expecting your visit. On the drive over, take five minutes to do the following:

▸ Recall your notes or conversation from your last meeting.
▸ Create a valuable purpose for your sales visit (introduce a new product, provide status on an existing loan, provide industry news, etc.).
▸ Create an icebreaker (comment on his favorite sports team, hobby, family vacation, award or recognition received, etc.).
▸ Check your professional image in the rear view mirror.
▸ Put a smile on and walk in.

Getting lazy with your existing Realtor or builder referral clients is an easy trap to fall into. This leads to sloppy sales calls where you just show up and wing it. Eventually, the client will see your visits as unproductive interruptions of his busy day. Is that how you want your clients to see you? If the answer is no, make sure you're prepared with an agenda for every sales call.

4 **Delivering a Group Presentation.** Whether it's a group presentation to an audience of Realtors, homebuyers, or any gathering of prospective clients, you want things to go well. When you're not prepared, your presentation flops, and with it your chance at new business. If you don't want that to happen, make sure you arrive at least twenty minutes ahead of time to do the following:

▸ Meet the facilities helper or representative or both.
▸ Set up the room the way you want it.
▸ Arrange your own presentation notes and materials.

- Place materials at each seat along with pens or pencils to take notes.
- Set out refreshments. (Never leave donuts in a closed box or bagels under wrap. People will want one but will feel uncomfortable taking it.)
- Attach your name tag to your lapel.
- Place a stack of business cards on the table.
- Visit the restroom to check your professional image.
- Put a smile on and stand by the door to greet everyone entering the room.

Group presentations are an ideal way to meet many new prospects at once and impress them with who you are and what you offer. Don't blow this chance by not being fully prepared and ready to go.

5 **Starting off a Productive Day** A great day starts with a great plan. Loan originators who don't take the time to prepare for a productive day wind up in a reactionary mode, running around fighting fires with no real sense of purpose. This leads to wasted time, wasted energy, and above all, stress. When you arrive for work each morning, your fifteen-minute set-up routine should look something like this:

- Turn on your computer.
- While your computer warms up, get a cup of coffee and check the fax machine for any overnight faxes.
- Update your telephone voice mail for the day.
- Review your calendar or PDA for scheduled meetings and appointments.

- ▸ Scan your pipeline report for loans scheduled to close that day.
- ▸ Make your to-do list.
- ▸ Plug important activities into your calendar (Time Frame).
- ▸ Get to work.

Remember the Boy Scout motto? *Be prepared.* The same rule applies to running a successful mortgage business. Prepared loan officers are on top of their game, in control, and more effective in every customer interaction.

— Lesson 14 —

Don't Be a Part-Time Originator

One of the best things about being a mortgage loan originator is the luxury of working on your own time. You can come and go as you please. You can set your own schedule. This luxury we have is also one of the worst things about being a mortgage loan originator. Without the self-discipline to manage your time and activities as productively as possible, it's all too easy to become a part-time loan originator.

What is a part-time loan originator? Ask yourself how many times you have been guilty of the following:

- Arriving at work at 9:30 A.M. (or later)
- Spending thirty minutes or so reading the morning paper in your office
- Making personal phone calls at work
- Balancing your checkbook at your desk
- Taking extended lunch breaks
- Running out for errands like picking up the dry cleaning, getting your hair cut, having your nails done, or stopping off at the bank

- ▸ Picking up the kids from soccer practice in the early afternoon
- ▸ Heading home at 4:00 P.M. just because you feel like it

Hard-working, top producing loan originators who consistently put in a solid fifty to sixty hour workweek know there's nothing wrong with enjoying the flexible schedule we all have. The problem is that far too many originators who are not top producers or who desperately need to produce more volume, take advantage of this flexibility to the point that they may be working, truly *working*, only 25 to 30 hours each week without realizing it. They grow frustrated wondering why they can't put enough loans on the books to take them to the level of results and income they need. Most often, they look to their company for answers in the form of better pricing or a broader product line. The real answer to increased production might just lie in how much time they spend actually *working* every single day.

It takes discipline to manage your time wisely. Many of us came from more structured jobs that required us to be at certain places at certain times and to be accountable for our activities to a supervisor or manager. Upon entering our position as an originator in the mortgage business we quickly discover a wide-open format, no watchful supervisor, and no time clock. So, we start to come and go as we please, and before we realize it, we're working part-time. Again, some people can adapt and manage this freedom effectively. Some simply cannot.

Does all this sound a little too familiar? Are you finding yourself guilty of becoming a part-time loan originator? Do you want to do something about it? The first step is to create the discipline you need to stay focused on your job and put in the time and energy it takes to succeed. Here are some suggestions that might help:

I Force yourself to be an early bird in the office.
Get to work at or before 8:00 A.M. and get a jump on the day. Plan

your activities for a productive day with a to-do list of three to five marketing and sales activities. Use this early morning quiet time to get yourself and your day organized before everyone gets in. You won't be interrupted and you'll get more accomplished.

2 **Use the system of *time framing* to block out specific activities on your calendar.** Schedule reading time, marketing time, letter writing time, telephone prospecting time, etc. right on your calendar. Make appointments with yourself and keep them. If you schedule activities and install them into your calendar, day planner or PDA you are more likely to remember to do them.

3 **Get out of the office.** Office time can often be very non-productive time. Hanging around the office leaves you susceptible for coffeepot gossip and personal phone calls. Make a firm commitment to get out and see your clients on a regular basis, and see lots of them. You'll be tempted less often to make and take personal calls, balance your checkbook, surf the net and read the paper if you are not in a place where you can do so.

4 **Have make-up hours.** If you decide to run errands during work time for two hours, schedule specific time on your calendar when you will make it up later in the week. Remember that two hours of a forty-hour week is 5% of your workweek. If you are guilty of doing this every week for fifty weeks a year, you are spending one hundred hours a year running errands. One hundred hours! That's two weeks worth of work. Makes you think, huh?

5 Schedule client lunches. Make it a habit to schedule at least one or two lunches a week with your key referral clients (Realtors, builders, etc.) This will keep you from long personal lunches, swinging by the mall, or taking extended lunches with other loan officers. On the days you lunch alone, take your checkbook and balance it, read the paper or stop by the bank on your own time.

6 Work a full day. Challenge yourself to put in a full eight to ten hour day every day. I've met hundreds of very successful, very wealthy loan originators in my career, none of whom work ten to four. They are rich and successful because they've developed the discipline to work. They learned early on that you can't make much money in this business working a five or six-hour day.

While you look for new and better ways to climb your ladder of success in this business, don't overlook the obvious. You're a professional salesperson to whom time is money. That's the trade off you make every day.

Don't get caught becoming a part-time loan originator. Invest your time wisely each day. The results will astound you.

— Lesson 15 —

Satisfied Customers Are not Enough

As a consumer, you are a customer. In the course of a normal week you might buy gas, shop for groceries, sign up for a new cellular phone service, or purchase a sandwich at a deli. At each buying event, you become one of three types of customer: dissatisfied, satisfied or extremely satisfied. The experience you have will determine whether you'll return again or recommend that company or both.

As a mortgage originator, you have customers. In the course of a normal week you might deal with a rate shopper, pre-qualify a prospect, take a loan application, make a sales call, or attend a closing. At each encounter, you create customers that are either dissatisfied with you, satisfied with you or extremely satisfied with you. Your entire business and livelihood depends on what type of customers you create.

It is obvious that none of us want dissatisfied customers. We know that dissatisfied customers either choose not to work with us the first time, or if they do, they never come back. We also know that dissatisfied customers talk, and if they have a negative experience with us or our companies, what they say can damage both our reputations and our business. A recent consumer research study showed that 92% of dissatisfied customers will never offer repeat business.

Most companies, and for that matter, most mortgage loan originators, shoot for satisfied customers. They feel that if they can get a borrower from application through closing with a minimal amount of problems, life is good. If the post-closing customer survey is returned with the word *satisfied* circled, they feel they have done their job. In fact they have failed. Statistics show that two out of three consumers that say they were merely satisfied with a company will never return. That's right, two out of three. The customer expected to be satisfied; you have done nothing special or memorable. All you have done is met their expectations, and you'll never see two out of three of these borrowers again.

So what does it take to get a customer back for their next refinance or purchase loan? What is required to secure an endorsement to their family or friends? Nothing less than *extremely* satisfied customers. The vast majority of people will not return or refer companies where they did not experience an extremely satisfied buying experience. Research shows that, of consumers who rate their reaction to a company as extremely satisfied, 85% will return again or recommend at least one other person to buy from you. Think about yourself as a customer. What restaurants do you recommend to a friend? One that you feel O.K. about or one where you had a great dining experience and know that he will too? Do you return to hotels or vacation resorts where you would say you had a good experience or a great experience? We are all customers in one way or another, and we frequent and recommend services and companies where we are more than satisfied with what we get.

I remember working with a sizable group of young loan originator recruits many years ago at a large mortgage company. I told them that their mission was to get to the point in their careers where they would never have to prospect for business again. The four-step plan follows:

I Build a strong base of excellent referral clients (Realtors, builders, etc.)

2 Provide an overwhelmingly positive experience for every borrower.
3 Ask every borrower for referrals.
4 Keep in touch with borrowers down the road so they would remember them, come back, and refer their friends.

Correctly followed, this plan would ensure that in five years, these originators would have built such a loyal following of customers that they could be done prospecting for life. No more sales calls, no more donut deliveries to real estate offices. In five years they would have an army of five hundred to one thousand extremely satisfied customers who sold for them. Like a pyramid, their base of customers could potentially double every year.

Unfortunately, most of these loan officers didn't follow the plan. They chased down deals, got them processed and closed, refrained from doing anything special and created satisfied customers. Most of them are long gone by now. Those still in business today most likely continue to beat the street every day looking for their next deal.

I recall one of these rookie originators who took the plan to heart. Ron bought into the *wow factor* of customer service. He tried to make each borrower experience special. He made personal follow-up phone calls. Ron sent out handwritten thank you cards. He showed up at closings with gift baskets. Ron so impressed each borrower that within just a few years he had hundreds of people out selling for him. The last time I saw Ron, seven years after presenting the four-step plan, he was still in the business in Florida, now one of his company's top producers, running his own branch office and making a fortune. Ron told me he doesn't prospect much anymore. He doesn't have to.

So, if 85% of extremely satisfied customers will provide a continual stream of referrals, loans and income, why doesn't every originator try to create them? The answer can be one or more of the following attitudes:

1 I don't have time.

2 I think it's silly.

3 I don't know how.

Let's tackle these one at a time.

1 I don't have time. The fact is you do have the time. As Steven Covey, author of *The 7 Habits of Highly Effective People* states, "We always will find the time to do the things we feel are important." Chances are you work forty to sixty hours a week. You have plenty of time for a personal follow-up call (1 minute) or to write a thank you note (2 minutes) or stop by a closing (30 minutes). You choose not to do these things because (and this may sting a little) because you don't think these things are important. Some originators are so busy chasing down loans and putting out fires, great customer service takes a back seat to their busywork. The fact is, you don't have time *not* to provide great service. Perhaps if more of your customers were extremely satisfied, you wouldn't have to prospect so much, giving you the time to take great care of all the referrals those customers would send you.

2 I think it's silly. Some loan originators think they're above giving great service. They feel the customer owes them, not the other way around. The friendly gesture of a phone call to a buyer asking how they're enjoying their new house or a Christmas card to the family are for someone else. That's too bad, because these originators are missing the point. As a test, think about when you're a customer. Think about a time someone went out of his way to ensure you had a great experience. How did you react? Did you think it was corny, silly, or unnecessary? No! Did you feel it was unprofessional? Certainly not! You loved it. That's how your customers would feel if you started providing them with an extremely satisfying experience.

3 I don't know how. Perhaps you believe in great customer service but aren't sure of what you can do to create the wow factor. First, remember that the wow factor isn't created with one big thing, but often a pattern of little things. A great experience at a restaurant is the product of an attentive valet, a welcoming hostess, a knowledgeable and helpful waiter, a clean dining environment, and a wonderful chef. To create a similar great experience in your business, ask yourself, *If I was a borrower, what would really impress me? What would a loan officer or mortgage lender do that would make me one of their raving fans?* Draft a list of what you would like to experience, and that's probably what your customers want as well. Once you have your total customer experience mapped out, integrate those actions and little touches into your system:

▸ A *Thank you for applying* card goes out twenty-four hours after the loan application.
▸ A personal welcome call from the loan processor is made within forty-eight hours.
▸ A gift basket is sent to the place of employment on the day of loan approval.
▸ A *Congratulations* card is mailed one day after closing.
▸ A magazine gift subscription is started thirty days later.

Everything is easier, even customer service, when you have it built into a system.

Think about how many borrowers you will help this year. Perhaps it will be fifty, one hundred, two hundred or more. What if everyone, because of their fantastic experiences, sent at least one family member, co-worker, neighbor, or friend to you next year? Theoretically, you could double your volume without any more prospecting. You would have calls coming in every day from pre-sold prospects being referred to you by someone they trust, who raved about you and your service. You might even have more business than you think you can handle. What a wonderful problem that would be!

For many years now, I have delivered seminars on the subject of customers for life. I love to share story after story about the ways successful loan originators wow their customers with special service. As I deliver these presentations, I can see many participants shaking their heads. Their facial reactions say to me, *Are you serious? Does this guy expect me to do this stuff?* I also notice a few nodding heads and smiling faces from originators who get it. They understand what this truly means and what extremely satisfied customers can do for their results.

Thank goodness not everyone in this business gives great customer service. It makes it that much easier for you to shine.

— Lesson 16 —

Put Your Ideas into Action

An energetic young loan officer approached me after one of my seminars. "I have this idea," he told me. "I've tried first-time homebuyer seminars a few times, but I just can't get people to show up. So my idea is to partner with my local Home Depot. A friend of mine is a manager there. Since their business comes mostly from people that own homes, they should want to promote home ownership. Right? We co-market a homebuyer's event as a free seminar, I pay the costs, we hold the seminar at the Home Depot store, and I leverage their credibility and name recognition to get lots of people to show up! What do you think?"

After listening to the idea and hearing his genuine enthusiasm I replied, "Sounds terrific! How long have you had this idea?" The loan officer smiled sheepishly, "About two years."

We all come up with good ideas for our business from time to time—some big ideas and some small ideas. Perhaps you have an idea for a new consumer direct marketing campaign, or an idea to generate more purchase mortgage leads from apartment buildings. Right now you may be harboring an idea for developing a new referral source, an idea for a new closing gift, or even an idea for how to streamline your backshop file flow operations. Ideas are everywhere. They're easy to create and best of all, they're free.

The challenge is making the leap from idea to action. Thomas Edison, among the greatest inventors in history, once stated, "The value of an idea lies in the using of it." He's right. The Edison Electric Company patented dozens of ideas, such as the phonograph and the electric light bulb. What most people don't know is that Edison and his team experimented with thousands of different ideas to achieve their results. They weren't afraid to take ideas to action. They were willing, as we should be, to take that leap of faith.

Like my loan officer friend and his homebuyer seminar idea, many originators have equally good ideas they have never taken to action. There are several reasons for this:

1 **They fear failure.** *What if the idea doesn't work?* some think. *What if it's a waste of time and energy? What will my boss think? Will my peers tease me about my foolhardy idea?* Many of us are haunted by negative possibilities. We conclude that the safe bet is not to act. Because of this fear of failure, we keep the idea in our head forever, never knowing if it might work and never reaping the rewards if it does.

2 **They fear success.** *What if this idea actually works?* some wonder. *What if my idea generates more business than I can handle? Can I risk that?* It sounds silly to fear success, but it is a harsh reality for many salespeople. Most ideas I hear from mortgage originators are truly good ideas that I believe will work. I think the reason they have never made their own personal leap from idea to action is that they, too, know their idea will work, and they are afraid

of handling the success and business that will come along with it.

3 They resist investing effort. Ideas take effort to get off the ground. That effort may include time, energy, brainpower, and even money. Some originators are in love with their ideas, but are not in love with the work it will take to bring them to life. Although a $200 investment can bring $10,000 in added income, they're hesitant to spend the $200. Even though five hours spent working a Saturday at a trade show may yield ten to twenty leads, they'd rather not spend a Saturday working. As with a new diet or exercise program, we can get really excited about the possible result. But if it means expending time, money, energy, and sacrifice, many of us will elect to pass.

4 They don't know where to start. For some of us, it's not about the time, money or risk. Our hesitancy to leap from idea to action comes from simply not knowing how and where to start. Actualizing some big ideas may involve as many as fifteen to twenty smaller actions or steps. We can become overwhelmed as we look at the big picture all at once. Because we see our idea as more than we can manage, we never take action and it remains just an idea.

If knowing where to start has stopped you from implementing your ideas, here's the best way to take an idea to action: take baby steps one at a time. Start with a clean piece of paper and write your idea on the top in bold letters: NEW HOMEBUYER SEMINAR. Then, brainstorm all the things that need to be done. Don't worry about the order of the items; just get them down on paper so you can see them all together. For example:

- Select location
- Put together my presentation
- Design flyers
- Run radio ads
- Newspaper announcements
- Put together attendee packets
- Design visual aids for session
- Handouts for attendees
- Refreshments
- Door prizes and/or discount coupons
- Partner with favorite real estate agent
- Create follow up mailers
- Process for registration

You won't think of everything on this first pass, but you will think of roughly 90% of the most important activities you need to do.

Once you have your list of things to do, place them in order of execution. Place a heading on a new piece of paper: NEW HOMEBUYER SEMINAR PROJECT PLAN. Then, list your plan in order of individual action steps. For example:

1 Set first delivery date on calendar.
2 Select and secure location.
3 Design advertising and marketing plan.
4 Solicit favorite real estate agent as partner and presenter.
5 Create registration system with contact name and phone number.
6 Finalize advertising and place ads (radio, paper, community bulletin, etc.).
7 Design the presentation along with visuals and handouts.
8 Arrange giveaways and door prizes.

9 Arrange for refreshments, seating, and room setup.

10 Create follow-up mailers (3) for post-seminar prospecting.

How do you eat an elephant? One bite at a time. Don't concern yourself with ten things to do, just one. Get step one accomplished, check it off, and move on to step two. It may take my loan officer friend who had this idea three months to finally get it into action, but that's better than two years (or never).

Do you have a great idea floating around in your head? Perhaps you've been considering a consumer direct advertising campaign or targeting a new area of town. Maybe you've been thinking about sponsoring a golf tournament or community event. Start to make the leap from idea to action today by writing down your favorite idea. Make a commitment to see this idea really happen and then build a step-by-step plan. As you look at your idea in a series of small, manageable steps you'll likely think, *This is achievable. I can do this!*

— Lesson 17 —

Move up to the Next Level

Mortgage companies and loan originators often talk about moving their business up to the next level. The term has been mentioned several times in this book. But what is the next level? And how do you know when you've arrived?

In a performance-driven business like ours, the next level is simply an arbitrary escalation of your results. Here's a good benchmark: the next level of performance for any loan originator should be 50% more results than currently generated. For example, if you are closing, on average, four units a month, your next level is a minimum of six units. If you are originating $2,000,000 a month in closed loan volume, your next level is $3,000,000. If you write ten loan applications a week, your next level is fifteen applications.

A 50% increase in performance at any level is a significant jump. Do you have what it takes to get there? There are four things you must do:

1 **You must create a plan.** For you to grow your results by at least 50%, you must have a specific plan to get there. *I'll just work harder*, is not a plan. You're going to have to identify and list the

specific action steps that need to be taken to achieve a 50% growth rate. That might include these examples:

▸ Increase my number of Realtor clients from three to five.
▸ Add another builder client.
▸ Open up a channel of consumer-direct advertising.
▸ Hire an operations assistant to free up more sales time.
▸ Double my frequency of outbound calls and contacts.
▸ Begin a quarterly database marketing campaign.

There's an old saying: *If you always do what you've always done, you will always get what you always got.* Too many loan originators today are trying to get to the next level by repeating exactly what they've always done. That's why they never move up. Executing the same activities month after month will usually get you the same result month after month. To increase your results you must first increase your efforts in at least one critical area. Talk with a top performer who has moved up in her career from level to level. Most likely, she'll describe significant steps taken to get there. You are going to have to do the same. And it all starts with your plan.

2 You must maximize your operating efficiencies.

Once you have identified your plan to grow your business by 50%, you need to consider another important factor: Can your backshop handle it? Suppose you plan to move from an average of ten loans a month to fifteen loans a month. Do you have the excess capacity in your backshop to deliver fifteen loans a month smoothly? Just think, if closing ten loans a month creates chaos at your office, what will happen with five more loans on top of that? Believe it or not, it's this barrier that keeps many loan originators from achieving their potential success and income levels. They can produce the business, but their system can't close it.

There are several questions you can ask to evaluate the current strength of your backshop operations:

▸ Do I pre-qualify and prepare borrowers thoroughly before they apply with me?
▸ Do I take complete and clear loan applications?
▸ Am I clogging up my backshop with low-quality loan applications that will likely never close?
▸ Are my loan processor and I working from a detailed checklist defining what is needed on each loan file and who is accountable for what?
▸ Am I actively requesting and using alternative documentation paperwork on every available loan?
▸ Am I organized? Really organized?
▸ Am I taking advantage of available LOS or AUS technology programs or both to the fullest extent? (If you don't know what those acronyms stand for, the answer is no.)
▸ Do I have enough support people working behind me, and are they the kind of people who can help take my business up another 50%?

As mentioned before, the mortgage approval process in any branch or company is essentially an assembly line that moves loan opportunities from start to finish. Like any assembly line, it is built to handle a certain amount of units. Start taking steps now to outfit your system (and yourself) for a capacity of 50% more volume.

3 You must change your habits. The third thing you may need to do to get your production to the next level is change your old work habits. I've known originators that have been in this business for ten years who still produce only seven or eight loans a month. Why doesn't their business grow? Because even with a great plan and a fully supported backshop system, they are unwilling to change how they run their business. Consider the following:

▸ Some originators come cruising into work at 10:00 A.M. and are gone by 4:00 P.M. To get to the next level, they may need to start coming in at 8:00 A.M. and not leave before 6:00 P.M.

▸ Some originators spend most of their time hanging around the office waiting for opportunities to call. To get to the next level, they may need to schedule and make ten sales call presentations each week.

▸ Some originators coddle their files and spend most of their time processing and chasing down paperwork. To get to the next level, they may need to let go, delegate processing duties, and spend more time out selling.

▸ Some originators still approach the business the way they did five years ago. To get to the next level, they may need to seek out and attend good sales training and marketing courses to update their strategies and practices.

▸ Some originators only know and sell about three or four loan programs. To get to the next level, they may need to expand their product knowledge into new and niche loan opportunities.

▸ Some originators are reluctant to embrace technology. To

get to the next level, they may need to get with the twenty-first century—get a web site, get an online application system, input on DU or LP and get their business up to speed.

In working with thousands of loan originators over the past twenty years, I firmly believe that one of the biggest things that keeps people from achieving greater success is themselves. They remain at the same level year after year because they fear change. Habits are hard things to break. But until you break them, you may never move up the ladder of success.

4 You must move forward. The fourth and final step in moving up to the next level is action—and action is all about initiative. Getting from ten to fifteen loans a month won't happen overnight, but it can happen. Moving forward takes guts. It's all too easy to retreat into a comfortable way of doing things. The best originators in the business are always looking forward, always asking, *Where do I go from here? What is my next step toward success?*

- Put together a think tank of three or four other originators and meet once a quarter to share successful ideas.
- Gather the names of fifteen new Realtors and get on the phone making appointments.
- Attend a class on self-employed borrowers or sub-prime lending opportunities.
- Buy a great book on personal marketing. Read it!
- Contact a community newspaper or real estate magazine and inquire about advertising there.

- ▸ Start interviewing potential assistants.
- ▸ Initiate weekly progress and status meetings with your loan processor.
- ▸ Get your web site up and running.
- ▸ Schedule your calendar out one day each week. Spend that day in the field making sales calls and visits.

Perhaps you're ready for the next level. If you need an extra incentive to get going, remember that a 50% increase in your performance results shows up as a 50% increase in your paycheck. Consider what you earned last year and add 50%. Does that sound good to you? Then get moving!

— Lesson 18 —

Start Thinking Like a Superstar

By now, you've probably heard stories about the superstars in our business. Perhaps you've even met one. How is it that some mortgage loan originators can consistently produce $50,000,000 to $200,000,000 a year and earn such enormous incomes? How do they do it? What do they have that you don't have?

As you study the habits and practices of various originators in the mortgage business, you'll quickly uncover a noticeable contrast between the truly successful producer—the superstar—and the average producer. This difference begins with the superstar's mindset. Superstar originators think differently than most average or mainstream originators. And as we all know, how we think forms the basis of how we act.

Let's look at the difference between the way a superstar producer thinks as opposed to most average producers. You'll begin to distinguish a pattern. You may even see where you now stand in your career and how thinking differently could propel you to even greater success, maybe even to superstar levels.

Superstar originators are in this business for the long run. Most average originators are in it to

make a few quick bucks. Superstar loan originators have burned their bridges and their resumes behind them. This is their chosen career and there's no turning back. This full-throttle commitment fuels their passion for excellence. Failure is not an option to them.

Many average originators see their job as a temporary stopover on the road to something else. They really don't envision themselves writing mortgage loans for more than a couple of years, so it's difficult for them to pour themselves into the business. As a result, things like training, studying, relationship building and other long-term activities seem unimportant to them. Thousands of migratory originators come into the industry year after year, stay for a short while, write a few loans, and move on. Superstars are in it for life. Are you?

Superstar originators work to build life-long relationships with their clients. Most average originators work from one loan to the next. With a mindset of transactional selling, many average producers can't see past their next deal. To them it's just, get the loan, get it processed, approved, closed, and go get another. Their focus remains on the details of the transaction, with little concern for what can come of it.

By contrast, superstar originators are sold on the idea of clients for life. They see every customer encounter as an opportunity to meet another prospect, another advocate, another referral client. That's why they take the extra time to take care of their customers. That's why they send out thank you cards, birthday cards, closing gifts, referral letters and more. Since their plan is to originate loans for a lifetime, their mindset is to have customers coming back again and again throughout that lifetime. Is that your plan?

Superstar originators operate from a game plan of personal goals and deliberate actions. Many average originators just come in every day and wing it. Ask a superstar originator about his goals, business plan or target book of clients. He'll immediately cite specific, well thought-out strategies now being executed. Ask average originators about the same. "Goals? Business plan? Target list?" they'll reply. "I guess I don't have a plan. I just work really hard." Because they have no clear direction in their business, they wander month after month from priority to priority. Some months are good; some months are bad. They're at the mercy of the market.

Superstar originators, by comparison, are deliberate about doing everything with keen intentions for consistent results. They have clearly defined production goals and a specific series of steps mapped out to take them where they want to go. Is that what you have?

Superstar originators are focused on their customers—their wants and their needs. Many average originators are focused primarily on themselves. Have you ever met a superstar in this business who didn't have a passion for helping others? Have you ever heard a successful producer say she really can't stand working with people? Of course not. That's not how superstars think. Superstars truly like people and enjoy the opportunity to help them. This translates into taking the time and energy to get to know their borrowers and referral clients well, so that strong personal relationships can be built.

Many average originators often see people as a necessary evil in the business and a challenge to be dealt with as painlessly as possible. "I hate Realtors!" they proclaim. "Borrowers are a pain in the rear!" they shout. Their focus remains on themselves thinking only about: *How much am I going to make on this deal? How fast can I get this done? What's in it for me?* This ego-driven attitude reveals itself in how they think, how they act and what they say. And believe it or not, the customers see it. What do your customers see?

Superstar originators view themselves as professional salespeople and look for new and more sales opportunities every day. Average originators really don't like to sell and therefore, don't. It's hard for many average originators to view themselves as salespeople. Selling is not part of their mindset. This thought process creates an aversion to prospecting and selling and can lead to call reluctance. They prefer to sit around the office and wait for an opportunity to find them. If they do engage in any proactive selling, it's usually last on their week's priority list.

By contrast, superstar originators are selling-machines. They understand that to grow their business they must first grow their number of opportunities each and every day. You see these people handing out business cards to everyone they meet, making frequent contacts and visits to their clients, delivering seminars, making presentations, taking referral clients to lunch and planting thousands of seeds for future business each year. Superstars love to sell. Do you?

Superstar originators maintain a positive, upbeat, can-do attitude. Most average originators look for something to complain about or criticize. While many less-than-successful producers are griping about how something can't work, superstar originators are already making it happen. As some originators say their business is off because the market is down, their company's rates aren't competitive or they don't have the right products, superstar producers (many who work for the same company in the same market with the same products and rates) are booking a steady pipeline of loans.

Superstar originators are positive people. These high performers attract clients and business opportunities every day because of their let's-make-it-happen attitude. If positive success starts with a positive attitude, superstars cannot be denied. Does that describe you?

Superstar originators view themselves as entrepreneurs and run their business like they own it. Many average originators have a job and expect their company to do it all for them. Evidence of this is seen everywhere. Most superstar mortgage originators hire personal assistants. They invest in consumer advertising and client marketing. They purchase contact management systems, personal web sites, and database mining fulfillment services. They employ a personal coach. They attend industry events, training seminars and personal development workshops. Who pays for all this? They do! This is their business and they run it like they own it. It's great to have a good company behind you, but that alone won't make you a superstar.

Unfortunately, many average originators have no skin in the game because they have yet to see this as their business. Their lack of commitment to their career holds them back. Do you run your business like you own it?

Superstar originators are consistent in their approach and can be counted on to perform. Many average originators fly by the seat of their pants. Talk with a superstar producer and you'll hear him use the word systems repeatedly. Superstars have a system for prospecting, for the application process, for referral client contact, for status reporting and for just about everything else. When you systematize your business, you create efficiencies and capacities to free up time to grow your volume.

Many average loan originators struggle with their internal operations. Their lack of established systems creates inconsistency in how they work. Calls go unreturned and loan opportunities slip through the cracks because of poor follow-up procedures and a loosely defined process. The result is wasted time, aggravation, and a blemished reputation, both internally and externally. This flying by the seat of your pants way of doing business forces them to work harder days, longer hours and later nights because of their propensity to reinvent the wheel with almost everything they do. Do you have systems built for your business?

Superstar originators maintain a strong work ethic and put in a full day, every day. Many average originators don't like to work very hard. Many average producers come in late, leave early, and spend the day in unproductive tasks. They waste the day reading paperwork, surfing the Internet, chatting with peers, working dead loans, over-processing files and running personal errands.

You won't catch superstar loan originators delivering packets around town, processing loans, spending a half-hour in the break room talking about a basketball game, or pouring hours into a loan that they know isn't going to fly. A superstar's time is too precious to waste because she understands that her time is like money. Her relentless focus on productive activities means she gets more profitable things done each day. It's not hard to make twice as much as the next guy when you work twice as hard and twice as smart as he does. What is your work ethic?

Superstar originators take responsibility for their own success. Many average originators make excuses for why they're not successful. We can always blame something for our lot in life. Many average producers blame their lack of success on their boss, their company, their insufficient training, the market, the economy, their support staff, their office location, the weather, you name it. It's never them; it's always something else.

Superstar mortgage loan originators empower themselves by taking full responsibility for their success. This accountability drives their motivation. This is why even in a slow economy, superstars still produce amazing results. It seems that no matter what the problem or obstacle, they find a way through. They live by the age-old mantra of success: *If it is to be, it is up to me.* Is that what you believe?

Some aspire to greatness while others are busy achieving it. Perhaps you've set your sights on becoming a superstar mortgage originator. If your thoughts create your actions and your actions create your results, the first step to becoming a superstar is to start thinking like a superstar. It doesn't happen overnight, but it does happen. Who knows? One day you, too, may be celebrated by your company, and your peers as one of the best in the business, a superstar. Wouldn't that be great?

— Lesson 19 —

It's All About Commitment

Motivational guru Tony Robbins taught me the most important lesson I have ever learned about success. Success is about answering three simple questions:

1 What do I want?
2 How bad do I want it?
3 Am I willing to do what it takes to get it?

The first question defines your direction: *What do I want?* What is it that you truly want? Do you want to get in shape? Do you want to retire rich? Do you want to be a top producer in the mortgage business? Many people don't achieve the success they want because they've not yet figured out what they really want. Without direction, we go on living and working day to day wondering what it's all about. The only thing worse than knowing what you want and not having it is not knowing what you want in the first place.

Question two is the question of motivation: *How bad do I want it?* People find ways to harness the resources and motivation they need to accomplish things that are extremely important to them. If getting in shape, retiring rich or being a top producer isn't really all that important to you in the big scheme of your life's agenda, then you probably won't ever get there.

The third and final question tests your commitment: *Am I willing to do what it takes to get it?* If you're clear on what you want, and you want it bad enough, you'll be willing to do whatever it takes to achieve that goal. Want to get in shape? Then you must be willing to change the way you eat, exercise, drink, and think about physical health. Are you serious about retiring rich? Plan to save a lot of money every month, invest it for the long run, curtail major spending and work harder in your job to earn a lot more money than you do now. If you're committed to become a top producer, you'll have to start doing what it takes to eventually get there. And that's what this final lesson is all about.

I don't think there's a mortgage loan originator out there today who doesn't want to be successful. Nobody takes this job fully expecting to fail miserably. If we define success in this business as doing something we enjoy, helping people and making great money along the way, then we must be committed to doing whatever it takes to earn that success. Many people in this business talk about success, but we all know talk is cheap; commitment is what counts.

I **Commitment to a Dream** Everyone has a dream. For some it's driving a Ferrari. For others it's owning a vacation cabin in the mountains or running their very own mortgage company. I've met many successful people in our industry who've achieved their dreams because of a total commitment to what they truly want this business to provide for them. What are your dreams? Write them down. How serious are you about doing what it takes to make them come true? Measure your resolve. Then, set a course of action that will lead you there. Dreams come true not by luck, but by hard work and planning over the long run.

2 Commitment to a Goal On January 1 of this year, you had likely set new income and production goals for yourself. Are you really committed to those goals, or are they just random numbers you pulled out of the air? Have you sat down and calculated what it will take to reach those goals? Do you know how many units, closings, applications and referrals you will need to reach your production or income goals? The mortgage business is a numbers game, and if you don't know the numbers, you can't play it. On the other hand, if you know your goals and are committed to them, you'll find a way to reach them.

3 Commitment to Your Business As we have already mentioned, the best loan originators view the business they are in as *their* business. That means they invest the time, money, energy, and passion necessary for success. If you are shy about spending money to advertise, you are not committed. If you are working with old technology or resources because you are too cheap to buy new ones, you are not committed. If you are afraid to hire an assistant because of risk, you are not committed. If you still see yourself as an employee of a mortgage company, you are not fully committed. Make the commitment to take command of your future and your life by taking command of your business. When does that commitment start? It starts TODAY.

4 Commitment to Your Profession We are fortunate to be employed in a prestigious field of work. What other profession can you think of that allows normal, hard working people like you and me to make fantastic money while helping people fulfill the American Dream?

With that luxury comes responsibility. Are you committed to your personal growth in this profession? Are you committed to continual learning by attending training classes and seminars throughout the year? Are you committed to staying current on changes and trends in the home financing and real estate industries by reading quality industry periodicals each week? Most importantly, are you committed to upholding the ethics of this business? Nobody has to tell us that mortgage loan originators as a whole do not enjoy a great reputation. Why is that? It's because today there are thousands of unscrupulous, poorly-educated lenders who will take advantage of their clients at every opportunity. I sincerely hope your commitment to this noble profession is above that.

5 Commitment to Your Clients Your referral and borrower clients put an enormous amount of trust in you. Are you equally committed to them? By taking the time to really get to know your clients and their needs, you act in their best interests. Do you get out to see your real estate agents on a regular basis? Do you send personal thank you cards for their referrals? Do you phone homebuyers a few weeks after closing and ask how they are enjoying their new house? Are you executing a client database-marketing program to keep in touch with them as clients for life? Speaker and author Zig Ziglar has long professed that we, as sales professionals, can achieve whatever we want in our lives by helping others achieve what they want. His message makes sense.

6 Commitment to Your Team Many people helped you get to the level of success you now enjoy (or will one day enjoy). This might include your company, your boss, your loan processors, underwriters, closers, investors, MI reps, appraisers, receptionists, assistants and maybe even your spouse and family. They have proven their commitment to you. Have you proven your commitment to them? What are you actively doing to make them feel a part of your winning team? Do you celebrate success together? Do you remember important days? Do you lend support and understanding when they need it? One of the hallmarks of successful mortgage originators is the genuine commitment they have to their teams. This business is challenging enough, let alone having to go it alone.

Our commitment is measured every day in what we do, what we say, and how we run our businesses. In the last twenty years, I have met many dedicated, committed people in this industry. I can with great confidence state that those loan originators that are committed to their dreams, goals, clients, teams, and professions climb the ladder of success faster and higher than anyone else. This is not only a lesson for success in our journey through mortgage loan origination; it is a lesson for success in our journey through life.

For more information on Doug Smith's
presentations, seminars, coaching programs,
newsletters and books, please contact:

Douglas Smith & Associates

by calling us toll free at
877-430-2329

Or visit our website at
www.DougSmithOnline.com

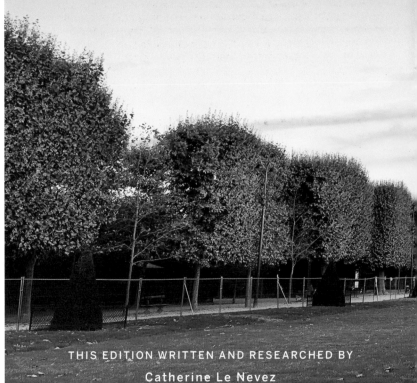

PARIS

TOP SIGHTS, AUTHENTIC EXPERIENCES

THIS EDITION WRITTEN AND RESEARCHED BY

Catherine Le Nevez

Lonely Planet's
Paris

Plan Your Trip

This Year in Paris 4
Need to Know.....................................18
Top Days in Paris 20
Hotspots For... 28
What's New 30
For Free 31
Family Travel.....................................32

Top Experiences......................35

Eiffel Tower 36
Arc de Triomphe 42
Notre Dame....................................... 46
The Louvre 52
Sacré-Coeur......................................58
Musée d'Orsay..................................62
Musée Rodin 66
Jardin du Luxembourg...................... 68
Cruising the Seine............................72
Centre Pompidou..............................74
Cimetière du Père Lachaise 78
Street Markets..................................82
Day Trip: Château de Versailles 84
Musée National du Moyen Âge 88
Jardin des Tuileries 90
Sainte-Chapelle................................92
Les Catacombes 94
Cooking & Wine-Tasting Courses 96
Day Trip: Maison et Jardins
de Claude Monet 98
Palais Garnier 100
Walking Tour: Seine-Side
Romantic Meander...........................102
Hôtel des Invalides..........................104
Jardin des Plantes...........................106
Walking Tour: Paris'
Covered Passages 110
Discovering Paris' Street Art 112
Musée National Picasso 114

Dining Out................................. 117

The Best... 120
Eiffel Tower & Western Paris 122
Champs-Élysées &
Grands Boulevards 123
Louvre & Les Halles 125
Montmartre & Northern Paris...............127
Le Marais, Ménilmontant
& Belleville 130
Bastille & Eastern Paris 132
The Islands 134
Latin Quarter.................................... 136
St-Germain & Les Invalides................. 138
Montparnasse & Southern Paris 141

Treasure Hunt 143

The Best... 146
Champs-Élysées &
Grands Boulevards 148
Louvre & Les Halles 149
Montmartre & Northern Paris...............151
Le Marais, Ménilmontant
& Belleville 151
Bastille & Eastern Paris 153
The Islands 154
Latin Quarter.................................... 155
St-Germain & Les Invalides.................. 156

Bar Open 163

The Best... 166
Eiffel Tower & Western Paris 168
Champs-Élysées &
Grands Boulevards 168
Louvre & Les Halles 170
Montmartre & Northern Paris...............173
Le Marais, Ménilmontant
& Belleville 176

**tre &
n Paris**
rtre's en-
hilly streets
e red-light
strict, home
oulin Rouge.
249)

**que du
-Cœur**

e & Les Halles
t streets fan out
d the mighty
e and the
g-edge Centre
dou.
p250)

**Centre
Pompidou**
🚇

**nte-
pelle**
⛪

⛪
**Notre
Dame**
⊙

**Jardin des
Plantes**
⊙

**Musée
National
Picasso** 🚇

**Le Marais,
Ménilmontant &
Belleville**
Hip boutiques, bars
and restaurants
squeeze alongside a
celebrity-filled ceme-
tery. *(Map p254)*

⊙ **Cimetière du
Père Lachaise**

The Islands
Notre Dame domi-
nates the larger Île
de la Cité, while little
Île St-Louis is graced
with elegant build-
ings. *(Map p250)*

⊙ **Gare de
Lyon**

🚉
**Gare
d'Austerlitz**

**Bastille &
Eastern Paris**
The Parisians' Paris,
with fabulous markets,
intimate gourmet
bistros and lively
drinking and dancing
venues. *(Map p254)*

n Quarter
e to beautiful
nic gardens and
ed with vibrant
ent haunts.
p252)*

Welcome to Paris

La Ville Lumière *(the City of Light)*
acquired its enduring moniker due to
its leading role in the Age of Enlight-
enment, and it's as apt as ever today,
with enduring icons alongside ground-
breaking innovations.

The enchanting French capital is awash with landmarks that need no introduction – the Eiffel Tower,
Arc de Triomphe and Notre Dame among them –
along with a trove of specialist museums and
galleries. Creamy-stone, grey-metal-roofed apartment buildings, lamp-lit bridges and geometrically
laid-out formal parks are equally integral parts of
the city's fabric.

Contrary to its magnificently preserved
cityscapes, however, Paris has never stood still,
but has constantly evolved throughout the eras,
leading the way in industrial, artistic, scientific and
architectural endeavours. This innovative spirit
continues today, with pioneering green transport
initiatives and dazzling new architectural projects that include skyscraping towers along the
periphery and re-energised urban spaces, such as
the Île Seguin-Rives de Seine development on a
Seine island being transformed into a cultural hub
of the city's ambitious Grand Paris (Greater Paris)
expansion. Creativity is evident everywhere, from
neobistro kitchens, cutting-edge cocktail bars,
fashion ateliers and vibrant street art to the 1920s
former railway depot housing Station F, the world's
largest start-up hub.

contrary to its magnificently
preserved cityscapes, Paris
has never stood still

Eiffel Tower (p36) overlooking Parc du Champ de Mars

PARIS

Mon
Nort
Mon
chan
adjo
Piga
to th
(Map

St-Germain &
Les Invalides
Literature lovers and
fashionistas flock to
this fabled cafe- and
boutique-filled Left
Bank neighbourhood.
(Map p246)

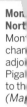

Ba
Sa

Champs-Élysées
& Grands Boulevards
Paris' grandest
avenue, art nouveau
department stores
and a 19th-century
opera house.
(Map p246)

Arc de
Triomphe
◎

Champs-
Élysées
◎

⊙ Gare St-
Lazare

Palais
Garnier
◎

Lo
Ma
are
Lo
cu
Po
(M

Jardin des
Tuileries
⊕

Louvre
⊕

Eiffel Tower &
Western Paris
Stately boulevards
flank the city's signa-
ture spire and major
museums.
(Map p246)

Eiffel
⊙ Tower

Hôtel des
Invalides
❶

Musée
d'Orsay
⊕

Seine

Musée
Rodin
⊕

Musé
National d
Moyen Âg

Jardin du
Luxembourg ⊕

Gare
Montparnasse
⊕

Les
Catacombes
◎

Montparnasse &
Southern Paris
Brasseries from the
mid-20th-century and
re-energised back-
streets buzzing with
local life. *(Map p246)*

Bastille & Eastern Paris 179
The Islands 180
Latin Quarter..180
St-Germain & Les Invalides...................181
Montparnasse & Southern Paris 183

Showtime 185
The Best... ....**187**
Eiffel Tower & Western Paris 188
Champs-Élysées &
Grands Boulevards 188
Louvre & Les Halles 188
Montmartre & Northern Paris..............189
Le Marais, Ménilmontant
& Belleville 191
Bastille & Eastern Paris 192
Latin Quarter...193
St-Germain & Les Invalides..................193

Active Paris 195
The Best... ....**197**
Spectator Sports 198
Swimming Pools 198
Inline Skating..198
Parks..199
Forests...200
Guided Tours 201

Rest Your Head 203
Accommodation Types.........................206
Need to Know 207
Where to Stay..209

In Focus
Paris Today 212
History 214
Architecture 219
Arts 223

Survival Guide
Directory A–Z..................................230
Transport...233
Language.. 238
Index 240
Paris Maps.......................................245
Symbols & Map Key.......................257

Plan Your Trip
This Year in Paris

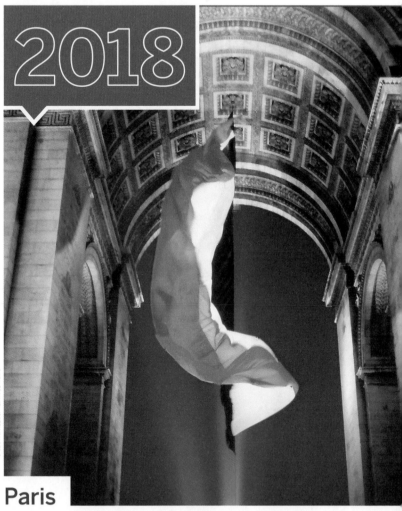

2018

Paris

Art fairs, music festivals, open-air cinema and epicurean events are just some of the highlights of Paris' calendar in 2018, with many more in the works: check www.parisinfo.com for updates.

From left: National flag waving under the Arc de Triomphe on Bastille Day (p12); Paris Plages (p12); Cocktails

2018

★ **Top Festivals & Events**

Paris Plages – Jul (p12)
Bastille Day – Jul (p12)
Paris Cocktail Week – Jan (p6)
Taste of Paris – May (p10)
Nuit Blanche – Oct (p15)

Plan Your Trip
This Year in Paris

January

The frosty first month of the year isn't the most festive in Paris, but cocktails – as well as the winter soldes *(sales) – certainly brighten the mood.*

✥ Grande Parade — 1 Jan
The New Year kicks off in style when carnival floats and brass bands make their way along the av des Champs-Élysées (pictured above).

✥ Epiphany — 6 Jan
On this Christian feast day (also known as Three Kings' Day), Parisian patisseries bake frangipane-filled puff-pastry *galettes des rois* (kings' cakes), which conceal a *fève* (small trinket). Whoever finds the *fève* is crowned 'king' for the day and wears the cardboard crown that comes with the cake.

✥ Louis XVI Commemorative Mass — 21 Jan
Royalists and right-wingers attend a mass at the Chapelle Expiatoire (www.monuments-nationaux.fr) marking the execution by guillotine of King Louis XVI in 1793.

☉ Gauguin. L'alchimiste — Until 22 Jan
This is your last chance to catch the blockbuster *Gauguin. L'alchimiste* (Gauguin. Alchemist) exhibition at Paris' magnificent glass-roofed, art nouveau Grand Palais (www.grandpalais.fr), showcasing the artist's diversity across painting, drawing, engraving, sculpture, ceramics and more.

🍷 Paris Cocktail Week — Late Jan
Each of the 50-plus cocktail bars all over the city that take part in Paris Cocktail Week (www.pariscocktailweek.fr) creates two signature cocktails for the event. There are also workshops, guest bartenders, masterclasses and food pairings. Sign up for a free pass for cut-price cocktails.

KIEV.VICTOR/SHUTTERSTOCK ©

2018

02

February

Festivities still aren't in full swing in February, but couples descend on France's romantic capital for Valentine's Day, when virtually all restaurants offer special menus.

✿ Carnaval de Paris   11 Feb

Now in its 21st year, Paris' carnival (www.carnaval-paris.org) sees Latin American, Creole, Caribbean and European communities take part in a vibrant street parade. The theme for 2018 is the fairytales of Charles Perrault (author of 'Little Red Riding Hood', 'Sleeping Beauty' and 'Cinderella' et al).

✿ Chinese New Year   16 Feb

Paris' largest lantern-lit festivities and dragon parades take place in the city's main Chinatown in the 13e. Parades are also held in Belleville and Le Marais.

✕ Salon International de l'Agriculture   Late Feb–Early Mar

Appetising nine-day international agricultural fair (www.salon-agriculture.com; pictured above), with produce (and animals) from all over France turned into delectable fare at the Parc des Expositions at Porte de Versailles, 15e.

Plan Your Trip
This Year in Paris

March

Blooms appear in Paris' parks and gardens, leaves start greening the city's avenues and festivities begin to flourish. And days get longer – the last Sunday morning of the month ushers in daylight-saving time.

🔒 Foire de Chatou   Mid-Mar
Just 10 minutes outside Paris on the île des Impressionnistes (reached by RER A to Rueil-Malmaison with a free shuttle from the station), some 500 antique and second-hand dealers, jewellers and art galleries set up at this nine-day fair (www. foiredechatou.com).

☆ Printemps du Cinéma   Mid-Mar
Selected cinemas across Paris offer film-goers a unique entry fee of €4 per session (excluding special screenings such as 3D films) over three days (www.printemps ducinema.com).

☆ Banlieues Bleues   Mid-Mar–Mid-Apr
Big-name acts from more than 40 groups and some 28 nationalities perform during the month-long Suburban Blues (www. banlieuesbleues.org) jazz, blues and R&B festival at venues in Paris' northern suburbs.

🎎 Salon du Livre   Late Mar
France's largest international book fair (pictured above; www.salondulivreparis. com) takes place over four days at the Parc des Expositions at Porte de Versailles, 15e.

☆ Cinéma du Réel   Late Mar–Early Apr
Dozens of French and international documentary films screen in and out of competition at this prestigious festival (www. cinemadureel.org). Tickets are available from Fnac, the Centre Pompidou and the Forum des Images.

2018

04

April

Sinatra sang about April in Paris, and the month sees the city's 'charm of spring' in full swing, with chestnuts blossoming and cafe terraces coming into their own. Easter Sunday is 1 April 2018.

🏃 Foire du Trône
Early Apr–Early Jun
Going strong since 957 AD, huge funfair Foire du Trône features some 350 attractions over 10 hectares on the Pelouse de Reuilly of the Bois de Vincennes from around Easter to early June.

🏃 Salon du Running
Early Apr
In the run-up to the Marathon International de Paris, the three-day Salon du Running ('Running Show'; www.salondurunning.fr) draws more than 80,000 visitors (including competitors picking up their bibs) and 200-plus professional exhibitors at the Parc des Expositions at Porte de Versailles, 15e.

🏃 Marathon International de Paris
Early Apr
Paris' international marathon, the Marathon International de Paris (pictured above) starts on the av des Champs-Élysées, 8e, and finishes on av Foch, 16e, attracting more than 57,000 runners from some 145 countries.

⊙ Foire de Paris
Late Apr–Early May
Gadgets, widgets, food and wine feature at this huge contemporary-living fair (www.foiredeparis.fr), held at the Parc des Expositions at Porte de Versailles, 15e.

Plan Your Trip
This Year in Paris

May

05

The temperate month of May has more public holidays than any other in France. Watch out for widespread closures, particularly on May Day (1 May).

🍺 Paris Beer Week   Early May
Craft beer's popularity in Paris peaks during Paris Beer Week (www.laparis beerweek.com), when scores of events take place across the city's bars, pubs, breweries, specialist beer shops and other venues.

🍴 Taste of Paris   Mid-May
Big-name chefs, such as Alain Ducasse and Guy Savoy, create dazzling dishes at the gourmet showcase Taste of Paris (http://paris.tastefestivals.com) inside the Grand Palais.

👁 La Nuit
Européenne des Musées   19 May
Key museums across Paris stay open late for the European Museums Night (http://nuitdesmusees.culturecommunication.gouv.fr), on one Saturday in mid-May. Most offer free entry.

☆ French
Open   Late May–Early Jun
The glitzy Internationaux de France de Tennis Grand Slam (www.rolandgar-ros.com) takes place from late May to early June at Stade Roland Garros at the Bois de Boulogne.

👁 Portes Ouvertes des Ateliers
d'Artistes de Belleville   Late May
More than 250 painters, sculptors and other artists in Belleville open their studio doors (http://ateliers-artistes-belleville.fr) to visitors over four days (Friday to Monday).

2018

ANDREY MALGIN/SHUTTERSTOCK ©

06

June

Paris is positively jumping in June, thanks to warm temperatures and long daylight hours. Watch for pop-up events in outdoor spaces – from rooftops to disused rail yards – citywide.

☆ Festival de St-Denis   Jun
Book ahead for this prestigious cycle of classical-music concerts at the Basilique de St-Denis (http://festival-saint-denis.com) and nearby venues held throughout the month.

☆ Paris Jazz Festival   Mid-Jun–Late Jul
Jazz concerts swing during June and July in the Parc Floral de Paris in the Bois de Vincennes during the Paris Jazz Festival (www.parisjazzfestival.fr).

☆ Fête de la Musique   21 Jun
Staged and impromptu live performances of jazz, reggae, classical and more take place all over the city during this national music festival (http://fetedelamusique.culturecommunication.gouv.fr) on the summer solstice.

🎉 Gay Pride March   Late Jun
Late June's colourful Saturday-afternoon Marche des Fiertés (pictured above; www.gaypride.fr) through Le Marais to Bastille celebrates Gay Pride Day with over-the-top floats and outrageous costumes.

☆ La Goutte d'Or en Fête   Late Jun–Early Jul
Raï, reggae and rap feature at this three-day world-music festival (http://goutte dorenfete.wordpress.com) on square Léon in the 18e's multiethnic Goutte d'Or neighbourhood.

Plan Your Trip
This Year in Paris

July

07

During the Parisian summer, 'beaches' – complete with sunbeds, umbrellas, atomisers, lounge chairs and palm trees – line the banks of the Seine, while shoppers hit the summer soldes *(sales).*

🎆 Bastille Day   14 Jul

France's national day begins with a morning military parade along av des Champs-Élysées accompanied by a fly-past of fighter aircraft. *Feux d'artifice* (fireworks) light up the night-time sky above the Champ de Mars and *Bals des Pompiers* (Firemen's Balls) see dancing at Parisian fire stations. (The flag-lined Champs-Élysées is pictured above.)

☆ Tour de France   Late Jul

The last of the 21 stages of this legendary, 3500km-long cycling event (www.letour.com) finishes with a dash up av des Champs-Élysées on the third or fourth Sunday of July.

🏃 Paris Plages   Mid-Jul–Mid-Aug

From mid-July to around mid-August (later in good weather), 'Paris Beaches' (www.paris.fr) take over the Right Bank between the Louvre, 1er, and Pont de Sully, 4e; and the Rotonde de la Villette and rue de Crimée, 19e. All beaches are open from 8am to midnight.

2018

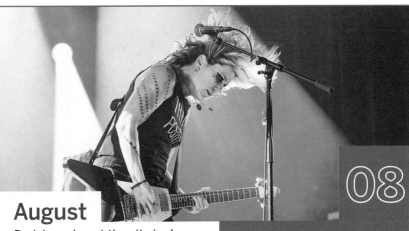

DAVID WOLFF - PATRICK/GETTY IMAGES ©

08

August

Parisians desert the city in droves during the summer swelter when, despite an influx of tourists, many restaurants and shops shut. It's a prime time to cycle, with far less traffic on the roads.

☆ Classique
au Vert Early Aug–Mid-Sep
In Paris' eastern forest, the Bois de Vincennes, the Parc Floral de Paris (www.classiqueauvert.paris.fr) hosts classical music concerts amid the greenery.

☆ Rock en Seine Late Aug
Headlining acts rock the Parc de St-Cloud, on the city's southwestern edge, at this wildly popular three-day, late-August music festival (www.rockenseine.com; Donita Sparks of L7 pictured above). A campsite sets up in the gardens.

☆ Silhouette Late Aug–Early Sep
Out-of-the-box short films by boundary-pushing independent film-makers screen in competition during this film festival (www.association-silhouette.com) along-

☢ Fête
des Tuileries Jun–Aug
Carousels (merry-go-rounds) of all vintages are the centrepiece of this funfair in the Jardin des Tuileries French formal gardens, along with bumper cars, giant slides and a scenic (if vertigo-inducing) Ferris wheel. Entry's free; rides are charged individually.

PICTUREREFLEX/SHUTTERSTOCK ©

side open-air concerts and workshops, attracting audiences of more than 20,000 people.

Plan Your Trip
This Year in Paris

September

Tourists leave and Parisians come home: la rentrée marks residents' return to work and study after the summer break. Cultural life shifts into top gear and the weather is often at its blue-skied best.

☆ Jazz à
La Villette   Early Sep

This super two-week jazz festival (www.jazzalavillette.com) in the first half of September has sessions in Parc de la Villette, at the Cité de la Musique and at surrounding venues.

⊙ Journées Européennes
du Patrimoine   15–16 Sep

The third weekend in September sees Paris open the doors of otherwise off-limits buildings – embassies, government ministries and so forth – during European Heritage Days (http://journeesdupatrimoine.culturecommunication.gouv.fr).

✕ Fête de
la Gastronomie   Mid-Sep

Food markets, cookery workshops and demonstrations, and tasting sessions, as well as events from aperitifs to dinners, make up this gastronomic festival (www.economie.gouv.fr/fete-gastronomie) held at venues Paris-wide.

☆ Techno Parade   Mid-Sep

On one Saturday in mid-September, floats carrying musicians and DJs pump up the volume as they travel between place de la République and place d'Italie during the Techno Parade (pictured above; www.technoparade.fr).

✿ Festival
d'Automne   Mid-Sep–Late Dec

The long-running Autumn Festival of arts (www.festival-automne.com) incorporates painting, music, dance and theatre at venues throughout the city.

2018

October

October heralds an autumnal kaleido-scope in the city's parks and gardens, along with bright, crisp days, cool, clear nights and excellent cultural offerings. Daylight saving ends on the last Sunday morning of the month.

◉ Nuit Blanche   6–7 Oct
From sundown until sunrise on the first Saturday and Sunday of October, museums and recreational facilities such as swimming pools stay open, along with bars and clubs, for one 'White Night' (ie 'All-Nighter'; www.paris.fr).

♟ Fête des Vendanges de Montmartre   Early Oct
The grape harvest from the Clos Montmartre in early October is followed by five days of festivities including a parade (www.fetedesvendangesdemontmartre.com).

◉ Foire Internationale d'Art Contemporain   Mid-Oct
Scores of galleries are represented at the contemporary-art fair known as FIAC (www.fiac.com), held over four days at venues including the Grand Palais.

☆ Cirque d'Hiver Bouglione   Oct–Mar
Clowns, trapeze artists and acrobats have entertained children of all ages at the city's winter circus, Cirque d'Hiver Bouglione (www.cirquedhiver.com), inside a 20-sided polygon building in Le Marais since 1852.

☆ Pitchfork Music Festival Paris   Late Oct
The Grande Halle de la Villette at the Parc de la Villette is the venue for this fest of pop, rock, indie and electro music (http://pitchforkmusicfestival.fr; M.I.A. pictured above).

Plan Your Trip
This Year in Paris

KIEV.VICTOR/SHUTTERSTOCK ©

November

Dark, chilly days and long, cold nights see Parisians take refuge indoors: the opera and ballet seasons are going strong and there are plenty of cosy bistros and bars.

☆ Africolor
Mid-Nov–Dec

This six-week-long African-music festival (www.africolor.com) is primarily held in outer suburbs, such as St-Denis, St-Ouen and Montreuil.

☉ Illuminations de Noël
Mid-Nov–Early Jan

Festive lights are switched on along the av des Champs-Élysées, and animated Christmas window displays at Grands Boulevards department stores Galeries Lafayette and Le Printemps enchant children and adults alike.

⌂ Champs-Élysées Christmas Market
Mid-Nov–Early Jan

Paris stages several Christmas markets from mid-November to early January; this one on the Champs-Élysées (pictured above), with over 100 food, gift and mulled-wine 'chalets' set up along the famous avenue, is the largest.

⛸ Ice Skating
Mid-Nov–Early Mar

Ice-skating rinks pop up at picturesque spots all over the city, such as inside the Grand Palais, on the 1st floor of the Eiffel Tower and on the rooftop of Tour Montparnasse. Dates vary; check ahead as venues can change.

CORIN/SHUTTERSTOCK ©

🍷 Beaujolais Nouveau
21–22 Nov

At midnight on the third Thursday (ie Wednesday night) in November – as soon as French law permits – the opening of the first bottles of cherry-bright, six-week-old Beaujolais Nouveau is celebrated in Paris wine bars, with more celebrations on the Thursday itself.

2018

12

December

Twinkling fairy lights, brightly decorated Christmas trees and shop windows, and outdoor ice-skating rinks make December a magical month to be in the City of Light.

☆ **Salon du
Cheval de Paris**   Late Nov–Early Dec
Sporting events and competitions including show jumping and dressage, plus a horse-back parade through Paris, are part of the Paris Horse Fair (www.salon-cheval.com).

◉ **Le Festival
du Merveilleux**   Late Dec–Early Jan
Normally accessible only by pre-booked guided tours, the magical private museum Musée des Arts Forains (www.arts-forains.com), filled with fairground attractions of yesteryear, opens for around 12 days

from late December to early January, with enchanting rides, attractions and shows.

🎄 **Christmas Eve Mass**   24–25 Dec
Mass is celebrated at midnight on Christmas Eve at many Paris churches, including Notre Dame – arrive early to find a place.

🎄 **New Year's Eve**   31 Dec–1 Jan
Bd St-Michel, 5e; place de la Bastille, 11e; the Eiffel Tower, 7e; and especially av des Champs-Élysées (pictured above), 8e, are the Parisian hotspots to welcome in the new year, although no New Year's fireworks have taken place in recent years.

Plan Your Trip
Need to Know

Daily Costs

Budget
Less than €100

○ Dorm bed: €25–50

○ Coffee/glass of wine/ 33cL craft beer: from €2.50/4/4.50

○ Inexpensive self-catering options include street markets

○ Book of 10 metro tickets: €14.50

○ Same-day, half-price theatre tickets: from €15

○ Frequent free concerts and events

Midrange
€100–250

○ Double room in a mid-range hotel: €130–250

○ Two-course meal: €20–40

○ Museum admission: free to around €15

○ Admission to clubs: free to around €20

Top End
More than €250

○ Historic luxury hotel double room: from €250

○ Gastronomic restaurant meal: from €40

○ Glass of Champagne/ cocktail: from €6/10

Advance Planning

Two months before Book accommodation; organise opera, ballet or cabaret tickets; check events calendars to find out what festivals will be on; and make reservations for high-end/popular restaurants.

Two weeks before Sign up for a local-led tour and start narrowing down your choice of museums, pre-purchasing tickets online where possible.

Two days before Pack your comfiest shoes!

Useful Websites

○ **Lonely Planet** (www. lonelyplanet.com/paris) Destination information, bookings, traveller forum and more.

○ **Paris Info** (www.paris info.com) Comprehensive tourist-authority website.

○ **Paris by Mouth** (www. parisbymouth.com) Restaurants searchable by *arrondissement*.

○ **Sortiraparis** (www.sor tiraparis.com) Up-to-date calendar listing what's on around town.

○ **HiP Paris** (www.hipparis. com) Not only vacation rentals ('Haven in Paris'), but switched-on articles and reviews by expat locals, too.

○ **My Little Paris** (www.mylittleparis.com) Little-known local treasures.

Currency
Euro (€)

Language
French

Visas
There are generally no restrictions for EU citizens. Usually not required for most other nationalities for stays of up to 90 days.

Money
ATMs are widely available. Visa and Master-Card accepted in most hotels, shops and restaurants; fewer accept American Express.

Mobile Phones
Check with your provider before you leave home about roaming costs and/or ensuring your phone is unlocked to use a French SIM card (available cheaply in Paris).

Time
Central European Time (GMT/UTC plus one hour).

Tourist Information
Paris Convention & Visitors Bureau (p232) sells tickets for tours and attractions, and museum and transport passes.

For more, see the Survival Guide (p229)

When to Go

Spring and autumn are ideal. Summer is the main tourist season but many establishments (restaurants, shops etc) close during August. Sights are quieter during winter.

Paris

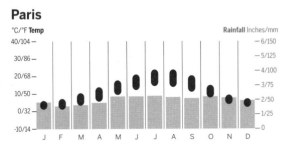

Arriving in Paris

Charles de Gaulle Airport
Trains (RER), buses and night buses to the city centre €6 to €17.50; taxi €50 to €55, 15% higher evenings and Sundays.

Orly Airport Trains (Orlyval then RER), buses and night buses to the city centre €8 to €12; T7 tram to Villejuif-Louis Aragon then metro to centre (€3.80); taxi €30 to €35, 15% higher evenings and Sundays.

Beauvais Airport Buses (€17) to Porte Maillot then metro (€1.90); taxi at least €150 (probably more than the cost of your flight!).

Gare du Nord train station
Within central Paris; served by metro (€1.90).

Getting Around

Walking is a pleasure in Paris, and the city also has one of the most efficient and inexpensive public-transport systems in the world, making getting around a breeze.

○ **Metro & RER** The fastest way to get around. Runs from about 5.30am and finishes around 12.35am or 1.15am (to around 2.15am on Friday and Saturday nights), depending on the line.

○ **Bicycle** Virtually free pick-up, drop-off Vélib' bikes operate across 1800 stations citywide.

○ **Bus** Good for parents with prams/strollers and people with limited mobility.

○ **Boat** The Batobus is a handy hop-on, hop-off service stopping at nine key destinations along the Seine.

Arrondissements

Within the *périphérique* (ring road), Paris is divided into 20 *arrondissements* (city districts), which spiral clockwise like a snail shell from the centre. *Arrondissement* numbers (1er, 2e etc) form an integral part of all Parisian addresses. Each *arrondissement* has its own personality, but it's the *quartiers* (quarters, ie neighbourhoods), which often overlap *arrondissement* boundaries, that give Paris its village atmosphere.

Sleeping

Paris has a range of accommodation for all budgets, but it's often *complet* (full) well in advance. Reservations are recommended year-round and essential during the warmer months (April to October) and all public and school holidays.

Although marginally cheaper, accommodation outside central Paris is invariably a false economy given travel time and costs. Choose somewhere within Paris' 20 *arrondissements* to experience Parisian life the moment you step out the door.

Top Days in Paris

SCIROCCO340/SHUTTERSTOCK ©

Central Right Bank

The central Right Bank is the ideal place to kick off your Parisian trip. As well as the ancient art and artefacts in Paris' mightiest museum, the Louvre, you'll also see ground-breaking modern and contemporary art inside the striking Centre Pompidou.

❶ Jardin des Tuileries (p90)

Start your day with a stroll through the elegant Jardin des Tuileries, stopping to view Monet's enormous *Waterlilies* at the Musée de l'Orangerie and/or photography exhibits at the Jeu de Paume.

➲ Jardin des Tuileries to Musée du Louvre

🚶 Stroll through the gardens to the Louvre.

❷ Musée du Louvre (p52)

Visiting the world's largest museum could easily consume a full day, but bear in mind that tickets are valid all day, so you can come and go as you please. Various tours (guided and self-guided) help you maximise your time.

➲ Musée du Louvre to Chez La Vieille

🚶 From the Louvre's Cour Carée, walk east via rue de Rivoli.

❸ Lunch at Chez La Vieille (p125)

Dine on updated versions of timeless bistro dishes at Chez La Vieille.

Day

01

○ Chez La Vieille to Jardin du Palais Royal

🏃 Walk northwest via rue St-Honoré to place du Palais Royal.

❹ Jardin du Palais Royal (p101)

Browse the colonnaded arcades of the exquisite Jardin du Palais Royal.

○ Jardin du Palais Royal to Église St-Eustache

🏃 Head back down rue St-Honoré, turn north into rue du Louvre and east on rue Coquillière.

❺ Église St-Eustache (p76)

One of Paris' most beautiful churches, Église St-Eustache has a magnificent organ – catch a classical concert here if you can.

○ Église St-Eustache to Centre Pompidou

🏃 Continue east on rue Rambuteau to place Georges-Pompidou.

❻ Centre Pompidou (p74)

Head to the late-opening Centre Pompidou for amazing modern and contemporary art.

○ Centre Pompidou to Brasserie Bofinger

Ⓜ Take Line 1 from Hôtel de Ville to Bastille; Brasserie Bofinger is just northwest.

❼ Dinner at Brasserie Bofinger (p131)

Dine beneath the stained-glass cupola on classic brasserie fare.

○ Brasserie Bofinger to PasDeLoup

Ⓜ Line 8 from Bastille to Filles du Calvaire.

❽ Drinks at PasDeLoup (p177)

Le Marais really comes into its own at night, with a cornucopia of hip clubs and top-notch cocktail bars such as PasDeLoup.

From left: Jardin des Tuileries; Église St-Eustache

Plan Your Trip
Top Days in Paris

Western & Southern Paris

It's a day of Parisian icons today – from the triumphal span of the Arc de Triomphe to the world-famous avenue, the Champs-Élysées, and, of course, the city's stunning art-nouveau Eiffel Tower, with some surprises, too, such as floating nightclubs.

Day
02

❶ Arc de Triomphe (p42)

Climb the mighty Arc de Triomphe for a pinch-yourself Parisian panorama. Back down on ground level, take the time to check out the intricate sculptures and historic bronze plaques, and pay your respects to the Tomb of the Unknown Soldier.

➲ Arc de Triomphe to Champs-Élysées

✈ Walk downhill along the Champs-Élysées.

❷ Champs-Élysées (p148)

Promenade along Paris' most glamorous avenue, the Champs-Élysées, and perhaps give your credit card a workout in the adjacent Triangle d'Or (Golden Triangle), home to flagship *haute couture* fashion houses.

➲ Champs-Élysées to Musée du Quai Branly

Ⓜ Line 9 from Franklin D Roosevelt to Alma Marceau.

❸ Musée du Quai Branly (p40)

From Alma Marceau metro station, cross the Pont d'Alma and turn right along quai Branly to check out indigenous art as

well as the awesome architecture of the Musée du Quai Branly. For lunch, drop by the museum's Café Branly or head to its elegant restaurant, Les Ombres (named 'the Shadows' for the webbed patterns cast by the adjacent Eiffel Tower).

➡ Musée du Quai Branly to Palais de Tokyo

🚶 Cross the Passerelle Debilly. Walk uphill along rue de la Manutention, turning east on av du Président Wilson.

❹ Palais de Tokyo (p41)

This stunning building takes on major temporary cutting-edge exhibits – the rooftop, for example, has been the setting for attention-getting projects such as the transient Hotel Everland and the see-through restaurant Nomiya.

➡ Palais de Tokyo to Eiffel Tower

Ⓜ Line 9 from Iéna to Trocadéro.

❺ Eiffel Tower (p36)

Exiting the Trocadéro metro station, walk east through the Jardins du Trocadéro for the ultimate Eiffel Tower snapshot, and cross Pont d'Iéna to the tower itself. Sunset is the best time to ascend the Eiffel Tower, to experience both the dazzling views during daylight and then the twinkling *Ville Lumière* (City of Light) by night. (Pre-purchase your tickets to minimise queuing!)

➡ Eiffel Tower to Le Casse Noix

🚶 Walk southeast through Parc du Champ de Mars, turn southwest on av Joseph Bouvard then rue Desaix to Le Casse Noix.

❻ Dinner & Drinks

Dining inside the Eiffel Tower itself is unforgettable. Alternatively, book ahead for cracking modern French cuisine at Le Casse Noix. Take metro line 6 to party aboard floating nightclubs such as Le Batofar.

From left: Arc de Triomphe; Champs-Élysées

Plan Your Trip
Top Days in Paris

MAZIARZ/SHUTTERSTOCK ©

The Islands & Left Bank

Begin the day in the heart of Paris at the city's colossal cathedral, then venture across to Paris' elegant Left Bank to see impressionist masterpieces in the Musée d'Orsay, and to visit the city's oldest church and its loveliest gardens.

Day

03

❶ Notre Dame (p46)

Starting your day at the Notre Dame gives you the best chance of beating the crowds. In addition to viewing its stained-glass interior, allow an hour to climb to the top for exceptional views, and another to descend below ground to explore the crypt.

➔ Notre Dame to Sainte-Chapelle

✈ Follow the Seine northwest to bd du Palais.

❷ Sainte-Chapelle (p92)

Don't miss the exquisite chapel Sainte-Chapelle. Consecrated in 1248, its stained glass forms a curtain of glazing on the 1st floor.

➔ Sainte-Chapelle to Musée d'Orsay

Ⓜ RER C from St-Michel–Notre Dame to Gare Musée d'Orsay.

❸ Musée d'Orsay (p62)

Set inside a magnificent art-nouveau former railway station, the Musée d'Orsay

is filled with impressionist tours de force by masters including Renoir, Monet, Van Gogh, Degas and dozens more. It's also an ideal place to dine, at casual Café Campana or the ornate Restaurant Musée d'Orsay.

○ Musée d'Orsay to Église St-Germain des Prés

Ⓜ Solférino to Sèvres-Babylone (line 12), then change for Mabillon (line 10).

❹ Église St-Germain des Prés (p105)

Paris' oldest church sits in the heart of the buzzing St-Germain des Prés district, with chic boutiques and historic literary cafes, including Les Deux Magots, just opposite.

○ Église St-Germain des Prés to Jardin de Luxembourg

🏃 Head south on rue Bonaparte to place St-Sulpice and continue on to rue Vaugirard.

❺ Jardin du Luxembourg (p68)

Enter this lovely garden from rue Vaugirard and stroll among its chestnut groves, paths and statues.

○ Jardin de Luxembourg to Bouillon Racine

🏃 From rue Vaugirard, take rue Monsieur-le-Prince northwest to rue Racine.

❻ Dinner at Bouillon Racine (p139)

Feast on French classics in this art-nouveau jewel. Afterwards, head to Shakespeare & Company for late-night book shopping.

From left: Sainte-Chapelle; Jardin du Luxembourg

Plan Your Trip
Top Days in Paris

Northern & Eastern Paris

Montmartre's slinking streets and steep staircases lined with crooked ivy-clad buildings are especially enchanting to meander in the early morning when there are fewer tourists. Afterwards, explore charming Canal St-Martin and futuristic Parc de la Villette before drinking, dining and dancing in lively Bastille.

Day

04

❶ Musée de Montmartre (p61)

Brush up on the area's fascinating history at the local museum, the Musée de Montmartre. Not only was Montmartre home to seminal artists, but Renoir and Utrillo are among those who lived in this very building.

➲ Musée de Montmartre to Sacré-Cœur

🚶 Walk east to Sacré-Cœur along rue Cortot, rue du Mont Cenis then rue Azais.

❷ Sacré-Cœur (p58)

Head to the hilltop Sacré-Cœur basilica and, for an even more extraordinary panorama over Paris, climb up into the basilica's main dome. Regular metro tickets are valid on the funicular that shuttles up and down the steep Butte de Montmartre.

➲ Sacré-Cœur to Le Miroir

🚶 At the bottom of the hill, walk west along rue Tardieu and rue Yvonne le Tac, turning south on rue des Martyrs.

❸ Lunch at Le Miroir (p129)

Locals' favourite Le Miroir offers great-value lunch *menu* specials. You'll also find wonderful gourmet food shops scattered nearby, such as Mesdemoiselles Madeleines.

⊙ Le Miroir to Canal St-Martin

Ⓜ Line 2 Pigalle to Jaurès.

❹ Canal St-Martin (p152)

A postcard-perfect vision of iron foot-bridges, swing bridges and shaded tow paths, Canal St-Martin's banks (and the surrounding streets) are lined with a steadily growing number of hip cafes and boutiques. Also here is cultural centre Point Éphemère, whose restaurant, Animal Kitchen, combines gourmet cuisine with music from Animal Records.

⊙ Canal St-Martin to Parc de la Villette

Ⓜ Line 5 Jacques Bonsergent to Porte de Pantin.

❺ Parc de la Villette (p199)

In addition to its striking geometric gardens, innovative Parc de la Villette has a slew of attractions, including the kid-friendly Cité des Sciences museum and the Cité de la Musique – Philharmonie de Paris complex.

⊙ Parc de la Villette to Le Bistrot Paul Bert

Ⓜ Porte de Pantin to République (line 5), changing for Faidherbe-Chaligny (line 8).

❻ Dinner at Le Bistrot Paul Bert (p132)

After a pre-dinner *apéro* (aperitif) at the classic, cherry-red Le Pure Café, head around the corner to enjoy exceptional bistro classics at Le Bistrot Paul Bert. After dinner head west to the Bastille neighbourhood's buzzing bars; there's a great concentration on rue de Lappe.

From left: Sacré-Cœur; Canal St-Martin

Plan Your Trip
Hotspots For...

EPICUREANS

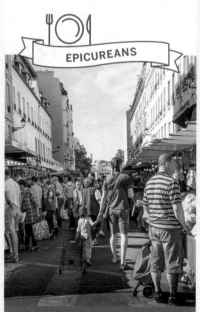

👁 **Musée du Louvre** Follow the Louvre's 'Art of Eating' thematic trail. (p52)

🍲 **Le Cordon Bleu** Take a cooking class at one of the world's foremost culinary institutions. (p96)

🛍 **E Dehillerin** Stock up on kitchen accoutrements alongside Paris' chefs. (p149)

🍴 **Bustronome** Dine on gourmet cuisine aboard a glass-roofed bus cruising Paris' boulevards. (p123)

🍴 **Marché d'Aligre** Shop for fresh produce and delectable specialities at this outstanding Parisian market. (pictured above; p83)

PHOTOGRAPHERS

👁 **Arc de Triomphe** Capture the spectacular panoramas radiating from the top of the arch. (view from Arc de Triomphe pictured below; p42)

👁 **Notre Dame** Exceptional opportunities exist inside, out and above all next to the rooftop's gargoyles. (p46)

📷 **Paris Photography Tours** Architecture, street life and nature are among the focal points of these inspiring tours. (p201)

⛵ **Vedettes de Paris** Get a different perspective of the city from a Seine river cruise. (p72)

🍴 **Le Jules Verne** Enjoy sublime vantage points at this Michelin-starred restaurant within the Eiffel Tower. (p122)

ART NOUVEAU FANS

⊙ **Musée d'Orsay** Impressionist art is matched only by the magnificent art-nouveau train station housing it. (p62)

⊙ **Musée Maxim's** Some 550 art-nouveau artworks, objets d'art and furniture above the famed belle époque–era restaurant. (p91)

✘ **Bouillon Racine** With mirrored walls, floral motifs and ceramic tiling, this 1906 brasserie is a listed monument. (p139)

🛍 **Belle du Jour** Browse perfume bottles from the belle époque. (p151)

☆ **Le Carreau du Temple** This beautiful wrought-iron covered market is now a vibrant cultural centre. (p191)

CREATIVES

⊙ **Art 42** Book ahead for a free tour of Paris' new street art museum. (p113)

⊙ **59 Rivoli** Drop by this central, now-legalised artists' squat. (p77)

☆ **Le 104** Eclectic events are programmed by this former funeral parlour turned city-funded art space. (p190)

🍷 **Beans on Fire** This fabulous collaborative coffee roastery/cafe also offers roasting workshops. (p176)

🛍 **Magasin Sennelier** Former clients of this 1887-founded art supply shop include Cézanne and Picasso. (p157)

ROMANTICS

⊙ **Musée Rodin** Contemplate Rodin's entwined figures in *Le Baiser* (The Kiss) and more sculptures in the gardens. (*Le Penseur* sculpture pictured above; p66)

⊙ **Jardin du Luxembourg** Stroll through Paris' most enchanting park. (p68)

⊙ **Eiffel Tower** Sip Champagne at the top of the city's emblematic tower. (p36)

✘ **La Tour d'Argent** Gaze out over Notre Dame from this culinary icon. (p138)

🍷 **Le Très Particulier** Sip cocktails in the walled garden of this Montmartre mansion-housed hotel. (p173)

Plan Your Trip
What's New

CATHERINE LE NEVEZ/LONELY PLANET ©

City Scents

A beautiful 17th-century *hôtel particulier* (private mansion) once occupied by Christian Lacroix' fashion house is now the setting for Paris' new, interactive fragrance museum, Le Grand Musée du Parfum (p91).

Sunday Shopping

The creation of shopping-friendly 'tourist zones', which take in department stores such as the Grands Boulevards' cupola-topped showpiece Galeries Lafayette (p148), has proved popular with visitors and locals alike.

All-Night Clubbing

France's high-density residential capital hasn't had an all-night clubbing scene but that's changing with the country's first-ever 24-hour club licence granted to Concrete (p179), aboard a barge moored on the Seine.

Street Art Showcase

Striking street art murals continue to stake a claim as one of the most influential art movements in Paris today, cemented by the opening of new street-art and post-graffiti 'anti-museum' Art 42 (p113).

Hip-Hop Hub

Graffiti and street-art workrooms are also part of Paris' new hip-hop centre La Place (p188), under the golden-hued Forum des Halles canopy, with recording and broadcast studios and concerts.

Above: La Place (p188)

Plan Your Trip
For Free

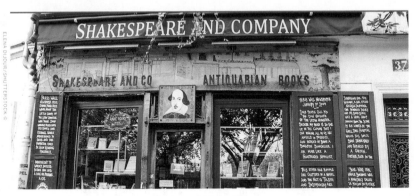

Free Museums

If you can, time your trip to be in Paris on the first Sunday of the month when you can visit the *musées nationaux* (www.rmn.fr) for free as well as certain monuments (some during certain winter-time months only).

European citizens under 26 get free entry to national museums and monuments.

At any time, you can visit the permanent collections of selected *musées municipaux* (www.paris.fr) for free.

Several other museums throughout the city are free, including the Pavillon de l'Arsenal (p115), covering urbanism and architecture in Paris, and two street-art showcases,

Galerie Itinerrance (p113) and the new Art 42 (p113) museum.

Some museums have reduced entry at various times of the day or week.

Free Music

Concerts, DJ sets and recitals regularly take place for free (or for the cost of a drink) at venues throughout the city.

Busking musicians and performers entertain crowds on Paris' streets, squares and aboard the metro.

Free Literary Events

This literary-minded city is an inspired place to catch a reading, author signing or writing workshop. English-language bookshops such as

Shakespeare & Company (p155) and Abbey Bookshop (p156) host literary events throughout the year and can point you towards others.

Free Fashion Shows

Reserve ahead to attend free weekly fashion shows (p148) at Galeries Lafayette's Grands Boulevards department store. While you're here, don't miss one of the best free views over the Parisian skyline from the store's rooftop.

Free Festivals & Events

Loads of Paris' festivals and events are free, such as the summertime Paris Plages riverside beaches.

Above: Shakespeare & Company (p155)

ELENA DIJOUR/SHUTTERSTOCK ©

Plan Your Trip
Family Travel

Sights & Activities

In addition to classic playgrounds, Paris' parks also have a host of children's activities, such as the toy boats, marionettes (puppets), pony rides and carousel of the Jardin du Luxembourg (p68); the new millennium playgrounds of Parc de la Villette (p199), adjacent to the fabulous interactive science museum **Cité des Sciences** (🎫01 85 53 99 74; www.cite-sciences.fr; 30 av Corentin Cariou, Parc de la Villette, 19e; per attraction adult/child €12/9; ⊘10am-6pm Tue-Sat, to 7pm Sun, La Géode 10.30am-8.30pm Tue-Sun; Ⓜ Porte de la Villette); and the Bois de Boulogne's adorable **Jardin d'Acclimatation** (http://jardindacclimatation.fr; av du Mahatma Gandhi; admission €3.50, per attraction €2.90; ⊘11am-6pm Mon-Fri, 10am-7pm Sat & Sun; Ⓜ Les Sablons) amusement park.

Animal-mad kids will love the lions, cougars, white rhinos and a gaggle of other creatures at the Bois de Vincennes' state-of-the-art Parc Zoologique de Paris (p200); the kid-friendly natural-history–focused Muséum National d'Histoire Naturelle (p107); and the shark tank inside the **Cinéaqua** (🎫01 40 69 23 23; www.cineaqua. com; av des Nations Unies, 16e; adult/child €20.50/16; ⊘10am-7pm; Ⓜ Trocadéro) aquarium. A trip to the Louvre (p52) can be a treat, particularly following thematic trails such as hunting for lions or galloping horses.

Every kid, big and small, loves a voyage down the Seine with Bateaux-Mouches (p73) or Bateaux Parisiens (p73). But there's something extra special about the one-hour 'Paris Mystery' tours designed especially for children by Vedettes de Paris (p72).

Further afield, theme parks within day-trip distance include Disneyland Paris (www.disneylandparis.com) and Parc Astérix (www.parcasterix.fr).

Eating Out with Kids

Many restaurants accept little diners (confirm ahead), but they're expected to behave. Children's menus are common, but most restaurants don't have high chairs. A wave of gourmet pizza, pasta, bagel and

ELENA DIJOUR/SHUTTERSTOCK ©

burger restaurants throughout the city offer kid-friendly fare. In fine weather, good options include picking up sandwiches and crêpes from a street stall or packing a market-fresh picnic and heading to parks and gardens where kids can play to their hearts' content.

Getting Around with Kids

Paris' narrow streets and metro stairways are a trial if you have a stroller (pram or pushchair) in tow; buses offer an easier, scenic alternative. Children under four years of age travel free on public transport and generally receive free admission to sights. For older kids, discounts vary from place to place – anything from a euro off for over-fours to free entry up to the age of 18.

Need to Know

Baby food and nappies Supermarkets stock a wide choice of baby food, infant formula, soy and cow's milk, nappies (diapers) and the like, but remember that opening hours may be more

> ### Top Five Parks & Playgrounds
>
> Jardin du Luxembourg (p68)
> Parc de la Villette (p199)
> Parc Montsouris (p199)
> Bois de Boulogne (p201)
> Bois de Vincennes (p200)

limited. Pharmacies – of which a handful are open 24/7 – also sell baby paraphernalia.

Babysitters Most hotels can arrange *gardes d'enfants* (babysitting) services. Weekly listings magazine *L'Officiel des Spectacles* advertises babysitters.

Cots When booking accommodation, check availability and costs for a *lit bébé* (cot/crib).

Rental equipment Rent strollers, scooters, car seats and anything else you need while in Paris from 2kids1bag (www.2kids1bag.com).

From left: Amusement ride at Jardin d'Acclimatation; Kite flying at Bois de Vincennes (p200)

MATTEO COLOMBO/SHUTTERSTOCK ©

Eiffel Tower................................ 36

Arc de Triomphe 42

Notre Dame 46

The Louvre..................................52

Sacré-Cœur 58

Musée d'Orsay 62

Musée Rodin............................... 66

Jardin du Luxembourg 68

Cruising the Seine 72

Centre Pompidou.......................74

Cimetière du
Père Lachaise.............................78

Street Markets...........................82

Day Trip: Château
de Versailles 84

Musée National
du Moyen Âge............................. 88

Jardin des Tuileries 90

Sainte-Chapelle 92

Les Catacombes 94

Cooking &
Wine-Tasting Courses 96

Day Trip: Maison et Jardins
de Claude Monet....................... 98

Palais Garnier........................... 100

Walking Tour: Seine-Side
Romantic Meander 102

Hôtel des Invalides................. 104

Jardin des Plantes..................106

Walking Tour: Paris'
Covered Passages 110

Discovering Paris'
Street Art................................... 112

Musée National Picasso 114

TOP EXPERIENCES

The very best to see & do

Eiffel Tower

Paris today is unimaginable without its signature spire. Originally only constructed as a temporary 1889 Exposition Universelle exhibit, it went on to become the defining fixture of the city's skyline.

Great For...

ⓘ Need to Know

Map p246; ☏08 92 70 12 39; www.toureiffel. paris; Champ de Mars, 5 av Anatole France, 7e; adult/child lift to top €17/8, lift to 2nd fl €11/4, stairs to 2nd fl €7/3; ⊙lifts & stairs 9am-12.45am mid-Jun-Aug, lifts 9.30am-11pm, stairs 9.30am-6.30pm Sep–mid-Jun; Ⓜ Bir Hakeim or RER Champ de Mars–Tour Eiffel

★**Top Tip**

Head here at dusk for the best day-time vistas and glittering night-time city views.

Named after its designer, Gustave Eiffel, the Tour Eiffel was built for the 1889 Exposition Universelle (World Fair). It took 300 workers, 2.5 million rivets and two years of nonstop labour to assemble. Upon completion the tower became the tallest human-made structure in the world (324m or 1063ft) – a record held until the completion of the Chrysler Building in New York (1930). A symbol of the modern age, it faced massive opposition from Paris' artistic and literary elite, and the 'metal asparagus', as some Parisians derided it, was originally slated to be torn down in 1909. It was spared only because it proved an ideal platform for the transmitting antennas needed for the newfangled science of radio-telegraphy.

Tickets & Queues

Buying tickets in advance online usually means you avoid the monumental queues at the ticket offices. Print your ticket or show it on a smartphone screen. If you can't reserve your tickets ahead of time, expect waits of well over an hour in high season.

Stair tickets can't be reserved online. They are sold at the south pillar, where the staircase can also be accessed: the climb to the 2nd floor consists of 704 steps.

Ascend as far as the 2nd floor (either on foot or by lift), from where it is lift-only to the top floor. Pushchairs must be folded in lifts and you are not allowed to take bags or backpacks larger than aeroplane-cabin size.

If you have reservations for either restaurant, you are granted direct access to the lifts.

First Floor

Of the tower's three floors, the 1st (57m) has the most space, but the least impressive views. The glass-enclosed **Pavillon Ferrié** houses an immersion film along with a small cafe and souvenir shop, while the outer walkway features a discovery circuit to help visitors learn more about the tower's ingenious design. Check out the sections of glass flooring that proffer a dizzying view of the ant-like people walking on the ground far below.

☑ **Don't Miss**

Views of the tower from the Jardins du Trocadéro outside Palais de Chaillot.

This level also hosts the 58 Tour Eiffel (p122) restaurant.

Not all lifts stop at the 1st floor (check before ascending), but it's an easy walk down from the 2nd floor should you accidentally end up one floor too high.

Second Floor

Views from the 2nd floor (115m) are the best – impressively high, but still close enough to see the details of the city below. Telescopes and panoramic maps placed around the tower pinpoint locations in Paris and beyond. Story windows give an overview of the lifts' mechanics, and the vision well allows you to gaze through glass panels to the ground. Also up here are toilets, a macaron bar and Michelin-starred restaurant Le Jules Verne (p122).

Top Floor

Views from the wind-buffeted top floor (276m) stretch up to 60km on a clear day, though at this height the panoramas are more sweeping than detailed. Celebrate your ascent with a glass of bubbly (€12 to €21) from the Champagne bar (open noon to 10pm). Afterwards peep into Gustave Eiffel's restored top-level office where lifelike wax models of Eiffel and his daughter Claire greet Thomas Edison. To access the top floor, take a separate lift on the 2nd floor (closed during heavy winds).

Nightly Sparkles

Every hour on the hour, the entire tower sparkles for five minutes with 20,000 6-watt lights. They were first installed for Paris' millennium celebration in 2000 – it took 25 mountain climbers five months to install the current bulbs and 40km of electrical cords. For the best view of the light show, head across the Seine to the Jardins du Trocadéro.

✕ **Take a Break**

At the tower's two restaurants, snack bars, macaron bar or top-floor Champagne bar.

What's Nearby?

Parc du Champ de Mars   Park
(Map p246; Champ de Mars, 7e; MÉcole Militaire or RER Champ de Mars–Tour Eiffel) Running southeast from the Eiffel Tower, the grassy Champ de Mars – an ideal summer picnic spot – was originally used as a parade ground for the cadets of the 18th-century **École Militaire**, the vast French-classical building at the southeastern end of the park, which counts Napoléon Bonaparte among its graduates. The steel-and-etched-glass **Wall for Peace Memorial** (http://wallforpeace.org), erected in 2000, is by Clara Halter.

Musée du Quai Branly   Museum
(Map p246; ☏01 56 61 70 00; www.quaibranly.fr; 37 quai Branly, 7e; adult/child €10/free; ☺11am-7pm Tue, Wed & Sun, 11am-9pm Thu-Sat; MAlma Marceau or RER Pont de l'Alma) A tribute to the diversity of human culture, Musée du Quai Branly inspires travellers, armchair anthropologists, and anyone who appreciates the beauty of traditional craftsmanship, through an overview of indigenous and folk art. Spanning four main sections – Oceania, Asia, Africa and the Americas – an impressive array of masks, carvings, weapons, jewellery and more makes up the body of the rich collection, displayed in a refreshingly unique interior without rooms or high walls. Look out for excellent temporary exhibitions and performances.

Palais de Chaillot   Historic Building
(Map p246; place du Trocadéro et du 11 Novembre, 16e; MTrocadéro) The two curved, colonnaded wings of this building (built for the 1937 International Expo) and central terrace afford an exceptional panorama of the **Jardins du Trocadéro**, Seine and Eiffel Tower. The eastern wing houses the standout **Cité de l'Architecture et du Patrimoine** (www.citechaillot.fr; 1 place du Trocadéro et du 11 Novembre, 16e; adult/child €8/free; ☺11am-7pm Wed & Fri-Sun, to 9pm Thu), devoted to French architecture and heritage, as well as the Théâtre National de Chaillot (p188), staging dance and theatre. The western wing houses the **Musée de la Marine** (Maritime Museum; ☏01 53 65 69 69; www.musee-marine.fr; 17 place du Trocadéro et du 11 Novembre, 16e), closed for renovations until 2021, and the **Musée de l'Homme** (Museum of Humankind; ☏01 44 05 72 72; www.museedelhomme.fr; 17 place Trocadéro et du 11 Novembre, 16e; adult/child €10/free; ☺10am-6pm Wed-Mon).

Palais de Chaillot

★ Man on a Wire
In 1989 tightrope artist Philippe Petit walked up an inclined 700m cable across the Seine, from Palais Chaillot to the Eiffel Tower's 2nd floor. The act, performed before an audience of 250,000 people, was held to commemorate the French Republic's bicentennial.

Musée Guimet des Arts Asiatiques   Gallery

(Map p246; ☎01 56 52 53 00; www.guimet.fr; 6 place d'Iéna, 16e; adult/child €7.50/free; ⊙10am-6pm Wed-Mon; Ⓜ Iéna) France's foremost Asian art museum has a superb collection. Observe the gradual transmission of both Buddhism and artistic styles along the Silk Road in pieces ranging from 1st-century Gandhara Buddhas from Afghanistan and Pakistan to later Central Asian, Chinese and Japanese Buddhist sculptures and art. Part of the collection is housed in the **Galeries du Panthéon Bouddhique** (Map p246; 19 av d'Iéna, 16e; incl in Musée Guimet des Arts Asiatiques admission; ⊙10am-5.45pm Wed-Mon, garden to 5pm; Ⓜ Iéna) with a Japanese garden.

Palais de Tokyo   Gallery

(Map p246; www.palaisdetokyo.com; 13 av du Président Wilson, 16e; adult/child €12/free;

❶ Did You Know?

Slapping a fresh coat of paint on the tower is no easy feat. It takes a 25-person team 18 months to complete the 60-tonnes-of-paint task, redone every seven years.

⊙noon-midnight Wed-Mon; Ⓜ Iéna) The Tokyo Palace, created for the 1937 Exposition Internationale des Arts et Techniques dans la Vie Moderne (International Exposition of Art and Technology in Modern Life), has no permanent collection. Instead, its shell-like interior of concrete and steel is a stark backdrop to interactive contemporary-art exhibitions and installations. Its bookshop is fabulous for art and design magazines, and its eating and drinking options are magic.

Arc de Triomphe

If anything rivals the Eiffel Tower as the symbol of Paris, it's this magnificent 1836-built triumphal arch commemorating Napoléon's 1805 victory at Austerlitz, which he commissioned the following year.

Great For...

Charles de Gaulle–Étoile

Charles de Gaulle–Étoile

Av de Friedland

Arc de Triomphe

Av des Champs-Élysées

Kléber Ⓜ

George V Ⓜ

❶ Need to Know

Map p246; www.paris-arc-de-triomphe.fr; place Charles de Gaulle, 8e; viewing platform adult/child €12/free; ☺10am-11pm Apr-Sep, to 10.30pm Oct-Mar; ⓂCharles de Gaulle–Étoile

★ **Top Tip**
Don't risk getting skittled by traffic by taking photos while crossing the Champs-Elysées.

History

Napoléon's armies never did march through the Arc de Triomphe showered in honour. At the time it was commissioned, his victory at Austerlitz seemed like a watershed moment that confirmed the tactical supremacy of the French army, but a mere decade later, Napoléon had already fallen from power and his empire had crumbled.

The Arc de Triomphe was never fully abandoned – simply laying the foundations had taken an entire two years – and in 1836, after a series of starts and stops under the restored monarchy, the project was finally completed. In 1840 Napoléon's remains were returned to France and passed under the arch before being interred at Invalides.

Accessing the Arch

Don't try to cross the traffic-choked roundabout above ground! Stairs on the Champs Élysées' northeastern side lead beneath the Étoile to pedestrian tunnels that bring you out safely beneath the arch.

There is a lift/elevator at the arch, but it's only for visitors with limited mobility or those travelling with young children, and there are still 46 unavoidable steps.

Beneath the Arch

Beneath the arch at ground level lies the **Tomb of the Unknown Soldier**. Honouring the 1.3 million French soldiers who lost their lives in WWI, the Unknown Soldier was laid to rest in 1921, beneath an eternal flame that is rekindled daily at 6.30pm.

Also here are a number of bronze plaques laid into the ground. Take the time to try and decipher some: these mark significant moments in modern French history, such as the proclamation of the Third French Republic (4 September 1870) and the return of Alsace and Lorraine to French rule (11 November 1918). The most notable plaque is the text from Charles de Gaulle's famous London broadcast on 18 June 1940, which sparked the French Resistance to life: 'Believe me, I who am speaking to you with full knowledge of the facts, and who tell you that nothing is lost for France. The same means that overcame us can bring us victory one day. For France is not alone! She is not alone!'

☑ **Don't Miss**

Some of the best vistas in Paris from the top of the arch.

Sculptures

The arch is adorned with four main sculptures, six panels in relief, and a frieze running beneath the top. Each was designed by a different artist; the most famous sculpture is the one to the right as you approach from the Champs-Élysées: *La Marseillaise* (Departure of the Volunteers of 1792). Sculpted by François Rude, it depicts soldiers of all ages gathering beneath the wings of victory, en route to drive back the invading armies of Prussia and Austria. The higher panels depict a series of important victories for the Revolutionary and imperial French armies, from Egypt to Austerlitz, while the detailed frieze is divided into two sections: the *Departure of the Armies* and the *Return of the Armies*. Don't miss the multimedia section beneath the viewing platform, which provides more detail and historical background for each of the sculptures.

Viewing Platform

Climb the 284 steps to the viewing platform at the top of the 50m-high arch and you'll be suitably rewarded with magnificent panoramas over western Paris. From here, a dozen broad avenues – many of them named after Napoléonic victories and illustrious generals – radiate towards every compass point. The Arc de Triomphe is the highest point in the line of monuments known as the *axe historique* (historic axis, also called the grand axis); it offers views that swoop east down the Champs-Élysées to the gold-tipped obelisk at place de la Concorde (and beyond to the Louvre's glass pyramid), and west to the skyscraper district of La Défense, where the colossal **Grande Arche** (⊕ Parvis de la Défense; Ⓜ La Défense) marks the western terminus of the *axe*.

✕ **Take a Break**

Pair an evening visit with a traditional French dinner at Le Hide (p123).

ESPIEGLE/GETTY IMAGES ©

Notre Dame

A vision of stained-glass rose windows, flying buttresses and frightening gargoyles, Paris' glorious cathedral, on the larger of the two inner-city islands, is the city's geographic and spiritual heart.

Great For...

☑ Don't Miss

Climbing the bell towers, which brings you face to face with the cathedral's ghoulish gargoyles.

When you enter the cathedral its grand dimensions are immediately evident: the interior alone is 127m long, 48m wide and 35m high, and can accommodate some 6000 worshippers.

Architecture

Built on a site occupied by earlier churches and, a millennium prior, a Gallo-Roman temple, Notre Dame was begun in 1163 and largely completed by the early 14th century. The cathedral was badly damaged during the Revolution, prompting architect Eugène Emmanuel Viollet-le-Duc to oversee extensive renovations between 1845 and 1864. Enter the magnificent forest of ornate flying buttresses that encircle the cathedral chancel and support its walls and roof.

Notre Dame is known for its sublime balance, though if you look closely you'll see all sorts of minor asymmetrical elements

❶ Need to Know

Map p250; ☎01 42 34 56 10; www.notredame-deparis.fr; 6 place du Parvis Notre Dame, 4e; cathedral free, adult/child towers €10/free, treasury €4/2; ⏱cathedral 7.45am-6.45pm Mon-Fri, to 7.15pm Sat & Sun, towers 10am-6.30pm Sun-Thu, to 11pm Fri & Sat Jul & Aug, 10am-6.30pm Apr-Jun & Sep, 10am-5.30pm Oct-Mar, treasury 9.30am-6pm Apr-Sep, 10am-5.30pm Oct-Mar; Ⓜ Cité

✕ Take a Break

On hidden place Dauphine, Le Caveau du Palais (p135) serves contemporary French fare.

★ Top Tip

Invariably huge queues get longer throughout the day – arrive as early as possible.

introduced to avoid monotony, in accordance with standard Gothic practice. These include the slightly different shapes of each of the three main portals, the statues of which were once brightly coloured to make them more effective as a *Biblia pauperum* – a 'Bible of the poor' to help the illiterate understand Old Testament stories, the Passion of the Christ and the lives of the saints.

Rose Windows & Pipe Organ

The most spectacular interior features are three rose windows, particularly the 10m-wide window over the western façade above the organ – one of the largest in the world, with 7800 pipes (900 of which have historical classification), 111 stops, five 56-key manuals and a 32-key pedalboard – and the window on the northern side of the transept (virtually unchanged since the 13th century).

Towers

A constant queue marks the entrance to the **Tours de Notre Dame**, the cathedral's bell towers. Climb the 400-odd spiralling steps to the top of the western façade of the North Tower, where you'll find yourself on the rooftop **Galerie des Chimères** (Gargoyles Gallery), face to face with frightening and fantastic gargoyles. These grotesque statues divert rainwater from the roof to prevent masonry damage, with the water exiting through the elongated, open mouth; they also, purportedly, ward off evil spirits. Although they appear medieval, they were installed by Eugène Viollet-le-Duc in the 19th century. From the rooftop there's a spectacular view over Paris.

In the South Tower hangs Emmanuel, the cathedral's original 13-tonne bourdon bell (all of the cathedral's bells are named).

During the night of 24 August 1944, when the Île de la Cité was retaken by French, Allied and Resistance troops, the tolling of the Emmanuel announced Paris' approaching liberation.

As part of 2013's celebrations for Notre Dame's 850th anniversary since construction began, nine new bells were installed, replicating the original medieval chimes.

Treasury

In the southeastern transept, the *trésor* (treasury) contains artwork, liturgical objects and first-class relics; pay a small fee to enter. Among its religious jewels and gems is the **Ste-Couronne** (Holy Crown), purportedly the wreath of thorns placed on Jesus' head before he was crucified. It is exhibited between 3pm and 4pm on the first Friday of each month, 3pm to 4pm every Friday during Lent, and 10am to 5pm on Good Friday.

Easier to admire is the treasury's wonderful collection, **Les Camées des Papes** (Papal cameos). Sculpted with incredible finesse in shell and framed in silver, the 268-piece collection depicts every pope in miniature from St Pierre to Pope Benoit XVI. Note the different posture, hand gestures and clothes of each pope.

The Mays

Walk past the choir, with its carved wooden stalls and statues representing the Passion of the Christ, to admire the cathedral's wonderful collection of paintings in its nave side chapels. From 1449 onwards, city goldsmiths offered to the cathedral each year on 1 May a tree strung with devotional ribbons and banners to honour

the Virgin Mary – to whom Notre Dame (Our Lady) is dedicated. Fifty years later the goldsmiths' annual gift, known as a May, had become a tabernacle decorated with scenes from the Old Testament, and, from 1630, a large canvas – 3m tall – commemorating one of the Acts of the Apostles, accompanied by a poem or literary explanation. By the early 18th century, when the brotherhood of goldsmiths was dissolved, the cathedral had received 76 such monumental paintings – just 13 can be admired today.

★ The Heart of Paris

Distances from Paris to metropolitan France destinations are measured from **Point Zéro des Routes de France** (Map p250; place du Parvis Notre Dame, 4e; Ⓜ Cité), marked by a bronze star.

ANDERSEN ROSS/GETTY IMAGES ©

Crypt

Under the square in front of Notre Dame lies the **Crypte Archéologique** (Archaeological Crypt; www.crypte.paris.fr; 4e; adult/child €8/free; ◷ 10am-6pm Tue-Sun), a 117m-long and 28m-wide area displaying in situ the remains of structures built on this site during the Gallo-Roman period, a 4th-century enclosure wall, the foundations of the medieval foundlings hospice and a few of the original sewers sunk by Haussmann.

Audioguides & Tours

Pick up an audioguide (€5) from Notre Dame's information desk, just inside the entrance. Audio-guide rental includes admission to the treasury.

Free one-hour English-language tours take place at 2pm Wednesday and Thursday and 2.30pm Saturday.

Landmark Occasions

Historic events that have taken place at Notre Dame include Henry VI of England's 1431 coronation as King of France, the 1558 marriage of Mary, Queen of Scots, to the Dauphin Francis (later Francis II of France), the 1804 coronation of Napoléon I by Pope Pius VII and the 1909 beatification and 1920 canonisation of Joan of Arc.

Music at Notre Dame

Music has been a sacred part of Notre Dame's soul since birth. The best day to appreciate its musical heritage is on Sunday at a Gregorian or polyphonic Mass (10am and 6.30pm respectively) or a free organ recital (4.30pm).

From October to June the cathedral stages evening concerts; find the programme online at www.musique-sacree-notredamedeparis.fr.

★ Square Jean XXIII

One of the best views of the cathedral's forest of flying buttresses is from square Jean XXIII, the little park behind the cathedral.

Notre Dame

TIMELINE

1160 Maurice de Sully becomes bishop of Paris. Mission: to grace growing Paris with a lofty new cathedral.

1182–90 The ❶ **choir with double ambulatory** is finished and work starts on the nave and side chapels.

1200–50 The ❷ **west façade**, with rose window, three portals and two soaring towers, goes up. Everyone is stunned.

1345 Some 180 years after the foundation stone was laid, the Cathédrale de Notre Dame is complete. It is dedicated to notre dame (our lady), the Virgin Mary.

1789 Revolutionaries smash the original ❸ **Gallery of Kings**, pillage the cathedral and melt all its bells except the great bell Emmanuel. The cathedral becomes a Temple of Reason then a warehouse.

1831 Victor Hugo's novel *The Hunchback of Notre Dame* inspires new interest in the half-ruined Gothic cathedral.

1845–64 Architect Viollet-le-Duc undertakes its restoration. Twenty-eight new kings are sculpted for the west façade. The heavily decorated ❹ **portals** and ❺ **spire** are reconstructed. The neo-Gothic ❻ **treasury** is built.

1860 The area in front of Notre Dame is cleared to create the parvis, an al fresco classroom where Parisians can learn a catechism illustrated on sculpted stone portals.

1935 A rooster bearing part of the relics of the Crown of Thorns, St Denis and Ste Geneviève is put on top of the cathedral spire to protect those who pray inside.

1991 The architectural masterpiece of Notre Dame and its Seine-side riverbanks become a Unesco World Heritage Site.

2013 Notre Dame celebrates 850 years since construction began with a bevy of new bells and restoration works.

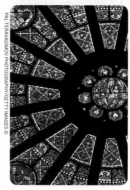

PAL TERAVAGIMOV PHOTOGRAPHY/GETTY IMAGES ©

Virgin & Child
Spot all 37 artworks representing the Virgin Mary. Pilgrims have revered the pearly-cream sculpture of her in the sanctuary since the 14th century. Light a devotional candle and write some words to the *Livre de Vie* (Book of Life).

North Rose Window
See prophets, judges, kings and priests venerate Mary in vivid blue and violet glass, one of three beautiful rose blooms (1225–70), each almost 10m in diameter.

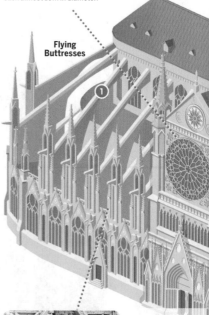

Flying Buttresses

❶

DIGITAL IMAGINATION/GETTY IMAGES ©

Choir Screen
No part of the cathedral weaves biblical tales more evocatively than these ornate wooden panels, carved in the 14th century after the Black Death killed half the country's population. The faintly gaudy colours were restored in the 1960s.

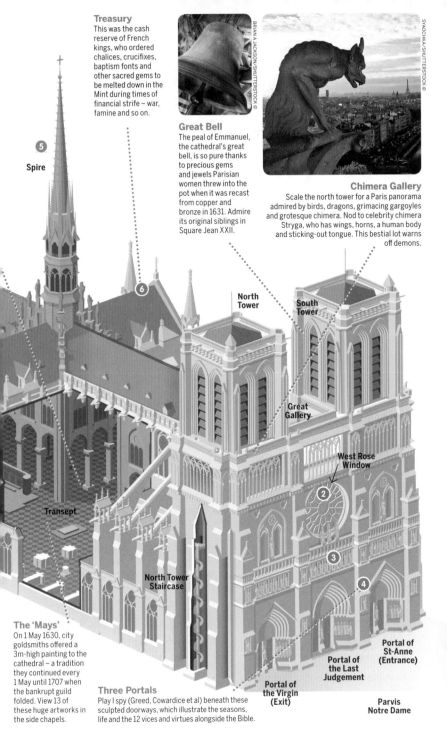

Treasury
This was the cash reserve of French kings, who ordered chalices, crucifixes, baptism fonts and other sacred gems to be melted down in the Mint during times of financial strife – war, famine and so on.

BRIAN A JACKSON/SHUTTERSTOCK ©

STADOCHKA/SHUTTERSTOCK ©

5 **Spire**

Great Bell
The peal of Emmanuel, the cathedral's great bell, is so pure thanks to precious gems and jewels Parisian women threw into the pot when it was recast from copper and bronze in 1631. Admire its original siblings in Square Jean XXII.

Chimera Gallery
Scale the north tower for a Paris panorama admired by birds, dragons, grimacing gargoyles and grotesque chimera. Nod to celebrity chimera Stryga, who has wings, horns, a human body and sticking-out tongue. This bestial lot warns off demons.

6

North Tower

South Tower

Great Gallery

West Rose Window

2

Transept

North Tower Staircase

3

4

The 'Mays'
On 1 May 1630, city goldsmiths offered a 3m-high painting to the cathedral – a tradition they continued every 1 May until 1707 when the bankrupt guild folded. View 13 of these huge artworks in the side chapels.

Three Portals
Play I spy (Greed, Cowardice et al) beneath these sculpted doorways, which illustrate the seasons, life and the 12 vices and virtues alongside the Bible.

Portal of the Virgin (Exit)

Portal of the Last Judgement

Portal of St-Anne (Entrance)

Parvis Notre Dame

NAUGHTYNUT/SHUTTERSTOCK ©

The Louvre

The **Mona Lisa** *and the* **Venus de Milo** *are just two of the priceless treasures resplendently housed inside the fortress turned royal palace turned France's first national museum.*

Few art galleries are as prized or as daunting as the Musée du Louvre – one of the world's largest and most diverse museums. Showcasing 35,000 works of art, it would take nine months to glance at every piece, rendering advance planning essential.

Works of art from Europe form the permanent exhibition, alongside priceless collections of Mesopotamian, Egyptian, Greek, Roman and Islamic art and antiquities – a fascinating presentation of the evolution of Western art up through the mid-19th century.

Visiting

You need to queue twice to get in: once for security and then again to buy tickets. The longest queues are outside the Grande Pyramide; use the Carrousel du Louvre entrance (99 rue de Rivoli or direct from the metro).

Great For...

☑ **Don't Miss**

The museum's thematic trails – from the 'Art of Eating' to 'Love in the Louvre'.

ℹ Need to Know

Map p250; ☎01 40 20 53 17; www.louvre.fr; rue de Rivoli & quai des Tuileries, 1er; adult/child €15/free; ⊙9am-6pm Mon, Thu, Sat & Sun, to 9.45pm Wed & Fri; Ⓜ Palais Royal–Musée du Louvre

✕ Take a Break

The Hall Napoléon sells sandwiches; ideal for a Jardin des Tuileries (p91) picnic.

★ Top Tip

Tickets are valid for the whole day, meaning you can come and go.

A Paris Museum Pass or Paris City Passport gives you priority; buying tickets in advance (on the Louvre website) will also help expedite the process.

You can download self-guided, thematic-trail brochures from the website. Another good option is to rent a Nintendo 3DS multimedia guide (adult/child €5/3; ID required). More formal, English-language **guided tours** (☎01 40 20 52 63; adult/child €12/7; ⊙11.30am & 2pm except 1st Sun of month) depart from the Hall Napoléon. Reserve a spot up to 14 days in advance or sign up on arrival at the museum.

In 2014, the Louvre embarked on a 30-year renovation plan. Phase 1 increased the number of main entrances, to reduce wait times to get through security. It also revamped the Hall Napoléon to improve what was previously bewildering chaos. Changes to come include increasing the number of English-language signs and artwork texts to aid navigation.

Palais du Louvre

The Louvre today rambles over four floors and through three wings: the **Sully Wing** creates the four sides of the Cour Carrée (literally 'Square Courtyard') at the eastern end of the complex; the **Denon Wing** stretches 800m along the Seine to the south; and the northern **Richelieu Wing** skirts rue de Rivoli. The building started life as a fortress built by Philippe-Auguste in the 12th century – medieval remnants are still visible on the Lower Ground Floor (Sully). In the 16th century it became a royal residence, and after the Revolution, in 1793, it was turned into a national museum. At the time, its booty was no more than 2500 paintings and objets d'art.

Over the centuries French governments amassed the paintings, sculptures and artefacts displayed today. The 'Grand Louvre' project, inaugurated by the late President Mitterrand in 1989, doubled the museum's exhibition space, and both new and renovated galleries have since opened, including the **Islamic art galleries**.

Priceless Antiquities

Whatever your plans are, don't rush by the Louvre's astonishing cache of treasures from antiquity: both Mesopotamia (ground floor, Richelieu) and Egypt (ground and 1st floors, Sully) are well represented, as seen in the *Code of Hammurabi* (Room 3, ground floor, Richelieu) and the *Seated Scribe* (Room 22, 1st floor, Sully). Room 12 (ground floor, Sackler Wing) holds impressive friezes and an enormous two-headed-bull column from the Darius Palace in ancient Iran, while an enormous seated statue of Pharaoh Ramesses II highlights the temple room (Room 12, Sully).

Also worth a look are the mosaics and figurines from the Byzantine empire (lower ground floor, Denon), and the Greek statuary collection, culminating with the world's most famous armless duo, the *Venus de Milo* (Room 16, ground floor, Sully) and the *Winged Victory of Samothrace* (top of Daru staircase, 1st floor, Denon).

French & Italian Masterpieces

The 1st floor of the Denon Wing, where the *Mona Lisa* is found, is easily the most popular part of the Louvre – and with good reason. Rooms 75 through 77 are hung with monumental French paintings, many iconic.

Rooms 1, 3, 5 and 8 are also must-visits. Filled with classic works by Renaissance masters – Raphael, Titian, Uccello, Botticini – this area culminates with the crowds around the *Mona Lisa*. But you'll find plenty else to contemplate, from Botticelli's graceful frescoes (Room 1) to the superbly detailed *Wedding Feast at Cana* (Room 6).

Dining room in the Napoleon III Apartments

Mona Lisa

Easily the Louvre's most admired work (and the world's most famous painting) is Leonardo da Vinci's *La Joconde* (in French; *La Gioconda* in Italian), the lady with that enigmatic smile known as *Mona Lisa* (Room 6, 1st floor, Denon).

Mona (*monna* in Italian) is a contraction of *madonna*, and Gioconda is the feminine form of the surname Giocondo. Canadian scientists used infrared technology to peer through paint layers and confirm *Mona Lisa's* identity as Lisa Gherardini

(1479–1542?), wife of Florentine merchant Francesco de Giocondo. Scientists also discovered that her dress was covered in a transparent gauze veil typically worn in early 16th-century Italy by pregnant women or new mothers; it's surmised that the work was painted to commemorate the birth of her second son around 1503, when she was aged about 24.

Louis XV's Crown

French kings wore their crowns only once – at their coronation. Lined with embroidered satin and topped with openwork arches and a fleur-de-lis, Louis XV's 1722-crafted crown (Room 66, 1st floor, Denon) was originally adorned with pearls, sapphires, rubies, topazes, emeralds and diamonds.

> ★ **Italian Sculptures**
>
> On the ground floor of the Denon Wing, take time for the Italian sculptures, including Michelangelo's *The Dying Slave* and Canova's *Psyche and Cupid* (Room 4).

The Pyramid Inside & Out

Almost as stunning as the masterpieces inside is the 21m-high glass pyramid designed by Chinese-born American architect IM Pei that bedecks the main entrance to the Louvre in a dazzling crown. Beneath Pei's Grande Pyramide is the **Hall Napoléon**, the main entrance area, comprising an information booth, temporary exhibition hall, bookshop, souvenir store, cafe and auditoriums. To revel in another Pei pyramid of equally dramatic dimensions, head toward the **Carrousel du Louvre** (Map p250; http://carrouseldulouvre. com; 99 rue de Rivoli, 1er; ⏰8.30am-11pm, shops 10am-8pm; 🛜), a shopping mall that loops underground from the Grande Pyramide to the Arc de Triomphe du Carrousel (p91) – its centrepiece is Pei's **Pyramide Inversée** (inverted glass pyramid).

BRIAN KINNEY/SHUTTERSTOCK ©

> ★ **Northern European Painting**
>
> The 2nd floor of the Richelieu Wing, directly above the gilt and crystal of the **Napoleon III Apartments** (1st floor), allows for a quieter meander through the Louvre's collection of Flemish and Dutch paintings, spearheaded by works by Peter Paul Rubens and Pieter Bruegel the Elder. Vermeer's *The Lacemaker* can be found in Room 38, while Room 31 is devoted chiefly to works by Rembrandt.

The Louvre

A HALF-DAY TOUR

Successfully visiting the Louvre is a fine art. Its complex labyrinth of galleries and staircases spiralling three wings and four floors renders discovery a snakes-and-ladders experience. Initiate yourself with this three-hour itinerary – a playful mix of *Mona Lisa*–obvious and up-to-the-minute unexpected.

Arriving in the newly renovated **1 Hall Napoléon** beneath IM Pei's glass pyramid, pick up colour-coded floor plans at an information stand, then ride the escalator up to the Sully Wing and swap passport or credit card for a multimedia guide (there are limited descriptions in the galleries) at the wing entrance.

The Louvre is as much about spectacular architecture as masterful art. To appreciate this, zip up and down Sully's Escalier Henri II to admire **2 Venus de Milo**, then up parallel Escalier Henri IV to the palatial displays in **3 Cour Khorsabad**. Cross Room 1 to find the escalator up to the 1st floor and the opulent **4 Napoleon III apartments**. Next traverse 25 consecutive galleries (thank you, floor plan!) to flip conventional contemplation on its head with Cy Twombly's **5 The Ceiling**, and the hypnotic **6 Winged Victory of Samothrace sculpture**, which brazenly insists on being admired from all angles. End with the impossibly famous **7 The Raft of the Medusa**, **8 Mona Lisa** and **9 Virgin & Child**.

TOP TIPS

➡ Don't even consider entering the Louvre's maze of galleries without a floor plan, free from the information desk in the Hall Napoléon.

➡ The Denon Wing is always packed; visit on late nights (Wednesday or Friday) or trade Denon in for the notably quieter Richelieu Wing.

➡ The 2nd floor isn't for first-timers: save its more specialist works for subsequent visits.

Napoleon III Apartments
1st Floor, Richelieu
Napoleon III's gorgeous gilt apartments were built from 1854 to 1861, featuring an over-the-top decor of gold leaf, stucco and crystal chandeliers that reaches a dizzying climax in the Grand Salon and State Dining Room.

Jardin du Carrousel

Galerie du Carrousel Entrances

Porte des Lions Entrance

LOUVRE AUDITORIUM

Classical-music concerts are staged several times a week at the Louvre Auditorium (off the main entrance hall). Don't miss the Thursday lunchtime concerts featuring emerging composers and musicians. The season runs from September to April or May, depending on the concert series.

Mona Lisa
Room 6, 1st Floor, Denon
No smile is as enigmatic or bewitching as hers. Da Vinci's diminutive *La Joconde* hangs opposite the largest painting in the Louvre – sumptuous, fellow Italian Renaissance artwork *The Wedding at Cana*.

The Raft of the Medusa
Room 77, 1st Floor, Denon
Decipher the politics behind French romanticism in Théodore Géricault's *Raft of the Medusa*.

Cour Khorsabad
Ground Floor, Richelieu
Time travel with a pair of winged human-headed bulls to view some of the world's oldest Mesopotamian art. DETOUR» Night-lit statues in Cour Puget.

The Ceiling
Room 32, 1st Floor, Sully
Admire the blue shock of Cy Twombly's 400-sq-metre contemporary ceiling fresco – the Louvre's latest, daring commission. DETOUR» *The Braque Ceiling*, Room 33.

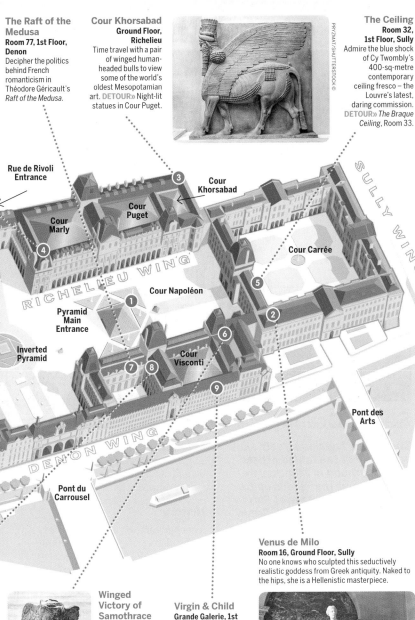

PRYZMAT/SHUTTERSTOCK ©

Rue de Rivoli Entrance

❸ **Cour Khorsabad**

Cour Puget

Cour Marly

❹

Cour Carrée

❺

R I C H E L I E U   W I N G

Cour Napoléon

❶

Pyramid Main Entrance

❷

Inverted Pyramid

❻

Cour Visconti

❼ ❽

D E N O N   W I N G

❾

Pont des Arts

Pont du Carrousel

S U L L Y   W I N G

Venus de Milo
Room 16, Ground Floor, Sully
No one knows who sculpted this seductively realistic goddess from Greek antiquity. Naked to the hips, she is a Hellenistic masterpiece.

PRYZMAT/SHUTTERSTOCK ©

Winged Victory of Samothrace
Escalier Daru, 1st Floor, Sully
Draw breath at the aggressive dynamism of this headless, handless Hellenistic goddess. DETOUR» The razzle-dazzle of the Apollo Gallery's crown jewels.

Virgin & Child
Grande Galerie, 1st Floor, Denon
In the spirit of artistic devotion save the Louvre's most famous gallery for last: a feast of Virgin-and-child paintings by Da Vinci, Raphael, Domenico Ghirlandaio, Giovanni Bellini and Francesco Botticini.

TUTTI FRUTTI/SHUTTERSTOCK ©

BIGLANNIE/BUDGET TRAVEL ©

Sacré-Cœur

Staircased, ivy-clad streets slink up the hill of the fabled artists' neighbourhood of Montmartre to a funicular that glides up to the dove-white domes of Paris' landmark basilica, Sacré-Cœur.

More than just a basilica, Sacré-Cœur is a veritable experience, from the musicians performing on the steps to the groups of friends picnicking on the hillside park.

History

It may appear to be a place of peacefulness and worship today, but in truth Sacré-Cœur's foundations were laid amid bloodshed and controversy. Its construction began in 1875, in the wake of France's humiliating defeat by Prussia and the subsequent chaos of the Paris Commune. Following Napoléon III's surrender to von Bismarck in September 1870, angry Parisians, with the help of the National Guard, continued to hold out against Prussian forces – a harrowing siege that lasted four long winter months. By the time a ceasefire was negotiated in early 1871, the split between the

Great For...

☑ **Don't Miss**

Dizzying vistas across Paris, especially from up inside the basilica's main dome.

❶ Need to Know

Map p249; ☎01 53 41 89 00; www.
sacre-coeur-montmartre.com; Parvis du
Sacré-Cœur; basilica admission free, dome
adult/child €6/4, cash only; ⏱basilica 6am-
10.30pm, dome 8.30am-8pm May-Sep, to 5pm
Oct-Apr; Ⓜ Anvers, Abbesses

✕ Take a Break

Head to the terrace of L'Été en Pente
Douce (p129) for French classics.

★ Top Tip

To skip walking up the hill, use a
regular metro ticket aboard the
funicular.

---

radical working-class Parisians (supported
by the National Guard) and the conservative national government (supported by the
French army) had become insurmountable.

Over the next several months, the
rebels, known as Communards, managed
to overthrow the reactionary government
and take over the city. It was a particularly
chaotic and bloody moment in Parisian
history, with mass executions on both
sides and a wave of rampant destruction
that spread throughout Paris. Montmartre
was a key Communard stronghold – it was
on the future site of Sacré-Cœur that the
rebels won their first victory – and it was
consequently the first neighbourhood to be
targeted when the French army returned
in full force in May 1871. Ultimately, many
Communards were buried alive in the gypsum mines beneath the Butte.

The Basilica

In this context, the construction of an
enormous basilica to expiate the city's
sins seemed like a gesture of peace and
forgiveness – indeed, the seven million
French francs needed to construct the
church's foundations came solely from the
contributions of local Catholics. However,
the Montmartre location was certainly no
coincidence: the conservative old guard desperately wanted to assert its power in what
was then a hotbed of revolution. The battle
between the two camps – Catholic versus
secular, royalists versus republican –
raged on, and in 1882 the construction of
the basilica was even voted down by the city
council (on the grounds that it would continue to fan the flames of civil war), only to be
overturned in the end by a technicality.

Six successive architects oversaw construction of the Romano-Byzantine–style
basilica, and it wasn't until 1919 that Sacré-
Cœur was finally consecrated, even then

standing in utter contrast to the bohemian lifestyle that surrounded it. While criticism of its design and white travertine stone has continued throughout the decades (one poet called it a giant baby's bottle for angels), the interior is enlivened by the glittering apse mosaic *Christ in Majesty*, designed by Luc-Olivier Merson in 1922 and one of the largest in the world.

In 1944, 13 Allied bombs were dropped on Montmartre, falling just next to Sacré-Cœur. Although the stained-glass windows all shattered from the force of the explosions, miraculously no one died and the basilica sustained no other damage.

In a sense, atonement here has never stopped: a prayer 'cycle' that began in 1885 before the basilica's completion still continues around the clock, with perpetual adoration of the Blessed Sacrament contin-

ually on display above the high altar. The basilica's travertine stone exudes calcite, ensuring it remains white despite weathering and pollution.

The Dome

Some 300 spiralling steps lead you to the basilica's dome, which affords one of Paris' most spectacular panoramas; it's said you can see for 30km on a clear day. Weighing in at 19 tonnes, the bell called La Savoyarde in the tower above is the largest in France.

What's Nearby?

Place du Tertre   Square

(Map p249; 18e; M Abbesses) Today filled with visitors, buskers and portrait artists, place du Tertre was originally the main square of the village of Montmartre before it was incorporated into the city proper.

Place du Tertre

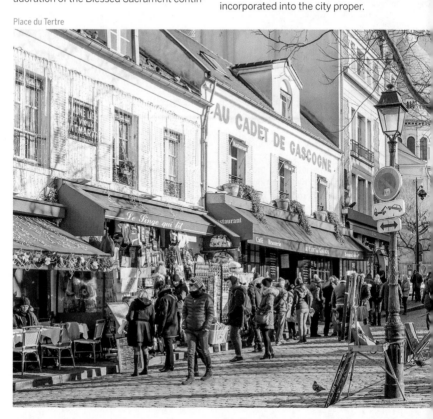

One of the more popular claims of Montmartre mythology is staked to La Mère Catherine at No 6: in 1814, so it's said, Cossack soldiers first introduced the term *bistro* (Russian for 'quickly') into the French lexicon.

Espace Dalí   Gallery

(Map p249; ☎01 42 64 40 10; www.daliparis. com; 11 rue Poulbot, 18e; adult/child €11.50/7; ◷10am-6pm Sep-Jun, to 8pm Jul & Aug; Ⓜ Abbesses) More than 300 works by Salvador Dalí (1904–89), the flamboyant Catalan surrealist printmaker, painter, sculptor and self-promoter, are on display at this

> ★ **Did You Know?**
> On Christmas Eve 1898, Louis Renault's first car was driven up the Montmartre Butte to the place du Tertre, igniting the start of the French auto industry.

surrealist-style basement museum located just west of place du Tertre. The collection includes Dalí's strange sculptures, lithograph, and many of his illustrations and furniture, including the famous Mae West Lips Sofa.

Clos Montmartre   Vineyard

(Map p249; www.clos-montmartre.com; 18 rue des Saules, 18e; Ⓜ Lamarck–Caulaincourt) Epitomising Montmartre's enchanting village-like atmosphere, the *quartier* even has its own small vineyard. Planted in 1933, its 2000 vines produce an average of 800 bottles of wine a year. Each October the grapes are pressed, fermented and bottled in Montmartre's town hall, then sold by auction to raise funds for local community projects. It's closed to the public except for a handful of special events.

Musée de Montmartre   Museum

(Map p249; ☎01 49 25 89 39; www.musee demontmartre.fr; 12 rue Cortot, 18e; adult/ child €9.50/5.50; ◷10am-6pm; Ⓜ Lamarck–Caulaincourt) One of Paris' most romantic spots, this enchanting 'village' museum showcases paintings, lithographs and documents illustrating Montmartre's bohemian, artistic and hedonistic past – one room is dedicated entirely to the French cancan! It's housed in a 17th-century manor where several artists, including Renoir and Raoul Dufy, had their studios in the 19th century. You can also visit the studio of painter Suzanne Valadon, who lived and worked here with her son Maurice Utrillo and partner André Utter between 1912 and 1926.

Moulin Blute Fin   Windmill

(Moulin de la Galette; Map p249; rue Lepic, 18e; Ⓜ Abbesses) Sister windmill to surviving **Moulin Radet** (83 rue Lepic, 18e) on the same street, this abandoned 18th-century windmill ground flour on its hillock perch. It later became known as Moulin de la Galette after the *guinguette* (dance hall) – immortalised in Renoir's painting, *Bal du Moulin de la Galette* (1876), now in the Musée d'Orsay – that sprung up around its feet in the 1930s.

BORIS B/SHUTTERSTOCK ©

Musée d'Orsay

The grand former railway station in which the Musée d'Orsay is located is an art nouveau marvel, but the masterpieces from 1848 to 1914 are the star of the show.

Great For...

❶ Need to Know

Map p246; www.musee-orsay.fr; 1 rue de la Légion d'Honneur, 7e; adult/child €12/free; ◷9.30am-6pm Tue, Wed & Fri-Sun, to 9.45pm Thu; Ⓜ Assemblée Nationale, RER Musée d'Orsay)

★ Top Tip
Musée d'Orsay admission drops to €9 after 4.30pm (after 6pm on Thursday).

History

The Gare d'Orsay railway station was designed by competition-winning architect Victor Laloux. On its completion, just in time for the 1900 Exposition Universelle, painter Edouard Detaille declared that the new station looked like a Palais des Beaux Arts. But although it had all the mod-cons of the day – including luggage lifts and passenger elevators – by 1939 the increasing electrification of the rail network meant the platforms were too short for mainline trains, and within a few years all rail services ceased.

The station was used as a mailing centre during WWII, and in 1962 Orson Welles filmed Kafka's *The Trial* in the then-abandoned building. Fortunately, it was saved from being demolished and replaced with a hotel complex by a Historical Monument listing in 1973, before the government set about establishing the palatial museum.

Transforming the languishing building into the country's premier showcase for art dating from 1848 to 1914 was the grand project of President Valéry Giscard d'Estaing, who signed off on it in 1977. The museum opened its doors in 1986.

Far from resting on its laurels, the Musée d'Orsay's recent renovations incorporated a re-energised layout and increased exhibition space. Rather than being lost in a sea of white, prized paintings now gleam from richly coloured walls that create an intimate, stately home–like atmosphere, with high-tech illumination literally casting the masterpieces in a new light.

Paintings & Graphic Arts

On the top of every visitor's must-see list is the world's largest collection of impression-

Views of Paris from the glass clockface

ist and post-impressionist art. Just some of its highlights include Manet's *On the Beach* and *Woman with Fans*; Monet's gardens at Giverny and *Rue Montorgueil, Paris, Celebration of June 30, 1878*; Cézanne's card players, *Green Apples* and *Blue Vase*; Renoir's *Ball at the Moulin de la Galette* and *Young Girls at the Piano*; Degas' ballerinas; Toulouse-Lautrec's cabaret dancers; Pissarro's *The Seine and the Louvre*; Sisley's *View of the Canal St-Martin*; and Van Gogh's self-portraits, *Bedroom in Arles* and *Starry Night over the Rhône*. One of the museum's newer acquisitions is James Tissot's 1868 painting *The Circle of the Rue Royale*, classified a National Treasure.

> **☑ Don't Miss**
>
> The Parisian panorama through the railway station's giant glass clockface and from the adjacent terrace.

Drawings, pastels and sketches from major artists are another of the d'Orsay's lesser-known highlights. Look for Georges Seurat's *The Black Bow* (c 1882), which uses crayon on paper to define forms by contrasting between black and white, and Paul Gauguin's poignant self-portrait (c 1902–03), drawn near the end of his life.

Decorative Arts & Sculpture

Household items such as hat and coat stands, candlesticks, desks, chairs, bookcases, vases, pot-plant holders, freestanding screens, wall mirrors, water pitchers, plates, goblets and bowls become works of art in the hands of their creators from the era, incorporating exquisite design elements.

The cavernous former station is also a magnificent setting for sculptures, including works by Degas, Gauguin, Camille Claudel, Renoir and Rodin.

Visiting

Combined tickets with the Musée de l'Orangerie (p90) cost €16, while combined tickets with the Musée Rodin (p66) are €18; both combination tickets are valid for a single visit to the museums within three months.

The museum is busiest Tuesday and Sunday, followed by Thursday and Saturday. Save time by buying tickets online and head directly to entrance C.

For a thorough introduction to the museum, 90-minute 'Masterpieces of the Musée d'Orsay' guided tours (€6) in English run at 11.30am and 2.30pm on Tuesday and 11.30am from Wednesday to Saturday. Kids under 13 aren't permitted on tours. An audioguide costs €5.

Non-professional photography is permitted but flash photography and tripods are not. There's an excellent book and gift shop.

✖ Take a Break

Time has scarcely changed the museum's (originally the station's) **Restaurant Musée d'Orsay** (✆01 45 49 47 03; Musée d'Orsay; 2-/3-course lunch menus €22/32, mains €16-29; ⏱11.45am-5.30pm Tue, Wed & Fri-Sun, 11.45am-2.45pm & 7-9.30pm Thu; ♿).

Musée Rodin

Paris' most romantic museum displays Auguste Rodin's sculptural masterpieces in his former workshop and showroom, the 1730-built, beautifully restored Hôtel Biron, as well as in its rambling, rose gardens.

Sculptor, painter, sketcher, engraver and collector Auguste Rodin donated his entire collection to the French state in 1908 on the proviso they dedicate his former workshop and showroom to displaying his works. They're now installed not only in the mansion itself, but also in its rose-filled garden – one of the most peaceful places in central Paris.

Sculptures

The first large-scale cast of Rodin's famous sculpture *Le Penseur* (The Thinker), made in 1902, resides in the garden – the perfect place to contemplate this heroic naked figure conceived by Rodin to represent intellect and poetry (it was originally titled 'The Poet').

La Porte de l'Enfer (The Gates of Hell) was commissioned in 1880 as the entrance

---

Great For...

☑ **Don't Miss**

Rodin's collection of works by artists including Van Gogh, Renoir and Camille Claudel.

Le Penseur (The Thinker)

WJAREK/SHUTTERSTOCK ©

❶ Need to Know

Map p246; www.musee-rodin.fr; 79 rue de Varenne, 7e; adult/child museum incl garden €10/free, garden only €4/free; ⏰10am-5.45pm Tue-Sun; Ⓜ Varenne

✖ Take a Break

Paris' oldest restaurant, À la Petite Chaise (p140), still serves excellent traditional fare.

★ Top Tip

Cheaper garden-only entry is available.

Grey, by British company Farrow & Ball, which now provides a backdrop to the sculptures.

The Rodin at the Hôtel Biron room incorporates original furniture to recreate the space as it was when he lived and worked here.

Visiting

Prepurchase tickets online to avoid queuing. Audioguides cost €6. A combined ticket with the Musée d'Orsay costs €18; combination tickets are valid for a single visit to each of the museums within three months.

for a never-built museum, and Rodin worked on his sculptural masterwork up until his death in 1917. Standing 6m high by 4m wide, its 180 figures comprise an intricate scene from Dante's *Inferno*.

Marble monument to love *Le Baiser* (The Kiss) was originally part of The Gates of Hell. The sculpture's entwined lovers caused controversy on its completion due to Rodin's then-radical approach of depicting women as equal partners in ardour.

The museum also features many sculptures by Camille Claudel, Rodin's protégé.

Rodin at the Hôtel Biron

Magnificent recent renovations to the museum – the first since Rodin worked here until his death in 1917 – included the creation of a new paint colour, Biron

What's Nearby?

Hôtel Matignon Landmark

(Map p246; 57 rue de Varenne, 7e; Ⓜ Solférino)
Hôtel Matignon has been the official residence of the French prime minister since the start of the Fifth Republic (1958). It's closed to the public.

Jardin du Luxembourg

The city's most beautiful park, the Jardin du Luxembourg, is an inner-city oasis encompassing 23 gracefully laid-out hectares of formal terraces, chestnut groves and lush lawns.

Great For...

❶ Need to Know

Map p252; www.senat.fr/visite/jardin; numerous entrances; ⊘hours vary; Ⓜ Mabillon, St-Sulpice, Rennes, Notre Dame des Champs, RER Luxembourg

★ **Top Tip**

For a quick snack or drink, kiosks and cafes are dotted throughout the park.

ALEXKOZLOV/GETTY IMAGES ©

The Jardin du Luxembourg has a special place in Parisians' hearts. Napoléon dedicated the gardens to the children of Paris, and many residents spent their childhood prodding little wooden sailboats with long sticks on the octagonal pond, watching puppet shows, and riding the carousel or ponies.

All those activities are still here today, as are modern playgrounds and sporting and games venues.

History

The Jardin du Luxembourg's history stretches further back than Napoléon's dedication. The gardens are a backdrop to the Palais du Luxembourg, built in the 1620s for Marie de Médici, Henri IV's consort, to assuage her longing for the Pitti Palace in Florence. The Palais is now home to the French Senate, which, in addition to parliamentary-assembly activities like voting on legislation, is charged with promoting the palace and its gardens.

Numerous overhauls over the centuries have given the Jardin du Luxembourg a blend of traditional French- and English-style gardens that is unique in Paris.

Grand Bassin

All ages love the octagonal Grand Bassin, a serene ornamental pond where adults can lounge and kids can play with 1920s **toy sailboats** (per 30min €3.50; ☉Apr-Oct). Nearby, littlies can take **pony rides** (rides €3.50; ☉3-6pm Wed, Sat, Sun & school holidays) or romp around the **playgrounds** (adult/child €1.50/2.50; ☉hours vary) – the green half is for kids aged seven to 12 years, the blue half for under-sevens.

Fontaine des Médici

Puppet Shows

You don't have to be a kid or speak French to be delighted by marionette shows, which have entertained audiences in France since the Middle Ages. The lively puppets perform in the Jardin du Luxembourg's little **Théâtre du Luxembourg** (www.marionnettesduluxem bourg.fr; tickets €6; ⏰usually 11am & 3.30pm Wed, Sat & Sun, 11am, 3pm & 4.15pm daily during school holidays). Show times can vary; check online and arrive half an hour ahead.

Orchards

Dozens of apple varieties grow in the orchards in the gardens' south. Bees have

---

☑ Don't Miss

Discovering the park's many sculptures, which include statues of Stendhal, Chopin, Baudelaire and Delacroix.

MARINA DA/SHUTTERSTOCK ©

---

produced honey in the nearby apiary, the **Rucher du Luxembourg** (Map p252), since the 19th century. The annual Fête du Miel (Honey Festival) offers two days of tasting and buying its sweet harvest around late September in the ornate **Pavillon Davioud** (Map p252; 55bis rue d'Assas, 6e).

Palais du Luxembourg

The **Palais du Luxembourg** (Map p252; www.senat.fr; rue de Vaugirard, 6e; Ⓜ Mabillon, RER Luxembourg) was built in the 1620s and has been home to the Sénat (French Senate) since 1958. It's occasionally open for visits by guided tour.

East of the palace is the ornate, Italianate **Fontaine des Médici** (Map p252; Ⓜ Mabillon, RER Luxembourg), built in 1630. During Baron Haussmann's 19th-century reshaping of the roads, the fountain was moved 30m, and the pond and dramatic statues of the giant bronze Polyphemus discovering the white-marble lovers Acis and Galatea were added.

Musée du Luxembourg

Prestigious temporary art exhibitions, such as *Cézanne et Paris*, take place in the beautiful **Musée du Luxembourg** (Map p252; http://museeduluxembourg.fr; 19 rue de Vaugirard, 6e; most exhibitions adult/child €12/8.50; ⏰10.30am-7pm Sat-Thu, to 10pm Fri; Ⓜ St-Sulpice, RER Luxembourg).

Around the back of the museum, lemon and orange trees, palms, grenadiers and oleanders shelter from the cold in the palace's **orangery**. Nearby, the heavily guarded **Hôtel du Petit Luxembourg** was where Marie de Médici lived while the Palais du Luxembourg was being built. The president of the Senate has called it home since 1825.

✗ Take a Break

Park picnics aside, nearby options include family-style French cuisine at historic Polidor (p140).

PHOTO UA/SHUTTERSTOCK ©

Cruising the Seine

The lifeline of Paris, the Seine sluices through the city, spanned by 37 bridges. Cruises along the river are an idyllic way to observe its Unesco World Heritage–listed riverbanks.

Great For...

☑ **Don't Miss**

Floating past Parisian landmarks such as the Louvre and Notre Dame.

Boat Trips & Cruise Companies

A plethora of companies run day- and night-time boat tours (usually lasting around an hour) with commentary in multiple languages.

An alternative to traditional boat tours is the Batobus (p237), a handy hop-on, hop-off service that stops at quintessentially Parisian attractions: the Eiffel Tower, Champs-Élysées, Musée d'Orsay, Musée du Louvre, St-Germain des Prés, Hôtel de Ville, Notre Dame and Jardin des Plantes. Single- and multiday tickets allow you to spend as long as you like sightseeing between stops.

Vedettes de Paris   Boating

(Map p246; ☎01 44 18 19 50; www.vedettesde paris.fr; Port de Suffren, 7e; adult/child €14/6; Ⓜ Bir Hakeim or RER Pont de l'Alma) These one-hour sightseeing cruises on smaller boats are a more intimate experience than the

❶ Need to Know

There are no barriers at the water's edge; keep a close eye on young children.

✖ Take a Break

Many cruise companies offer brunch, lunch and dinner cruises with high-quality food.

★ Top Tip

Floodlights illuminate the iconic riverside buildings at night.

major companies. It runs themed cruises too, including imaginative 'Mysteries of Paris' tours for kids (adult/child €14/8).

Vedettes du Pont Neuf   Boating

(Map p250; ☑ 01 46 33 98 38; www.vedettesdu pontneuf.com; square du Vert Galant, 1er; adult/child €14/7; ⊙10.30am-9pm; M Pont Neuf) One-hour cruises depart year-round from Vedettes' centrally located dock at the western tip of Île de la Cité; commentary is in French and English. Tickets are cheaper if you buy in advance online (adult/child €10/5). Check the website for details of its one-hour lunch cruises (adult/child €41/35) and two-hour dinner and Champagne cruises (adult/child €104/35).

Bateaux Parisiens   Boating

(Map p246; ☑ 01 76 64 14 45; www.bateauxparisiens. com; Port de la Bourdonnais, 7e; adult/child €15/10;

🛜; M Bir Hakeim or RER Pont de l'Alma) This vast operation runs hour-long river circuits with audioguides in 14 languages (every 30 minutes 10am to 11pm April to September, hourly 10am to 10.30pm October to March), and a host of themed lunch and dinner cruises. It has two locations: one by the Eiffel Tower, the other south of Notre Dame.

Bateaux-Mouches   Boating

(Map p246; ☑ 01 42 25 96 10; www.bateaux-mouches.fr; Port de la Conférence, 8e; adult/child €13.50/6; M Alma Marceau) Bateaux-Mouches, the largest river cruise company in Paris, is a favourite with tour groups. Departing just east of the Pont de l'Alma on the Right Bank, cruises (70 minutes) run regularly from 10.15am to 10.30pm April to September and 13 times a day between 11am and 9.20pm the rest of the year. Commentary is in French and English.

Paris Canal Croisières   Boating

(Map p246; ☑ 01 42 40 96 97; www.pariscanal.com; quai Anatole France, 7e; adult/child €20/13; ⊙mid-Mar–mid-Nov; M Solférino, RER Musée d'Orsay) Seasonal 2½-hour Seine-and-canal cruises depart from quai Anatole France near the Musée d'Orsay and from Parc de la Villette.

CENTRE POMPIDOU STUDIO PIANO & ROGERS, ARCHITECT: TAKASHI IMAGES/SHUTTERSTOCK. ©

Centre Pompidou

The primary-coloured, inside-out Centre Pompidou building houses France's national modern and contemporary art museum, the Musée National d'Art Moderne (MNAM), showcasing creations from 1905 to the present day.

Galleries and exhibitions, hands-on workshops, dance performances, a bookshop, a design boutique, cinemas and other entertainment venues here are an irresistible cocktail.

Architecture & Views

Former French President Georges Pompidou wanted an ultracontemporary artistic hub and he got it: competition-winning architects Renzo Piano and Richard Rogers designed the building inside out, with utilitarian features like plumbing, pipes, air vents and electrical cables forming part of the external façade. The building was completed in 1977.

Viewed from a distance (such as from Sacré-Cœur), the Centre Pompidou's primary-coloured, boxlike form amid a sea of muted grey Parisian rooftops makes it look like a child's Meccano set abandoned

---

Great For...

☑ **Don't Miss**

The sweeping panorama of Paris from the rooftop.

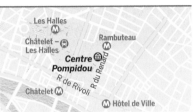

❶ Need to Know

Map p250; ☏01 44 78 12 33; www.centre
pompidou.fr; place Georges Pompidou, 4e;
museum, exhibitions & panorama adult/
child €14/free, panorama ticket only €5;
⏰11am-10pm Wed & Fri-Mon, to 11pm Thu; 🛜;
Ⓜ Rambuteau

✖ Take a Break

For a meal or a casual drink, head to
nearby Café La Fusée (p173).

> ### ★ Top Tip
>
> The Centre Pompidou opens late;
> head here around 5pm to avoid
> daytime crowds.

on someone's elegant living-room rug.
Although the Centre Pompidou is just six
storeys high, the city's low-rise cityscape
means stupendous views extend from
its roof (reached by external escalators
enclosed in tubes). Rooftop admission
is included in museum and exhibition
admission – or buy a panorama ticket (€5;
11am to 10pm Wednesday to Monday) just
for the roof.

Musée National d'Art Moderne

Europe's largest collection of modern art
fills the bright and airy, well-lit galleries of
the National Museum of Modern Art, covering two complete floors of the Pompidou.
For art lovers, this is one of the jewels of
Paris. On a par with the permanent collection are the two temporary exhibition halls
(on the ground floor/basement and the top
floor), which showcase some memorable

blockbuster exhibits. Also of note is the
fabulous children's gallery on the 1st floor.

The permanent collection changes every
two years, but the basic layout generally
stays the same. The 5th floor showcases
artists active between 1905 and the 1960s;
the 4th floor focuses on more contemporary creations, roughly from the 1990s
onward.

The dynamic presentation of the 5th
floor mixes up works by Picasso, Matisse,
Chagall and Kandinsky with lesser-known
contemporaries from as far afield as
Argentina and Japan, as well as more famous cross-Atlantic names such as Arbus,
Warhol, Pollock and Rothko.

One floor down on the 4th, you'll find
monumental paintings, installation pieces,
sculpture and video taking centre stage. The
focus here is on contemporary art, architecture and design. The 4th floor also has an
Espace des Collections Nouveaux Médias et
Film, where visitors can discover 40 years of
image and sound experimentation.

Tours & Guides

Guided tours in English lasting 1½-hours take place at noon on Saturday (€4.50); there are also regular guided tours in French. The information desk in the central hall on the ground floor has details. Alternatively, download a free app from the Centre Pompidou's website for a self-guided tour.

Atelier Brancusi

West of the Centre Pompidou main building, this reconstruction of the **studio** (Map p250; 55 rue de Rambuteau, 4e; incl in admission to Centre Pompidou €14/free; ⊘2-6pm Wed-Mon; MRambuteau) of Romanian-born sculptor Constantin Brancusi (1876–1957) – known for works such as *The Kiss* and *Bird in Space* – contains over 100

sculptures in stone and wood. You'll also find drawings, pedestals and photographic plates from his original Paris studio.

Street Fun

The full-monty Pompidou experience is as much about hanging out in the busy streets and squares around it, packed with souvenir shops and people, as absorbing the centre's contents. West of the Centre Pompidou, fun-packed place Georges Pompidou and its nearby pedestrian streets attract bags of buskers, musicians, jugglers and mime artists.

What's Nearby?
Église St-Eustache   Church
(Map p250; www.st-eustache.org; 2 impasse St-Eustache, 1er; ⊘9.30am-7pm Mon-Fri, 9am-7pm Sat & Sun; MLes Halles) Just north

Forum des Halles

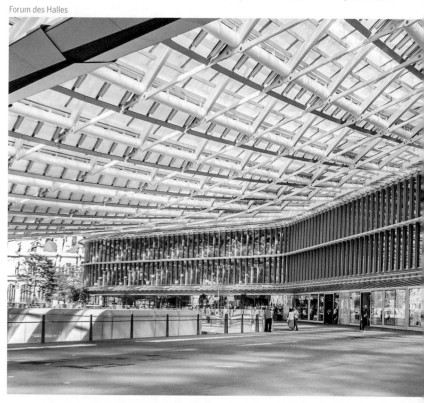

of the gardens adjoining the city's old marketplace, now the Forum des Halles, is one of the most beautiful churches in Paris. Majestic, architecturally magnificent and musically outstanding, St-Eustache was constructed between 1532 and 1632. It's primarily Gothic, though a neoclassical façade was added on the western side in the mid-18th century. Highlights include a work by Rubens, Raymond Mason's colourful bas-relief of market vendors (1969) and Keith Haring's bronze triptych (1990) in the side chapels.

> ### ★ Don't Miss
> Nearby place Igor Stravinsky with its fanciful mechanical fountains of skeletons, hearts, treble clefs, and a big pair of ruby-red lips by Jean Tinguely and Niki de St-Phalle.

Outside the church is a gig[...]ture of a head and hand entit[...](Listen; 1986) by Henri de M[...]

One of France's largest organs, ab[...]church's western entrance, has 101 stops and 8000 pipes dating from 1854. Free organ recitals at 5.30pm on Sunday are a must for music lovers; there are also various concerts during the week – schedules and prices are listed online. Audioguides are available for €3.

Forum des Halles   Notable Building
(Map p250; http://forumdeshalles.com; 1 rue Pierre Lescot, 1er; ⊗shops 10am-8pm Mon-Sat, 11am-7pm Sun; MChâtelet, Les Halles) Paris' main wholesale food market stood here for nearly 800 years before being replaced by this underground shopping mall in 1971. Long considered an eyesore by many Parisians, the mall's exterior was finally demolished in 2011 to make way for its golden-hued translucent canopy, unveiled in 2016. Below, four floors of stores (over 100), 18 eateries and entertainment venues including cinemas extend down to the city's busiest metro hub.

Spilling out from the canopied centre, new gardens have *pétanque* (a variant on the game of bowls) courts and chess tables, a central patio and pedestrian walkways. The project has also opened up the shopping centre, allowing for more natural light.

59 Rivoli   Gallery
(Map p250; www.59rivoli.org; 59 rue de Rivoli, 1er; ⊗1-8pm Tue-Sun; MChâtelet, Pont Neuf) FREE In such a classical part of Paris filled with elegant historic architecture, 59 Rivoli is a bohemian breath of fresh air. Take time out to watch artists at work in the 30 ateliers (studios) strung on six floors of the long-abandoned bank building, now a legalised squat where some of Paris' most creative talent works (but doesn't live). The ground-floor gallery hosts a new exhibition every fortnight and free gigs, concerts and shows pack the place out at weekends.

NADJA_FOTO/SHUTTERSTOCK ©

Cimetière du Père Lachaise

Paris is a collection of villages and this sprawling cemetery of cobbled lanes and elaborate tombs, with a 'population' of over one million, qualifies as one in its own right.

The world's most visited cemetery was founded in 1804, and initially attracted few funerals because of its distance from the city centre. The authorities responded by exhuming famous remains and resettling them here. Their marketing ploy worked and Cimetière du Père Lachaise has been Paris' most fashionable final address ever since.

Famous Occupants

Paris residency was the only criterion needed to be buried in Père Lachaise, hence the cemetery's cosmopolitan population, which includes Irish playwright Oscar Wilde and 1960s rock god Jim Morrison. Other famous occupants buried here are the composer Chopin; the playwright Molière; the poet Apollinaire; writers Balzac, Proust, Gertrude Stein and

Great For...

☑ Don't Miss

Oscar Wilde, Jim Morrison, Édith Piaf and countless other famous names.

Tombstone of Louis-Sébastien Gourlot

❶ Need to Know

Map p254; ☏01 55 25 82 10; www.pere-lachaise.com; 16 rue du Repos & 8 bd de Ménilmontant, 20e; ⊕8am-6pm Mon-Fri, 8.30am-6pm Sat, 9am-6pm Sun mid-Mar–Oct, shorter hours Nov–mid-Mar; Ⓜ Père Lachaise, Gambetta

✖ Take a Break

Stroll to nearby Le Servan (p133) for neobistro fare.

★ Top Tip
Arriving at Gambetta metro station allows you to walk downhill through the cemetery.

Bendewald, or simply start with architect Étienne-Hippolyte Godde's neoclassical chapel and portal at the main entrance and get wonderfully lost.

Colette; the actors Simone Signoret, Sarah Bernhardt and Yves Montand; the painters Pissarro, Seurat, Modigliani and Delacroix; the *chanteuse* Édith Piaf alongside her two-year-old daughter; and the dancer Isadora Duncan.

Art & Architecture

For those visiting Paris for its exceptional art and architecture, this vast cemetery – the city's largest – is not a bad starting point. It's one of central Paris' biggest green spaces, with 5300 trees and a treasure trove of magnificent 19th-century sculptures by artists such as David d'Angers, Hector Guimard, Visconti and Chapu. Consider the walking tour detailed in the photographic book *Meet Me At Père Lachaise* by Anna Eriksson and Mason

Visiting

The cemetery has five entrances, two of which are on bd de Ménilmontant.

To save time searching for famous graves, pick up cemetery maps at the **conservation office** (Bureaux de la Conservation; ☏01 55 25 82 10; 16 rue du Repos, 20e; ⊕8.30am-12.30pm & 2-5pm Mon-Fri; Ⓜ Philippe Auguste, Père Lachaise) near the main bd de Ménilmontant entrance.

Alternatively, you can pre-book a themed guided tour led by entertaining cemetery historian Thierry Le Roi (www.necro-romantiques.com).

Cimetière du Père Lachaise

A HALF-DAY TOUR

There is a certain romance to getting lost in Cimetière du Père Lachaise, a jungle of graves spun from centuries of tales. But to search for one grave among one million in this 44-hectare land of the dead is no joke – narrow the search with this itinerary.

From the main bd de Ménilmontant entrance (metro Père Lachaise or Philippe Auguste), head up av Principale, turn right onto av du Puits and collect a map from ❶ the Bureaux de la Conservation.

Backtrack along av du Puits, turn right onto av Latérale du Sud, scale the stairs and bear right along chemin Denon to New Realist artist ❷ Arman, film director ❸ Claude Chabrol and ❹ Chopin.

Follow chemin Méhul downhill, cross av Casimir Périer and bear right onto chemin Serré. Take the second left (chemin Lebrun – unsigned), head uphill and near the top leave the footpath to weave through graves on your right to rock star ❺ Jim Morrison. Back on chemin Lauriston, continue uphill to roundabout ❻ Rond-Point Casimir Périer.

Admire the funerary art of contemporary photographer ❼ André Chabot, av de la Chapelle. Continue uphill for energising city views from the ❽ chapel steps, then zig-zag to ❾ Molière & La Fontaine, on chemin Molière.

Cut between graves onto av Tranversale No 1 – spot potatoes atop ❿ Parmentier's headstone. Continue straight onto av Greffülhe and left onto av Tranversale No 2 to rub ⓫ Monsieur Noir's shiny crotch.

Navigation to ⓬ Édith Piaf and the ⓭ Mur des Fédérés is straightforward. End with lipstick-kissed ⓮ Oscar Wilde near the Porte Gambetta entrance.

TOP TIPS

➡ Père Lachaise is a photographer's paradise any time of the day or year, but best are sunny autumn mornings after the rain.
➡ Cemetery-lovers will appreciate themed guided tours (two hours) led by entertaining cemetery historian Thierry Le Roi (www.necro-romantiques.com).

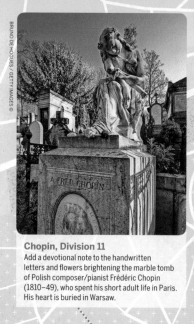

BRUNO DE HOGUES / GETTY IMAGES ©

Chopin, Division 11
Add a devotional note to the handwritten letters and flowers brightening the marble tomb of Polish composer/pianist Frédéric Chopin (1810–49), who spent his short adult life in Paris. His heart is buried in Warsaw.

Jim Morrison, Division 6
The original bust adorning the disgracefully dishevelled grave of Jim Morrison (1943–71), lead singer of The Doors, was stolen. Pay your respects to rock's greatest legend – no chewing gum or padlocks please.

DAN HERRICK / GETTY IMAGES ©

André Chabot, Division 20
Contemporary photographer André Chabot (b 1941) shoots funerary art, hence the bijou 19th-century chapel he's equipped with monumental granite camera – and a QR code – in preparation for the day he departs.

BRUNO DE HOGUES / GETTY IMAGES ©

Molière & La Fontaine, Division 25
Parisians refused to leave their local *quartier* for Père Lachaise so in 1817 the authorities moved in popular playwright Molière (1622–73) and poet Jean de la Fontaine (1621–95). The marketing strategy worked.

Oscar Wilde, Division 89
Irish writer Oscar Wilde (1854–1900) was forever scandalous: check the enormous packet of the sphinx on his tomb, sculpted by British-American sculptor Jacob Epstein 11 years after he died.

BRUNO DE HOGUES / GETTY IMAGES ©

Monsieur Noir, Division 92
Cemetery sex stud Mr Black, alias 21-year-old journalist Victor Noir (1848–70), was shot by Napoléon III's nephew in a botched duel. Urban myth means women rub his crotch to boost fertility.

BRUNO DE HOGUES / GETTY IMAGES ©

av des Combattants Étrangers morts pour la France

Porte Gambetta Entrance

84

88

av Circulaire

av Tranversale No 3

Crematorium

89

14

Chapel

50

51

av Tranversale No 2

93

8

av de Saint Morys

92

chemin Berthollé

24

av Tranversale No 1

11

av Greffülhe

21

chemin Molière

25

42

94

av de la Chapelle

7

20

9

26

10

41

95

6

Rond-Point Casimir Périer

av Pacthod

Commemorative war memorials

39

12   97

13

14

chemin Lauriston

76

5

6

96

Édith Piaf, Division 97
The archbishop of Paris might have refused Parisian diva Édith Piaf (1915–63) the Catholic rite of burial, but that didn't stop more than 100,000 mourners attending her internment at Père Lachaise.

5

chemin Lebrun

av Circulaire

Porte de la Réunion

Mur des Fédérés, Division 76
This plain brick wall was where 147 Communard insurgents were lined up and shot in 1871. Equally emotive is the sculpted walkway of commemorative war memorials surrounding the mass grave.

ALAN COPSON / GETTY IMAGES ©

Marché d'Aligre

BRUNO DE HOGUES/SHUTTERSTOCK ©

Street Markets

Not simply places to shop, the city's street markets are social gatherings for the entire neighbourhood, and visiting one will give you a true appreciation for Parisian life.

Stall after stall of cheeses, stacked baguettes, sun-ripened tomatoes, freshly lopped pigs' trotters, horsemeat sausages, spit-roasted chickens, glass bottles of olives and olive oils, quail eggs, duck eggs, boxes of chanterelle mushrooms and knobbly truffles, long-clawed langoustines and prickly sea urchins on beds of crushed ice – along with belts, boots, wallets, cheap socks, chic hats, colourful scarves, striped t-shirts, wicker baskets, wind-up toys, buckets of flowers... Paris' street markets are a feast for the senses.

Great For...

☑ **Don't Miss**

The city is also home to some wonderful covered food markets.

Top Choices
Marché Bastille   Market €

(Map p254; bd Richard Lenoir, 11e; ⊙7am-2.30pm Thu, 7am-3pm Sun; Ⓜ Bastille, Bréguet–Sabin) If you only get to one open-air street market in Paris, this one – stretching

ⓘ Need to Know

The website www.paris.fr lists every market by *arrondissement*, including speciality markets.

✕ Take a Break

Paris' markets have aromatic snacks and meals cooked on-site.

★ Top Tip

Neighbourhood street markets take place at least once a week, but never Mondays.

between the Bastille and Richard Lenoir metro stations – is among the city's very best.

Marché d'Aligre   Market €

(Map p254; rue d'Aligre, 12e; ☺8am-1pm Tue-Sun; ⓂLedru-Rollin) A real favourite with Parisians, this chaotic street market's stalls are piled with fruit, vegetables and seasonal delicacies such as truffles. Behind them, specialist shops stock cheeses, coffee, chocolates, meat, seafood and wine. More stands are located in the adjoining covered market hall, **Marché Beauvau** (place d'Aligre, 12e; ☺9am-1pm & 4-7.30pm Tue-Fri, 9am-1pm & 3.30-7.30pm Sat, 9am-1.30pm Sun). The small but bargain-filled flea market Marché aux Puces d'Aligre (☺8am-1pm Tue-Sun) takes place on the square.

Marché Raspail   Market €

(Map p246; bd Raspail btwn rue de Rennes & rue du Cherche Midi, 6e; ☺regular market 7am-2.30pm Tue & Fri, organic market 9am-2pm Sun; ⓂRennes) ✔ A traditional open-air market on Tuesday and Friday, Marché Raspail is especially popular on Sunday, when it's filled with *biologique* (organic) produce.

Marché Biologique des Batignolles   Market €

(34 bd des Batignolles, 17e; ☺9am-3pm Sat; ⓂPlace de Clichy) ✔ Abuzz with market stalls, this busy boulevard in northern Paris had its own covered market from 1846 until 1867 (when it shut and moved to its current location on nearby rue Lemercier). These days it's the organic produce that pulls in the punters. Many of the stalls offer tastings and everything is super fresh.

Marché Edgar Quinet   Market €

(Map p246; bd Edgar Quinet, 14e; ☺7am-2.30pm Wed, 7am-3pm Sat; ⓂEdgar Quinet, Montparnasse Bienvenüe) Opposite Tour Montparnasse, this open-air street market teems with neighbourhood shoppers. There's always a great range of cheeses, as well as stalls sizzling up snacks to eat on the run, from crêpes to spicy falafels.

Hall of Mirrors

FREDERIC LEGRAND · COMEO/SHUTTERSTOCK ©

Day Trip: Château de Versailles

This monumental, 700-room palace and sprawling estate – with its gardens, fountains, ponds and canals – is a Unesco World Heritage–listed wonder situated an easy 40-minute train ride from central Paris.

Great For...

☑ Don't Miss

Summertime 'dancing water' displays set to music by baroque- and classical-era composers.

Amid magnificently landscaped formal gardens, this splendid and enormous palace was built in the mid-17th century during the reign of Louis XIV – the Roi Soleil (Sun King) – to project the absolute power of the French monarchy, which was then at the height of its glory. The château has undergone relatively few alterations since its construction, though almost all the interior furnishings disappeared during the Revolution and many of the rooms were rebuilt by Louis-Philippe (r 1830–48).

Some 30,000 workers and soldiers toiled on the structure, the bills for which all but emptied the kingdom's coffers.

Work began in 1661 under the guidance of architect Louis Le Vau (Jules Hardouin-Mansart took over from Le Vau in the mid-1670s); painter and interior

❶ Need to Know

☎ 01 30 83 78 00; www.chateauversailles.fr; place d'Armes; adult/child passport ticket incl estate-wide access €20/free, with musical events €27/free, palace €15/free; ⏱ 9am-6.30pm Tue-Sun Apr-Oct, to 5.30pm Tue-Sun Nov-Mar; Ⓜ RER Versailles-Château–Rive Gauche

✖ Take a Break

Nearby rue de Satory is lined with restaurants and cafes.

> ### ★ Top Tip
> Arrive early morning and avoid Tuesday, Saturday and Sunday, Versailles' busiest days.

designer Charles Le Brun; and landscape artist André Le Nôtre, whose workers flattened hills, drained marshes and relocated forests as they laid out the seemingly endless **gardens** (free except during musical events; ⏱ 8am-8.30pm Apr-Oct, to 6pm Nov-Mar, park 7am-8.30pm Apr-Oct, 8am-6pm Nov-Mar), ponds and fountains.

Le Brun and his hundreds of artisans decorated every moulding, cornice, ceiling and door of the interior with the most luxurious and ostentatious of appointments: frescos, marble, gilt and woodcarvings, many with themes and symbols drawn from Greek and Roman mythology. The King's Suite of the Grands Appartements du Roi et de la Reine (King's and Queen's State Apartments), for example, includes rooms dedicated to Hercules, Venus, Diana, Mars and Mercury. The opulence

reaches its peak in the Galerie des Glaces (Hall of Mirrors), a 75m-long ballroom with 17 huge mirrors on one side and, on the other, an equal number of windows looking out over the gardens and the setting sun.

To access areas that are otherwise off limits and to learn more about Versailles' history, prebook a 90-minute **guided tour** (☎ 01 30 83 77 88; tours €7, plus palace entry; ⏱ English-language tours 9.30am Tue-Sun) of the Private Apartments of Louis XV and Louis XVI and the Opera House or Royal Chapel. Tours also cover the most famous parts of the palace.

The château is situated in the leafy, bourgeois suburb of Versailles, about 22km southwest of central Paris. Take the frequent RER C5 (€4.20) from Paris' Left Bank RER stations to Versailles-Château–Rive Gauche station.

Versailles

A DAY IN COURT

Visiting Versailles – even just the State Apartments – may seem overwhelming at first, but think of it as a house where people ate, drank, worked, slept and conspired and you'll be on the right path.

Some two decades into his long reign, Louis XIV began turning his father's hunting lodge into a palace large enough to house his entire court (to keep closer tabs on the 6000-strong army of courtiers). Sparing no expense, the Sun King employed the greatest artists and craftspeople of the day and by 1682 he'd created the most extravagant dormitory in history.

The royal schedule was as accurate and predictable as a Swiss watch. By following this itinerary of rooms you can recreate the king's day, starting with the ❶ King's Bedchamber and the ❷ Queen's Bedchamber, where the royal couple was roused at about the same time. The royal procession then leads through the ❸ Hall of Mirrors to the ❹ Royal Chapel for morning Mass and returns to the ❺ Council Chamber for late-morning meetings with ministers. After lunch the king might ride or hunt or visit the ❻ King's Library. Later he could join courtesans for an 'apartment evening' starting from the ❼ Hercules Drawing Room or play billiards in the Diana ❽ Drawing Room before supping at 10pm.

VERSAILLES BY NUMBERS

Rooms 700 (11 hectares of roof)

Windows 2153

Staircases 67

Gardens and parks 800 hectares

Trees 200,000

Fountains 50 (with 620 nozzles)

Paintings 6300 (measuring 11km laid end to end)

Statues and sculptures 2100

Objets d'art and furnishings 5000

Visitors 5.3 million per year

Queen's Bedchamber
Chambre de la Reine
The queen's life was on constant public display and even the births of her children were watched by crowds of spectators in her own bedchamber. DETOUR » The Guardroom, with a dozen armed men at the ready.

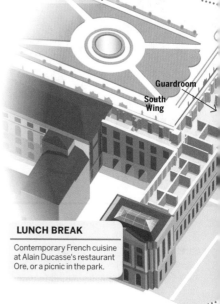

Guardroom

South Wing

LUNCH BREAK

Contemporary French cuisine at Alain Ducasse's restaurant Ore, or a picnic in the park.

Hercules Drawing Room
Salon d'Hercule
This salon, with its stunning ceiling fresco of the strong man, gave way to the State Apartments, which were open to courtiers three nights a week. DETOUR » Apollo Drawing Room, used for formal audiences and as a throne room.

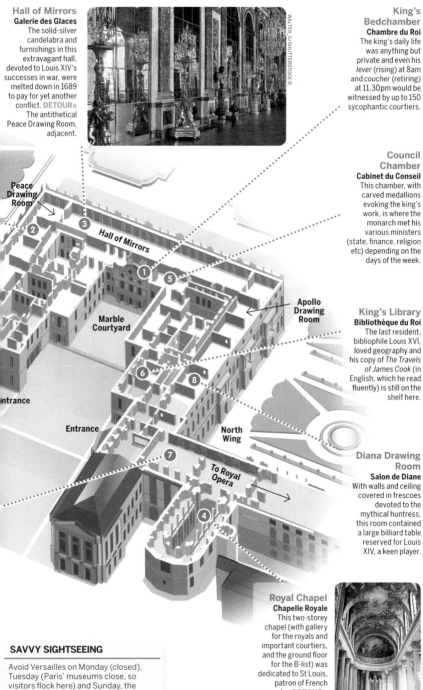

Hall of Mirrors
Galerie des Glaces
The solid-silver candelabra and furnishings in this extravagant hall, devoted to Louis XIV's successes in war, were melted down in 1689 to pay for yet another conflict. DETOUR» The antithetical Peace Drawing Room, adjacent.

King's Bedchamber
Chambre du Roi
The king's daily life was anything but private and even his *lever* (rising) at 8am and *coucher* (retiring) at 11.30pm would be witnessed by up to 150 sycophantic courtiers.

Council Chamber
Cabinet du Conseil
This chamber, with carved medallions evoking the king's work, is where the monarch met his various ministers (state, finance, religion etc) depending on the days of the week.

King's Library
Bibliothèque du Roi
The last resident, bibliophile Louis XVI, loved geography and his copy of *The Travels of James Cook* (in English, which he read fluently) is still on the shelf here.

Diana Drawing Room
Salon de Diane
With walls and ceiling covered in frescoes devoted to the mythical huntress, this room contained a large billiard table reserved for Louis XIV, a keen player.

Royal Chapel
Chapelle Royale
This two-storey chapel (with gallery for the royals and important courtiers, and the ground floor for the B-list) was dedicated to St Louis, patron of French monarchs. DETOUR» The sumptuous Royal Opera.

Peace Drawing Room

Hall of Mirrors

Marble Courtyard

Entrance

Entrance

Apollo Drawing Room

North Wing

To Royal Opera

WALTER.G/SHUTTERSTOCK ©

COJATO/BUDGET TRAVEL ©

SAVVY SIGHTSEEING

Avoid Versailles on Monday (closed), Tuesday (Paris' museums close, so visitors flock here) and Sunday, the busiest day. Also, book tickets online so you don't have to queue.

CHRISTIAN MUELLER/SHUTTERSTOCK ©

Musée National du Moyen Âge

An enormous Roman-era bathhouse (c AD 200) and the ornate 15th-century mansion, the Hôtel de Cluny, house France's fascinating National Museum of the Middle Ages, famed for its medieval tapestries.

Great For...

☑ **Don't Miss**

The extraordinary Gallo-Roman remains.

The Hôtel de Cluny

Initially the residential quarters of the Cluny Abbots, the Hôtel de Cluny was later occupied by Alexandre du Sommerard, who moved here in 1833 with his collection of medieval and Renaissance objects. Bought by the state after his death, the museum opened a decade later, retaining the Hôtel de Cluny's original layout and features.

Today it holds some fascinating relics, not least of which is an entire room (No 8) dedicated to statuary from Notre Dame's façade, removed during the Revolution and later used to support the foundations of a private mansion.

The restored 1st-floor late-Gothic chapel, La Chapelle de l'Hôtel de Cluny, with rich carvings of Christ on the cross, 13 angels, floral and foliage ornaments, has direct access to the garden.

ⓘ Need to Know

Map p252; www.musee-moyenage.fr; 6 place Paul Painlevé, 5e; adult/child incl audioguide €8/free, during temporary exhibitions €9/free; ⊙9.15am-5.45pm Wed-Mon; ⓜCluny–La Sorbonne

✕ Take a Break

Bouillon Racine (p139) serves time-honoured French fare in historic art nouveau surrounds.

★ Top Tip

Arrive after 3.30pm on Mondays, Thursdays and Fridays to bypass school groups.

Gallo-Roman Bathhouse

The museum's northwestern corner is where you'll find the remains of the Gallo-Roman bathhouse, built around AD 200. Look for the display of the fragment of mosaic *Love Riding a Dolphin*, as well as a gorgeous marble bathtub from Rome. Outside the museum, remnants of the other rooms – a *palestra* (exercise room), *tepidarium* (warm bath) and *calidarium* (hot bath) – are visible.

Tapestries

Upstairs on the 1st floor (room 13) are the unicorn tapestries, representing the five senses and an enigmatic sixth, perhaps the heart. It's believed that they were originally commissioned around 1500 by the Le Viste family in Paris. Discovered in 1814 in the Chateau de Boussac, they were acquired by the museum in 1882 and have since provided inspiration to many.

Gardens

Small gardens to the museum's northeast, including the Jardin Céleste (Celestial Garden) and the Jardin d'Amour (Garden of Love), are planted with flowers, herbs and shrubs that appear in works hanging throughout the museum.

What's Nearby?

Panthéon   Mausoleum

(Map p252; www.paris-pantheon.fr; place du Panthéon, 5e; adult/child €9/free; ⊙10am-6.30pm Apr-Sep, to 6pm Oct-Mar; ⓜMaubert-Mutualité or RER Luxembourg) Overlooking the city from its Left Bank perch, the Panthéon's stately dome is an icon of the Parisian skyline. The vast interior is an architectural masterpiece: originally a church and now a mausoleum, it has served since 1791 as the resting place of some of France's greatest thinkers, including Voltaire, Rousseau, Braille and Hugo. A copy of Foucault's pendulum, first hung from the dome in 1851 to demonstrate the rotation of the earth, takes pride of place.

WSIATI/GETTY IMAGES ©

Jardin des Tuileries

Filled with fountains, classical sculptures and magnificent panoramas at every turn, this quintessentially Parisian 28-hectare formal park constitutes part of the Banks of the Seine Unesco World Heritage Site.

Great For...

☑ Don't Miss

Monet's enormous mural-like Water Lilies in the Musée de l'Orangerie.

The park was laid out in its present form in 1664 by André Le Nôtre.

Musée de l'Orangerie   Museum

(Map p246; ☎01 44 77 80 07; www.musee-orang erie.fr; place de la Concorde, 1er; adult/child €9/ free; ◷9am-6pm Wed-Mon; ⓂConcorde) Monet's extraordinary cycle of eight enormous *Decorations des Nymphéas* (Water Lilies) occupies two huge oval rooms purpose-built in 1927. The lower level houses more of Monet's impressionist works and many by Sisley, Renoir, Cézanne, Gauguin, Picasso, Matisse and Modigliani. Audioguides cost €5.

Jeu de Paume   Gallery

(Map p246; ☎01 47 03 12 50; www.jeudepaume. org; 1 place de la Concorde, 1er; adult/child €10/free; ◷11am-9pm Tue, to 7pm Wed-Sun; ⓂConcorde) This gallery, which stages innovative photography exhibitions, is housed

Arc de Triomphe du Carrousel

ARYAIVANOVA/GETTY IMAGES ©

ⓘ Need to Know

Map p246; rue de Rivoli, 1er; ⏱7am-9pm late Mar–late Sep, 7.30am-7.30pm late Sep–late Mar; ♿; Ⓜ Tuileries, Concorde

✗ Take a Break

Famed hot chocolate at Angelina (p173) comes with a pot of whipped cream.

★ Top Tip

Kids will love the Fête des Tuileries funfair in July and August.

in an erstwhile *jeu de paume* (royal tennis court) of the former Palais des Tuileries in the northwestern corner of the Jardin des Tuileries. Cinema screenings and concert performances also take place.

What's Nearby?

Arc de Triomphe du Carrousel · Monument

(Map p250; place du Carrousel, 1er; Ⓜ Palais Royal–Musée du Louvre) This triumphal arch, erected by Napoléon to celebrate his battlefield successes of 1805, rises from the **Jardin du Carrousel**, the gardens immediately next to the Louvre. The eastern counterpoint to the more famous Arc de Triomphe, it is one of several monuments that comprise the *axe historique* (historical axis), which terminates with the statue of Louis XIV next to the Pyramide du Louvre.

Musée Maxim's · Museum

(Map p246; ☎01 42 65 30 47; http://maxims-de-paris.com; 3 rue Royale, 8e; adult/child €20/free; ⏱English tours 2pm Wed-Sun, closed Jul & Aug; Ⓜ Concorde) During the belle époque, Maxim's bistro was the most glamorous place to be in Paris. The restaurant has lost much of its cachet (though the food is actually excellent), but for art buffs, the real treasure is the museum. Opened by Maxim's owner, fashion designer Pierre Cardin, its 12 rooms are filled with some 550 pieces of art nouveau artworks, objets d'art and furniture detailed during one-hour guided tours.

Le Grand Musée du Parfum · Museum

(Map p246; www.grandmuseeduparfum.fr; 73 rue du Faubourg St-Honoré, 8e; adult/child €14.50/9.50; ⏱10.30am-7pm Tue-Thu, Sat & Sun, to 10pm Fri; Ⓜ Miromesnil) History exhibits (ancient perfume bottles, interpretive French/English panels and dioramas) fill the basement of this museum, but the most engaging sections are upstairs. The 1st floor is a heady sensory guide, revealing the chemical processes while you identify scents. The 2nd floor showcases the art of fragrance creation.

Sainte-Chapelle

This gemlike Holy Chapel is Paris' most exquisite Gothic monument. Try to save it for a sunny day, when Paris' oldest, finest stained glass is at its dazzling best.

Sainte-Chapelle was built in just six years (compared with nearly 200 years for Notre Dame) and consecrated in 1248. The chapel was conceived by Louis IX to house his personal collection of holy relics, including the famous Ste-Couronne (Holy Crown), acquired by the French king in 1239 from the emperors of Constantinople for a sum of money easily exceeding the amount it cost to build the chapel. The wreath of thorns is safeguarded today in the treasury at Notre Dame.

Statues, foliage-decorated capitals, angels and so on decorate this sumptuous, bijou chapel. But it is the 1113 scenes depicted in its 15 floor-to-ceiling stained-glass windows – 15.5m high in the nave, 13.5m in the apse – that stun visitors. From the bookshop in the former ground-floor chapel reserved for palace staff, spiral up the staircase to the upper chapel, where only the king and his close friends were allowed.

Great For...

☑ **Don't Miss**

The ethereal experience of classical- and sacred-music concerts amid the stained glass.

❶ Need to Know

Map p250; ☏01 53 40 60 80, concerts 01 42 77 65 65; www.sainte-chapelle.fr; 8 bd du Palais, 1er; adult/child €10/free, joint ticket with Conciergerie €15; ⊙9am-7pm Apr-Sep, to 5pm Oct-Mar; Ⓜ Cité)

❶ Take a Break

Enjoy artistically presented dishes at Seine-side Sequana (p135).

★ Top Tip

Combination tickets pre-purchased at the Conciergerie allow you to skip the ticket queues.

What's Nearby?

Conciergerie Monument

(Map p250; www.paris-conciergerie.fr; 2 bd du Palais, 1er; adult/child €9/free, joint ticket with Sainte-Chapelle €15; ⊙9.30am-6pm; Ⓜ Cité) A royal palace in the 14th century, the Conciergerie later became a prison. During the Reign of Terror (1793–94) alleged enemies of the Revolution were incarcerated here before being brought before the Revolutionary Tribunal next door in the **Palais de Justice**. Top-billing exhibitions take place in the beautiful, Rayonnant Gothic **Salle des Gens d'Armes**, Europe's largest surviving medieval hall.

Of the almost 2800 prisoners held in the dungeons during the Reign of Terror (in various 'classes' of cells, no less) before being sent in tumbrels to the guillotine, star prisoner was Queen Marie-Antoinette – see a reproduction of her cell. As the Revolution began to turn on its own, radicals Danton and Robespierre made an appearance at the Conciergerie and, finally, the judges of the tribunal themselves.

Before arriving, download a free storyboard in English from the website to 'read' the 15-window biblical story – from Genesis through to the resurrection of Christ. Once here, rent an audioguide (€4.50 for two people) or join a free 45-minute guided tour in English between 11am and 3pm.

Sainte-Chapelle's location within the Palais de Justice (Law Courts) means security is tight; be sure to leave pocket knives, scissors and the like at your accommodation. Even combination ticket-holders still need to go through the security queue.

You can peek at Sainte-Chapelle's exterior from across the street (albeit not a patch on its interior), by the law courts' magnificently gilded 18th-century gate facing rue de Lutèce.

Les Catacombes

Paris' most macabre sight is its series of subterranean passages lined with skulls and bones. It's a 2km walk through the creepy ossuary and definitely not for the faint-hearted.

In 1785 it was decided to rectify the hygiene problems of Paris' overflowing cemeteries by exhuming the bones and storing them in disused quarry tunnels; the Catacombes were created in 1810.

The route through Les Catacombes begins at a small, dark-green belle époque building in the centre of a grassy area of av Colonel Henri Roi-Tanguy, adjacent to place Denfert Rochereau. After descending 20m below street level (via 130 narrow, dizzying spiral steps), you follow the dark, subterranean passages to reach the ossuary itself, with a mind-boggling number of bones and skulls of millions of Parisians neatly packed along the walls.

The exit is back up 83 steps onto rue Rémy Dumoncel, 14e (metro Mouton-Duvernet), 700m southwest of av Colonel Henri Roi-Tanguy. Bag searches are carried

Great For...

☑ **Don't Miss**

Combining a visit to Les Catacombes with a wander through Cimetière du Montparnasse.

VIACHESLAV LOPATIN/SHUTTERSTOCK ©

❶ Need to Know

Map p246; www.catacombes.paris.fr; 1 av Colonel Henri Roi-Tanguy, 14e; adult/child €12/free, online booking incl audioguide €27/5; ⏱10am-8pm Tue-Sun; Ⓜ Denfert Rochereau

✕ Take a Break

Neighbourhood favourite Félicie (p183) is great for a drink of classic bistro fare.

★ Top Tip

Wear sturdy shoes for the uneven, often muddy surface and loose stones.

out to prevent visitors 'souveniring' bones. A **gift shop** (Map p246; www.compoirdes-catacombes.com; 31 rue Rémy Dumoncel, 14e; ⏱10.30am-8.30pm Tue-Sun; Ⓜ Alésia) selling quirky skull-and-bone-themed items (Jenga, candles, shot glasses) is across the street from the exit.

Visiting

A maximum of 200 people are allowed in the tunnels at a time and queues can be huge – when the queue extends beyond a 20-minute wait, you'll be handed a coupon with a return entry time later that day. Last entry is at 7pm.

Renting an audioguide (€5) greatly enhances the experience.

Bear in mind that the catacombes are not suitable for young children. Also be aware there are no toilets, flash photogra-phy isn't permitted and the temperature is a cool 14°C below ground.

What's Nearby?

Cimetière du Montparnasse   Cemetery

(Map p246; www.paris.fr; 3 bd Edgar Quinet, 14e; ⏱8am-6pm Mon-Fri, 8.30am-6pm Sat, 9am-6pm Sun; Ⓜ Edgar Quinet) **FREE** Opened in 1824, Montparnasse Cemetery, Paris' second largest after Père Lachaise, sprawls over 19 hectares shaded by 1200 trees, including maples, ash, lime trees and conifers. Among its illustrious 'residents' are poet Charles Baudelaire, writer Guy de Maupassant, playwright Samuel Beckett, sculptor Constantin Brancusi, painter Chaim Soutine, photographer Man Ray, industrialist André Citroën, Captain Alfred Dreyfus of the infamous Dreyfus Affair, actress Jean Seberg, and philosopher-writer couple Jean-Paul Sartre and Simone de Beauvoir, as well as legendary singer Serge Gainsbourg.

Macarons at La Cuisine Paris

MATT MUNRO/LONELY PLANET©

Cooking & Wine-Tasting Courses

If dining in the city's restaurants whets your appetite, Paris has oustanding cookery schools. And where there's food in Paris, wine is never more than an arm's length away.

Great For...

☑ **Don't Miss**

Even during a lightning-quick trip there are myriad short-course options, but book ahead.

Le Cordon Bleu   Cooking

(Map p246; ☏01 85 65 15 00; www.cordonbleu. edu/paris; 13-15 quai André Citroën, 15e; Ⓜ Javel–André Citroën or RER Javel) One of the world's foremost culinary arts schools, Le Cordon Bleu relocated in summer 2016 to state-of-the-art, shiny, steel-encased new premises overlooking the Seine and **Statue of Liberty** (Map p246; Île aux Cygnes; Ⓜ Javel–André Citroën), with views of the nearby Eiffel Tower from its terrace. Prices start at €85 for three-hour classes and €410 for two-day courses.

La Cuisine Paris   Cooking

(Map p254; ☏01 40 51 78 18; https://lacuis ineparis.com; 80 quai de l'Hôtel de Ville, 4e; 2hr cooking classes or walking tours from €69; Ⓜ Pont Marie, Hôtel de Ville) Classes in English range from how to make bread and croissants to macarons, market classes and gourmet 'foodie walks'.

Need to Know

Establishments often run classes in English or offer translation; check when booking.

✕ Take a Break

Culinary courses' highlights often include meals you've created (with wine, of course).

★ Top Tip

Junior chefs needn't miss out – many establishments offer children's classes.

Cook'n With Class   Cooking

(📞01 42 57 22 84; https://cooknwithclass.com; 6 rue Baudelique, 18e; ⊘2hr classes from €85; Ⓜ Simplon, Jules Joffrin) A bevy of international chefs, small classes and an enchanting Montmartre location are ingredients for success at this informal cooking school, which organises dessert classes for kids, cheese and wine courses, market visits, gourmet food tours and six-course dinners with the chef and sommelier as well as regular cookery classes.

Ô Chateau   Wine Bar

(Map p250; 📞01 44 73 97 80; http://o-chateau.com; 68 rue Jean-Jacques Rousseau, 1er; ⊘4pm-midnight Mon-Sat; 🛜; Ⓜ Les Halles, Étienne Marcel) Wine aficionados can thank this young, fun, cosmopolitan wine bar for bringing affordable tasting to Paris. Choose from 50 *grands vins* served by the glass (or 1000-plus by the bottle!). Or sign up in advance for a 'tour de France' of French wines (€55) or a guided cellar tasting in English over lunch (€75) or dinner (€99).

Le Foodist   Cooking

(Map p252; 📞06 71 70 95 22; www.lefoodist.com; 59 rue du Cardinal Lemoine, 5e; Ⓜ Cardinal Lemoine) Classes at this culinary school include classic French cookery and patisserie courses, allowing you to create your own eclairs and choux pastry, macarons or croissants. Market tours and wine and cheese tastings and pairings are also available. Instruction is in English. Three-hour classes start at €95.

Wine Tasting in Paris   Wine

(Map p252; 📞06 76 93 32 88; www.wine-tasting-in-paris.com; 14 rue des Boulangers, 5e; tastings from €60; ⊘tastings 5-7.30pm Tue, Thu & Sat; Ⓜ Jussieu) Situated on a winding cobblestone Latin Quarter backstreet, this wine-tasting school offers various options for tastings, including its popular French Wine Tour (2½ hours, six wines). All classes are in English.

Meeting the French   Cultural, Tours

(📞01 42 51 19 80; www.meetingthefrench.com; tours & courses from €25) Cosmetics workshops, backstage cabaret tours, fashion designer showroom visits, French table decoration, art embroidery classes, market tours, baking with a Parisian baker – the repertoire of cultural and gourmet tours and behind-the-scenes experiences offered by Meeting the French is truly outstanding. All courses and tours are in English.

ERIC VALENNE GEOSTORY/SHUTTERSTOCK ©

Day Trip: Maison et Jardins de Claude Monet

Monet lived in Giverny from 1883 until his death in 1926, in a rambling house – surrounded by flower-filled gardens – that's now the immensely popular Maison et Jardins de Claude Monet.

Great For...

☑ **Don't Miss**

Monet's trademark lily pond, immortalised in his *Nymphéas* (Water Lilies) series.

Monet's home for the last 43 years of his life is now a delightful house-museum. His pastel-pink house and Water Lily studio stand on the periphery of the Clos Normand, with its symmetrically laid-out gardens bursting with flowers. Monet bought the Jardin d'Eau (Water Garden) in 1895 and set about creating his trademark lily pond, as well as the famous Japanese bridge (since rebuilt).

The charmingly preserved house and beautiful bloom-filled gardens (rather than Monet's works) are the draws here.

Draped with purple wisteria, the Japanese bridge blends into the asymmetrical foreground and background, creating the intimate atmosphere for which the 'painter of light' was renowned.

Seasons have an enormous effect on Giverny. From early to late spring, daffodils, tulips, rhododendrons, wisteria and irises

Maison et Jardins
de Claude Monet

Vernon
Giverny
Vétheuil
Seine
Pacy-
sur-Eure
Mantes-
la-Jolie

❶ Need to Know

02 32 51 28 21; http://fondation-monet.
com; 84 rue Claude Monet; adult/child
€9.50/5.50, incl Musée des Impressionn-
ismes Giverny €16.50/8.50; 9.30am-6pm
Easter-Oct

✖ Take a Break

Michelin-starred dishes are exquisite at
country estate **Le Jardin des Plumes**
(02 32 54 26 35; www.jardindesplumes.fr; 1
rue du Milieu; 3-course/tasting menu €48/95,
mains €32-42; 12.15-1.30pm & 7.30-9pm Wed-
Sun, hotel closed Mon & Tue Nov-Mar;).

★ Top Tip

Note the sight closes from November
to Easter, along with most accommodation and restaurants.

appear, followed by poppies and lilies. By
June, nasturtiums, roses and sweet peas
are in flower. Around September, there are
dahlias, sunflowers and hollyhocks.

Combined tickets with Paris' **Musée
Marmottan Monet** (01 44 96 50 33; www.
marmottan.fr; 2 rue Louis Boilly, 16e; adult/child
€11/7.50; 10am-6pm Tue, Wed & Fri-Sun, to
9pm Thu; La Muette) cost €20.50/12 per
adult/child, and combined adult tickets
with Paris' Musée de l'Orangerie (p90) cost
€18.50.

Visiting

The tiny country village of Giverny is 74km
northwest of Paris.

From Paris' Gare St-Lazare there are
up to 15 daily trains to Vernon (€14.70, 45
minutes to one hour), 7km to the west of
Giverny, from where buses, taxis and cycle/
walking tracks run to Giverny.

Shuttle buses (€10 return, 20 minutes,
up to five daily Easter to October) meet
most trains from Paris at Vernon. There are
limited seats, so arrive early for the return
trip from Giverny.

Rent bikes (cash only) at the **Café L'Ar-
rivée de Giverny** (02 32 21 16 01; 1-3 place
de la Gare, Vernon; per day €14; 8am-11pm),
opposite the train station in Vernon, from
where Giverny is a signposted 5km along a
direct (and flat) cycle/walking track.

Taxis (02 32 51 10 24) usually wait outside
the train station in Vernon and charge around
€15 for the one-way trip to Giverny. There's
no taxi rank in Giverny, so you'll need to
phone one for the return trip to Vernon.

A 10-minute stroll from the museum, Le
Jardin des Plumes has beautiful rooms and
suites (€180 to €350) and exquisite cuisine.

Be aware that the village has no public
toilets, ATMs or bureaux de change.

GARY YIM/SHUTTERSTOCK ©

Palais Garnier

The fabled 'phantom of the opera' lurked in this opulent opera house designed in 1860 by Charles Garnier (then an unknown 35-year-old architect), which offers behind-the-scenes tours.

Reserve a spot on an English-language guided tour or take an unguided tour of the attached museum, with posters, costumes, backdrops, original scores and other memorabilia, which includes a behind-the-scenes peek (except during matinees and rehearsals). Highlights include the Grand Staircase and gilded auditorium with a massive chandelier and Chagall's gorgeous ceiling mural. A prop man at the opera set up beehives on the roof in 1983 – the honey is now sold at the gift shop when available.

Great For...

☑ **Don't Miss**

Taking a stroll through the beautiful Jardin des Tuileries (p90) nearby.

What's Nearby

Église de la Madeleine Church
(Church of St Mary Magdalene; Map p246; www.eglise-lamadeleine.com; place de la Madeleine, 8e; ⏱9.30am-7pm; Ⓜ Madeleine) Place de la Madeleine is named after the 19th-century neoclassical church at its centre, the Église

Chaussée d'Antin

Auber

Palais Garnier

R Auber

R Halévy

Opéra

❶ Need to Know

Map p246; ☎08 25 05 44 05; www.operade-paris.fr; cnr rues Scribe & Auber, 9e; audio-guided tours €5, guided tours adult/child €15.50/11; ⏱audio-guided tours 10am-5pm, to 1pm on matinee performance days, guided tours by reservation; ⓂOpéra

✕ Take a Break

Close at hand, place de la Madeleine (p149) is a gourmet fantasyland.

★ Top Tip

Catching a performance (p188) here is a treat.

de la Madeleine. Constructed in the style of a massive Greek temple, 'La Madeleine' was consecrated in 1842 after almost a century of design changes and construction delays.

The church is a popular venue for classical-music concerts (some free); check the posters outside or the website for dates.

On the south side, the monumental staircase affords one of the city's most quintessential Parisian panoramas. From here, you can see down rue Royale to place de la Concorde and its obelisk and across the Seine to the Assemblée Nationale.

Jardin du Palais Royal   Gardens

(Map p250; www.domaine-palais-royal.fr; 2 place Colette, 1er; ⏱8am-10.30pm Apr-Sep, to 8.30pm Oct-Mar; ⓂPalais Royal–Musée du Louvre) The Jardin du Palais Royal is a perfect spot to sit, contemplate and picnic between boxed hedges, or shop in the trio of beautiful

arcades that frame the garden: the **Galerie de Valois** (east), **Galerie de Montpensier** (west) and **Galerie Beaujolais** (north). However, it's the southern end of the complex, polka-dotted with sculptor Daniel Buren's 260 black-and-white striped columns, that has become the garden's signature feature. This elegant urban space is fronted by the neoclassical **Palais Royal** (closed to the public), constructed in 1633 by Cardinal Richelieu but mostly dating to the late 18th century. Louis XIV hung out here in the 1640s; today it is home to the **Conseil d'État** (Council of State; 1 place du Palais Royal, 1er).

The Galerie de Valois is the most upmarket arcade, with designer boutiques like Stella McCartney and Pierre Hardy. Across the garden, in the Galerie de Montpensier, the Revolution broke out on a warm mid-July day, just three years after the galleries opened, in the Café du Foy. The third arcade, tiny Galerie Beaujolais, is crossed by **Passage du Perron**, a passageway above which the writer Colette (1873–1954) lived out the last dozen years of her life.

Seine-Side Romantic Meander

The world's most romantic city has no shortage of beguiling spots, but the Seine and its surrounds are Paris at its most seductive. Descend the steps along the quays wherever possible to stroll along the water's edge.

Start: Place de la Concorde
Distance: 7km
Duration: 3 hours

3 Take the steps to **Square du Vert Galant** (p200), before ascending to place du Pont Neuf and place Dauphine.

Classic Photo: Enjoy fountain views in this elegant 28-hectare garden.

1 After taking in the panorama at place de la Concorde, stroll through the **Jardin des Tuileries** (p90).

MING TANG-EVANS/LONELY PLANET ©

2 Walk through the Jardin de l'Oratoire to the **Cour Carrée** (p53) and exit at the Jardin de l'Infante.

PAVEL L PHOTO AND VIDEO/SHUTTERSTOCK ©

7 End your romantic meander at the tranquil **Jardin des Plantes** (p106). Cruise back along the Seine by Batobus.

RRRAINBOW/GETTY IMAGES ©

0 500 m
0 0.25 miles

4 Curl up with a volume of poetry in the magical **Shakespeare & Company** (p155) bookshop.

ALESSIO CATELLI/SHUTTERSTOCK ©

Jardin du Palais Royal

R du Louvre

Palais-Royal – Musée du Louvre

Louvre Rivoli

Pont Neuf

Q du Louvre

Pont Neuf

Q des Grands Augustins

Île de la Cité

Bd du Palais

Cité

Châtelet

Hôtel de Ville

4E

Q de l'Hôtel de Ville

Bd St-Germain

St-Michel

St-Michel–Notre Dame

Sq Jean XXIII

Pont St-Louis

Pont Marie

Île St-Louis

Take a Break...
Morning or night, try hip **Café Saint Régis** (p135).

5 Cross to Île St-Louis and share an ice cream from *glacier* (ice-cream maker) **Berthillon** (p134).

Pont de Sully

Bd St-Germain

Q Henri IV

Q St-Bernard

Seine

Jardin du Luxembourg

6 Wander among late-20th-century unfenced sculptures at the **Musée de la Sculpture en Plein Air** (Open-Air Sculpture Museum; p109).

R Cuvier

Jardin des Plantes

Place Monge

FINISH

R Buffon

Place Monge

Gare d'Austerlitz

Dome interior

WIN-INITIATIVE/GETTY IMAGES ©

Hôtel des Invalides

Flanked by the 500m-long Esplanade des Invalides lawns, this massive military complex built in the 1670s by Louis XIV to house 4000 invalides (disabled war veterans) contains Napoléon's tomb.

Great For...

☑ **Don't Miss**

France's largest military museum, the Musée de l'Armée.

On 14 July 1789, a mob broke into the building and seized 32,000 rifles before heading on to the prison at Bastille and the start of the French Revolution.

In the **Cour d'Honneur**, the nation's largest collection on the history of the French military is displayed at the **Musée de l'Armée** (Army Museum; included in Hôtel des Invalides entry). South is **Église St-Louis des Invalides**, once used by soldiers, and **Église du Dôme** (included in Hôtel des Invalides entry) which, with its sparkling golden dome (1677–1735), is one of the finest religious edifices erected under Louis XIV and was the inspiration for the United States Capitol building. It received the remains of Napoléon in 1840. The extravagant **Tombeau de Napoléon 1er**, in the centre of the church, comprises six coffins fitting into one another like a Russian doll. Scale

Église du Dôme

❶ Need to Know

Map p246; www.musee-armee.fr; 129 rue de Grenelle, 7e; adult/child €11/free; ⊙10am-6pm Apr-Oct, to 5pm Nov-Mar, hours can vary; Ⓜ Varenne, La Tour Maubourg

✕ Take a Break

Coutume (p181) brews up some of Paris' best coffee from its own-roasted beans.

★ Top Tip

Atmospheric classical concerts (ranging from €5 to €30) take place regularly here year-round.

models of towns, fortresses and châteaux across France fill the esoteric **Musée des Plans-Reliefs**.

Admission includes entry to all Hôtel des Invalides sights. Their individual hours often vary – check the website for updates.

What's Nearby?
Église St-Germain des Prés
Church

(Map p250; www.eglise-stgermaindespres. fr; 3 place St-Germain des Prés, 6e; ⊙8am-7.45pm; Ⓜ St-Germain des Prés) Paris' oldest standing church, the Romanesque St Germanus of the Fields, was built in the 11th century on the site of a 6th-century abbey and was the main place of worship in Paris until the arrival of Notre Dame.

It's since been altered many times, but the **Chapelle de St-Symphorien** (to the right as you enter) was part of the original abbey and is believed to be the resting place of St Germanus (496–576), the first bishop of Paris.

The Merovingian kings were buried here during the 6th and 7th centuries, but their tombs disappeared during the Revolution. Over the western entrance, the **bell tower** has changed little since 990, although the spire dates only from the 19th century.

An English brochure (€10) is available; proceeds go towards the current restoration works (the church will stay open throughout). Free organ concerts are held on the last Sunday of the month; check the website's calendar for times. Other concerts take place on Thursdays and Fridays at 8.30pm; details including prices are listed online.

DENNISVDW/GETTY IMAGES ©

Jardin des Plantes

Founded in 1626 as a medicinal herb garden for Louis XIII, Paris' 24-hectare botanic gardens are an idyllic spot to stroll or visit its museums or zoo.

Visually defined by the double alley of plane trees that run the length of the park, these sprawling gardens allow you to escape the city concrete for a spell.

Highlights here include peony and rose gardens, an alpine garden, and the gardens of the École de Botanique, used by students of the school and green-fingered Parisians. The gorgeous glass-and-metal **Grandes Serres** (Map p252; www.jardindesplantes.net; Jardin des Plantes; adult/child €6/4; ⊗10am-6pm Apr-Sep, to 5pm Oct-Mar; Ⓜ Jussieu) – a series of four greenhouses – have been in use since 1714, and several of Henri Rousseau's jungle paintings, sometimes on display in the Musée d'Orsay, were inspired by his frequent visits here.

Great For...

☑ **Don't Miss**

The gardens' beautiful glass-and-metal Grandes Serres (greenhouses).

ℹ️ Need to Know

Map p252; www.jardindesplantes.net; place Valhubert & 36 rue Geoffroy-St-Hilaire, 5e; ⏱7.30am-8pm early Apr–mid-Sep, shorter hours rest of year; Ⓜ Gare d'Austerlitz, Censier Daubenton, Jussieu

✖️ Take a Break

Bring a picnic with you (but watch out for the automatic sprinklers!).

> ## ★ Top Tip
> A tranquil way to travel to/from here is by Batobus (p237) along the Seine.

Museums & Zoo

Muséum National d'Histoire Naturelle   Museum

(Map p252; www.mnhn.fr; place Valhubert & 36 rue Geoffroy-St-Hilaire, 5e; Ⓜ Gare d'Austerlitz, Censier Daubenton, Jussieu) Despite the name, the Natural History Museum is not a single building, but a collection of sites throughout France. Its historic home is in the Jardin des Plantes , and it's here you'll find the greatest number of branches: taxidermied animals in the excellent **Grande Galerie de l'Évolution** (Map p252; www.grandegaleriede levolution.fr; 36 rue Geoffroy-St-Hilaire, 5e; adult/child €9/free; ⏱10am-6pm Wed-Mon Apr-Sep, to 5pm Wed-Mon Oct-Mar; Ⓜ Censier Daubenton); fossils and dinosaur skeletons in the **Galeries d'Anatomie Comparée et de Paléontologie** (Map p252; www.mnhn.fr; 2 rue Buffon, 5e; adult/child €7/5; ⏱10am-6pm Wed-

Mon Apr-Sep, to 5pm Wed-Mon Oct-Mar; Ⓜ Gare d'Austerlitz); and meteorites and crystals in the **Galerie de Minéralogie et de Géologie** (Map p252; www.grandegaleriedelevolution. fr; 36 rue Geoffroy-St-Hilaire, 5e; adult/child €6/4; ⏱10am-6pm Wed-Mon Apr-Sep, to 5pm Wed-Mon Oct-Mar; Ⓜ Censier Daubenton).

Created in 1793, the National Museum of Natural History became a site of significant scientific research in the 19th century. Of the three museums here, the four-floor Grande Galerie de l'Évolution is a particular winner if you're travelling with kids: life-sized elephants, tigers and rhinos play safari, and imaginative exhibits on evolution, extinction and global warming fill 6000 sq metres. The temporary exhibits are generally excellent. Within this building is a separate attraction, the **Galerie des Enfants** (Map p252; www.galeriedesenfants.fr; 36 rue Geoffroy-St-Hilaire, 5e; adult/child €11/9; ⏱10am-6pm Wed-Mon Apr-Sep, to 5pm Wed-Mon Oct-Mar, final entry 1hr prior to closing; Ⓜ Censier

Daubenton) – a hands-on science museum tailored to children from ages six to 12.

Ménagerie du Jardin des Plantes

Zoo

(Map p252; www.zoodejardindesplantes.fr; 57 rue Cuvier, 5e; adult/child €13/9; ☺9am-6pm Mon-Sat, to 6.30pm Sun early Mar–mid-Oct, shorter hours rest of year; Ⓜ Gare d'Austerlitz) Like the Jardin des Plantes in which it's located, this 1000-animal zoo is more than a tourist attraction, also doubling as a research centre for the reproduction of rare and endangered species. During the Prussian siege of 1870, the animals of the day were themselves endangered, when almost all were eaten by starving Parisians.

Note that the recently renovated zoo (p200) in Vincennes is considerably larger.

What's Nearby?

Mosquée de Paris

Mosque

(Map p252; ☎01 45 35 97 33; www.mosqueede paris.net; 2bis place du Puits de l'Ermite, 5e; adult/child €3/2; ☺9am-noon & 2-7pm Sat-Thu Apr-Sep, 9am-noon & 2-6pm Sat-Thu Oct-Mar; Ⓜ Place Monge) Paris' central mosque, with a striking 26m-high minaret, was complet-ed in 1926 in an ornate art deco Moorish style. You can visit the interior to admire the intricate tile work and calligraphy. A separate entrance leads to the wonderful North African–style **hammam** (Map p252; ☎01 43 31 14 32; www.la-mosque.com; 39 rue Geoffroy-St-Hilaire, 5e; admission €18, spa pack-age from €43; ☺10am-9pm Wed-Mon; Ⓜ Censier Daubenton, Place Monge), **restaurant** (☎01 43 31 14 32; www.restaurantauxportesdelorient. com; 39 rue Geoffroy-St-Hilaire, 5e; mains €11-26; ☺kitchen noon-midnight) and **tearoom**

Mosquée de Paris

(www.restaurantauxportesdelorient.com; 39 rue Geoffroy-St-Hilaire, 5e; ☺noon-midnight), and a small *souk* (actually more of a gift shop). Visitors must be modestly dressed.

Musée de la Sculpture en Plein Air
Museum

(Map p252; quai St-Bernard, 5e; Ⓜ Gare d'Austerlitz) FREE Along quai St-Bernard, this open-air sculpture museum (also known as the Jardin Tino Rossi) has more than 50 late-20th-century unfenced sculptures, and makes a great picnic spot. A salad beneath a César or a baguette beside a Brancusi is a pretty classy way to see the Seine up close.

★ **Don't Miss**
The incredible views from the top (9th) floor observation terrace of the Institut du Monde Arabe.

EQROY/SHUTTERSTOCK ©

Institut du Monde Arabe
Museum

(Arab World Institute; Map p252; www.imarabe. org; 1 place Mohammed V, 5e; adult/child €8/4; ☺10am-6pm Tue-Fri, to 7pm Sat & Sun; Ⓜ Jussieu) The Arab World Institute was jointly founded by France and 18 Middle Eastern and North African nations in 1980, with the aim of promoting cross-cultural dialogue. In addition to hosting concerts, film screenings and a research centre, the stunning building houses a museum and temporary exhibition space. Architect Jean Nouvel took his inspiration from traditional latticed-wood windows, creating thousands of modern *mashrabiya*, photo-electrically sensitive apertures built into the glass walls that regulate the amount of light that enters the interior.

Docks en Seine
Cultural Centre

(Cité de la Mode et du Design; www.citemode design.fr; 34 quai d'Austerlitz, 13e; ☺10am-midnight; Ⓜ Gare d'Austerlitz) Framed by a lurid-lime wave-like glass façade, a transformed Seine-side warehouse now houses the French fashion institute, the **Institut Français de la Mode** (hence the docks' alternative name, Cité de la Mode et du Design), mounting fashion and design exhibitions and events through-out the year. Other draws include an entertainment-themed contemporary art museum **Art Ludique-Le Musée** (www. artludique.com; Docks en Seine, 34 quai d'Auster-litz, 13e; adult/child €16.50/11; ☺11am-7pm Mon, Wed & Fri, 11am-10pm Thu, 10am-8pm Sat & Sun; Ⓜ Gare d'Austerlitz), along with ultra-hip bars, clubs and restaurants and huge riverside terraces.

✗ **Take a Break**
Sip a sweet mint tea and nibble on a *pâtisserie orientale* at the Mosquée de Paris' tearoom.

Paris' Covered Passages

Stepping into Paris' *passages couverts* (covered shopping arcades) is a superb way to get a feel for what life was like in early-19th-century Paris. This walking tour is tailor-made for a rainy day, but it's best avoided on a Sunday, when some arcades shut.

Start: Galerie Véro Dodat
Distance: 3km
Duration: 2 hours

Take a Break...
Dine and drink within the arcades.

Classic Photo: Stroll through this elegant passage, designed by Jacques Billaud.

3 The 1826-built **Galerie Colbert** features a huge glass dome and rotunda.
KIEV.VICTOR/SHUTTERSTOCK ©

7 There's lots to explore in **Passage Verdeau**: vintage comic books, antiques, old postcards and more.

4 The 1824-built **Passage Choiseul** has discount and vintage clothing, beads and costume jewellery, and cheap eateries.
KIEV.VICTOR/SHUTTERSTOCK ©

R St-Augustin

R des Petits Champs

R de Richelieu

R Vivienne

Ⓜ Pyramides

Av de l'Opéra

Jardin du Palais Royal

R de Valois

1ER

Pl Colette

R du Colonel Driant

R de Rohan

Palais Royal – Musée du Louvre Ⓜ R de Rivoli

R Croix des Petits Champs

R Richer

FINISH

7

0   200 m
0   0.1 miles

6

6 Inside **Passage Jouffroy** (1847) there's a wax museum, the Musée Grévin, and wonderful boutiques.

Grands
Boulevards
Ⓜ
Bd Poissonnière

Passage des Panoramas

5

R Vivienne

R Montmartre

Pl de la
Bourse
Ⓜ
Bourse

Notre Dame des Victoires

R de Réaumur

5 Paris' oldest covered arcade (1800), **Passage des Panoramas**, was expanded in 1834 and is full of eateries and unusual shops.
KIEV.VICTOR/SHUTTERSTOCK ©

2 Built in 1826, **Galerie Vivienne** is decorated with floor mosaics and bas-reliefs on the walls.

Pl des
Victoires

1 Galerie Véro Dodat retains its 19th-century skylights, murals, Corinthian columns, and shopfronts.
ANDERSPHOTO/SHUTTERSTOCK ©

R du Bouloi

R du Louvre

1

START

Street art on Point Éphémère (p189)

BRUNO DE HOGUES/SHUTTERSTOCK ©

Discovering Paris' Street Art

Vibrant street art continues to splash colour across neighbourhoods throughout the city, and, in a sign of its cultural cachet, a ground-breaking street-art museum, Art 42, recently opened its doors.

The City of Light inspires artists of all genres, including urban art. In 2016, the Mairie de Paris confirmed funds from the *budget participatif*, the allocation of which is voted on by city residents, would be set aside to create *murs d'expression* (street art murals), in all 20 *arrondissements*.

Belleville has some of the city's best street art. From Belleville metro station, walk east uphill along rue de Belleville then turn right into pedestrian rue Dénoyez, 20e. Artists' workshops pepper the small pedestrian street, where everything from litter bins and flower pots to lamp posts and window shutters is covered in colourful graffiti.

Some 1.6km east, look for more street art on rue Laurence Savart, 20e, photo-

Great For...

☑ Don't Miss

Check out works by French and international artists, including Banksy, at Art 42.

graphed by Willy Ronis in 1947 and now a contantly evolving canvas.

On rue Oberkampf, 11e, look out for Le Mur (www.lemur.fr), a wall adjoining Café Charbon (p177) overseen by a collective, with hundreds of incarnations to date.

Street Art Paris (http://streetartparis.fr) runs tours in English of Oberkampf, Belleville and Ménilmontant's street art lasting 2½ hours (€20) and departing at 11am on Saturdays; book ahead online.

Other hotspots for street art include Canal St-Martin (especially in and around cultural centre Point Ephémère, p189), Canal de l'Ourcq, the 13e, and, beyond the bd Périphérique, Vitry sur Seine (reached by RER C).

ⓘ Need to Know
Book well ahead for compulsory Art 42 guided tours.

✕ Take a Break
Next to Le Mur, Café Charbon (p177) is great for a drink or bistro fare.

★ Top Tip
See graffiti street artists in action at the workrooms in hip-hop centre La Place (p188).

Street Art Museums & Galleries

Art 42 — Gallery
(http://art42.fr; 96 bd Bessières, 17e; ⊘tours 7-9pm Tue, 11am-3pm Sat; Ⓜ Porte de Clichy) **FREE** Street art and post-graffiti now have their own dedicated space at this 'anti-museum', with works by Banksy, Bom.K, Miss Van, Ericailcane, and Invader (who's behind the Space Invader motifs on buildings all over Paris), among other boundary-pushing urban artists. Compulsory guided tours (English generally available; confirm ahead) lead you through 4000 sq metres of subterranean rooms sheltering some 150 works. Entry's free but you need to reserve tours online (ideally several weeks in advance, although last-minute cancellations can arise).

Galerie Itinerrance — Gallery
(http://itinerrance.fr; 24 bd du Général d'Armée Jean Simon, 13e; ⊘noon-7pm Tue-Sat; Ⓜ Bibliothèque) **FREE** Testament to the 13e's ongoing creative renaissance, this gallery showcases graffiti and street art, and can advise on self-guided and guided street-art tours of the neighbourhood that take in many landmark works by artists represented by the gallery. Exhibitions and events change regularly.

Musée National Picasso

An exquisite 17th-century mansion in Le Marais is the wonderfully intimate setting for an exceptional collection of works by long-time Paris resident, Pablo Picasso.

One of Paris' most beloved art collections is showcased inside the mid-17th-century Hôtel Salé, an exquisite private mansion owned by the city since 1964. The Musée National Picasso is a staggering art museum devoted to Spanish artist Pablo Picasso (1881–1973), who spent much of his life living and working in Paris. The collection includes more than 5000 drawings, engravings, paintings, ceramic works and sculptures by the *grand maître* (great master), although they're not all displayed at the same time.

The extraordinary collection was donated to the French government by the artist's heirs in lieu of paying inheritance taxes. In addition to the permanent collection, the museum mounts two major temporary exhibitions per year (included in the admission price).

Great For...

☑ Don't Miss

The museum's bi-annual temporary exhibitions.

❶ Need to Know

Map p254; ☎01 85 56 00 36; www.museepicassoparis.fr; 5 rue de Thorigny, 3e; adult/child €12.50/free; ☺10.30am-6pm Tue-Fri, 9.30am-6pm Sat & Sun; Ⓜ St-Paul, Chemin Vert

✕ Take a Break

Stop by the museum's 1st-floor 'rooftop cafe', overlooked by an ancient stone sphinx.

★ Top Tip

To best appreciate the artworks and building's history, rent an audio-guide (€5).

---

a museum, this magnificent glass-roofed building with arched wrought-iron girders wasn't actually used as one until over a century later, when it opened as a centre for Parisian urbanism and architecture. Exhibitions (30 per year) showcase the city's past, present and future. Interpretative information is in French but it's fascinating for anyone with an interest in the evolution of Paris. Every second Saturday, the farmers market here features produce from a 250km radius. There's a small but excellent architectural bookshop on the ground floor.

Marché des Enfants Rouges Market

(Map p254; 39 rue de Bretagne & 33bis rue Charlot, 3e; ☺8.30am-1pm & 4-7.30pm Tue-Fri, 4-8pm Sat, 8.30am-2pm Sun; Ⓜ Filles du Calvaire) Built in 1615, Paris' oldest covered market is secreted behind an inconspicuous green-metal gate. A glorious maze of 20-odd food stalls selling ready-to-eat dishes, produce, cheese and flower stalls, it's a great place for a meander and to dine with locals at communal tables.

What's Nearby

Musée d'Art et d'Histoire du Judaïsme Museum

(Map p254; ☎01 53 01 86 62; www.mahj.org; 71 rue du Temple, 3e; adult/child €9/free; ☺11am-6pm Tue-Fri, 10am-6pm Sat & Sun; Ⓜ Rambuteau) To delve into the historic heart of Le Marais' Jewish community in Pletzl (from the Yiddish for 'little square'), visit this fascinating museum inside Hôtel de St-Aignan, dating from 1650. The museum traces the evolution of Jewish communities from the Middle Ages to the present, with particular emphasis on French Jewish history. Highlights include documents relating to the Dreyfus Affair, and works by Chagall, Modigliani and Soutine.

Pavillon de l'Arsenal Museum

(Map p254; www.pavillon-arsenal.com; 21 bd Morland, 4e; ☺10.30am-6.30pm Tue-Sat, 11am-7pm Sun; Ⓜ Sully–Morland) **FREE** Built in 1879 as

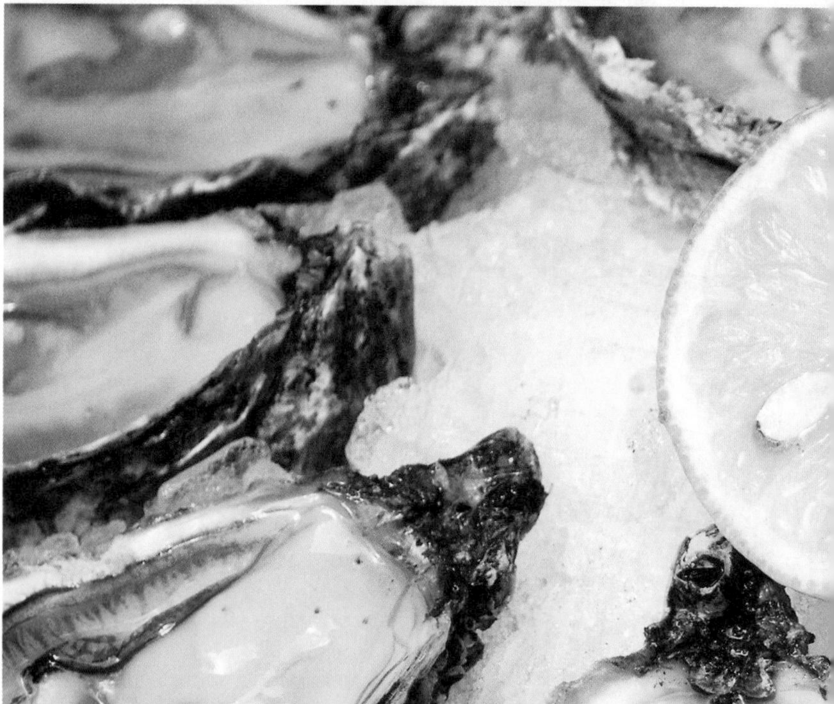

JOHN HARPER/GETTY IMAGES ©

DINING OUT

Produce-laden markets, intimate bistros, gastronomic temples and more

Dining Out

The inhabitants of some cities rally around local sports teams, but in Paris, they rally around la table. Pistachio macarons, shots of tomato consommé, decadent bœuf bourguignon, a gooey wedge of Camembert running onto the cheese plate...food is not fuel here, it's the reason you get up in the morning. Paris doesn't have its own 'local' cuisine, but is the crossroads for the regional flavours of France. Dishes from the hot south favour olive oil, garlic and tomatoes; the cooler, pastoral northern regions turn to cream and butter; and coastal areas concentrate on seafood. The freshness of ingredients and reliance on natural flavours combined with refined, often very complex cooking methods – and, of course, wine – means you're in a gourmet's paradise.

In This Section

Eiffel Tower & Western Paris 122

Champs-Élysées &
Grands Boulevards 123

Louvre & Les Halles 125

Montmartre & Northern Paris............127

Le Marais, Ménilmontant
& Belleville 130

Bastille & Eastern Paris 132

The Islands 134

Latin Quarter.......................................136

St-Germain & Les Invalides................138

Montparnasse &
Southern Paris 141

Price Ranges/Tipping

Price Ranges

The following price ranges refer to the cost of a two-course meal.

€ Less than €20

€€ €20 to €40

€€€ More than €40

Tipping

A *pourboire* (tip) is unnecessary, as service is always included in the bill. It's not uncommon to round up the bill for good service.

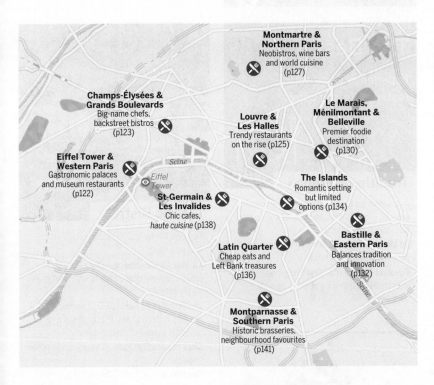

Montmartre & Northern Paris
Neobistros, wine bars and world cuisine (p127)

Champs-Élysées & Grands Boulevards
Big-name chefs, backstreet bistros (p123)

Louvre & Les Halles
Trendy restaurants on the rise (p125)

Le Marais, Ménilmontant & Belleville
Premier foodie destination (p130)

Eiffel Tower & Western Paris
Gastronomic palaces and museum restaurants (p122)

Seine

Eiffel Tower

St-Germain & Les Invalides
Chic cafes, *haute cuisine* (p138)

The Islands
Romantic setting but limited options (p134)

Bastille & Eastern Paris
Balances tradition and innovation (p132)

Latin Quarter
Cheap eats and Left Bank treasures (p136)

Seine

Montparnasse & Southern Paris
Historic brasseries, neighbourhood favourites (p141)

Useful Phrases

I'd like to reserve a table for... *Je voudrais réserver une table pour*...

... **(eight) o'clock** *(vingt) heures*

...**two/three people** ...*deux/trois personnes*

I don't eat... *Je ne mange pas*...

Please bring the bill. *Apportez-moi l'addition, s'il vous plaît.*

Must Try/Classic Dishes

Bœuf bourguignon Beef marinated and cooked in young red wine with mushrooms, onions, carrots and bacon.

Confit de canard Duck cooked slowly in its own fat.

Entrecôte Thin, boneless rib-eye steak.

Tarte Tatin Upside-down apple tart.

The Best...

Experience Paris' top restaurants and cafes

Traditional French

À la Biche au Bois (p134) Game, especially *la biche* (doe), is the speciality of the countrified 'doe in the woods'.

Le Miroir (p129) Excellent French standards at this Montmartre favourite.

Bouillon Racine (p139) Art-nouveau jewel with traditional fare inspired by age-old recipes.

Classic Bistros

Le Petit Rétro (p122) Zinc bar and art-nouveau tiling.

La Tour de Montlhéry – Chez Denise (p126) Red-chequered tablecloths and snails on the menu.

Le Bistrot Paul Bert (p132) Legendary address with timeless vintage decor and perfectly executed classic dishes.

Chez Paul (p133) Paris as your grandmother knew it.

Chez Dumonet (p139) The quintessential Parisian bistro experience.

Neobistros

Richer (p123) Smart setting and genius flavour combinations, but no reservations, so arrive early.

Semilla (p139) Edgy, modern dishes in factory-style premises.

Le Beurre Noisette (p141) Creative, locally loved cooking.

Wine-Bar Dining

Le Verre Volé (p127) Excellent wines, expert advice and hearty *plats du jour*.

Floquifil (p123) The backstreet Parisian wine-bar dining experience of your imagination.

Frenchie Bar à Vins (p125) Can't get a reservation at Frenchie? Try the wine bar instead.

Bakeries

Poilâne (pictured above; p139) Turning out distinctive wood-fired, rounded sourdough loaves since 1932.

Besnier (p141) Watch baguettes being made through the viewing window.

Du Pain et des Idées (p127) Traditional bakery near Canal St-Martin with an exquisite 1889 interior.

Views

Le Jules Verne (p122) A magical, Michelin-starred address perched in the Eiffel Tower.

Le Comptoir du Panthéon (p138) Cafe right by the Panthéon with Eiffel Tower views.

La Tour d'Argent (p138) Gastronomic dining overlooking Notre Dame.

Le Ciel de Paris (p141) City panoramas from 'the Sky of Paris' atop Tour Montparnasse.

★ Lonely Planet's Top Choices

Restaurant AT (p136) Abstract-art-like masterpieces made from rare ingredients.

Restaurant Guy Savoy (p138) Resplendent triple-Michelin-starred flagship rehoused in the neoclassical mint.

Le Pantruche (p129) Superb modern French cuisine at fantastic value.

Hugo Desnoyer (p122) Feast for meat lovers courtesy of Paris' most famous butcher.

⊗ Eiffel Tower & Western Paris

Hugo Desnoyer Modern French €€€

(☎01 46 47 83 00; www.hugodesnoyer.com; 28 rue du Docteur Blanche, 16e; 2-course lunch menu €22, mains €28-46; ☺restaurant 11.30am-3.30pm Tue & Thu-Sat, 8-11pm Wed, closed Aug; Ⓜ Jasmin) Hugo Desnoyer is Paris' most famous butcher and the trip to his 16e premises, done out with cowhide-covered seats, is well worth it. Reserve ahead to feast on exceptional homemade terrines, quiches, foie gras and cold cuts followed by the finest meat in Paris, including an exceptional *côte de bœuf* (rib steak; for two or three people).

Le Jules Verne Gastronomy €€€

(Map p246; ☎01 45 55 61 44; www.leju-lesverne-paris.com; 2nd fl, Eiffel Tower, Champ de Mars, 7e; 5-/6-course menus €190/230, 3-course lunch menu €105; ☺noon-1.30pm & 7-9.30pm; Ⓜ Bir Hakeim or RER Champ de Mars–Tour Eiffel) Book way ahead (online only) to feast on Michelin-starred cuisine and the most beautiful view of Paris at this magical spot on the Eiffel Tower's 2nd floor, accessed by a private lift (elevator) in the south pillar. Cuisine is contemporary, with a five- or six-course 'experience' menu allowing you to taste the best of chef Pascal Féraud's stunning gastronomic repertoire.

Le Petit Rétro Bistro €€

(Map p246; ☎01 44 05 06 05; http://petit retro.fr; 5 rue Mesnil, 16e; 2-/3-course menus lunch €26/31, dinner €31/36, mains €19-33; ☺noon-2.30pm & 7-10.30pm Mon-Sat; Ⓜ Victor Hugo) From the gorgeous 'Petit Rétro' em-blazoned on the zinc bar to the ceramic, floral art-nouveau tiles on the wall, this 1904-opened old-style bistro is now a historic monument. Fare prepared using seasonal ingredients is classic French: for example, blood sausage, *blanquette de veau* (veal in a butter and cream sauce) and *oreilles de cochon* (pig's ears). Delicious.

58 Tour Eiffel French €€€

(Map p246; ☎01 76 64 14 64; www.restau-rants-toureiffel.com; 1st fl, Eiffel Tower, Champ de Mars, 7e; menus lunch €41.50, dinner €85-180;

Le Jules Verne

⊙11.30am-4.30pm & 6.30-11pm; 🖉🛉; Ⓜ Bir Hakeim or RER Champ de Mars–Tour Eiffel) You'll certainly remember a meal here – the location on the Eiffel Tower's 1st floor is only bested by the Michelin-starred Jules Verne, one floor up. Walk-ins are possible for a 'picnic' lunch delivered in a wire basket; reservations are essential for dinner (and allow you to skip the lift queues), with guaranteed window-table options. Vegetarian and kids' menus are available.

⊗ Champs-Élysées & Grands Boulevards

Richer   Bistro €
(Map p250; www.lericher.com; 2 rue Richer, 9e; mains €18-20; ⊙noon-2.30pm & 7.30-10.30pm; Ⓜ Poissonière, Bonne Nouvelle) Run by the same team as across-the-street neighbour L'Office (www.office-resto.com), Richer's pared-back, exposed-brick decor is a smart setting for genius creations like smoked duck breast ravioli in miso broth, and quince and lime cheesecake for dessert. It doesn't take reservations, but it serves up snacks and Chinese tea, and has a full bar (open until midnight). Fantastic value.

Le Hide   French €€
(🖉01 45 74 15 81; www.lehide.fr; 10 rue du Général Lanrezac, 17e; 2-/3-course menus €30/38; ⊙6-10.30pm Mon-Sat; Ⓜ Charles de Gaulle–Étoile) A perpetual favourite, Le Hide is a tiny neighbourhood bistro serving scrumptious traditional French fare: snails, seared duck breast with celery puree and truffle oil, baked shoulder of lamb, and monkfish with *beurre blanc* (white sauce). This place fills up faster than you can scamper down the steps of the nearby Arc de Triomphe (p42) – reserve well in advance.

Crabe Royal   Seafood, Deli €€
(Map p246; 🖉01 81 69 96 70; http://craberoyal. com; 19 place de la Madeleine, 8e; sandwiches €9.50-17, mains €21-38; ⊙noon-10.30pm Mon-Sat; Ⓜ Madeleine) Royal Kamchatka (Alaskan king crab) is the star of the show at this restaurant-deli on gourmet place

🍽 Bustronome

A true moveable feast, **Bustronome** (Map p246; 🖉09 54 44 45 55; www.bustronome. com; 2 av Kléber, 16e; 4-course lunch menu €65, with paired wines €85, 6-course dinner menu €100, with paired wines €130; ⊙by reservation 12.15pm, 12.45pm, 7.45pm & 8.45pm; 🖉🛉; Ⓜ Kléber, Charles de Gaulle–Étoile) is a voyage into French gastronomy aboard a glass-roofed bus, with Paris' famous monuments – the Arc de Triomphe, Grand Palais, Palais Garnier, Notre Dame and Eiffel Tower – gliding by as you dine on seasonal creations prepared in the purpose-built vehicle's lower-deck galley. Children's menus for lunch/dinner cost €40/50; vegetarian, vegan and gluten-free menus are available.

Exquisite dishes might include escabeche of shrimp with candied lemon, roast pigeon and artichokes with apricot and rosemary jus, melon meringue with vanilla-bean syrup and mint-and-lime sorbet, and the finest French cheeses.

IMAGE COURTESY OF BUSTRONOME ©

de la Madeleine – styles range from gratin to miso-caramelised, grilled with yuzu and coriander marinade or ceviche – but lobster, salmon and oysters also get a supporting role. If the restaurant is beyond your budget, pick up a brioche crab roll to take away.

Floquifil   French €
(Map p250; 🖉01 42 46 11 19; 17 rue de Montyon, 9e; mains €16-21; ⊙11am-midnight Mon-Sat; Ⓜ Grands Boulevards) If you were to envision

Paris on a Plate

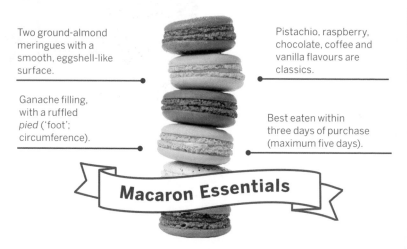

Two ground-almond meringues with a smooth, eggshell-like surface.

Pistachio, raspberry, chocolate, coffee and vanilla flavours are classics.

Ganache filling, with a ruffled *pied* ('foot'; circumference).

Best eaten within three days of purchase (maximum five days).

Macaron Essentials

BUTSAYA/SHUTTERSTOCK ©

Brought to Paris in the 1600s by Catherine de' Medici's Italian chefs, today's ganache-filled Parisian macarons were created by patisserie Ladurée in the 1930s, and updated in the 1990s by its then-pastry chef Pierre Hermé (who now helms his own empire). Exquisite tearooms and patisseries citywide sell these rainbow-coloured delicacies (beautifully boxed to take away). Macaron Day (20 March) sees free samples, workshops and more.

Macarons at La Cuisine Paris cooking school (p96)
MATT MUNRO/LONELY PLANET ©

★ **Top Macaron Suppliers**

Ladurée (Map p246; www.laduree.com; 75 av des Champs-Élysées, 8e; ⊙7.30am-11.30pm Mon-Thu, 7.30am-12.30am Fri, 8.30am-12.30am Sat, 8.30am-11.30pm Sun; 🖟; ⓜGeorge V) **Ladurée has been around since 1862 and first created the lighter-than-air, ganache-filled macaron in the 1930s. Its tearoom is the classiest spot to indulge on the Champs.**

Pierre Hermé (Map p252; www.pierreherme.com; 72 rue Bonaparte, 6e; ⊙10am-7pm Sun-Fri, to 8pm Sat; ⓜOdéon) **The size of a chocolate box, it's a veritable feast of perfectly presented petits fours, cakes, chocolates, nougats, jams and dazzling macarons.**

Fou de Pâtisserie (Map p250; 45 rue Montorgueil, 2e; ⊙11am-8pm Mon-Fri, 10am-8pm Sat, 10am-6pm Sun; ⓜÉtienne Marcel, Sentier) **A Paris first, this is the brainchild of the publishers of pastry magazine *Fou de Pâtisserie* (sold here).**

the ultimate backstreet Parisian wine bar, it would probably look a lot like Floquifil: table-strewn terrace, dark timber furniture, aquamarine-painted walls and bottles galore. But while the by-the-glass wines are superb, you're missing out if you don't dine here (on rosemary-roasted lamb with ratatouille, pot-au-feu, frogs legs or at the very least a charcuterie platter).

❽ Louvre & Les Halles

Frenchie   Bistro €€€
(Map p250; ☎01 40 39 96 19; www.frenchie-restaurant.com; 5 rue du Nil, 2e; 4-course lunch menu €45, 5-course dinner menu €74, with wine €175; ◷6.30-11pm Mon-Wed, noon-2.30pm & 6.30-11pm Fri; ⓂSentier) Tucked down an inconspicuous alley, this tiny bistro with wooden tables and old stone walls is always packed and for good reason: excellent-value dishes are modern, market-driven and prepared with unpretentious flair by French chef Gregory Marchand. Reserve well in advance; arrive at 6.30pm and pray for a cancellation (it does happen); or head to neighbouring **Frenchie Bar à Vins** (Map p250; www.frenchie-restaurant.com; 6 rue du Nil, 2e; dishes €9-23; ◷6.30-11pm Mon-Fri; ⓂSentier).

No reservations at the latter – write your name on the sheet of paper strung outside and wait for your name to be called.

During the day, swing by its adjacent deli-style takeaway outlet **Frenchie to Go** (Map p250; www.frenchietogo.com; 9 rue du Nil, 2e; dishes €8-14; ◷8.30am-4.30pm Mon-Fri, 9.30am-5.30pm Sat & Sun; ☎; ⓂSentier).

Bambou   Southeast Asian €€
(Map p250; ☎01 40 28 98 30; www.bambouparis.com; 23 rue des Jeûneurs, 2e; mains €19-28; ◷noon-2.30pm & 7-11pm, bar to midnight; ☏; ⓂSentier) One of Paris' most sizzling recent openings, this spectacular Southeast Asian restaurant occupies a 500-sq-metre former fabric warehouse, with vintage bird-cages and a giant metal dragon adorning the main dining room, a downstairs billiards room/bar, vast terrace and Zen-like garden.

Chef Antonin Bonnet's specialities include squid with black pepper and basil, and aromatic shrimp pad thai.

Chez La Vieille   French €
(Map p250; ☎01 42 60 15 78; 1 rue Bailleul, 1er; mains €15-20; ◷noon-2pm & 7-10.30pm Tue-Sat; ⓂLouvre–Rivoli) In salvaging this history-steeped eatery within a 16th-century building, star chef Daniel Rose pays homage to the former wholesale markets, the erstwhile legendary owner Adrienne Biasin (many of whose timeless dishes he's updated, from terrines and rillettes to veal blanquette), and the soul of Parisian bistro cooking itself. Dine at the street-level bar or upstairs in the peacock-blue dining room.

Da Roco   Italian €€
(Map p250; ☎01 42 21 93 71; 6 rue Vivienne, 2e; mains €15-28; ◷noon-3pm & 7pm-midnight; ☏; ⓂBourse) Mirrored ceilings created a space-defying effect in this former JP Gaultier boutique, now transformed into a spectacular trattoria. Premium ingredients are used in mains such as dorade fillet with orange jus and fennel salad, three daily pastas such as linguine with clams, and 10 different pizzas. On the mezzanine, award-winning mixologist Nicolas de Soto reigns over cocktail bar Da Nico.

Stohrer   Patisserie €
(Map p250; www.stohrer.fr; 51 rue Montorgueil, 2e; ◷7.30am-8.30pm; ⓂÉtienne Marcel, Sentier) Opened in 1730 by Nicolas Stohrer, the Polish pastry chef of queen consort Marie Leszczyńska (wife of Louis XV), Stohrer's house-made specialities include its own inventions, the *baba au rhum* (rum-soaked sponge cake) and *puits d'amour* (caramel-topped, vanilla cream-filled puff pastry). The beautiful pastel murals were added in 1864 by Paul-Jacques-Aimé Baudry, who also decorated the Palais Garnier's Grand Foyer.

Le Grand Véfour   Gastronomy €€€
(Map p250; ☎01 42 96 56 27; www.grand-vefour.com; 17 rue de Beaujolais, 1er; lunch/dinner menu €115/315, mains €98-135; ◷noon-2.30pm & 7.30-10.30pm Mon-Fri; ⓂPyramides) Holding

Tradi

two Michelin stars, this 18th-century jewel on the northern edge of the Jardin du Palais Royal (p101) has been a dining favourite since 1784; the names ascribed to each table span Napoléon and Victor Hugo to Colette (who lived next door). Expect a voyage of discovery from chef Guy Martin in one of the most beautiful restaurants in the world.

La Tour de Montlhéry – Chez Denise   French €€

(Map p250; ☎01 42 36 21 82; 5 rue des Prouvaires, 1er; mains €17-27; ⏰noon-3pm & 7.30pm-5am Mon-Fri mid-Aug–mid-Jun; MChâtelet, Louvre Rivoli) The most traditional eatery near the former Les Halles marketplace, this boisterous old half-timbered bistro with red-chequered tablecloths stays open until dawn and has been run by the same family since 1966. If you're ready to feast on all the French classics – snails in garlic sauce, veal liver, steak tartare, braised beef cheeks and house-made pâté – reservations are in order.

Tradi   Bistro €€

(Map p250; ☎01 44 82 07 83; www.tradi.paris; 4 rue du Mail, 2e; mains €16-29; ⏰7-11pm Mon & Sat, noon-3pm & 7-11pm Tue-Fri; MSentier) 🍴 This traditional bistro has been reborn and now only uses sustainable French produce, which can be traced from farm to plate. Everything is made on site, including the foie gras, smoked salmon and freshly baked bread. Menus change daily but might feature roast duck with honey and pistachios, or line-caught dorade with tarragon leaves and white beans.

Le Cochon à l'Oreille   French €€

(Map p250; ☎01 42 36 07 56; 15 rue Montmartre, 1er; mains €17-24; ⏰10am-2am Tue-Sat; MLes Halles) A Parisian jewel, the hole-in-the-wall Le Cochon à l'Oreille – a listed monument – retains 1890-laid tiles depicting vibrant market scenes of the old *halles*, while an iron staircase leads to a second dining room upstairs. Bistro-style dishes are traditional French (the steak tartare is excellent), and are accompanied by well-chosen wines. Hours can vary. Cash only.

Miss Kale Health Food €

(Map p250; http://misskale.fr; 104 rue de Réaumur, 2e; dishes €9-14; ⊗8.30am-6.30pm Mon-Fri; ⊿; Ⓜ Sentier) Buddha bowls, salads, sandwiches, soups, superb *tartines* such as roasted beetroot with goat's cheese and hazelnuts, and ultrahealthy desserts provide a vitamin fix at this bare-brick warehouse-style space. The eponymous superfood finds its way into many of the menu items as well as cold-pressed juices. Vegetarian and vegan options are plentiful, but there are also chicken and fish dishes.

⦿ Montmartre & Northern Paris

Matière à. Modern French €€

(Map p254; ⏺09 83 07 37 85; 15 rue Marie et Louise, 10e; 2-/3-course lunch menu €21/25, 4-course dinner menu €46; ⊗12.30-2pm & 7.30-11pm Mon-Fri, 7.30-11pm Sat; Ⓜ Goncourt) The short but stunning seasonal menu changes daily at this unique space. *Table d'hôte*–style dining for up to 14 is around a shared oak table lit by dozens of naked light bulbs. In the kitchen is young chef Anthony Courteille, who prides himself on doing everything *fait maison* (homemade), including bread and butter to die for. Reservations essential.

Du Pain et des Idées Bakery €

(Map p254; www.dupainetdesidees.com; 34 rue Yves Toudic, 10e; ⊗6.45am-8pm Mon-Fri; Ⓜ Jacques Bonsergent) This traditional bakery with an exquisite interior from 1889 is famed for its naturally leavened bread, orange-blossom brioche and *escargots* (scroll-like 'snails') in four sweet flavours. Its mini savoury *pavés* (breads) flavoured with reblochon cheese and fig, or goat's cheese, sesame and honey are perfect for lunch on the run. A wooden picnic table sits on the pavement outside.

Le Verre Volé Bistro €€

(Map p254; ⏺01 48 03 17 34; http://leverrevole. fr; 67 rue de Lancry, 10e; 2-/3-course lunch menu €19/22, mains €16.50-26; ⊗bistro 12.30-2.30pm &

🍽 When to Eat

Petit déjeuner (breakfast) The French kick-start the day with a *tartine* (slice of baguette smeared with unsalted butter and jam) and *un café* (espresso) or – for kids – hot chocolate. Parisians might grab a coffee and croissant on the way to work, but otherwise croissants (eaten straight, never with butter or jam) are more of a weekend or 4pm treat along with *pains au chocolat* (chocolate-filled croissants) and other *viennoiseries* (sweet pastries).

Déjeuner (lunch) The traditional main meal of the day, lunch translates to a starter and main course with wine, followed by a short sharp *café*. During the work week this is less likely to be the case – many busy Parisians now grab a sandwich to go and pop off to run errands – but the standard hour-long lunch break, special *prix-fixe* menus and *tickets restaurant* (company-funded meal vouchers) ensure that many restaurants fill up at lunch.

Apéritif Otherwise known as an *apéro,* the premeal drink is sacred. Cafes and bars get packed out from around 5pm onwards as Parisians wrap up work for the day and relax over a chit-chat-fuelled glass of wine or beer.

Dîner (dinner) Traditionally lighter than lunch, but a meal that is being treated more and more as the main meal of the day. In restaurants the head chef will almost certainly be in the kitchen, which is not always the case during lunch.

Croissants, coffee and juice
MATT MUNRO/LONELY PLANET ©

From left: Le Verre Volé (p127); Mesdemoiselles Madeleines; Café des Deux Moulins

7.30-11.30pm, wine bar 10am-2am; 🛜; MJacques Bonsergent) The tiny 'Stolen Glass' – a wine shop with a few tables – is one of the most popular wine bar–restaurants in Paris, with outstanding natural and unfiltered wines and expert advice. Unpretentious and hearty *plats du jour* are excellent. Reserve well in advance for meals, or stop by to pick up a gourmet sandwich (€7.90) and a bottle.

Le Bistrot de la Galette   Modern French €

(Map p249; 📞01 46 06 19 65; http://bistrotdela galette.fr; 102ter rue Lepic, 18e; mains €14-17; 🕙11am-10pm Tue-Sun; MAbbesses) 🍴 In the shadow of Montmartre windmill Moulin de la Galette, this seemingly timeless vintage-fitted bistro is the creation of pastry chef Gilles Marchal, who uses locally hand-milled flour in *feuilletés* (delicately laminated pastry puffs) that accompany most dishes, such as *Galette Parisienne* (roast ham, sautéed mushrooms and Comté) and *Galette Provençale* (shredded roast lamb, aubergine, garlic and sun-dried tomatoes).

Fric-Frac   Sandwiches €

(Map p254; http://fricfrac.fr; 79 quai de Valmy, 10e; sandwiches €11.50-15; 🕙noon-3pm & 7.30-11pm Tue-Fri, noon-11pm Sat & Sun; MJacques Bonsergent) Traditional snack croque monsieur (a toasted cheese and ham sandwich) gets a contemporary makeover at this quayside space. Gourmet Winnie (Crottin de Chavignol cheese, dried fruit, chestnut honey, chives and rosemary) and exotic Shaolin (king prawns, lemongrass paste, shitake mushrooms and Thai basil) are among the creative combos served with salad and fries. Eat in or head to the canal.

Mesdemoiselles Madeleines   Pastries €

(Map p249; www.mllesmadeleines.com; 37 rue des Martyrs, 9e; madeleines small €0.70, large €2.50-4.50; 🕙10.30am-7pm Tue-Sat, 10.30am-2pm & 3.30-6.30pm Sun; MSt-Georges) Shell-shaped French madeleine cakes, immortalised by Marcel Proust, are the sole product of this ingenious spot, in a dazzling array of flavours: 'simple' (Tahitian vanilla; Ethiopian coffee), 'savoury' (red onion,

chives and crème fraîche; basil, feta and pine nuts), and 'gourmet' (Rhône valley raspberries with raspberry coulis; caramelised hazelnuts, salted caramel mousse and a caramel shell), along with bite-sized mini-madeleines.

L'Été en Pente Douce   Cafe €

(Map p249; ☎01 42 64 02 67; 8 rue Paul Albert, 18e; mains €10.50-18; ✆noon-midnight; MChâteau Rouge) Parisian terraces don't get much better than 'Summer on a Gentle Slope' (named after the 1987 French film): a hidden square wedged between two flights of steep staircases on the back side of Montmartre, in a neighbourhood that's the real thing. Quiches, giant salads and dishes such as organic tofu lasagna or veal stew with mushrooms make up the menu.

Le Pantruche   Modern French €€

(Map p249; ☎01 48 78 55 60; 3 rue Victor Massé, 9e; lunch/dinner menus €19/35; ✆12.30-2.30pm & 7.30-10.30pm Mon-Fri; MPigalle) Named after a nearby 19th-century theatre, oak-furnished Pantruche woos foodies in the dining hotspot of south Pigalle with its intimate setting,

reasonable prices and seasonal neobistro fare. Daring creations might include oysters with green lettuce foam, lamb ravioli with mimolette and mint, wild hare with beetroot jus, or red mullet and bacon-wrapped polenta. Reserve well in advance.

Le Miroir   Bistro €€

(Map p249; ☎01 46 06 50 73; 94 rue des Martyrs, 18e; lunch menu €19.50, dinner menus €35-46; ✆noon-2pm & 7.30-10pm; MAbbesses) This modern bistro is a local favourite, smack in the middle of the Montmartre tourist trail. There are lots of delightful pâtés and *rillettes* to start with – guinea hen with dates, duck with mushrooms, haddock and lemon – followed by its signature stuffed veal shoulder or daily changing specials like crispy chanterelle duck, salmon mille-feuille or filet mignon with foie gras.

Café des Deux Moulins   Cafe €

(Map p249; http://cafedesdeuxmoulins.fr; 15 rue Lepic, 18e; ✆7.30am-2am Mon-Fri, 8am-2am Sat & Sun; MBlanche) Midway along food-shop-lined rue Lepic is neon-lit Café des Deux Moulins; this is the much-loved cafe where

🍽️ Dining Tips

Bread Order a meal and within seconds a basket of fresh bread will be brought to the table. Butter is rarely an accompaniment. Except in the most upmarket of places, don't expect a side plate – simply put it on the table.

Water Asking for *une carafe d'eau* (jug of tap water) is perfectly acceptable, although some waiters will presume you don't know this and only offer mineral water, which you have to pay for. Should bubbles be more your cup of tea, ask for *de l'eau gazeuze* (fizzy mineral water). Ice *(glaçons)* can be hard to come by.

Service To state the obvious, France is not a service-oriented country. No one is working for tips here, so to get around this, think like a Parisian – acknowledge the expertise of your *serveur* by asking for advice (even if you don't really want it) and don't be afraid to flirt. In France flirtation is not the same as picking someone up, it is both a game that makes the mundane more enjoyable and a vital life skill to help you get what you want (such as the bill). Being witty and speaking French with an accent will often help your cause.

Dress Smart casual is best. How you look is very important, and Parisians favour personal style above all else. But if you're going somewhere dressy, don't assume this means suit and tie – that's more business-meal attire. On the other hand, running shoes may be too casual, unless, of course, they are more hip than functional, in which case you may fit right in.

MATT MUNRO/LONELY PLANET ©

Amélie worked in the eponymous film. Head beyond the tourist crowds posing for photographs outside into the cinematic interior to join locals for drinks, lunch (two-/three-course *menu* €14.90/17.50) or weekend brunch (€21). Happy hour is from 6pm to 9pm.

❌ Le Marais, Ménilmontant & Belleville

Jacques Genin   Pastries €

(Map p254; 📞01 45 77 29 01; http://jacques genin.fr; 133 rue de Turenne, 3e; pastries €9; ⏱11am-7pm Tue-Sun; 🚇Oberkampf, Filles du Calvaire) Wildly creative *chocolatier* Jacques Genin is famed for his flavoured caramels, *pâtes de fruits* (fruit jellies) and exquisitely embossed *bonbons de chocolat* (chocolate sweets). But what completely steals the show at his elegant chocolate showroom is the *salon de dégustation* (aka tearoom), where you can order a pot of outrageously thick hot chocolate and legendary Genin *millefeuille*, assembled to order.

La Maison Plisson   Cafe, Deli €

(Map p254; www.lamaisonplisson.com; 93 bd Beaumarchais, 3e; mains €8-15; ⏱9.30am-9pm Mon, 8.30am-9pm Tue-Sat, 9.30am-7pm Sun; 🚇St-Sébastien–Froissart) Framed by sage-green, glass-canopied wrought-iron girders, this gourmand's fantasyland incorporates a covered-market-style, terrazzo-floored food hall filled with exquisite, mostly French produce: meat, vegetables, cheese, wine, chocolate, jams, freshly baked breads and much more. If your appetite's whet, its cafe, opening to twin terraces, serves charcuterie, foie gras and cheese planks, bountiful salads and delicacies such as olive oil-marinated, Noilly Prat-flambéed sardines.

Le Clown Bar   Modern French €€

(Map p254; 📞01 43 55 87 35; www.clown-bar-paris.com; 114 rue Amelot, 11e; mains €28-36; ⏱kitchen noon-2.30pm & 7-10.30pm Wed-Sun, bar 7.30am-1.30am; 🚇Filles du Calvaire) The former staff dining room of the city's winter circus, the 1852-built Cirque d'Hiver, is a historic monument with colourful clown-themed ceramics and mosaics, painted glass ceilings and its original zinc bar. Fabulous modern French cuisine spans scallops with smoked rosemary ricotta to Mesquer pigeon, smoked eel with pear and mushrooms and sautéed veal's brains, accompanied by excellent natural wines.

Breizh Café   Crêpes €

(Map p254; ☑01 42 72 13 77; http://breizhcafe.com; 109 rue Vieille du Temple, 3e; crêpes & galettes €6.50-18.80; ⊙11.30am-11pm Tue-Sun; MSt-Sébastien–Froissart) Everything at the Breton Café (breizh is 'Breton' in Breton) is 100% authentic, making it top many Parisians' lists for the city's best crêpes. Be it the Cancale oysters, 20 types of cider or the buttery organic-flour crêpes, everything here is cooked to perfection. Tables are limited and there's often a wait; book ahead or try **L'Épicerie** (Map p254; www.breizhcafe.com; 111 rue Vieille du Temple, 3e; crêpes & galettes €6.50-18.80; ⊙11.30am-10pm Wed-Sun) next door.

Café Pinson   Cafe, Vegetarian €

(Map p254; ☑09 83 82 53 53; www.cafepinson.fr; 6 rue du Forez, 3e; 2-course lunch menu €17.50, mains €14; ⊙9am-10pm Mon-Fri, 10am-10pm Sat, noon-6pm Sun; �
⏚⏛; MFilles du Calvaire) ⏛ Tucked down a narrow side street in the fashionable Haut Marais, with an interior by celebrity designer Dorothée Meilichzon, this spacious cafe sees a stylish lunchtime crowd flock for its organic vegetarian and vegan dishes such as almond, carrot and ginger soup and dark chocolate pear crumble. Freshly squeezed juices are excellent, as is Sunday brunch (€27; 12.15pm and 2pm).

Chambelland   Bakery €

(Map p254; ☑01 43 55 07 30; http://chambelland.com; 14 rue Ternaux, 11e; lunch menu €10-12; ⊙9am-8pm Tue-Sun; MParmentier) In a city known for its bakeries, it's only right there's Chambelland – a 100% gluten-free bakery with breads to die for. Using rice and buck-

wheat flour milled at the bakery's own mill in southern France, this pioneering bakery creates exquisite cakes and pastries as well as sourdough loaves and brioches peppered with nuts, seeds, chocolate and fruit.

Istr   Seafood, Breton €€

(Map p254; ☑01 43 56 81 25; 41 rue Notre Dame de Nazareth, 3e; dozen oysters €24-40, mains €15-25, 2-/3-course lunch menu €19/23; ⊙kitchen noon-2.30pm & 6-10pm Tue-Fri, 6-11pm Sat, bar to 2am Tue-Sat; MTemple) Fabulously patterned wallpaper and a gleaming zinc bar set the stage for innovative Breton-inspired cuisine. The region's famed istr ('oyster' in Breton) is the star of the show here, served plain, as a Bloody Mary–style shot, or with sauces such as raspberry vinegar. Other culinary creations include buckwheat chips with smoked haddock fishcakes. It doubles as a rocking bar.

L'As du Fallafel   Jewish €

(Map p254; 34 rue des Rosiers, 4e; takeaway €5.50-8.50; ⊙noon-midnight Sun-Thu, to 4pm Fri; ⏛; MSt-Paul) The lunchtime queue stretching halfway down the street from this place says it all. This Parisian favourite, 100% worth the inevitable wait, is the address for kosher, perfectly deep-fried falafel (chickpea balls) and turkey or lamb shawarma sandwiches. Do as every Parisian does and get them to take away.

Brasserie Bofinger   Brasserie €€

(Map p254; ☑01 42 72 87 82; www.bofingerparis.com; 5-7 rue de la Bastille, 4e; 2-/3-course menus from €33/38, seafood platters €29.90-125; ⊙noon-3pm & 6.30pm-midnight Mon-Fri, noon-3.30pm & 6.30pm-midnight Sat, noon-11pm Sun; ⏛; MBastille) Founded in 1864, Bofinger is reputedly Paris' oldest brasserie, though its polished art-nouveau brass, glass and mirrors indicates redecoration a few decades later. Alsatian-inspired specialities include five kinds of choucroute (sauerkraut), along with oysters and magnificent seafood platters. Ask for a seat downstairs beneath the coupole (stained-glass dome). Kids are catered for with a two-course children's menu (€11.90).

🍽 Menu Advice

Carte Menu, as in the written list of what's cooking, listed in the order you'd eat it: starter, main course, cheese then dessert. Note that an entrée is a starter, not the main course (as in the US).

Menu Not at all what it means in English, *le menu* in French is a *prix-fixe* menu: a multicourse meal at a fixed price. It's by far the best-value dining there is and most restaurants chalk one on the board. In some cases, particularly at neobistros, there is no *carte* – only a stripped-down *menu* with one or two choices.

À la carte Order whatever you fancy from the menu (as opposed to opting for a *prix-fixe* menu).

Formule Similar to a *menu*, *une formule* is a cheaper lunchtime option comprising a main plus starter or dessert. Wine or coffee is sometimes included.

Plat du jour Dish of the day, invariably good value.

Menu enfant Two- or three-course kids' meal (generally up to the age of 12) at a fixed price; usually includes a drink.

Menu dégustation Fixed-price tasting menu served in many top-end restaurants, consisting of five to seven modestly sized courses.

Rainettes   Modern French €€
(Map p254; ☑09 86 59 63 85; 5 rue Caron, 4e; 2-/3-course lunch menu €16/20, mains €25-29; ⊙6-11.45pm Tue-Thu, noon-11.45pm Fri-Sun; Ⓜ St-Paul) *Bar à grenouilles* (frog legs bar) Rainettes serves five types of frog legs platters, including Normandes (with apples, calvados and crème fraîche), Alsaciennes (Riesling, shallots and parsley), and Provençales (aubergine and garlic), as well as a daily vegetarian and meat dish. The street-level dining room has a *mur végétal* (vertical garden); there are another 30 tables in the cellar.

✖ Bastille & Eastern Paris

Septime   Modern French €€€
(Map p254; ☑01 43 67 38 29; www.septime-charonne.fr; 80 rue de Charonne, 11e; 4-course lunch menu €42, dinner menu €80, with wine €135; ⊙7.30-10pm Mon, 12.15-2pm & 7.30-10pm Tue-Fri; Ⓜ Charonne) The alchemists in Bertrand Grébaut's Michelin-starred kitchen produce truly beautiful creations, while blue-aproned waitstaff ensure culinary surprises are all pleasant. Each dish on the menu is a mere listing of three ingredients, while the mystery *carte blanche* dinner menu puts you in the hands of the innovative chef. Reservations require planning and perseverance – book at least three weeks in advance.

For a pre- or post-meal drink, drop by its nearby wine bar **Septime La Cave** (Map p254; ☑01 43 67 14 87; www.septime-charonne.fr; 3 rue Basfroi, 11e; ⊙4-11pm; Ⓜ Charonne). For stunning seafood tapas, its sister restaurant **Clamato** (Map p254; www.septime-charonne.fr; 80 rue de Charonne, 11e; tapas €7-19, dozen oysters €18-48; ⊙7-11pm Wed-Fri, noon-11pm Sat & Sun; Ⓜ Charonne) is right next door.

Le Bistrot Paul Bert   Bistro €€
(Map p254; ☑01 43 72 24 01; 18 rue Paul Bert, 11e; 2-/3-course lunch/dinner menu €19/41; ⊙noon-2pm & 7.30-11pm Tue-Sat; Ⓜ Faidherbe-Chaligny) When food writers list Paris' best bistros, Paul Bert's name consistently pops up. The timeless vintage decor and classic dishes like *steak-frites* and hazelnut-cream Paris-Brest pastry merit booking ahead. Look for its siblings in the same street: **L'Écailler du Bistrot** (Map p254; ☑01 43 72 76 77; 22 rue Paul Bert; weekday lunch menu €19, mains €17-38; ⊙noon-2.30pm & 7.30-11pm Tue-Sat; Ⓜ Faidherbe-Chaligny) for seafood; **La Cave Paul Bert** (Map p254; ☑01 58 53 30 92; 16 rue Paul Bert; ⊙noon-midnight, kitchen noon-2pm & 7.30-11.30pm; Ⓜ Faidherbe-Chaligny), a wine bar with small plates; and **Le 6 Paul Bert** (Map p254; ☑01 43 79 14 32; 6 rue Paul Bert; 6-course menu €60; ⊙7-11pm Tue-Sat; Ⓜ Faidherbe-Chaligny) for modern cuisine.

Passerini   Italian, Neobistro €€

(Map p254; ☑01 43 42 27 56; www.passerini. paris; 65 rue Traversière, 12e; lunch menus €24-48, dinner mains €16-28; ⓗ12.30-2.15pm & 7.30-10.30pm Tue-Fri, 7.30-10.30pm Sat, closed early May & Aug; ⓂLedru-Rollin) Rome native Giovanni Passerini is one of the finest Italian chefs cooking in Europe today, and Saturday evenings are the ultimate showcase of his talents, when small plates cost just €10 apiece. Delectable specialities include roast pigeon with smoked ricotta, and tagliolini with red Sicilian shrimp. Pastas are made fresh and are also sold at its adjoining deli, Pastificio Passerini.

Le Servan   Neobistro €€

(Map p254; ☑01 55 28 51 82; http://leservan. com; 32 rue St-Maur, 11e; 3-course lunch menu €27, mains €23-38; ⓗ7.30-10.30pm Mon, noon-2.30pm & 7.30-10.30pm Tue-Fri; ⓂVoltaire, Rue St-Maur, Père Lachaise) Ornate cream-coloured ceilings with moulded cornices and pastel murals, huge windows and wooden floors give this neighbourhood neobistro near Père Lachaise (p78) a light, airy feel on even the greyest Parisian day.

Confit suckling pig with cauliflower and satay sauce, sea snails and razor clams in cider broth, and mackerel with green papaya and coriander are among the kitchen's inventive creations.

Chez Paul   Bistro €€

(Map p254; ☑01 47 00 34 57; www.chezpaul. com; 13 rue de Charonne, 11e; 2-/3-course lunch menu €18/21, mains €17-27; ⓗnoon-12.30am; ⓂLedru-Rollin) This is Paris as your grand-mother knew it: chequered red-and-white napkins, faded photographs on the walls, old red banquettes and traditional French dishes such as pig trotters, *andouillette* (a feisty tripe sausage) and *tête de veau et cervelle* (calf head and brains). If offal isn't for you, alternatives include a steaming bowl of *pot au feu* (beef stew).

Blé Sucré   Bakery €

(Map p254; 7 rue Antoine Vollon, 12e; ⓗ7am-7.30pm Tue-Sat, to 1.30pm Sun; ⓂLedru-Rollin) Some of the flakiest, most wonderfully buttery croissants in Paris are baked at this exceptional *boulangerie* near the foodie nexus of Marché d'Aligre (p83). It also turns

Rainettes

From left: Septime (p132); Berthillon; Steak meal

out sourdoughs, focaccia with sea salt and rosemary, crunchy baguettes, and a slew of sweet treats including award-winning madeleine cakes. On weekends especially, queues stretch well out the door.

À la Biche au Bois　French €€

(Map p254; ☎01 43 43 34 38; 45 av Ledru-Rollin, 12e; 3-course lunch menu €32.80, mains €17.50-23.50; ⓧnoon-2.30pm & 7-10.45pm Tue-Fri, 7-10.45pm Mon & Sat; Ⓜ Gare de Lyon) Game, especially *la biche*, is the speciality of convivial 'doe in the woods', but dishes like foie gras and coq au vin also add to the countryside ambience, as do the green awning and potted plants out front. The cheeses and wines are excellent, but game aside, top honours have to go to the sensational *frites* (fries).

Dersou　Bistro €€€

(Map p254; ☎09 81 01 12 73; www.dersouparis.com; 21 rue St-Nicolas, 12e; 5-/6-/7-course tasting menu with paired cocktails €95/115/135, mains €15-30; ⓧ7.30pm-midnight Tue-Fri, noon-3pm & 7.30pm-midnight Sat, noon-3pm Sun; Ⓜ Ledru-Rollin) Much of the seating at this hot spot turning out creative fusion cuisine is at the counter, offering first-class views of chef Taku Sekine at work. Intricately constructed tasting menus are a highlight, with each course exquisitely paired with a bespoke cocktail. There are two seatings per night, at 7.30pm and 10.30pm; reservations are essential.

❽ The Islands

Berthillon　Ice Cream €

(Map p252; www.berthillon.fr; 31 rue St-Louis en l'Île, 4e; 1/2/3 scoops take away €3/4/6.50, eat-in €4.50/7.50/10.50; ⓧ10am-8pm Wed-Sun, closed Aug; Ⓜ Pont Marie) Founded here in 1954, this esteemed *glacier* (ice-cream maker) is still run by the same family today. Its 70-plus all-natural, chemical-free flavours include fruit sorbets such as blackcurrant or pink grapefruit, and richer ice creams made from fresh milk and eggs, such as salted caramel, *marrons glacés* (candied chestnuts) and Agenaise (Armagnac and prunes), along with seasonal flavours like gingerbread.

Café Saint Régis Cafe €

(Map p252; www.cafesaintregisparis.com; 6 rue Jean du Bellay, 4e; breakfast & snacks €3.50-14.50, mains €18-32; ⊗kitchen 8am-midnight, bar to 2am; ⊛; MPont Marie) Waiters in long white aprons, a white ceramic-tiled interior and retro vintage decor make hip Le Saint Régis (as regulars call it) a deliciously Parisian hang-out any time of day – from breakfast pastries to mid-morning pancakes, lunchtime salads and burgers and early-evening oyster platters. Come midnight it morphs into a late-night hotspot.

Sequana Modern French €€€

(Map p250; ☑01 43 29 78 81; http://sequana. paris; 72 quai des Orfèvres, 1er; 2-/3-course lunch menu €24/32, 4-/6-course dinner menu €47/67, with wine €70/92; ⊗noon-2.30pm & 7.30-11pm Tue-Fri, 7.30-11pm Sat; ⊛; MPont Neuf) A sleek new addition to the Île de la Cité, with a chic aqua-and-grey dining room, Sequana sits near its southwestern tip overlooking the Seine (the restaurant's name comes from the Gallo-Roman name

of the goddess of the river). Artistic modern French dishes are influenced by chef Eugénie's Senegalese heritage. Vegetarian menus are available; kids under 12 dine for half-price.

Le Caveau du Palais Modern French €€

(Map p250; ☑01 43 26 04 28; www.caveaudu palais.fr; 19 place Dauphine, 1er; mains €21-28; ⊗noon-2.30pm & 7-10pm; MPont Neuf) Even when the western Île de la Cité shows few other signs of life, the Caveau's half-timbered dining areas and (weather permitting) al fresco terrace are packed with diners tucking into bountiful fresh fare: scallop carpaccio with pickled beetroot and lime, deconstructed red-onion and black-olive tapenade sandwich with parmesan, and chorizo- and cilantro-stuffed chicken leg with roast tomato mousse.

More informal dishes are served at its adjacent wine bar, **Le Bar du Caveau** (www.barducaveau.fr; 17 place Dauphine, 1er; ⊗bar 8am-6.30pm Mon-Fri, kitchen noon-4pm Mon-Fri).

⊗ Latin Quarter

Restaurant AT — Gastronomy €€€

(Map p252; ☑01 56 81 94 08; www.atsushitana
ka.com; 4 rue du Cardinal Lemoine, 5e; 6-course
lunch menu €55, 12-course dinner tasting menu
€95; ☺12.15-2pm & 8-9.30pm Tue-Sat; Ⓜ Cardinal Lemoine) Trained by some of the biggest
names in gastronomy (Pierre Gagnaire
included), chef Atsushi Tanaka showcases
abstract artlike masterpieces incorporating
rare ingredients (charred bamboo, kohlrabi
turnip cabbage, juniper berry powder, wild
purple fennel, Nepalese Timut pepper) in
a blank-canvas-style dining space on stunning outsized plates. Just off the entrance,
steps lead to his cellar wine bar, **Bar à Vins
AT** (dishes €12-16; ☺7pm-2am Tue-Sun).

Sola — Fusion €€€

(Map p252; ☑09 67 61 97 03; www.restaurant-
sola.com; 12 rue de l'Hôtel Colbert, 5e; menus
lunch €65, dinner €98; ☺6.30-9.30pm Mon-
Thu, noon-1.30pm & 6.30-9.30pm Fri & Sat;
Ⓜ St-Michel) Michelin-starred chef Hiroki
Yoshitake combines French technique
with Japanese sensibility, resulting in
gorgeous signature creations (such as
miso-marinated foie gras on *feuille de
brick* served on sliced tree trunk). The
artful presentations and attentive service
make this a perfect choice for a romantic meal – go for the full experience and
reserve a table in the vaulted stone dining
room downstairs.

Shakespeare & Company Café — Cafe €

(Map p252; www.shakespeareandcompany.com;
2 rue St-Julien le Pauvre, 5e; dishes €3.50-10.50;
☺9.30am-7pm Mon-Fri, to 8pm Sat & Sun;
🛜☑🚹; Ⓜ St-Michel) ⌀ Instant history was
made when this light-filled, literary-inspired
cafe opened in 2015 adjacent to magical
bookshop Shakespeare & Company
(p155), designed from long-lost sketches
to fulfil a dream of late bookshop founder
George Whitman from the 1960s. Its
primarily vegetarian menu (with vegan
and gluten-free dishes available) includes
homemade bagels, rye bread, soups, salads
and pastries, plus Parisian-roasted Café
Lomi (p174) coffee.

Meal preparation at La Tour d'Argent (p138)

Café de la Nouvelle Mairie Cafe €

(Map p252; ☑01 44 07 04 41; 19 rue des Fossés
St-Jacques, 5e; mains €9-19; ☺kitchen noon-
2.30pm & 8-10.30pm Mon-Thu, 8-10pm Fri;
Ⓜ Cardinal Lemoine) Shhhh...just around
the corner from the Panthéon but hidden
away on a small, fountained square, this
narrow wine bar is a neighbourhood secret,
serving blackboard-chalked natural wines
by the glass and delicious seasonal bistro
fare from oysters and ribs (*à la française*)
to grilled lamb sausage over lentils. It takes
reservations for dinner but not lunch –
arrive early.

Le Coupe-Chou French €€

(Map p252; ☑01 46 33 68 69; www.lecoupechou.
com; 9 & 11 rue de Lanneau, 5e; 2-/3-course menus
€27/33, mains €17.50-29.50; ☺noon-1.30pm
& 7-10.30pm Mon-Sat, 7-10.30pm Sun Sep-Jun,
7-10.30pm Jul & Aug; Ⓜ Maubert-Mutualité) This
maze of candlelit rooms inside a vine-clad
17th-century townhouse is overwhelmingly
romantic. Ceilings are beamed, furnishings
are antique, open fireplaces crackle and
background classical music mingles with
the intimate chatter of diners. As in the
days when Marlene Dietrich dined here, advance reservations are essential. Timeless
French dishes include Burgundy snails,
steak tartare and bœuf bourguignon.

Les Papilles Bistro €€

(Map p252; ☑01 43 25 20 79; www.lespapilles
paris.fr; 30 rue Gay Lussac, 5e; 2-/3-course
menus from €22/33, mains €17-27; ☺noon-
2pm & 7-10.30pm Tue-Sat; Ⓜ Raspail or RER
Luxembourg) This hybrid bistro, wine cellar
and *épicerie* (specialist grocer) with a
sunflower-yellow façade is one of those
fabulous Parisian dining experiences.
Meals are served at simply dressed tables
wedged beneath bottle-lined walls, and
fare is market driven: each weekday cooks
up a different *marmite du marché* (market
casserole). But what really sets it apart is
its exceptional wine list.

It only seats around 15 people; reserve a
few days in advance to guarantee a table.
After your meal, stock your own *cave* (wine
cellar) at Les Papilles' *cave à vins*.

🍽 The Five Basic Cheese Types

The choices on offer at a *fromagerie*
(cheese shop) can be overwhelming,
but vendors are usually very generous
with their guidance and pairing advice.

Fromage à pâte demi-dure 'Semi-hard
cheese' means uncooked, pressed
cheese. Among the finest are Tomme
de Savoie, Cantal, St-Nectaire and
Ossau-Iraty.

Fromage à pâte dure 'Hard cheese'
is always cooked and then pressed.
Popular varieties are Beaufort, Comté,
Emmental and Mimolette.

Fromage à pâte molle 'Soft cheese' is
moulded or rind-washed. Camembert
and Brie de Meaux are both made from
raw cow's milk. Munster, Chaource,
Langres and Époisses de Bourgogne are
rind-washed, fine-textured cheeses.

Fromage à pâte persillée 'Marbled' or
'blue cheese' is so called because the
veins often resemble *persille* (parsley).
Roquefort is a ewe's-milk veined cheese
that is to many the king of French
cheeses. Fourme d'Ambert is a mild
cow's-milk cheese from Rhône-Alpes.
Bleu du Haut Jura is a mild, blue-veined
mountain cheese.

Fromage de chèvre 'Goat's-milk
cheese' is usually creamy and both
sweet and slightly salty when fresh,
but hardens and gets much saltier as
it matures. Among the best varieties
are Ste-Maure de Touraine, Crottin de
Chavignol, Cabécou de Rocamadour
and soft, slightly aged Chabichou.

Le Comptoir du Panthéon   Cafe €

(Map p252; ☑01 43 54 75 36; 5 rue Soufflot, 5e; salads €11-13.50, mains €13-17.50; ⊘kitchen 7am-11pm Mon-Sat, 8am-11pm Sun; 🛜; Ⓜ Cardinal Lemoine or RER Luxembourg) Enormous, creative meal-size salads are the reason to choose this as a dining spot. Magnificently placed across from the domed Panthéon on the shady side of the street, its pavement terrace is big, busy and quintessentially Parisian – turn your head away from Voltaire's burial place and the Eiffel Tower pops into view. The bar closes at 1.45am every night.

La Tour d'Argent   Gastronomy €€€

(Map p252; ☑01 43 54 23 31; www.latourdargent.com; 15 quai de la Tournelle, 5e; mains €78-158; ⊘12.30-2pm & 7-10pm Tue-Sat, closed Aug; Ⓜ Cardinal Lemoine) The venerable Michelin-starred 'Silver Tower' is famous for its *caneton* (duckling), rooftop garden with glimmering Notre Dame views and fabulous history harking back to 1582 – from Henry III's inauguration of the first fork in France to inspiration for the winsome animated film *Ratatouille*. Its wine cellar is one of Paris' best; dining is dressy and exceedingly fine.

✪ St-Germain & Les Invalides

Restaurant Guy Savoy   Gastronomy €€€

(Map p250; ☑01 43 80 40 61; www.guysavoy.com; Monnaie de Paris, 11 quai de Conti, 6e; lunch menu via online booking €110, 12-/18-course tasting menus €420/490; ⊘noon-2pm & 7-10.30pm Tue-Fri, 7-10.30pm Sat; Ⓜ Pont Neuf) If you're considering visiting a three-Michelin-star temple of gastronomy, this should certainly be on your list. The world-famous chef needs no introduction (he trained Gordon Ramsay, among others) but now his flagship, entered via a red-carpeted staircase, is ensconced in the gorgeously refurbished neoclassical **Monnaie de Paris** (☑01 40 46 56 66; www.monnaiedeparis.fr). Monumental

cuisine to match includes Savoy icons like artichoke and black-truffle soup with layered brioche.

Look out for Guy Savoy's casual courtyard brasserie-cafe on the same site. Or try his famed brioche for a fraction of the price in his eponymous restaurant by heading around the corner to his brioche boutique, **Goût de Brioche** (Map p250; www.goutdebrioche.com; 54 rue Mazarine, 6e; brioche €5-7; ⊘11am-6pm Wed-Fri, 10.30am-6pm Sat, 10.30am-4pm Sun; Ⓜ Odéon).

Restaurant David Toutain   Gastronomy €€€

(Map p246; ☑01 45 50 11 10; http://davidtoutain.com; 29 rue Surcouf, 7e; 3-course lunch menu €55, 9-/15-course tasting menus €80/110; ⊘noon-2pm & 8-10pm Mon-Fri; Ⓜ Invalides) Prepare to be wowed: David Toutain pushes the envelope at his eponymous Michelin-starred restaurant with some of the most creative high-end cooking in Paris. Mystery degustation courses include unlikely combinations such as smoked eel in green-apple-and-black-sesame mousse, cauliflower, white chocolate and coconut truffles, or candied celery and truffled rice pudding with artichoke praline (stunning wine pairings available).

Tomy & Co   Gastronomy €€

(Map p246; ☑01 45 51 46 93; 22 rue Surcouf, 7e; 2-course lunch menu €25, 3-course dinner menu €45, tasting menu €65, with paired wines €100; ⊘noon-2pm & 7.30-9.30pm Mon-Fri; Ⓜ Invalides) The talk-of-the-town address of the moment is Tomy Gousset's inaugural restaurant (book ahead). Gousset previously cooked in some of Paris' top kitchens and now works his magic here on inspired seasonal dishes like roast duck with candied yellow beets and pickled grapes, and pork neck with spinach, black olives, micro herbs and raw mushrooms, using produce from his organic garden. Spectacular desserts are also seasonally inflected and might include chocolate tart with fresh figs, Cambodian palm sugar and fig ice cream.

Bouillon Racine   Brasserie €€

(Map p252; ☏01 44 32 15 60; www.bouillon racine.com; 3 rue Racine, 6e; weekday 2-course lunch menu €17, menus €33-46, mains €18.50-29; ⊙noon-11pm; ⏪; Ⓜ Cluny-La Sorbonne) Inconspicuously situated in a quiet street, this heritage-listed 1906 art-nouveau 'soup kitchen', with mirrored walls, floral motifs and ceramic tiling, was built in 1906 to feed market workers. Despite the magnificent interior, the food – inspired by age-old recipes – is no afterthought but superbly executed (stuffed, spit-roasted suckling pig, pork shank in Rodenbach red beer, scallops and shrimps with lobster coulis).

Finish off your foray into gastronomic history with an old-fashioned sherbet. Two-course children's menus (€14.50) mean kids don't miss out.

L'Avant Comptoir du Marché   Tapas €

(Map p252; 15 rue Lobineau, 6e; tapas €3.50-19; ⊙noon-11pm; Ⓜ Mabillon) The latest of Yves Camdeborde's casual 'small plates' eateries is this porcine-specialist tapas bar wedged in one corner of the Marché St-Germain covered market–shopping complex. A flying, fire-engine-red pig is the ceiling's centrepiece, surrounded by suspended menus listing dishes such as Bayonne ham croquettes, Bigorre pâté, and shots of Béarnaise pig's blood; wines are chalked on the blackboard. No reservations.

Camdeborde's neighbouring addresses include bistro **Le Comptoir du Relais** (Map p252; ☏01 44 27 07 97; www.hotel-paris-relais -saint-germain.com; 9 Carrefour de l'Odéon, 6e; lunch mains €14-28, dinner menu €60; ⊙noon-6pm & 8.30-11.30pm Mon-Fri, noon-11pm Sat & Sun; Ⓜ Odéon), tapas bar **L'Avant Comptoir** (Map p252; www.hotel-paris-relais-saint-germain. com; 3 Carrefour de l'Odéon, 6e; tapas €4-10; ⊙noon-midnight; Ⓜ Odéon) and seafood tapas bar **L'Avant Comptoir de la Mer** (Map p252; www.hotel-paris-relais-saint-germain.com; 3 Carrefour de l'Odéon, 6e; tapas €5-25; ⊙11am-11pm; Ⓜ Odéon).

Semilla   Neobistro €€

(Map p250; ☏01 43 54 34 50; www.semilla paris.com; 54 rue de Seine, 6e; lunch menu €23, 6-course menu €66, mains €16-28; ⊙12.30-2.30pm & 7-11pm Mon-Sat, 12.30-2.30pm & 7-10pm Sun, closed early–mid-Aug; Ⓜ Mabillon) Stark concrete, exposed pipes and an open kitchen (in front of which you can book front-row 'chef seats') set the factory-style scene for edgy, modern, daily changing dishes such as pork spare ribs with sweet potato and cinnamon, mushrooms in hazelnut butter, and trout with passionfruit and ginger (all suppliers are listed). Desserts here are outstanding. Be sure to book.

If you haven't made a reservation, head to its adjoining walk-in wine bar, **Freddy's** (small plates €6-13; ⊙kitchen 12.30-3pm & 6-11pm, bar noon-midnight), which serves small tapas-style plates.

Chez Dumonet   Bistro €€

(Joséphine; Map p246; ☏01 45 48 52 40; 117 rue du Cherche Midi, 6e; mains €23-43; ⊙noon-2.30pm & 7.30-9.30pm Mon-Fri; Ⓜ Duroc) Fondly known by its former name, Joséphine, this lace-curtained, mosaic-tiled place with white-clothed tables inside and out is the Parisian bistro of many people's dreams, serving timeless standards such as confit of duck, *millefeuille* of pigeon, and grilled *châteaubriand* steak with Béarnaise sauce. Be sure to order its enormous signature Grand Marnier soufflé at the start of your meal.

Poilâne   Bakery €

(Map p246; www.poilane.com; 8 rue du Cherche Midi, 6e; ⊙7am-8.30pm Mon-Sat; Ⓜ Sèvres-Babylone) Pierre Poilâne opened his *boulan-gerie* upon arriving from Normandy in 1932. Today his granddaughter Apollonia runs the company, which still turns out wood-fired, rounded sourdough loaves made with stone-milled flour and Guérande sea salt. A clutch of other outlets include one in the **15e** (Map p246; 49 bd de Grenelle, 15e; ⊙7am-8.30pm Tue-Sun; Ⓜ Dupleix).

Au Pied de Fouet   Bistro €

(Map p250; ☑01 42 96 59 10; www.aupied defouet.com; 3 rue St-Benoît, 6e; mains €9-12.50; ⊗noon-2.30pm & 7-11pm Mon-Sat; ⓂSt-Germain des Prés) At this tiny, lively, cherry-red-coloured bistro, wholly classic dishes such as *entrecôte* (steak), *confit de canard* with creamy potatoes and *foie de volailles sauté* (pan-fried chicken livers) are astonishingly good value. Round off your meal with a *tarte Tatin*, wine-soaked prunes, or deliciously rich *fondant au chocolat*.

Polidor   French €€

(Map p252; www.polidor.com; 41 rue Monsieur le Prince, 6e; menus €22-35, mains €11-25; ⊗noon-2.30pm & 7pm-12.30am Mon-Sat, noon-2.30pm & 7-11pm Sun; ⏁; ⓂOdéon) A meal at this quintessentially Parisian *crèmerie-restaurant* is like a trip to Victor Hugo's Paris: the restaurant and its decor date from 1845. *Menus* of family-style French cuisine ensure a stream of diners eager to sample *bœuf bourguignon*, *blanquette de veau à l'ancienne* (veal in white sauce) and Polidor's famous *tarte Tatin*. No credit cards or reservations (expect to wait).

Midnight in Paris fans might recognise it as the place where Owen Wilson's character meets Hemingway (who dined here in his day). More than 20,000 bottles are stocked in its wine cellar.

À la Petite Chaise   French €€

(Map p246; ☑01 42 22 13 35; www.alapetite chaise.fr; 36 rue de Grenelle, 6e; 2-/3-course lunch menus €25/33, 3-course dinner menu €26, mains €21; ⊗noon-2pm & 7-11pm; ⓂSèvres-Babylone) Paris' oldest restaurant hides behind an iron gate that's been here since it opened in 1680, when wine merchant Georges Rameau served food to the public to accompany his wares. Classical decor and cuisine (onion soup, foie gras, duck, lamb and unexpected delights such as venison terrine with hazelnuts) make it worth a visit above and beyond its history.

L'Amaryllis de Gérard Mulot   Pastries €

(Map p252; www.gerard-mulot.com; 12 rue des Quatre Vents, 6e; dishes €6.60-20, lunch menu €25; ⊗11am-6.30pm Tue-Sat; ⓂOdéon) Pastry maestro Gérard Mulot has three boutiques

La Rotonde Montparnasse

KATALENKAVA/SHUTTERSTOCK ©

in Paris, including one on nearby **rue de Seine** (Map p252; www.gerard-mulot.com; 76 rue de Seine, 6e; ◷6.45am-8pm Thu-Tue; Ⓜ Mabillon), but this branch also incorporates a *salon de thé* (tea room) where you can sit down to savour his famous fruit tarts on the spot. Other dishes include quiches, gourmet salads, omelettes and more filling lunch meals including a meat or fish *suggestion du chef*.

Besnier   Bakery €

(Map p246; 40 rue de Bourgogne, 7e; ◷7am-8pm Mon-Sat, closed Aug; Ⓜ Varenne) You can watch baguettes being made through the viewing window of this award-winning *boulangerie*. Fig bread made from chestnut flour is a speciality. Expect to queue around lunchtime.

⊗ Montparnasse & Southern Paris

Le Casse Noix   Modern French €€

(Map p246; ☑01 45 66 09 01; www.le-cassenoix. fr; 56 rue de la Fédération, 15e; 3-course menus €34; ◷noon-2.30pm & 7-10.30pm Mon-Fri; Ⓜ Bir Hakeim) Proving that a location footsteps from the Eiffel Tower doesn't mean compromising on quality, quantity or authenticity, 'the nutcracker' is a neighbourhood gem with a cosy retro interior, affordable prices, and exceptional cuisine that changes by season and by the inspiration of owner-chef Pierre Olivier Lenormand, who has honed his skills in some of Paris' most fêted kitchens. Book ahead.

Le Beurre Noisette   Neobistro €€

(Map p246; ☑01 48 56 82 49; www.restaurant beurrenoisette.com; 68 rue Vasco de Gama, 15e; 2-/3-course lunch menus €23/32, 3-/5-/7-course dinner menus €36/45/55, mains lunch/dinner €18/21; ◷noon-2pm & 7-10.30pm Tue-Sat; Ⓜ Lourmel) *Beurre noisette* (brown butter sauce, named for its hazelnut colour)

features in dishes such as scallops with cauliflower purée, and tender *bœuf fondante* with artichokes, courgette and carrot at pedigreed chef Thierry Blanqui's neighbourhood neobistro. Other treats include homemade blood sausage with apple compote. Filled with locals, the chocolate-toned dining room is wonderfully convivial – be sure to book. Fantastic value.

Le Ciel de Paris   French €€€

(Map p246; ☑01 40 64 77 64; www.cieldeparis. com; Level 56, Tour Montparnasse, 33 av du Maine, 14e; menus lunch/dinner from €30/68, mains €36-56; ◷kitchen 7.30-11am, noon-2.30pm & 7-11pm, bar 7.30am-1am; Ⓜ Montparnasse Bienvenüe) Views don't get much better than 'the sky of Paris', the Tour Montparnasse's 56th-floor restaurant, accessed by private lift/elevator. Starters include snails and pigs' trotters; seafood is a speciality. The gastronomic Grand Écran menu (€136), available at dinner daily and Sunday lunch, includes a guaranteed window table and bottle of Champagne per person.

La Rotonde
Montparnasse   Brasserie €€

(Map p246; ☑01 43 26 48 26; www.rotonde montparnasse.com; 105 bd du Montparnasse, 6e; 3-course menu €44, mains €16-48, seafood platters €29.50-118.50; ◷kitchen noon-3pm & 7-11pm, bar 6am-2am; Ⓜ Vavin) Opened in 1911 and recently restored to its former glory, La Rotonde may be awash with the same Les Montparnos history as its famous brasserie neighbours like Le Select, but the real reason to come is for the superior food. Meat comes from Parisian butcher extraordinaire Hugo Desnoyer, salmon and chicken are organic, and brasserie classics are cooked to perfection.

Extravagant seafood platters are piled high with prawns, lobsters, crabs and shellfish.

Swarovski Christmas tree at Galeries Lafayette (p148)

MATEJ KASTELIC/SHUTTERSTOCK ©

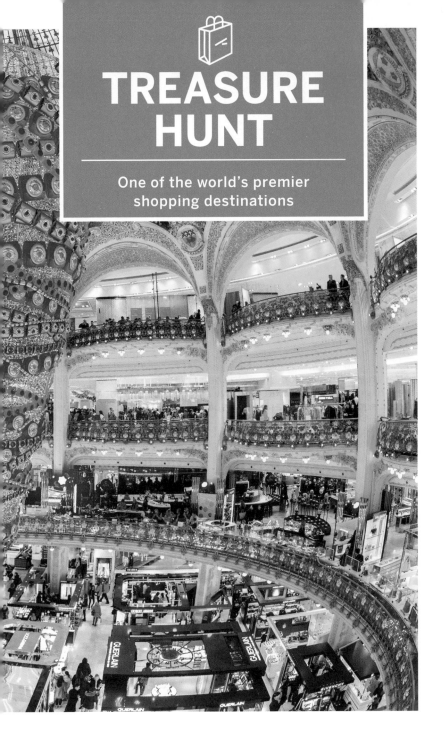

TREASURE HUNT

One of the world's premier
shopping destinations

Treasure Hunt

Paris has it all: broad boulevards lined with flagship fashion houses and international labels, famous grand magasins (department stores) and fabulous markets, along with tiny speciality shops and one-off boutiques. Fashion is Paris' forte. Browse haute couture creations, cutting-edge designs and original streetwear, along with statement-making accessories and adorable children's wear. Parisian fashion doesn't have to break the bank: you can find fantastic bargains at secondhand boutiques and outlet shops. But fashion is just the beginning. Paris is also a treasure chest of gourmet food, wine, tea, new and antiquarian books, stationery, classic and cutting-edge art, art supplies, antiques and collectables.

In This Section

Champs-Élysées &
Grands Boulevards 148

Louvre & Les Halles 149

Montmartre & Northern Paris............ 151

Le Marais, Ménilmontant
& Belleville 151

Bastille & Eastern Paris 153

The Islands 154

Latin Quarter 155

St-Germain & Les Invalides................156

Useful Phrases

○ Look for signs indicating *cabines d'essayage* (fitting rooms).

○ Most shops offer free (and beautiful) gift wrapping – ask for *un paquet cadeau*.

○ A *ticket de caisse* (receipt) is essential for returning/exchanging an item (within one month of purchase).

○ If you're happy browsing, tell sales staff *Je regarde* (I'm just looking).

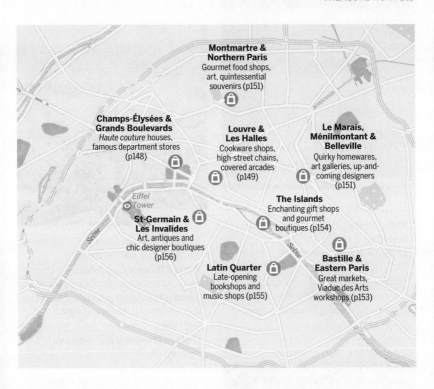

**Montmartre &
Northern Paris**
Gourmet food shops,
art, quintessential
souvenirs (p151)

**Champs-Élysées &
Grands Boulevards**
Haute couture houses,
famous department stores
(p148)

**Louvre &
Les Halles**
Cookware shops,
high-street chains,
covered arcades
(p149)

**Le Marais,
Ménilmontant &
Belleville**
Quirky homewares,
art galleries, up-and-
coming designers
(p151)

*Eiffel
Tower*

**St-Germain &
Les Invalides**
Art, antiques and
chic designer boutiques
(p156)

The Islands
Enchanting gift shops
and gourmet
boutiques (p154)

Latin Quarter
Late-opening
bookshops and
music shops (p155)

**Bastille &
Eastern Paris**
Great markets,
Viaduc des Arts
workshops (p153)

Opening Hours

Generally 10am and 7pm Monday to Saturday; in 'tourist zones', such as the Grands Boulevards and Champs-Élysées, shops also open similar hours on Sunday. Smaller shops often shut on Monday and/or close from around noon to 2pm. Larger stores hold *nocturnes* (late-night shopping), usually Thursday, until around 10pm.

Sales

Paris' twice-yearly *soldes* (sales) generally last five to six weeks. Winter sales start around mid-January and summer sales start around mid-June.

The Best...

Experience Paris' best shopping

Fashion Boutiques

Andrea Crews (p152) Bold art and fashion collective.

La Boutique Extraordinaire (p153) Exquisite hand-knitted garments.

Antoine et Lili (pictured below; p152) All the colours of the rainbow in this iconic boutique.

Pigalle (p151) Leading Parisian menswear brand.

For Kids

Smallable Concept Store (p161) One-stop shop for babies, children and teens.

Boîtes à Musique Anna Joliet (p149) Swiss music boxes to enchant in the Palais Royale.

Album (p156) Superb collection of *bandes desinées* (graphic novels) and related collectibles.

Finger in the Nose (p159) Streetwise Parisian label for kids.

Accessories

JB Guanti (pictured above; p158) Gorgeous gloves.

Marie Mercié (p159) Handmade hats.

Alexandra Sojfer (p161) Handcrafted umbrellas.

Concept Stores

Gab & Jo (p156) The country's first concept store stocking only French-made items.

Merci (pictured above; p151) Fabulously fashionable and unique: all profits go to a children's charity in Madagascar.

Colette (p149) Uber-hip designer fashion and basement 'water bar'.

Hermès (p158) Housed in an art deco swimming pool.

Gourmet Shops

Place de la Madeleine (p149) Single-item specialist shops and famous emporiums.

La Manufacture de Chocolat (p153) Alain Ducasse's bean-to-bar chocolate factory.

Fromagerie Goncourt (p151) Contemporary *fromagerie* unusually styled like a boutique.

La Dernière Goutte (p158) Wines from small, independent French producers.

★ Lonely Planet's Top Choices

Le Bonbon au Palais (p155) Artisan sweets from regions throughout France.

Didier Ludot (p149) Couture creations of yesteryear.

E Dehillerin (p149) Paris' professional chefs stock up at this 1820-opened cookware shop.

La Grande Épicerie de Paris (p156) Glorious food emporium.

Magasin Sennelier (p157) Historic art-supply shop with paints, canvases and paraphernalia galore.

Shakespeare & Company (pictured above; p155) A 'wonderland of books', as Henry Miller described it.

⑥ Champs-Élysées & Grands Boulevards

Galeries Lafayette
Department Store

(Map p246; http://haussmann.galerieslafayette.com; 40 bd Haussmann, 9e; ⊗9.30am-8.30pm Mon-Sat, 11am-7pm Sun; 🛜; MChaussée d'Antin or RER Auber) Grande-dame department store Galeries Lafayette is spread across the main store (whose magnificent stained-glass dome is over a century old), **men's store** (bd Haussmann, 9e; ⊗9.30am-8.30pm Mon-Sat, 11am-7pm Sun; 🛜; MChaussée d'Antin or RER Auber), and **homewares store** (bd Haussmann, 9e; ⊗9.30am-8.30pm Mon-Sat, 11am-7pm Sun; 🛜; MHavre Caumartin or RER Auber) with a **gourmet emporium** (bd Haussmann, 9e; ⊗8.30am-9.30pm Mon-Sat; MHavre Caumartin or RER Auber).

Catch modern art in the first-floor **gallery** (www.galeriedesgaleries.com; 40 bd Haussmann, 9e; ⊗11am-7pm Tue-Sat; MChaussée d'Antin or RER Auber) **FREE**, take in a **fashion show** (🕿bookings 01 42 82 81 98; 40 bd Haussmann, 9e; ⊗3pm Fri Mar-Jun & Sep-Dec by reservation;

MChaussée d'Antin or RER Auber), ascend to a free, windswept rooftop panorama, or take a break at one of its 24 restaurants and cafes.

The main store will stay open during renovations by architect Amanda Levete's studio AL_A. On the av des Champs-Élysées, a new Galeries Lafayette store is under construction and is expected to open in late 2018.

À la Mère de Famille
Food & Drinks

(Map p250; www.lameredefamille.com; 35 rue du Faubourg Montmartre, 9e; ⊗9.30am-8pm Mon-Sat, 10am-7.30pm Sun; MLe Peletier) Founded in 1761, this is the original location of Paris' oldest chocolatier. Its beautiful belle époque façade is as enchanting as the rainbow of sweets, caramels and chocolates inside.

Guerlain
Perfume

(Map p246; 🗹spa 01 45 62 11 21; www.guerlain.com; 68 av des Champs-Élysées, 8e; ⊗10.30am-8pm; MFranklin D Roosevelt) Guerlain is Paris' most famous parfumerie, and its shop (dating from 1912) is one of the most beautiful in the city. With its shimmering mirror and

Galeries Lafayette

marble art deco interior, it's a reminder of the former glory of the Champs-Élysées. For total indulgence, make an appointment at its heavenly spa.

ⓐ Louvre & Les Halles

Legrand Filles & Fils   Food & Drinks
(Map p250; www.caves-legrand.com; 1 rue de la Banque, 2e; ⊙11am-7pm Mon, 10am-7.30pm Tue-Sat; MBourse) Tucked inside Galerie Vivienne since 1880, Legrand sells fine wine and all the accoutrements: cork-screws, tasting glasses, decanters etc. It also has a fancy wine bar, *école du vin* (wine school; courses from €60 for two hours) and *éspace dégustation* with several tastings a month, including ones accompanied by live concerts; check its website for details.

Didier Ludot   Fashion & Accessories
(Map p250; ☑01 42 96 06 56; www.didierludot. fr; 24 Galerie de Montpensier, 1er; ⊙10.30am-7pm Mon-Sat; MPalais Royal–Musée du Louvre) In the rag trade since 1975, collector Didier Ludot sells the city's finest couture creations of yesteryear, hosts exhibitions and has published a book portraying the evolution of the little black dress.

Colette   Gifts & Souvenirs
(Map p246; www.colette.fr; 213 rue St-Honoré, 1er; ⊙11am-7pm Mon-Sat; MTuileries) Check the Parisian fashion forecast at this con-cept store. Browse designer fashion on the 1st floor, and streetwear, limited-edition sneakers, art books, music, gadgets and other high-tech, inventive and/or plain unusual items on the ground floor. End with a drink in the basement 'water bar' and pick up free design magazines and flyers for some of the city's hippest happenings.

E Dehillerin   Homewares
(Map p250; www.e-dehillerin.fr; 18-20 rue Coquillière, 1er; ⊙9am-12.30pm & 2-6pm Mon, 9am-6pm Tue-Sat; MLes Halles) Founded in 1820, this extraordinary two-level store – more like an old-fashioned warehouse than a shiny, chic boutique – carries an

 Place de la Madeleine

Ultragourmet food shops garland place de la Madeleine; many have in-house dining options. Notable names include truffle dealers **La Maison de la Truffe** (Map p246; ☑01 42 65 53 22; www.maison -de-la-truffe.com; 19 place de la Madeleine, 8e; ⊙noon-10.30pm Mon-Sat; MMade-leine); mustard specialist **Boutique Maille** (Map p246; www.maille.com; 6 place de la Madeleine, 8e; ⊙10am-7pm Mon-Sat, 11am-6pm Sun; MMadeleine); Paris' most famous caterer, **Fauchon** (Map p246; ☑01 70 39 38 00; www.fauchon.fr; 26 & 30 place de la Madeleine, 8e; ⊙8am-8.30pm Mon-Sat; MMadeleine), with delicacies from foie gras to jams, chocolates and pastries; and extravagant chocolate sculptures at **Patrick Roger** (Map p246; www. patrickroger.com; 3 place de la Madeleine, 8e; ⊙10.30am-7.30pm; MMadeleine). 'Honey house' **La Maison du Miel** (Map p246; ☑01 47 42 26 70; www.maisondumiel.com; 24 rue Vignon, 9e; ⊙9.30am-7pm Mon-Sat; MMadeleine) is nearby.

Chocolate sculptures and gift boxes at Patrick Roger
EQROY/SHUTTERSTOCK ©

incredible selection of professional-quality *matériel de cuisine* (kitchenware). Poultry scissors, turbot poacher, professional copper cookware or an Eiffel Tower–shaped cake tin – it's all here.

Boîtes à Musique Anna Joliet   Gifts & Souvenirs
(Map p250; Palais Royal, 9 rue de Beaujolais, 1er; ⊙noon-7pm Tue-Sat; MBourse) This wonderful shop at the northern end of the

Top Five Paris Souvenirs

Artistic Gems

At major museums, the Boutiques de Musées have painting-and-frame services: browse masterpieces, choose a frame and have replicas mailed to your home.

Perfume

Browse Parisian perfume at new innovators or department stores, or buy a bottle of Champs-Élysées from Guerlain's beautiful premises (p148) on its namesake street.

Chocolate

Exquisite chocolate boutiques throughout the city include star chef Alain Ducasse's bean-to-bar chocolate factory, La Manufacture de Chocolat (p153).

Candles

Candle-makers span from the world's oldest, Cire Trudon (p157), to La Note Parisienne's designs for each arrondissement, at Gab & Jo (p156).

Scarves

The ultimate Parisian accessory, whatever the season. Timeless silk designs are created by Hermès (p158).

Jardin du Palais Royal (p101) specialises in music boxes, new and old, from Switzerland.

Antoine   Fashion & Accessories
(Map p250; www.antoine1745.com; 10 av de l'Opéra, 1er; ⊘10.30am-1pm & 2-6.30pm Mon-Sat; Ⓜ Pyramides, Palais Royal–Musée du Louvre) Antoine has been the Parisian master of bespoke canes, umbrellas, fans and gloves since 1745.

⊙ Montmartre & Northern Paris

Fromagerie Alléosse   Cheese
(http://fromage-alleosse.com; 13 rue Poncelet, 17e; ⊘9am-1pm & 3-7pm Tue-Fri, 9am-7pm Sat, 9am-1pm Sun; Ⓜ Ternes) Alléosse is Paris' only *fromagerie* with its own cheese-ripening *caves* (cellars) spanning 300 sq metres with four separate environments. Its 250-plus cheeses are grouped into five main categories: *fromage de chèvre* (goat's-milk cheese), *fromage à pâte persillée* (veined or blue cheese), *fromage à pâte molle* (soft cheese), *fromage à pâte demi-dure* (semihard cheese) and *fromage à pâte dure* (hard cheese).

Belle du Jour   Fashion & Accessories
(Map p249; www.belle-de-jour.fr; 7 rue Tardieu, 18e; ⊘11am-1pm & 2-7pm Tue-Fri, 11am-1pm & 2-6pm Sat; Ⓜ Anvers) Be whisked back in time to the elegance of belle époque Paris at this Montmartre shop specialising in perfume bottles. Gorgeous 19th-century atomisers, smelling salts and powder boxes in engraved or enamelled Bohemian, Baccarat and Saint-Louis crystal share shelf space with more contemporary designs. Whether you're after art deco or art nouveau, pink-frosted or painted glass, it's here.

Pigalle   Fashion & Accessories
(Map p249; www.pigalle-paris.com; 7 rue Henry Monnier, 9e; ⊘noon-8pm Mon-Sat, 2-8pm Sun; Ⓜ St-Georges) Blend in with local hipsters with a hoodie emblazoned with the B&W Pigalle logo from this leading Parisian menswear

brand, created by wild-child designer and amateur basketball player Stéphane Ashpool, who grew up in the 'hood.

Spree   Fashion & Accessories
(Map p249; ☏01 42 23 41 40; www.spree.fr; 16 rue de la Vieuville, 18e; ⊘11am-7.30pm Tue-Sat, 3-7pm Sun & Mon; Ⓜ Abbesses) Allow plenty of time to browse this superstylish boutique-gallery, with a carefully selected collection of designer fashion put together by stylist Roberta Oprandi and artist Bruni Hadjadj. What makes shopping here fun is that all the furniture – vintage 1950s to 1980s pieces by Eames et al – is also for sale, as is the contemporary artwork on the walls.

⊙ Le Marais, Ménilmontant & Belleville

Merci   Gifts & Souvenirs
(Map p254; ☏01 42 77 00 33; www.merci-merci.com; 111 bd Beaumarchais, 3e; ⊘10am-7.30pm; Ⓜ St-Sébastien–Froissart) ✈ A Fiat Cinquecento marks the entrance to this unique concept store, which donates all its profits to a children's charity in Madagascar. Shop for fashion, accessories, linens, lamps and nifty designs for the home; and complete the experience with a coffee in its hybrid used-bookshop-cafe or lunch in its stylish **La Cantine de Mercia** (dishes €11-19; ⊘10am-7.30pm).

Paris Rendez-Vous   Gifts & Souvenirs
(Map p250; http://rendezvous.paris.fr; 29 rue de Rivoli, 4e; ⊘10am-7pm Mon-Sat; Ⓜ Hôtel de Ville) This chic city has its own designer line of souvenirs, sold in its own ubercool concept store inside Hôtel de Ville (city hall). Shop here for everything from clothing and homewares to Paris-themed books, wooden toy sailing boats and signature Jardin du Luxembourg Fermob chairs. *Quel style!*

Fromagerie Goncourt   Cheese
(Map p254; ☏01 43 57 91 28; 1 rue Abel Rabaud, 11e; ⊘9am-1pm & 4-8.30pm Tue-Fri, 9am-8pm Sat; Ⓜ Goncourt) Styled like a boutique, this contemporary *fromagerie* is a

Canal St-Martin

Bordered by shaded towpaths and traversed by iron footbridges, the quaint setting of **Canal St-Martin** (Map p254; MRépublique, Jaurès, Jacques Bonsergent) has lured artists, designers and students, who set up neoretro cafes, artists' collectives and offbeat boutiques.

One of the first designers to open on boutique-lined rue Beaurepaire was **Liza Korn** (Map p254; www.liza-korn.com; 19 rue Beaurepaire, 10e; ⊙11am-7.30pm Mon-Sat; MJacques Bonsergent), whose collections range from rock and roll fashion to a children's line. Vintage boutique **Frivoli** (Map p254; 26 rue Beaurepaire, 10e; ⊙1-7pm Mon, 11am-7pm Tue-Sat, 2-7pm Sun; MRépublique, Jacques Bonsergent) is across the street. Local artwork is often on display at **Espace Beaurepaire** (Map p254; ☑01 42 45 59 64; www.espacebeaurepaire.com; 28 rue Beaurepaire, 10e; MJacques Bonsergent) FREE, a gallery and cultural centre that also hosts events such as book signings, pop-up concept stores and dance performances.

Around the corner is rue de Marseille, another great shopping street; look out for **Medecine Douce** (Map p254; www.bijouxmedecinedouce.com; 10 rue de Marseille, 10e; ⊙11am-7pm Mon-Sat; MJacques Bonsergent), a studio-showroom displaying gorgeous jewellery handmade on-site.

Facing the canal, **Artazart** (Map p254; http://artazart.com; 83 quai de Valmy, 10e; ⊙10.30am-7.30pm Mon-Fri, 11am-7.30pm Sat, 1-7.30pm Sun; MJacques Bonsergent) is a leading design bookshop, while **Antoine et Lili** (Map p254; www.antoineetlili.com; 95 quai de Valmy, 10e; ⊙11am-8pm Tue-Fri, to 7pm Sun & Mon; MJacques Bonsergent, Gare de l'Est) has a candy-coloured trio of boutiques with designer clothing for women (pink store) and children (green store), and hip homewares (yellow store).

must-discover. Clément Brossault ditched a career in banking to become a *fromager* and his cheese selection – 70-plus types – is superb. Cheeses flagged with a bicycle symbol are varieties he discovered in situ during a two-month French cheese tour he embarked on as part of his training.

Made by Moi — Fashion, Homewares

(Map p254; ☑01 58 30 95 78; www.madebymoi.fr; 86 rue Oberkampf, 11e; ⊙2.30-8pm Mon, 10am-8pm Tue-Sat; MParmentier) 'Made by Me', aka handmade, is the driver of this appealing boutique on trendy rue Oberkampf – a perfect address to buy unusual gifts, from women's fashion to homewares such as 'Bobo brunch' scented candles by Bougies La Française and other beautiful objects such as coloured glass carafes, feathered headdresses, funky contact-lens boxes and retro dial telephones.

Edwart — Chocolate

(Map p254; http://edwart.fr; 17 rue Vielle du Temple, 4e; ⊙11am-8pm; MHôtel de Ville) Wunderkind chocolatiers Edwin Yansané and Arthur Heinze (collectively 'Edwart') take their inspiration from Paris (and – as a global melting pot – by extension, the world) to create feisty chocolates using unique ingredients such as Indian curry, Iranian saffron and Japanese whisky. Sparingly displayed in their sleek Marais boutique, their award-winning chocolates stand out, even in a city spoilt for choice.

Belleville Brûlerie — Coffee

(Map p254; ☑09 83 75 60 80; http://cafes belleville.com; 10 rue Pradier, 19e; ⊙11.30am-5.30pm Sat; MPyrénées) With its understated steel-grey facade, this ground-breaking roastery in Belleville is easy to miss. Don't! Belleville Brûlerie brought good coffee to Paris and its beans go into some of the best espressos in town. Taste the week's selection, compare tasting notes, and buy a bag to take home. Its own cafe, La Fontaine de Belleville (p174), is near Canal St-Martin.

Andrea Crews — Fashion & Accessories

(Map p254; www.andreacrews.com; 83 rue de Turenne, 3e; ⊙1-7.30pm Wed-Fri, to 7pm Sat; MSt-Sébastien–Froissart) Using everything from discarded clothing to electrical fittings and household bric-a-brac, this bold art and fashion collective sews, recycles and reinvents to create the most extraordinary pieces. Watch out for 'happenings' in its Marais boutique.

Mélodies Graphiques   Stationery

(Map p254; 10 rue du Pont Louis Philippe, 4e; ⊙2-7pm Mon, 11am-7pm Tue-Sat; M Pont Marie) On a street renowned for its fine paper and stationery boutiques, Mélodies Graphiques's soundtrack of classical music makes it an especially charming spot to browse its exquisite range of paper, notebooks, greeting cards, bookmarks, sealing wax, ink and calligraphy pens. Owner-calligraphist Eric de Tugny is also an entomologist and sells his intricate insect illustrations in store.

La Boutique
Extraordinaire   Fashion & Accessories

(Map p254; www.laboutiqueextraordinaire.com; 67 rue Charlot, 3e; ⊙11am-8pm Tue-Sat, 3-7pm Sun; M Filles du Calvaire) Mohair, silk, llama, camel, yak and other natural, organic and ethical materials are hand-knitted into exquisite garments, almost too precious to wear, at this unusual and captivating Haut Marais boutique.

Mariage Frères   Drinks

(Map p254; www.mariagefreres.com; 30, 32 & 35 rue du Bourg Tibourg, 4e; ⊙10am-7.30pm; M Hôtel de Ville) Founded in 1854, this is Paris' first and arguably finest tea shop. Choose from more than 500 varieties of tea sourced from some 35 countries. Mariage Frères has outlets in the 1er, 6e, 7e and 8e as well as international branches.

Its **tea room** (10.30am to 7.30pm), where you can sample its teas along with light dishes, and tiny **tea museum** (admission free; 10.30am to noon and 3pm to 5pm Thursday to Saturday) are on the same street.

🄰 Bastille & Eastern Paris

La Manufacture
de Chocolat   Food

(Map p254; www.lechocolat-alainducasse.com; 40 rue de la Roquette, 11e; ⊙10.30am-7pm Tue-Sat; M Bastille) If you dine at superstar chef Alain Ducasse's restaurants, the chocolate

Antoine et Lili

will have been made here at Ducasse's own chocolate factory (the first in Paris to produce 'bean-to-bar' chocolate), which he set up with his former executive pastry chef Nicolas Berger. Deliberate over ganaches, pralines and truffles and no fewer than 44 flavours of chocolate bar.

You can also buy Ducasse's chocolates at other outlets including his Left Bank boutique, **Le Chocolat Alain Ducasse** (Map p250; 26 rue St-Benoît, 6e; ⊘1.30-7.30pm Mon, 10.30am-7.30pm Tue-Sat; MSt-Germain des Prés).

Viaduc des Arts   Arts & Crafts

(Map p254; www.leviaducdesarts.com; 1-129 av Daumesnil, 12e; ⊘hours vary; MBastille, Gare de Lyon) Located beneath the red-brick arches of Promenade Plantée (p199), the Viaduc des Arts's line-up of traditional artisans and contemporary designers – including furniture and tapestry restorers, interior designers, cabinetmakers, violin- and flute-makers, embroiderers and jewellers – carry out antique renovations and create new items using time-honoured methods.

🔟 The Islands

Marché aux Fleurs
Reine Elizabeth II   Market

(Map p250; place Louis Lépin, 4e; ⊘8am-7.30pm Mon-Sat; MCité) Blooms have been sold at this flower market since 1808, making it the oldest market of any kind in Paris. On Sunday, it transforms into a cacophonous bird market, the **Marché aux Oiseaux** (⊘8am-7pm Sun).

L'Îles aux Images   Art

(Map p252; ☑01 56 24 15 22; www.vintage-photos -lithos-paris.com; 51 rue Saint-Louis en l'Île, 4e; ⊘2-7pm Mon-Sat & by appointment; MPont Marie) Original and rare vintage posters, photographs and lithographs dating from 1850 onwards from artists including Man Ray, Salvador Dalí, Paul Gauguin and Picasso are stocked at this gallery-boutique. Many depict Parisian scenes and make evocative home decorations. Framing can be arranged.

Clair de Rêve   Toys

(Map p252; www.clairdereve.com; 35 rue St-Louis en l'Île, 4e; ⊘11am-1pm & 2-7pm Mon-Sat; MPont

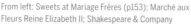

From left: Sweets at Mariage Frères (p153); Marché aux Fleurs Reine Elizabeth II; Shakespeare & Company

Marie) Stringed marionettes made of papier mâché, leather and porcelain bob from the ceiling of this endearing little shop. It also sells wind-up toys and music boxes.

🔒 Latin Quarter

Le Bonbon au Palais Food

(Map p252; www.bonbonsaupalais.fr; 19 rue Monge, 5e; ⓧ10.30am-7.30pm Tue-Sat; MCardinal Lemoine) Kids and kids-at-heart will adore this sugar-fuelled *tour de France*. The school-geography-themed boutique stocks artisan sweets from around the country. Old-fashioned glass jars brim with treats like *calissons* (diamond-shaped, icing-sugar-topped ground fruit and almonds from Aix-en-Provence), *rigolettes* (fruit-filled pillows from Nantes), *berlingots* (striped, triangular boiled sweets from Carpentras and elsewhere) and *papalines* (herbal liqueur-filled pink-chocolate balls from Avignon).

Shakespeare & Company Books

(Map p252; ☎01 43 25 40 93; www.shakespeareandcompany.com; 37 rue de la Bûcherie, 5e; ⓧ10am-11pm; MSt-Michel) Shakespeare's enchanting nooks and crannies overflow with new and secondhand English-language books. The original shop (12 rue l'Odéon, 6e; closed by the Nazis in 1941) was run by Sylvia Beach and became the meeting point for Hemingway's 'Lost Generation'. Readings by emerging and illustrious authors take place at 7pm most Mondays. There's a wonderful cafe (p136) and various workshops and festivals.

The bookshop is fabled for nurturing writers, and at night its couches turn into beds where writers stay in exchange for stacking shelves.

American-born George Whitman opened the present incarnation in 1951, attracting a beat-poet clientele, and scores of authors have since passed through its doors. In 2006 Whitman was awarded the Officier des Arts et Lettres by the French Minister of Culture, recognising his significant contribution to the enrichment of the French cultural inheritance. Whitman died in 2011, aged 98; he is buried in division 73 of Cimetière du Père Lachaise (p78). Today his daughter, Sylvia Beach Whitman, maintains Shakespeare & Company's serendipitous magic.

Bouquinistes along the Seine

With some 3km of forest-green boxes lining the Seine, containing over 300,000 secondhand, often out-of-print, books, rare magazines, postcards and old advertising posters, Paris' **bouquinistes** (Map p250; quai Voltaire, 7e to quai de la Tournelle, 5e & Pont Marie, 4e to quai du Louvre, 1er; ⏰11.30am–dusk), or used-book sellers, are as integral to the cityscape as Notre Dame. Many open only from spring to autumn (and many shut in August), but year-round you'll still find some to browse.

The *bouquinistes* have been in business since the 16th century, when they were itinerant peddlers selling their wares on Parisian bridges – back then their sometimes subversive (eg Protestant) materials would get them in trouble with the authorities. By 1859 the city had finally wised up: official licences were issued, space was rented (10m of railing) and eventually the permanent green boxes were installed.

Today, *bouquinistes* (the official count ranges from 200 to 240) are allowed to have four boxes, only one of which can be used to sell souvenirs. Look hard enough and you just might find some real treasures: old comic books, forgotten first editions, maps, stamps, erotica and prewar newspapers – as in centuries past, it's all there, waiting to be rediscovered.

Abbey Bookshop
Books

(Map p252; 📞01 46 33 16 24; 29 rue de la Parcheminerie, 5e; ⏰10am–7pm Mon-Sat; Ⓜ Cluny–La Sorbonne) In the 18th-century Hôtel Dubuisson, a protected monument, this welcoming Canadian-run bookshop serves free coffee (sweetened with maple syrup) to sip while you browse over 35,000 new and used books. It also organises literary events and countryside hikes.

Album
Comics

(Map p252; www.albumcomics.com; 67 bd St-Germain, 5e; ⏰10am–8pm Mon-Sat, noon–7pm Sun; Ⓜ Cluny–La Sorbonne) Album specialises in *bandes dessinées* (comics and graphic novels), which have an enormous following in France, with everything from Tintin and Babar to erotic comics and the latest Japanese manga. Serious comic collectors – and anyone excited by Harry Potter wands, *Star Wars*, *Superman* and other superhero figurines and T-shirts (you know who you are!) – shouldn't miss it.

🅐 St-Germain & Les Invalides

Gab & Jo
Fashion & Accessories

(Map p250; www.gabjo.fr; 28 rue Jacob, 6e; ⏰11am–7pm Mon-Sat; Ⓜ St-Germain des Prés) 🌿 Forget mass-produced, imported souvenirs: for quality local gifts, browse the shelves of the country's first-ever concept store stocking only made-in-France items. Designers include La Note Parisienne (scented candles for each Parisian *arrondissement*, such as the 6e, with notes of lipstick, cognac, orange blossom, tuberose, jasmine, rose and fig), Marius Fabre (Marseille soaps), Germaine-des-Prés (lingerie), MILF (sunglasses) and Monsieur Marcel (T-shirts).

La Grande Épicerie de Paris
Food & Drinks

(Map p246; www.lagrandeepicerie.com; 36 rue de Sèvres, 7e; ⏰8.30am–9pm Mon-Sat, 10am–8pm Sun; Ⓜ Sèvres-Babylone) The magnifi-

cent food hall of department store Le Bon Marché sells 30,000 rare and/or luxury gourmet products, including 60 different types of bread baked on site and delicacies such as caviar ravioli. Its fantastical displays of chocolates, pastries, biscuits, cheeses, fresh fruit and vegetables and deli goods are a Parisian sight in themselves. Wine tastings regularly take place in the basement.

Magasin Sennelier   Arts & Crafts

(Map p246; www.magasinsennelier.com; 3 quai Voltaire, 7e; ◷2-6.30pm Mon, 10am-12.45pm & 2-6.30pm Tue-Sat; ⓂSt-Germain des Prés) Cézanne and Picasso were among the artists who helped develop products for this venerable 1887-founded art supplier on the banks of the Seine, and it remains an exceptional place to pick up canvases, brushes, watercolours, oils, pastels, charcoals and more. The shop's forest-green facade with gold lettering, exquisite original timber cabinetry and glass display cases also fuel artistic inspiration.

Le Bon Marché   Department Store

(Map p246; www.bonmarche.com; 24 rue de Sèvres, 7e; ◷10am-8pm Mon-Wed & Sat, to 8.45pm Thu & Fri, 11am-8pm Sun; ⓂSèvres-Babylone) Built by Gustave Eiffel as Paris' first department store in 1852, Le Bon Marché is the epitome of style, with a superb concentration of men's and women's fashions, beautiful homewares, stationery, books and toys as well as chic dining options.

The icing on the cake is its glorious food hall, La Grande Épicerie de Paris.

Cire Trudon   Gifts & Souvenirs

(Map p252; https://trudon.com; 78 rue de Seine, 6e; ◷10am-7pm Mon-Sat; ⓂOdéon) Claude Trudon began selling candles here in 1643, and the company – which officially supplied Versailles and Napoléon with light – is now the world's oldest candle-maker (look for the plaque to the left of the shop's awning). A rainbow of candles and candlesticks fill the shelves inside.

 Flea Markets

Vast flea market **Marché aux Puces de St-Ouen** (http://marcheauxpuces-saint ouen.com; rue des Rosiers, St-Ouen; ◷Sat-Mon; ⓂPorte de Clignancourt), founded in the late 19th century and said to be Europe's largest, has more than 2500 stalls grouped into 15 *marchés* (markets), each with its own speciality (eg Marché Paul Bert Serpette for 17th-century furniture, Marché Biron for Asian art). Each market has different opening hours – check the website for details.

Close by, an abandoned Petite Ceinture train station has been repurposed as eco-hub **La REcyclerie** (www.larecyclerie.com; 83 bd Ornano, 18e; ◷8am-midnight Mon-Thu, to 2am Fri & Sat, to 10pm Sun; 🛜; ⓂPorte de Clignancourt) 🍴 with an urban farm along the old railway line featuring community vegetable and herb gardens and chickens. They provide ingredients for the mostly vegetarian cafe-canteen. In turn, food scraps replenish the chickens and gardens. There are regular flea markets and upcycling and repair workshops.

Across town in the city's south, **Marché aux Puces de la Porte de Vanves** (www.pucesdevanves.fr; av Georges Lafenestre & av Marc Sangnier, 14e; ◷7am-2pm Sat & Sun; ⓂPorte de Vanves) has over 380 stalls. Paris' most central flea market is the small but bargain-filled Marché aux Puces d'Aligre (p83).

Marché aux Puces de St-Ouen

From left: Le Bon Marché (p157); La Dernière Goutte;
Jardin du Luxembourg's signature chairs by Fermob

Mayaro · Design

(Map p246; ☎01 80 06 04 41; http://mayaro.
fr; 20 rue Amélie, 7e; ☺11am-5pm Mon-Sat,
hours can vary; ☒La Tour-Maubourg) Billing
itself as 'une maison inclassable', this truly
unclassifiable space spanning three floors
of a Haussmannian building is part gallery,
part concept store for men, part design
showcase and part collaborator, which
also variously hosts dinners by celebrated
chef Sven Chartier and sommelier Ewen
Le Moigne. Inspirational made-in-France
products include cabinets, leather shoes,
leather-framed eyewear, meteorite cufflinks
and digital art.

JB Guanti · Fashion & Accessories

(Map p246; www.jbguanti.com; 59 rue de Rennes,
6e; ☺10am-7pm Mon-Sat; ☒St-Sulpice) For the
ultimate finishing touch, the men's and
women's gloves at this boutique, which
specialises solely in gloves, are the epitome
of both style and comfort, whether unlined,
silk lined, cashmere lined, lambskin lined or
trimmed with rabbit fur.

Hermès · Fashion & Accessories

(Map p246; www.hermes.com; 17 rue de Sèvres,
6e; ☺10.30am-7pm Mon-Sat; ☒Sèvres-Babylone)
A stunning art-deco swimming pool now
houses luxury label Hermès' inaugural
concept store. Retaining its original mosaic
tiles and iron balustrades, and adding
enormous timber pod-like 'huts', the vast,
tiered space showcases new directions in
home furnishings, including fabrics and
wallpaper, along with classic lines such as
its signature scarves. Its cafe, Le Plongeoir
(the Diving Board), is equally chic.

La Dernière Goutte · Wine

(Map p250; ☎01 43 29 11 62; www.laderniere
goutte.net; 6 rue du Bourbon le Château, 6e;
☺3-8pm Mon, 10.30am-1.30pm & 3-8pm Tue-Fri,
10.30am-8pm Sat, 11am-7pm Sun; ☒Mabil-
lon) 'The Last Drop' is the brainchild of
Cuban-American sommelier Juan Sánchez,
whose tiny wine shop is packed with
exciting, mostly organic French vins de pro-
priétaires (estate-bottled wines) made by
small independent producers. Wine classes
lasting two hours (seven tastings) regularly
take place in English (per person €55);

phone for schedules and reservations. Free tastings with winemakers take place most Saturdays.

Au Plat d'Étain
Toys

(Map p252; www.soldats-plomb-au-plat-etain.fr; 16 rue Guisarde, 6e; ⊙10.30am-6.30pm Tue-Sat; MMabillon, St-Sulpice) Tiny tin *(étain)* and lead soldiers, snipers, cavaliers, military drummers and musicians (great for chessboard pieces) cram this fascinating boutique. In business since 1775, the shop itself is practically a collectable.

Finger in the Nose
Children, Fashion

(Map p250; www.fingerinthenose.com; 11 rue de l'Échaudé, 6e; ⊙2.30-7pm Mon, 11am-7.30pm Tue-Sat; MMabillon) This finger-on-the-pulse Parisian children's-wear label thumbs its nose at convention and offers edgy streetwear for kids, such as graphic T-shirts, fleeces and jackets along with sophisticated twists like its line of LBDs ('little black dresses') for teenage girls.

Sabbia Rosa
Fashion & Accessories

(Map p246; ☎01 45 48 88 37; 73 rue des Sts-Pères, 6e; ⊙10am-7pm Mon-Sat; MSt-Germain des Prés)

Only French-sourced fabrics (silk from Lyon, lace from Calais) are used by lingerie designer Sabbia Rosa for her ultra-luxe range. Every piece is unique; measurements can be taken and gorgeous items custom made in just 48 hours. The list of celebrity clients reads like a who's who: Madonna, Naomi Campbell, Claudia Schiffer and George Clooney have all shopped here.

Fermob
Homewares

(Map p246; www.paris.fermob.com; 17 bd Raspail, 7e; ⊙10am-1pm & 2-7pm Tue-Sat; MRue du Bac) Famed for manufacturing iconic French garden furniture, including the Jardin du Luxembourg's signature chairs in a spectacular array of colours (23 at last count) for your own garden or terrace, Fermob has opened this large, white 120-sq-metre Left Bank boutique in addition to its **Bastille premises** (Map p254; 81-83 av Ledru-Rollin, 12e; ⊙10am-7pm Mon-Sat; MLedru-Rollin).

Marie Mercié
Fashion & Accessories

(Map p252; www.mariemercie.com; 23 rue St-Sulpice, 6e; ⊙11am-7pm Mon-Sat; MMabillon) Stand out in the crowd in a unique hat

Street in Montmartre

handcrafted by Fontainebleau-born milliner Marie Mercié, who has collaborated with designers including Hermès, Kenzo, John Galliano and Agnès B, and combines traditional methods with modern materials and humorous twists. She's also authored two books on her work and the history of millinery.

Smallable
Concept Store   Children's Clothing
(Map p246; www.smallable.com; 81 rue du Cherche Midi, 6e; ⊘2-7.30pm Mon, 10.30am-7.30pm Tue-Sat; MVaneau) Set back behind a covered polished-concrete courtyard, this deceptively large Parisian-chic space is a one-stop shop for babies, children and teens, with over 20,000 items (strollers, shoes, furniture, clothes and toys) from 450 premium brands (Little Eleven Paris, Chloé Kids, Petit Bateau, Pom d'Api, Zadig & Voltaire and many more).

Alexandra
Sojfer   Fashion & Accessories
(Map p246; www.alexandrasojfer.com; 218 bd St-Germain, 7e; ⊘10am-7pm Mon-Sat; MRue du Bac) One-of-a-kind high-fashion *parapluies* and *ombrelles* (parasols and umbrellas) as well as *cannes* (walking sticks) are hand-made by Alexandra Sojfer, who bought this 1834-opened atelier in 2002, and whose family has been in the business for gener-ations. If nothing on display catches your fancy, you can have one custom-made.

 Vintage Style

Designer and vintage cast-offs at *dépôt-vente* (secondhand) boutiques can yield serious bargains.

Scattered along one street, **Chercheminippes** (Map p246; www.cherchemin ippes.com; 102, 106, 109-111, 114 & 124 rue du Cherche Midi, 6e; ⊘11am-7pm Mon-Sat; MVaneau) has seven beautifully present-ed boutiques selling secondhand pieces by current designers. Each specialises in a different genre (haute couture, kids, menswear etc); items are perfectly ordered by size and designer. There are changing rooms.

Fans of Chanel and Hermès should visit **Catherine B** (Map p252; http://les 3marchesdecatherineb.com; 1-3 rue Guisarde, 6e; ⊘11am-7pm Mon-Sat; MMabillon), who specialises exclusively in authentic items from these two iconic French fashion houses.

Chanel handbag
DKSSTYLE/SHUTTERSTOCK ©

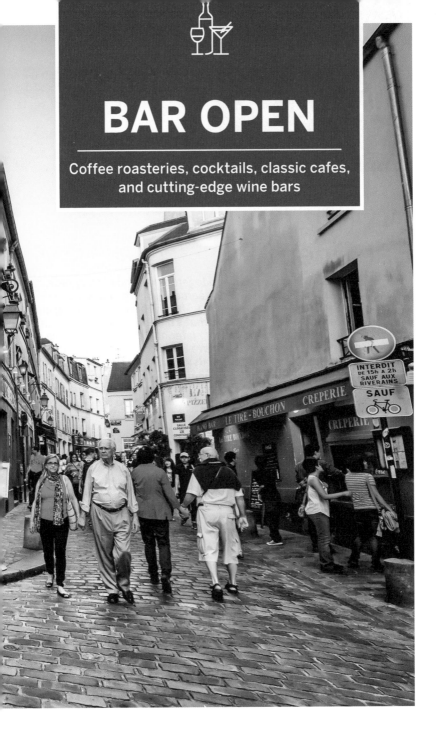

BAR OPEN

Coffee roasteries, cocktails, classic cafes, and cutting-edge wine bars

Bar Open

For the French, drinking and eating go together like wine and cheese, and the line between a cafe, salon de thé *(tearoom), bistro, brasserie, bar, and even bar à vins (wine bar) is blurred. The line between drinking and clubbing is often nonexistent – a cafe that's quiet midafternoon might have DJ sets in the evening and dancing later on. Many Parisians live in tiny apartments, and cafes and bars have traditionally served as the salon they don't have – a place to meet friends over un verre (glass of wine), read for hours over un café (coffee), debate politics while downing an espresso at a zinc counter, swill cocktails during apéro (aperitif; predinner drink) or get the party started aboard a floating club on the Seine.*

In This Section

Eiffel Tower & Western Paris 168

Champs-Élysées &
Grands Boulevards 168

Louvres & Les Halles................................170

Montmartre & Northern Paris................173

Le Marais, Ménilmontant
& Belleville...176

Bastille & Eastern Paris 179

The Islands 180

Latin Quarter.......................................180

St-Germain & Les Invalides................181

Montparnasse & Southern Paris 183

Opening Hours

Many cafes and bars open first thing in the morning, around 7am. Closing time for cafes and bars tends to be 2am, though some have licences until dawn. Club hours vary depending on the venue, day and event.

**Montmartre &
Northern Paris**
Local gems include
canal-side cafes
(p173)

**Champs-Élysées &
Grands Boulevards**
Swanky hotel bars,
glam nightclubs (p168)

**Louvre &
Les Halles**
Eclectic mix of
bars and clubs
(p170)

**Le Marais,
Ménilmontant &
Belleville**
Hip, edgy bars and
nightlife venues
(p176)

**Eiffel Tower &
Western Paris**
Classy bars and
sunny cafes
(p168)

**St-Germain &
Les Invalides**
Historic literary cafes,
stylish bars
(p181)

The Islands
Quaint tearooms
and wine bars
(p180)

**Bastille &
Eastern Paris**
Lively clubs and
bars galore (p179)

Latin Quarter
Spirited student
pubs and bars
(p180)

**Montparnasse &
Southern Paris**
Boulevard-facing
brasseries and
backstreet cafes
(p183)

Costs/Tipping

Costs A coffee starts at about €2.50, a glass of wine from €4, a cocktail €8 to €15 and a demi (half-pint) of beer €3.50 to €7. In clubs and chic bars, prices can be double this. Admission to clubs is free to around €20 and is often cheaper before 1am.

Tipping Tipping isn't necessary at the bar. If drinks are brought to your table, tip as you would in a restaurant.

Useful Phrases

Un café Single shot of espresso.

Un café allongé Espresso lengthened with hot water (sometimes served separately).

Un café au lait Coffee with milk.

Un café crème Shot of espresso lengthened with steamed milk.

Un double Double shot of espresso.

Une noisette Shot of espresso with a spot of milk.

The Best...

Experience Paris' finest drinking establishments

Wine Bars

Le Garde Robe (pictured below; p171) Affordable natural wines and unpretentious vibe.

La Quincave (p182) Bar stools fashioned from wine barrels and over 200 natural wines.

Au Sauvignon (p182) Original zinc bar and hand-painted ceiling.

Nightclubs

Le Rex Club (p173) Legendary house and techno club with a phenomenal sound system.

Concrete (p179) Top spot for electro dance music all hours, on a barge by Gare de Lyon.

Club Rayé (pictured above; p170) Classy club with live jazz and DJs in a 13th-century former convent.

Zig Zag Club (p169) Best of the Champs-Élysées venues.

La Dame de Canton (p183) Aboard a three-masted Chinese junk.

Pavement Terraces

Chez Prune (pictured above; p174) The boho cafe that put Canal St-Martin on the map.

Café des Anges (p179) Wrap up in a ginger blanket and live the Paris dream.

L'Ebouillanté (p178) On sunny days there is no prettier cafe terrace.

Tearooms

Mosquée de Paris (p108) Sip sweet mint tea and nibble delicious pastries in this peaceful haven.

Mariage Frères (pictured above; p153) Paris' oldest and finest tearoom, founded in 1854.

L'Amaryllis de Gérard Mulot (p140) Wonderful tearoom by patisserie maestro Gérard Mulot.

Coffee

Boot Café (p177) A fashionable must, if only to snap the enchanting façade.

Caffé Juno (p180) Aromatic little Latin Quarter roaster.

Café Lomi (p174) Coffee roastery and cafe in the multiethnic La Goutte d'Or neighbourhood.

Coutume (p181) Leading artisan roastery.

★ Lonely Planet's Top Choices

Le Mary Céleste (p176) Fashionable Marais cocktail bar.

Le Baron Rouge (pictured above; p179) Wonderfully convivial barrel-filled wine bar.

Lockwood (p170) Irrepressibly good all day long, from coffee to cocktails.

Le Batofar (p183) Red-metal tugboat with a rooftop bar and portholed club beneath.

🍸 Eiffel Tower & Western Paris

St James Paris   Bar

(Map p246; www.saint-james-paris.com; 43 av Bugeaud, 16e; ⏰7pm-1am Mon-Sat; 🛜; Ⓜ Porte Dauphine) Hidden behind a stone wall, this historic mansion-turned-hotel opens its bar each evening to nonguests – and the setting redefines extraordinary. Winter drinks are in the wood-panelled library, in summer they're on the impossibly romantic 300-sq-metre garden terrace with giant balloon-shaped gazebos (the first hot-air balloons took flight here). There are over 70 cocktails and an adjoining Michelin-starred restaurant.

Yoyo   Club

(Map p246; http://yoyo-paris.com; 13 av du Président Wilson, 16e; ⏰11.30pm-dawn Fri & Sat; Ⓜ Iéna) Deep in the basement of the Palais de Tokyo, Yoyo has an edgy, raw-concrete Berlin-style vibe and a capacity of 800. Techno and house dominate, with diversions into hip-hop, electro, funk, disco, R&B and soul. Hours can vary; check the website to see what's happening when.

Upper Crèmerie   Bar

(Map p246; 📞 01 40 70 93 23; 71 av Marceau, 16e; ⏰9am-midnight Mon-Fri; Ⓜ Kléber, George V) The sun-flooded tables at this hybrid cafe–cocktail bar in a quintessential Parisian pavement terrace heave at lunchtime and after work with a well-dressed crowd from surrounding offices, while inside, vivid colours and neon lighting reassure trendsetters that the place is anything but traditional. Cocktails (and food including a €10 *plat du jour*) hit the spot.

🍸 Champs-Élysées & Grands Boulevards

Honor   Coffee

(Map p246; www.honor-cafe.com; 54 rue du Faubourg St-Honoré, 8e; ⏰9am-6pm Mon-Fri, 10am-6pm Sat; Ⓜ Madeleine) Hidden off ritzy rue du Faubourg St-Honoré in a courtyard adjoining fashion house Comme des Garçons is Paris' 'first and only outdoor independent

Harry's New York Bar (p171)

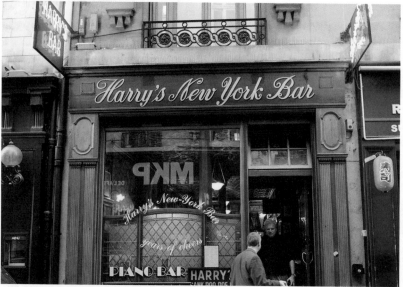

MEHDI FEDOUACH/GETTY IMAGES ©

coffee shop', an opaque-plastic-sheltered black-and-white timber kiosk brewing coffee from small-scale producers around the globe. It also serves luscious cakes, filled-to-bursting lunchtime sandwiches, quiches and salads (dishes €2.50 to €11.50), along with fresh juices, wine and beer.

Zig Zag Club · Club

(Map p246; http://zigzagclub.fr; 32 rue Marbeuf, 8e; ⏰11.30pm-7am Fri & Sat; Ⓜ Franklin D Roosevelt) With star DJs, a great sound and light system, and a spacious dance floor, Zig Zag has some of the hippest electro beats in western Paris. It can be pricey, but it still fills up quickly, so don't start the party too late.

Wine by One · Wine Bar

(Map p246; ✆01 45 63 18 98; www.winebyone. com; 27 rue de Marignan, 8e; ⏰noon-11pm Mon-Sat, 3-11pm Sun; Ⓜ Franklin D Roosevelt) At this serve-yourself wine bar off the Champs-Élysées, you load up a card (€2 deposit) with the amount you'd like to spend, then browse the bottles lining the walls and dispense one of three tasting sizes. There are over 100 choices; prices run from roughly €1.40 to €10. Substantial cheese-and-charcuterie plates could easily turn a visit into a full meal.

PanPan · Bar

(Map p250; ✆01 42 46 36 06; 32 rue Drouot, 9e; ⏰10am-2am Mon-Fri, 6pm-2am Sat; Ⓜ Le Peletier) This unassuming locals' hangout doesn't even bother with a sign, but it keeps things interesting with activities throughout the week. Favourites include Monday's cocktail workshop (where you learn to mix your own, in French, *bien sûr*) and Thursday's *aperitivo* (from 7pm), where you can nibble on quiche, charcuterie and the like for €1. Happy hour runs from 6pm to 8pm.

Blaine · Cocktail Bar

(Map p246; 65 rue Pierre Charron, 8e; ⏰8pm-7am Wed-Sat; Ⓜ Franklin D Roosevelt) Hidden in plain sight is this underground speakeasy: enter through an unmarked black door, relay the password (hint: research on

 Wine

Wine is easily the most popular beverage in Paris and house wine can cost less than bottled water. Of France's dozens of wine-producing regions, the principal ones are Burgundy, Bordeaux, the Rhône and the Loire valleys, Champagne, Languedoc, Provence and Alsace. Wines are generally named after the location of the vineyard rather than the grape varietal.

The best wines are Appellation d'Origine Contrôlée (AOC; soon to be re-labelled Appellation d'Origine Protégée, AOP), meaning they meet stringent regulations governing where, how and under what conditions they're grown, fermented and bottled.

Natural Wine

The latest trend in wine, *les vins naturels* (natural wines) have a fuzzy definition – no one really agrees on the details, but the general idea is that they are produced using little or no pesticides or additives. This means natural wines do not contain sulphites, which are added as a preservative in most wines. The good news is that this gives natural wines a much more distinct personality (or *terroir*, as the French say), the bad news is that these wines can also be more unpredictable.

For more specifics, see the website www.morethanorganic.com.

From left: Martini at Bar Hemingway; Club Rayé; Frog & Underground

social media) and enter into a recreated Prohibition-era bar. Elaborate cocktails start at €15; there's occasional live jazz and DJ sets.

⊖ Louvre & Les Halles

Bar Hemingway　　Cocktail Bar

(Map p246; www.ritzparis.com; Hôtel Ritz Paris, 15 place Vendôme, 1er; ⊙6pm-2am; 🛜; MOpéra) Black-and-white photos and memorabilia (hunting trophies, old typewriters and framed handwritten letters by the great writer) fill this snug bar inside the Ritz. Head bartender Colin Field mixes monumental cocktails, including three different Bloody Marys made with juice from freshly squeezed seasonal tomatoes. Legend has it that Hemingway himself, wielding a machine gun, helped liberate the bar during WWII.

Lockwood　　Cocktail Bar

(Map p250; ☑01 77 32 97 21; www.lockwoodparis. com; 73 rue d'Aboukir, 2e; ⊙6pm-2am Mon-Fri, 10am-4pm & 6pm-2am Sat, 10am-4pm Sun; MSentier) Cocktails incorporating premium spirits such as Hendrick's rose- and cucumber-infused gin and Pierre Ferrand Curaçao are served in Lockwood's stylish ground-floor lounge and subterranean candle-lit cellar. It's especially buzzing on weekends, when brunch stretches out between 10am and 4pm, with Bloody Marys, coffee brewed with Parisian-roasted Belleville Brûlerie (p152) beans and fare including eggs Benedict and Florentine (dishes €8.50 to €13).

Experimental Cocktail Club　　Cocktail Bar

(ECC; Map p250; www.experimentalevents.com; 37 rue St-Sauveur, 2e; ⊙7pm-2am; MRéaumur–Sébastopol) With a black curtain façade, this retro-chic speakeasy – with sister bars in London, Ibiza and New York – is a sophisticated flashback to those *années folles* (crazy years) of Prohibition New York. Cocktails (€13 to €15) are individual and fabulous, and DJs keep the party going until dawn at weekends. It's not a large space, however, and fills to capacity quickly.

Club Rayé　　Club

(Map p250; ☑01 40 13 72 93; http://clubraye.com; 26 rue Dussoubs, 2e; ⊙5pm-midnight Tue & Wed, to

2am Thu-Sat, closed Aug; MRéaumur–Sébastopol)
Boudoir-style, black-and-white decor forms
the backdrop for live jazz at this 13th-century
former convent. Music is on the ground floor
and in the cellar, and DJs spin electro jazz
from 11pm on Thursday to Saturday. Incredible cocktails include Chien Chaud ('hot dog';
coconut water, white rum, chartreuse and
bitters) and Midnight Express (walnut-infused
cognac, freshly brewed coffee and amaretto).

Harry's New York Bar   Cocktail Bar
(Map p246; ☎01 42 61 71 14; http://harrysbar.
fr; 5 rue Daunou, 2e; ⊗noon-2am Mon-Sat, 4pm-
1am Sun; MOpéra) One of the most popular
American-style bars in the prewar years,
Harry's once welcomed writers including
F Scott Fitzgerald and Ernest Hemingway,
who no doubt sampled the bar's unique
cocktail and creation: the Bloody Mary. The
Cuban mahogany interior dates from the
mid-19th century and was brought over
from a Manhattan bar in 1911.

There's a basement piano bar called
Ivories where Gershwin supposedly composed *An American in Paris* and, for the
peckish, old-school hot dogs and generous
club sandwiches to snack on. Its enduring
tagline is 'Tell the Taxi Driver Sank Roo
Doe Noo'.

Frog & Underground   Pub
(Map p250; www.frogpubs.com; 173 rue Montmartre, 2e; ⊗7.30am-4am Thu-Sat, to 2am Sun-Wed;
🛜; MGrands Boulevards) FrogPubs has been
brewing in Paris since 1993, and this central
new rue Montmartre venue is its best yet.
Spread over a cavernous ground floor and
opening to a terrace, vaulted cellar with a
dance floor, and upstairs lounge (spanning
370 sq metres in all), its exciting beers
include a wonderfully crisp dry-hopped
Hopster pale ale.

Le Garde Robe   Wine Bar
(Map p250; ☎01 49 26 90 60; 41 rue de l'Arbre
Sec, 1er; ⊗12.30-2.30pm & 6.30pm-midnight
Mon-Fri, 6.30pm-midnight Mon-Sat; MLouvre
Rivoli) Le Garde Robe is possibly the world's
only bar to serve alcohol alongside a detox
menu. While you probably shouldn't come
here for the full-on cleansing experience,
you can definitely expect excellent, affordable natural wines, a casual atmosphere
and a good selection of food, ranging from

Paris in a Glass

30mL Cognac

30mL fresh lemon juice

30mL Triple Sec/Cointreau

Celebrate the Sidecar

HORTIMAGES/SHUTTERSTOCK ©

The Sidecar

This enduring classic was allegedly invented in 1923 by the Ritz' first head bar tender, Frank Meier, for an American regular who arrived by sidecar. When current head bar tender Colin Peter Field updated it in 2001, his 'Ritz Sidecar', using pre-Phylloxera cognac, became a Guinness World Record holder for the world's most expensive cocktail (now €1500 at Bar Hemingway).

ANDREI MAYATNIK/SHUTTERSTOCK ©

★**Best Bars for a Sidecar**
Bar Hemingway (p170)
Harry's New York Bar (p171)
Le Syndicat (p173)
A La Française (p179)
Little Bastards (p180)

cheese and charcuterie plates to adventurous options (tuna gravlax with black quinoa and guacamole).

Hoppy Corner Craft Beer

(Map p250; www.facebook.com/hoppycorner; 34 rue des Petits Carreaux, 2e; ⊙5pm-2am Mon-Fri, 2pm-2am Sat; MSentier) Mainly French beers rotate on the 15 taps of this convivial craft beer specialist, such as Indigo IPA from Deck & Donohue, made in Montreuil just east of central Paris. A handful of European (and occasionally American) brews also make the blackboard listing the day's offerings; super-knowledgeable staff can help you decide. Dried hops are served as bar snacks.

Café La Fusée Bar

(Map p250; ☑01 42 76 93 99; 168 rue St-Martin, 3e; ⊙9am-2am; MRambuteau, Étienne Marcel) A short walk from the Centre Pompidou (p74), the Rocket is a lively, laid-back indie hang-out with a red-and-white-striped awning strung with fairy lights outside, and tobacco-coloured walls indoors. You can grab simple meals here (€8 to €13), and it's got a decent wine selection by the glass.

Le Rex Club Club

(Map p250; www.rexclub.com; 5 bd Poissonnière, 2e; ⊙midnight-7am Thu-Sat; MBonne Nouvelle) Attached to the art deco Grand Rex cinema, this is Paris' premier house and techno venue where some of the world's hottest DJs strut their stuff on a 70-speaker, multidiffusion sound system.

Angelina Teahouse

(Map p246; ☑01 42 60 82 00; www.angelina-paris.fr; 226 rue de Rivoli, 1er; ⊙7.30am-7pm Mon-Fri, 8.30am-7pm Sat & Sun; MTuileries) Clink china with lunching ladies, their posturing poodles and half the students from Tokyo University at Angelina, a grande-dame tearoom dating from 1903. Decadent pastries are served here, but it's the super-thick, wonderfully decadent 'African' hot chocolate (€8.20), which comes with a pot of whipped cream and a carafe of water, that prompts the constant queue for a table.

Le Tambour Bar

(Map p250; ☑01 42 33 06 90; 41 rue Montmartre, 2e; ⊙8.30am-6am; MÉtienne Marcel, Sentier) Insomniacs head to local landmark 'the Drummer' for its rowdy, good-natured atmosphere and filling, inexpensive French fare (including legendary desserts such as its *tarte Tatin* – traditional upside-down caramelised-apple tart) served until 3.30am or 4am. But what makes this place truly magical is its salvaged decor, such as an old Stalingrad metro map and Parisian street furniture.

🌑 Montmartre & Northern Paris

Le Syndicat Cocktail Bar

(Map p254; http://syndicatcocktailclub.com; 51 rue du Faubourg St-Denis, 10e; ⊙6pm-2am Mon-Sat, 7pm-2am Sun; MChâteau d'Eau) Plastered top to bottom in peeling posters, this otherwise unmarked facade conceals one of Paris' hottest cocktail bars, but it's no fly-by-night. Le Syndicat's subtitle, Organisation de Défense des Spiritueux Français, reflects its impassioned commitment to French spirits. Ingeniously crafted (and named) cocktails include Saix en Provence (Armagnac, chilli syrup, lime and lavender).

Le Très Particulier Cocktail Bar

(Map p249; ☑01 53 41 81 40; www.hotel-particulier-montmartre.com; Pavillon D, 23 av Junot, 18e; ⊙6pm-2am; MLamarck-Caulaincourt) The clandestine cocktail bar of boutique Hôtel Particulier Montmartre is an enchanting spot for a summertime al fresco cocktail. Ring the buzzer at the unmarked black gated entrance and make a beeline for the 1871 mansion's flowery walled garden (or, if it's raining, the adjacent conservatory-style interior). DJs spin tunes from 9.30pm Wednesday to Saturday and from 7pm on Sunday.

Gravity Bar Cocktail Bar

(Map p254; 44 rue des Vinaigriers, 10e; ⊙7pm-2am Tue-Sat; MJacques Bonsergent) Gravity's stunning wave-like interior crafted from

 Craft Breweries

Bière artisanale (craft beer) is exploding in Paris and there are some fabulous, flavour-packed beers being brewed right in the city centre. Behind-the-scenes tours and tastings are available at creative new breweries, including **Brasserie BapBap** (Map p254; ☎01 77 17 52 97; www.bapbap.paris; 79 rue St-Maur, 11e; guided tours €15; ☺guided tours 11am Sat, shop noon-8pm Tue-Sat; Ⓜ︎St-Maur) and **Brasserie la Goutte d'Or** (Map p249; ☎09 80 64 23 51; www.brasserielagouttedor.com; 28 rue de la Goutte d'Or, 18e; ☺5-7pm Thu & Fri, 2-7pm Sat; Ⓜ︎Château Rouge) **FREE**.

Dedicated craft-beer shops such as **Biérocratie** (☎01 53 80 16 10; www.bierocratie.com; 32 rue de l'Espérance, 13e; ☺11am-8pm Tue & Thu-Sat, 4-8pm Wed; Ⓜ︎Corvisart), **Bieregrad** (www.bieregrad.com; 18-20 rue de la Butte aux Cailles, 13e; ☺5-9.30pm Mon, 2-9.30pm Tue-Sat; Ⓜ︎Corvisart) and **Bières Cultes** (Map p252; http://bierescultes.fr; 44 rue des Boulangers, 5e; ☺3-8pm Mon, 11am-2pm & 3-8pm Tue-Thu, 11am-2pm & 3-9pm Fri & Sat; Ⓜ︎Cardinal Lemoine) also often host events. Craft beer devotees will want to time their trip to coincide with May's Paris Beer Week.

slats of plywood descending to the curved concrete bar threatens to distract from the business at hand – serious cocktails, such as Back to My Roots (Provence herb-infused vodka, vermouth, raspberry purée and lemon juice) best partaken in the company of excellent and inventive tapas-style small plates (€5 to €15) such as duck breast tartare.

Lulu White · Cocktail Bar

(Map p249; www.luluwhite.bar; 12 rue Frochot, 9e; ☺7pm-2am Mon-Thu, to 4am Fri & Sat; Ⓜ︎Pigalle) Sip absinthe-based cocktails in Prohibition-era New Orleans surrounds at this elegant, serious and supremely busy cocktail bar on rue Frochot, which hosts live jazz and folk music on Tuesday evenings. Several more bars line the same street, making for a fabulous evening out.

La Fontaine de Belleville · Coffee

(Map p254; http://lafontaine.cafesbelleville.com; 31-33 rue Juliette Dodu, 10e; ☺8am-10pm; Ⓜ︎Colonel Fabien) Beans roasted by Belleville Brûlerie (p152) are the toast of Paris and 2016 saw the roastery open its own cafe near Canal St-Martin, updating a long-standing local corner spot with gold lettering, woven sky-blue-and-cream bistro chairs and matching tables, and retaining its vintage fittings. Spectacular coffee is complemented by sandwiches, salads and small sharing plates (dishes €6.50 to €11).

Chez Prune · Bar

(Map p254; 36 rue Beaurepaire, 10e, cnr quai de Valmy; ☺9am-1am Mon-Sat, 10am-1am Sun; Ⓜ︎République) This boho cafe put Canal St-Martin on the map and its good vibes, original mosaic-tiled interior and rough-around-the-edges look show no sign of disappearing in the near future. Chez Prune remains one of those timeless classic Paris addresses, fabulous for hanging out and people-watching any time of day. Weekend brunch buzzes.

Café Lomi · Coffee

(☎09 80 39 56 24; https://lomi.paris; 3ter rue Marcadet, 18e; ☺10am-7pm; Ⓜ︎Marcadet–Poissonniers) Lomi's internationally sourced beans are roasted here on site in the multiethnic La Goutte d'Or neighbourhood adjacent to its cafe. Brews include filter coffee (mug, Aeropress or Chemex) and wacky creations such as Bleu d'Auvergne cheese dipped in espresso or tonic water with espresso. Two- to three-hour coffee workshops in English (filter techniques, world coffee tours, latte art) start from €72.

Le Progrès
Bar

(Map p249; 7 rue des Trois Frères, 18e; ⏱9am-2am; MAbbesses) A real live *café du quartier* perched in the heart of Abbesses, the Progress occupies a corner site with huge windows that attracts a relaxed mix of local artists, writers and more. It's great for convivial evenings, but it's also a good place to come for Auvergne specialities (mains €15 to €17.50) or coffee.

La Machine du Moulin Rouge
Club

(Map p249; www.lamachinedumoulinrouge.com; 90 bd de Clichy, 18e; admission €9-15; ⏱11pm-6am Fri & Sat, variable Sun-Thu; MBlanche) Part of the original Moulin Rouge (well, the boiler room, anyway), this club packs 'em in on weekends with a dance floor, a concert hall, a Champagne bar and an outdoor terrace. Check the agenda online for weekday soirées and happenings.

Le Coq
Cocktail Bar

(Map p254; 12 rue du Château d'Eau, 10e; ⏱6pm-2am Tue-Sat; MRépublique, Jacques Bonsergent) Pop art and concrete walls set the stage for the some of the 10e's best cocktails. Signature tipples tested in its in-house laboratory incorporate rare French spirits – consider a Les Fleurs du Mal (absinthe and rose-infused vodka) or Initials BB (Bénédictine and bourbon).

La Fourmi
Bar

(Map p249; 74 rue des Martyrs, 18e; ⏱8.30am-2am Sun-Thu, to 4am Fri & Sat; MPigalle) A Pigalle institution, sociable La Fourmi hits the mark with its high ceilings, long zinc bar, timber-panelled walls and unpretentious vibe. It's a great place to find out about live music and club nights or grab a drink before heading out to a show. Bonus: table football.

 Coffee & Tea

Coffee has always been Parisians' drink of choice to kick-start the day. So it's surprising, particularly given France's fixation on quality, that Parisian coffee has lagged behind world standards. But the city is in the throes of a coffee revolution, with local roasteries like Belleville Brûlerie (p152) and Coutume (p181) priming cafes citywide for outstanding brews made by professional baristas, often using cutting-edge extraction techniques. Caffeine fiends are now spoilt for choice and while there's still plenty of substandard coffee in Paris, you don't have to go far to avoid it.

Surprisingly, too, tea – more strongly associated with France's northwestern neighbours, the UK and Ireland – is extremely popular in Paris. Tearooms offer copious varieties; learn about its history at the tea museum within the original Marais branch of Mariage Frères (p153).

Mariage Frères
EQROY/SHUTTERSTOCK ©

Au P'tit Douai
Bar

(Map p249; 38 rue Douai, cnr 92 rue Blanche, 9e; ⏱11am-2am Mon-Sat; 🛜; MBlanche) This quirky neighbourhood cafe is just down the street from the Moulin Rouge. Trade the tourist mayhem for a mellow coffee, an excellent-value lunch (*plat du jour* €12 to €13.50) or tapas (€6.50 to €14), cocktails or 11 by-the-glass wines amid an eclectic array of bric-a-brac and vintage furniture. Kids love the welly boots of felt-tip pens adorning some tables.

🟢 Le Marais, Ménilmontant & Belleville

Candelaria   Cocktail Bar

(Map p254; www.quixotic-projects.com/venue/candelaria; 52 rue de Saintonge, 3e; ⏰bar 6pm-2am Mon-Fri, noon-4pm & 6pm-2am Sat & Sun, taqueria noon-10.30pm Sun-Wed, noon-11.30pm Thu-Sat; MFilles du Calvaire) A lime-green *taqueria* serving homemade tacos, quesadillas and tostadas (dishes €3.50 to €9) conceals one of Paris' coolest cocktail bars through an unmarked internal door. Evenings kick off with occasional DJ sets, tastings, pos t-gallery drinks and phenomenal cocktails made from agave spirits including mezcal. Reserve online for cocktail-fuelled weekend brunch (€20; noon to 4pm), featuring a feisty tequila-laced Bloody Maria.

Wild & the Moon   Juice Bar

(Map p254; www.wildandthemoon.com; 55 rue Charlot, 3e; ⏰8am-7pm Mon-Fri, 9am-7pm Sat & Sun; MFilles du Calvaire) A beautiful crowd hobnobs over nut milks, vitality shots, smoothies, cold-pressed juices and raw food in this sleek juice bar in the fashionable Haut Marais. Raw, all-vegan ingredients are fresh, seasonal and organic, and it's one of the few places in town where you can have dishes such as avocado slices on almond and rosemary crackers for breakfast.

Le Mary Céleste   Cocktail Bar

(Map p254; www.quixotic-projects.com/venue/mary-celeste; 1 rue Commines, 3e; ⏰6pm-2am, kitchen 7-11.30pm; MFilles du Calvaire) Snag a stool at the central circular bar at this uber-popular brick-and-timber-floored cocktail bar or reserve one of a handful of tables (in advance online). Creative cocktails such as Ahha Kapehna (grappa, absinthe, beetroot, fennel and Champagne) are the perfect partner to a dozen oysters (€29 to €38) or tapas-style 'small plates' to share (€7 to €14).

Beans on Fire   Coffee

(Map p254; https://thebeansonfire.com; 7 rue du Général Blaise, 11e; ⏰8am-5pm Mon-Thu, to 7pm Fri-Sun; 📶; MSt-Ambroise) 🖋 Outstanding coffee is guaranteed at this innovative space. Not only a welcoming local cafe, it's also a collaborative roastery, where movers and shakers on Paris' reignited

From left: La Machine du Moulin Rouge (p175); Chez Prune (p174); Café Charbon

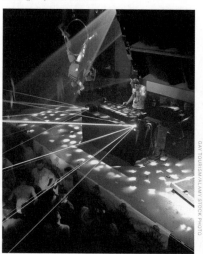

coffee scene come to roast their beans (two-hour roasting workshops, available in English, cost €24, if you're keen to roast your own). Overlooking a park, the terrace is a neighbourhood hotspot on sunny days. Hours can vary.

PasDeLoup   Cocktail Bar

(Map p254; ☎ 09 54 74 16 36; www.facebook. com/pasdelouparis; 108 rue Amelot, 11e; ⓢ 6pm-2am Tue-Sat, 12.30-3.30pm & 6pm-2am Sun; Ⓜ Filles du Calvaire) Next to the Cirque d'Hiver (Winter Circus), a small front bar with timber shelving gives way to a larger space out back where epicureans head for its interesting and superbly gourmet food pairings (dishes €4 to €12, pairings €17 to €25), accompanied by a loungey retro soundtrack. Sunday brunch (€23) is an event.

Café Charbon   Bar

(Map p254; www.lecafecharbon.fr; 109 rue Ober-kampf, 11e; ⓢ 8am-2am Mon-Wed, to 5am Thu, to 6am Fri & Sat; ☎; Ⓜ Parmentier) Canopied by a gold-stencilled navy-blue awning, the Charbon was the first of the hip bars to catch on in Ménilmontant and remains one

of the best. It's always crowded and worth heading to for the belle époque decor (high ceilings, chandeliers and leather booths) and sociable atmosphere. Happy hour is 4.30pm to 8pm; DJs and musicians play Thursday to Saturday.

Boot Café   Coffee

(Map p254; 19 rue du Pont aux Choux, 3e; ⓢ 10am-6pm; Ⓜ St-Sébastien–Froissart) The charm of this three-table cafe is its facade, which must win a prize for 'most photographed'. An old cobbler's shop, its original washed-blue exterior, 'Cordonnerie' lettering and fantastic red boot sign above are beautifully preserved. Excellent coffee is roasted in Paris, to boot.

La Belle Hortense   Bar

(Map p254; www.cafeine.com/belle-hortense; 31 rue Vieille du Temple, 4e; ⓢ 5pm-2am; Ⓜ Hôtel de Ville) Behind its charming chambray blue-painted facade, this creative wine bar named after a Jacques Roubaud novel fuses shelf after shelf of literary novels with an excellent wine list and an enriching weekly agenda of book readings, signings and art events.

Nightlife

Paris' residential make-up means nightclubs aren't ubiquitous. Lacking a mainstream scene, clubbing here tends to be underground and extremely mobile. The best DJs and their followings have short stints in a certain venue before moving on, and the scene's hippest *soirées clubbing* (clubbing events) float between venues – including the many dance-driven bars. Dedicated clubbers may also want to check out the growing suburban scene, much more alternative and spontaneous in nature, but also harder to reach.

Wherever you wind up, the beat is strong. Electronic music is of particularly high quality in Paris' clubs, with some excellent local house and techno. Funk and groove have given the predominance of dark minimal sounds a good pounding, and the Latin scene is huge; salsa dancing and Latino music nights pack out plenty of clubs. World music also has a following in Paris, where everything – from Algerian raï to Senegalese *mbalax* and West Indian *zouk* – goes at clubs. R&B and hip-hop pickings are decent, if less represented than elsewhere. Track tomorrow's hot 'n' happening soirée with these finger-on-the-pulse Parisian nightlife links:

Paris DJs (www.parisdjs.com) Free downloads on this site help to get you in the groove.

Paris Bouge (www.parisbouge.com) Comprehensive listings site.

Parissi (www.parissi.com) Search by date, then *la before, la soirée* and *l'after*.

Tribu de Nuit (www.tribudenuit.com) Parties, club events and concerts galore.

The Hood — Cafe

(Map p254; www.thehoodparis.com; 80 rue Jean-Pierre Timbaud, 11e; ⊙8am-6.30pm Mon & Wed-Fri, 10am-7pm Sat & Sun; 🛜; MParmentier) First and foremost this light-filled local hangout is about the coffee – Belleville Brûlerie (p152) beans are brewed to absolute perfection here – but it takes its music just as seriously with a great vinyl collection, spontaneous jam sessions and acoustic Sunday-afternoon 'folkoff' gigs. Fantastic lunches might include cinnamon-roasted chicken with red cabbage and soba noodles. Ask about English-language coffee-brewing workshops. Guest chefs pop in to cook for weekend brunch.

Gibus Club — Club

(Map p254; 📞01 47 00 59 14; http://gibusclub.fr; 18 rue du Faubourg du Temple, 11e; admission €15-20; ⊙11pm-7am Thu-Sat; MRépublique) What started out as a summer party thrown by Scream Club has now morphed into a permanent fixture on the city's gay scene, rebranded as Gibus Club and still working hard to stay top dog as one of Paris' biggest gay parties.

Le Pick-Clops — Bar

(Map p254; 16 rue Vieille du Temple, 4e; ⊙7am-2am Mon-Sat, 8am-2am Sun; 🛜; MHôtel de Ville) This buzzy 1950s-styled bar-cafe – all shades of yellow and lit by neon – has a mosaic-tiled facade, formica tables, red vinyl lounges and plenty of mirrors. Attracting a friendly flow of locals and passers-by, it's a great place for morning or afternoon coffee, occasional concerts, or that last drink alone or with friends.

L'Ebouillanté — Cafe

(Map p254; http://ebouillante.fr; 6 rue des Barres, 4e; ⊙noon-10pm Tue-Sun Jun-Aug, noon-7pm Tue-Sun Sep-May; MPont Marie, Hôtel de Ville) Set on a pedestrian, stone-flagged street just footsteps from the Seine, with one of the city's prettiest terraces, cornflower-blue-painted L'Ebouillanté buzzes with Parisians sipping refreshing glasses of homemade *citronnade* (ginger lemonade), hibiscus-flower cordial and over two dozen varieties of tea. Delicious cakes, jumbo salads and savoury crêpes complement the long drinks menu.

3w Kafé   Lesbian

(Map p254; 8 rue des Écouffes, 4e; ⊘7pm-3am Wed & Thu, to 5am Fri & Sat, to 4am Sun; Ⓜ St-Paul) The name of this flagship cocktail-bar-pub means 'women with women'. It's relaxed and there's no ban on men (but they must be accompanied by a woman). On weekends there's dancing downstairs with a DJ. Themed evenings take place regularly; check its Facebook page for events.

Ob-La-Di   Coffee

(Map p254; 54 rue de Saintonge, 3e; ⊘8am-5pm Wed-Fri, 9am-6pm Sat & Sun; Ⓜ Filles du Calvaire) Serious coffee roasted by Paris' Café Lomi is the big draw of this pocket-sized coffee shop, clad with large mirrors, geometric blue-and-white tiles and glass vases of fresh flowers. The stylish space is not designed for hanging out with your laptop, but the crowd is hip, and the *café*, cookies, cakes and fruity granola superb.

⊙ Bastille & Eastern Paris

Concrete   Club

(www.concreteparis.fr; 69 Port de la Rapée, 12e; ⊘Thu-Sun; Ⓜ Gare de Lyon) This wild-child club with two dance floors lures a young international set to a barge on the Seine, moored by Gare de Lyon. Famed for introducing an 'after-hours' element to Paris' somewhat staid clubbing scene, Concrete is a hugely popular place to party all hours. Watch for world-class electro DJ appearances and all-weekend events on social media. Admission is free on Thursday; prices average around €20 Friday to Sunday.

Le Baron Rouge   Wine Bar

(Map p254; ☑01 43 43 14 32; http://lebaron rouge.net; 1 rue Théophile Roussel, 12e; ⊘5-10pm Mon, 10am-2pm & 5-10pm Tue-Fri, 10am-10pm Sat, 10am-4pm Sun; Ⓜ Ledru-Rollin) Just about the ultimate Parisian wine-bar experi-

ence, this wonderfully unpretentious local meeting place where everyone is welcome has barrels stacked against the bottle-lined walls and serves cheese, charcuterie and oysters. It's especially busy on Sunday after the Marché d'Aligre (p83) wraps up. For a small deposit, you can fill up 1L bottles straight from the barrel for under €5.

Café des Anges   Cafe

(Map p254; ☑01 47 00 00 63; www.cafedes angesparis.com; 66 rue de la Roquette, 11e; ⊘7.30am-2am; 🛜; Ⓜ Bastille) With its pastel-shaded paintwork and locals sipping coffee beneath the terracotta-coloured awning on its busy pavement terrace, Angels Cafe lives up to the 'quintessential Paris cafe' dream. In winter wrap up beneath a blanket outside, or squeeze through the crowds at the zinc bar to snag a coveted table inside. Happy hour runs from 5pm to 9pm.

A La Française   Cocktail Bar

(Map p254; 50 rue Léon Frot, 11e; ⊘5pm-midnight Mon, to 2am Tue-Sat; 🛜; Ⓜ Charonne) House creations and revived ancient cocktail recipes at this cool neighbourhood bar are made only with spirits, liqueurs and wines produced in France and French-speaking countries, such as La Parisienne (d'Aloe Vera Maison Védrenne, Monson's dry gin and sauvignon blanc) and Le Sazerac (Martell cognac, Pernod absinthe, sugar and Amer d'Amédée Peychaud bitters). Happy hour runs from 6pm to 8pm.

Bluebird   Cocktail Bar

(Map p254; 12 rue St-Bernard, 11e; ⊘6pm-2am; Ⓜ Faidherbe-Chaligny) The ultimate neighbourhood hang-out, Bluebird is styled like a 1950s apartment with retro decor, a giant fish tank along one wall, and a soundtrack of smooth lounge music. Cocktail recipes date from the 1800s and early 1900s and change seasonally, but the menu always features six gin-based creations, six with other spirits, and three low-alcohol wine- and Champagne-based drinks.

Le Pure Café
Cafe

(Map p254; www.lepurecafe.fr; 14 rue Jean Macé, 11e; ⊙7am-1am Mon-Fri, 8am-1am Sat, 9am-midnight Sun; ⓂCharonne) A classic Parisian corner cafe, Le Pure is a charming spot to drop into for a morning coffee, aperitif, meal (mains €13.50 to €25) or Sunday brunch (€19). Its selection of natural and organic wines by the glass is particularly good. Film buffs might recognise its cherry-red facade and vintage-wood and zinc bar from the Richard Linklater film *Before Sunset*.

La Fée Verte
Bar

(Map p254; ☑01 43 72 31 24; 108 rue de la Roquette, 11e; ⊙7am-2am; 🛜; ⓂVoltaire) Absinthe is the speciality of the Green Fairy, a thronging neighbourhood bar with dark-wood furniture, huge mirrors and a zinc bar. It stocks 20-odd different types of the devilish drink (served traditionally, with slotted spoons and sugar cubes) as well as good food, including house-speciality burgers. Sunday brunch costs €24.

The Islands

Taverne Henri IV
Wine Bar

(Map p250; 13 place du Pont Neuf, 1er; ⊙noon-11pm Mon-Sat, closed Aug; ⓂPont Neuf) Dating from 1885, this venerable wine bar lures lawyers and paralegals from the nearby Palais de Justice (not to mention celeb writers and actors, as the autographed snaps testify). Classic French dishes such as garlic snails, charcuterie (cold cooked meats) and aromatic cheese platters complement its extensive wine list.

Les Jardins du Pont-Neuf
Cocktail Bar

(Map p250; http://lesjardinsdupontneuf.com; quai de l'Horloge, 1er; ⊙7pm-2am Tue-Sat, hours can vary; 🛜; ⓂPont Neuf) Decked out with art-nouveau-inspired decor including rattan furniture and hanging plants, this ultra-chic floating cocktail bar aboard a barge moored by the Pont Neuf has two vast terraces with magical views of the Seine and a dance floor. Check the website for upcoming soirées.

Latin Quarter

Little Bastards
Cocktail Bar

(Map p252; 5 rue Blainville, 5e; ⊙7pm-2am Mon, 6pm-2am Tue-Thu, 6pm-4am Fri & Sat; ⓂPlace Monge) Only house-creation cocktails are listed on the menu at uberhip Little Bastards – among them Fal' in Love (Beefeater gin, cranberry juice, lime, mint, guava puree and Falernum clove-, ginger- and almond-syrup), Be a Beet Smooth (Jameson, coriander, sherry, egg white and pepper) and Deep Throat (Absolut vodka, watermelon syrup and Pernod) – but they'll also mix up classics if you ask.

Le Verre à Pied
Cafe

(Map p252; http://leverreapied.fr; 118bis rue Mouffetard, 5e; ⊙9am-9pm Tue-Sat, 9.30am-4pm Sun; ⓂCensier Daubenton) This *café-tabac* is a pearl of a place where little has changed since 1870. Its nicotine-hued mirrored wall, moulded cornices and original bar make it part of a dying breed, but it epitomises the charm, glamour and romance of an old Paris everyone loves, including stallholders from the rue Mouffetard market who yo-yo in and out.

Caffè Juno
Coffee

(Map p252; www.caffe-juno.com; 58 rue Henri Barbusse, 5e; ⊙9am-7pm Mon-Sat; 🛜; ⓂRaspail or RER Port Royal) 🖋 Hole-in-the-wall Caffè Juno roasts its own Ethiopian, Indonesian, Colombian and Cameroonian beans and specialises in espressos, filters and lattes. Prices are impressively reasonable to drink on site in the industrial-style space strewn with hessian bags; you can also buy beans to take home.

Le Crocodile
Bar

(Map p252; 6 rue Royer-Collard, 5e; ⊙6pm-2am Mon-Sat; ⓂOdéon or RER Luxembourg) This green-shuttered bar has been dispensing affordable cocktails (350 at last count, with gummy-'bear' crocodiles in the glass) since 1966. Arrive late for a truly eclectic crowd, including lots of students, and raucous revelry. Hours can vary (dawn closings are common). Happy hour runs from 6pm to 11pm Monday to Thursday and 6pm to 10pm Friday and Saturday. Cash only.

Le Pub St-Hilaire   Pub

(Map p252; 2 rue Valette, 5e; ☺4pm-2am Mon-Thu, to 5am Fri & Sat; ⓜMaubert-Mutualité) 'Buzzing' fails to do justice to the pulsating vibe inside this student-loved pub. Generous happy hours last from 5pm to 9pm and the place is kept packed with a trio of pool tables, board games, music on two floors, hearty bar food and various gimmicks to rev up the party crowd (a metre of cocktails, 'be your own barman' etc).

🜚 St-Germain & Les Invalides

Tiger Bar   Cocktail Bar

(Map p252; www.tiger-paris.com; 13 rue Princesse, 6e; ☺6pm-2am Mon-Sat, 7pm-2am Sun; ⓜMabillon) Suspended bare-bulb lights and fretted timber make this split-level space a stylish spot for specialist gins (45 different varieties). Its 24 cocktails include a Breakfast Martini (gin, triple sec, orange marmalade and lemon juice) and Oh My Dog (white-pepper-infused gin, lime juice, raspberry and rose cordial and ginger ale). A *degustation* of four gins costs €25.

Gin aside, it also serves Japanese sake, wine and craft beer.

Les Deux Magots   Cafe

(Map p250; www.lesdeuxmagots.fr; 170 bd St-Germain, 6e; ☺7.30am-1am; ⓜSt-Germain des Prés) If ever there was a cafe that summed up St-Germain des Prés' early-20th-century literary scene, it's this former hang-out of anyone who was anyone. You will spend *beaucoup* to sip a coffee in a wicker chair on the terrace shaded by dark-green awnings and geraniums spilling from window boxes, but it's an undeniable piece of Parisian history.

Coutume   Coffee

(Map p246; www.coutumecafe.com; 47 rue de Babylone, 7e; ☺8am-6pm Mon-Fri, 9am-6pm Sat & Sun; 🛜; ⓜSt-François Xavier) 🍃 The

Les Deux Magots

Café de Flore

dramatic improvement in Parisian coffee in recent years is thanks in no small part to Coutume, artisan roaster of premium beans for scores of establishments around town. Its flagship cafe – a bright, light-filled, postindustrial space – is ground zero for innovative preparation methods including cold extraction and siphon brews. Fabulous organic fare and pastries are also available.

Café de Flore — Cafe

(Map p250; http://cafedeflore.fr; 172 bd St-Germain, 6e; ☺7am-1.30am; Ⓜ St-Germain des Prés) The red upholstered benches, mirrors and marble walls at this art-deco landmark haven't changed much since the days when Jean-Paul Sartre and Simone de Beauvoir essentially set up office here, writing in its warmth during the Nazi occupation. It also hosts a monthly English-language *philocafé* (philosophy discussion) session.

Au Sauvignon — Wine Bar

(Map p246; http://ausauvignon.com; 80 rue des Sts-Pères, 7e; ☺8am-11pm Mon-Sat, 9am-10pm Sun; Ⓜ Sèvres-Babylone) Grab a table in the evening light at this wonderfully authentic *bar à vins* or head to the quintessential bistro interior, with an original zinc bar, tightly packed tables and hand-painted ceiling celebrating French viticultural tradition. A plate of *casse-croûtes au pain Poilâne* – toast with ham, pâté, terrine, smoked salmon and foie gras – is the perfect accompaniment.

La Quincave — Wine Bar

(Map p246; 17 rue Bréa, 6e; ☺11am-1pm & 5-9pm Tue-Fri, 11am-9pm Sat, 11am-2pm Sun; Ⓜ Vavin) Bar stools at this lively wine bar–shop are fashioned from wine barrels, but on summer evenings most of the action spills onto the tiny street out front. More than 200 varieties of natural wines are available by the bottle, ranging from €9 to €35 (corkage costs €7), along with charcuterie and cheese platters to soak them up.

Le 10 — Pub

(Map p252; www.lebar10.com; 10 rue de l'Odéon, 6e; ☺5pm-2am Mon-Sat; ☎; Ⓜ Odéon) Plastered with posters, cellar pub 'Le Dix' is a student favourite, not least for its cheap sangria. An eclectic selection emerges from the jukebox – everything from jazz and The Doors to traditional French *chansons* (*à la* Édith Piaf). It's the ideal spot for plotting the next revolution or conquering a lonely heart.

Frog & Princess
Microbrewery

(Map p252; www.frogpubs.com; 9 rue Princesse, 6e; ⊗5.30pm-2am Mon-Thu, noon-2am Fri-Sun; 🖹; Ⓜ Mabillon) Part of the Frog family that includes several Parisian microbreweries, this good-time pub on one of the Left Bank's liveliest drinking streets is popular for its own-brewed beers (several of which recently took out medals at the World Beer Awards), burgers, American barbecue and soul food, and sports screenings.

Montparnasse & Southern Paris

Le Batofar
Club

(www.batofar.fr; opposite 11 quai François Mauriac, 13e; ⊗club 11.30pm-6am Tue-Sat, bar 6-11pm Tue-Sat May-Sep, 7pm-midnight Tue-Sat Oct-Apr; Ⓜ Quai de la Gare, Bibliothèque) This much-loved, red-metal tugboat has a rooftop bar that's terrific in summer, and a respected restaurant, while the club underneath provides memorable underwater acoustics between its metal walls and portholes. Le Batofar is known for its edgy, experimental music policy and live performances from 7pm, mostly electro-oriented but also incorporating hip hop, new wave, rock, punk and jazz.

Hexagone Café
Coffee

(Map p246; www.hexagone-cafe.fr; 121 rue du Château, 14e; ⊗8am-6pm Mon-Fri, 10am-6pm

Sat & Sun; 🖹; Ⓜ Pernety) Parisian furniture maker David Guillon designed the industrial-inspired metal-framed bar stools and textured blonde-wood bar for this chilled spot, which uses award-winning Breton roaster Caffè Cataldi beans for its addictive espressos, drip-filters and cappuccinos, and also serves loose-leaf teas and pastries. Fast wi-fi, big picture windows and downlights make it a favourite with freelancers, students and creatives.

Félicie
Bar

(Map p246; www.felicie.info; 174 av du Maine, 14e; ⊗7.30am-2am Mon-Fri, 8am-2am Sat & Sun; 🖹; Ⓜ Lourmel) Chances are your first visit won't be your last at this unpretentious neighbourhood cafe with a big heated pavement terrace, fun-loving staff and a laid-back vibe. It's a quintessentially Parisian spot to hang out any time of day, but especially during Sunday brunch and late at night. Bistro classics include steak tartare.

La Dame de Canton
Club

(www.damedecanton.com; opp 11 quai François Mauriac, 13e; ⊗7pm-midnight Tue-Thu, to 2am Fri, to 5am Sat; Ⓜ Bibliothèque) This floating *boîte* (club) aboard a three-masted Chinese junk with a couple of world voyages under its belt bobs beneath the Bibliothèque Nationale de France. Concerts cover pop and indie to electro, hip hop, reggae and rock; afterwards DJs keep the crowd hyped. There's also a popular bar and restaurant with wood-fired pizzas served on the terrace from May to September.

SHOWTIME

Renowned opera, ballet, jazz clubs, street performers and buskers

Showtime

Catching a performance in Paris is a treat. French and international opera, ballet and theatre companies and cabaret dancers take to the stage in fabled venues, and a flurry of young, passionate, highly creative musicians, thespians and artists make the city's fascinating fringe art scene what it is. Paris became Europe's most important jazz centre after WWII and the city has some fantastic jazz clubs, as well as venues for stirring French chansons, dazzling cabarets including the iconic Moulin Rouge, cutting-edge cultural centres, wonderful independent cinemas, and dozens of orchestral, organ and chamber-music concerts each week.

In This Section

Eiffel Tower & Western Paris 188

Champs-Élysées &
Grands Boulevards 188

Louvre & Les Halles 188

Montmartre & Northern Paris............189

Le Marais, Ménilmontant
& Belleville 191

Bastille & Eastern Paris 192

Latin Quarter..193

St-Germain & Les Invalides................193

Tickets

The most convenient place to purchase concert, theatre and other cultural and sporting-event tickets is from electronics and entertainment megashop Fnac (www.fnactickets.com), whether in person at the *billeteries* (ticket offices) or by phone or online. There are branches throughout Paris, including in the Forum des Halles (p77). Tickets generally can't be refunded.

MOULIN ROUGE® – HABAS·SMADJA ©

Moulin Rouge (p190)

The Best...

Entertainment Venues

Palais Garnier (p188) Paris' premier opera house.

Point Éphémère (p189) Canal St-Martin cultural centre.

Moulin Rouge (p190) The razzledazzle can-can creator.

Le 104 (p190) Cultural tour de force.

La Flèche d'Or (p192) Renowned for unearthing new musical talent.

Jazz Clubs

Café Universel (p193) Unpretentious vibe and no cover.

New Morning (p191) Solid and varied line-up.

Le Baiser Salé (p188) Focuses on Caribbean and Latin sounds.

Sunset & Sunside (p189) Blues, fusion and world sounds.

Le Caveau des Oubliettes (p193) Dungeon jam sessions.

Discount Tickets

Pick up half-price tickets for same-day performances of ballet, opera and music at **Kiosque Théâtre Madeleine** (Map p246; www.kiosqueculture.com; opposite 15 place de la Madeleine, 8e; ⊘12.30-7.30pm Tue-Sat, to 3.45pm Sun; MMadeleine), a freestanding kiosk by place de la Madeleine.

✪ Eiffel Tower & Western Paris

Théâtre National de Chaillot   Theatre
(Map p246; ☎01 53 65 30 00; http://theatre
-chaillot.fr; 1 place du Trocadéro, 16e; MTro-
cadéro) The French national theatre located beneath the Trocadéro esplanade primarily stages modern-dance productions.

✪ Champs-Élysées & Grands Boulevards

Palais Garnier   Opera, Ballet
(Map p246; www.operadeparis.fr; place de l'Opéra, 9e; MOpéra) The city's original opera house (p100) is smaller than its Bastille counterpart, but has perfect acoustics. Due to its odd shape, some seats have limited or no visibility – book carefully. Ticket prices and conditions (including last-minute discounts) are available from the **box office** (Map p246; ☎international calls 01 71 25 24 23, within

France 08 25 05 44 05; cnr rues Scribe & Auber; ⊘11am-6.30pm Mon-Sat; MOpéra). Online flash sales are held from noon on Wednesdays.

✪ Louvre & Les Halles

La Place   Cultural Centre
(Map p250; ☎01 70 22 45 48; http://laplace.paris; 10 passage de la Canopée, Forum des Halles, 1er; ⊘cultural centre 10am-11pm Tue-Sat, bar 1-7pm Tue-Sat, concert hours vary; MLes Halles, Châtelet or RER Châtelet–Les Halles) The overhaul of the vast shopping mall Forum des Halles (p77) saw the launch of Paris' inaugural hip-hop cultural centre under its custard-yellow glass canopy, with a 400-capacity concert hall, a 100-capacity broadcast studio, several recording studios and street-art graffiti workrooms, along with a relaxed bar. Some concerts are free, while ticket prices vary for others – check the programme online.

Le Grand Rex   Cinema
(Map p250; www.legrandrex.com; 1 bd Poissonnière, 2e; tours adult/child €11/9, cinema tickets €11/4.50; ⊘tours 10am-6pm Wed & Sun, 10am-6.30pm Sat, extended hours during school holidays; MBonne Nouvelle) Blockbuster screenings and concerts aside, this 1932 art deco cinematic icon runs 50-minute behind-the-scenes tours (English soundtracks available) during which visitors – tracked by a sensor slung around their neck – are whisked up (via a lift) behind the giant screen, tour a soundstage and experiment in a recording studio. Whizz-bang special effects along the way will stun adults and kids alike.

Le Baiser Salé   Live Music
(Map p250; ☎01 42 33 37 71; www.lebaiser-sale.com; 58 rue des Lombards, 1er; ⊘daily; MChâtelet) Known for its Afro and Latin jazz, and jazz fusion concerts, the Salty Kiss combines big names and unknown artists. The place has a relaxed vibe, with sets usually starting at 7.30pm or 9.30pm.

Sunset & Sunside   Live Music

(Map p250; 01 40 26 46 60; www.sunset-sunside.com; 60 rue des Lombards, 1er; daily; Châtelet) There are two venues in one at this well-respected club, which hosts electric jazz, fusion and occasional salsa at Sunset, in the vaulted cellar, and acoustics and concerts on the ground floor at Sunside.

Comédie Française   Theatre

(Map p250; 01 44 58 15 15; www.comedie-francaise.fr; place Colette, 1er; Palais Royal–Musée du Louvre) Founded in 1680 under Louis XIV, this state-run theatre bases its repertoire around the works of classic French playwrights. The theatre has its roots in an earlier company directed by Molière at the Palais Royal.

Forum des Images   Cinema

(Map p250; www.forumdesimages.fr; Forum des Halles, 2 rue du Cinéma, Porte St-Eustache, 1er; tickets adult/child €6/5; 12.30-9pm Tue-Fri, 2-9pm Sat & Sun; Les Halles) A five-screen cinema showing films set in Paris is the centrepiece of the city's film archive. Created in 1988 to establish an audiovisual archive of the city, and renovated in dramatic shades of pink, grey and black, the complex has a library and research centre with newsreels, documentaries and advertising. Its online programme lists thematic series, festivals and events.

❂ Montmartre & Northern Paris

Philharmonie de Paris   Concert Venue

(01 44 84 44 84; http://philharmoniedeparis.fr; 221 av Jean Jaurès, 19e; box office noon-6pm Tue-Fri, 10am-6pm Sat & Sun; Porte de Pantin) Major complex the Cité de la Musique – Philharmonie de Paris hosts an eclectic range of concerts – from classical to North African and Japanese – in the 2015-innaugurated Philharmonie building's Grande Salle Pierre Boulez, with an audience capacity of 2400 to 3600, and in

 Buskers in Paris

Paris' gaggle of clowns, mime artists, living statues, acrobats, in-line skaters, buskers and other street entertainers can be loads of fun and cost substantially less than a theatre ticket (a few coins in the hat is appreciated). Some excellent musicians perform in the long echo-filled corridors of the metro, a highly prized privilege that artists audition for. Outside, you can be sure of a good show at the following:

Place Georges Pompidou, 4e The huge square in front of the Centre Pompidou.

Pont St-Louis, 4e The bridge linking Paris' two islands (best enjoyed with a Berthillon ice cream in hand).

Pont au Double, 4e The pedestrian bridge linking Notre Dame with the Left Bank.

Place Joachim du Bellay, 1er Musicians and fire-eaters near the Fontaine des Innocents.

Place du Tertre, Montmartre, 18e Montmartre's original main square is Paris' busiest busker stage.

Arlette Denis busking in Montmartre

the adjacent Cité de la Musique's Salle des Concerts, with a capacity of 900 to 1600.

Point Éphémère   Live Music

(01 40 34 02 48; www.pointephemere.org; 200 quai de Valmy, 10e; 12.30pm-2am Mon-Sat, to 10pm Sun; ; Louis Blanc) On the banks of Canal St-Martin in a former fire

From left: La Place (p188); Le Grand Rex (p188); Maggie Rogers performs at Point Éphémère (p189)

station and later squat, this arts and music venue attracts an underground crowd for concerts, dance nights and art exhibitions. Its rockin' restaurant, Animal Kitchen, fuses gourmet cuisine with music from Animal Records (Sunday brunch from 1pm is a highlight); the rooftop bar, Le Top, opens in fine weather.

Moulin Rouge   Cabaret
(Map p249; 01 53 09 82 82; www.moulinrouge.fr; 82 bd de Clichy, 18e; show/dinner show from €87/165; shows 7pm, 9pm & 11pm; Blanche) Immortalised in Toulouse-Lautrec's posters and later in Baz Luhrmann's film, Paris' legendary cabaret twinkles beneath a 1925 replica of its original red windmill. Yes, it's packed with bus-tour crowds. But from the opening bars of music to the last high cancan-girl kick, it's a whirl of fantastical costumes, sets, choreography and Champagne. Book in advance online and dress smartly (no sneakers). No entry for children under six.

Le Divan du Monde   Live Music
(Map p249; 01 40 05 08 99; www.divandumonde.com; 75 rue des Martyrs, 18e; Pigalle)

Take some cinematographic events and *nouvelles chansons françaises* (new French songs). Add in soul/funk fiestas, air-guitar face-offs and rock parties of the Arctic Monkeys/Killers/Libertines persuasion... You may now be getting some idea of the inventive, open-minded approach at this excellent cross-cultural venue in Pigalle.

Café A   Arts Centre
(Map p254; www.cafea.fr; 148 rue du Faubourg St-Martin, 10e; 10am-5pm Mon, 10am-2am Tue-Sat, 11am-5pm Sun; Gare de l'Est) Hidden inside a convent dating from the 17th century and opening out back to a courtyard garden strung with coloured light bulbs, this multipurpose venue hosts regular live music (Cuban, jazz, African, classical and more), DJs, artistic performances, fashion shows, cinema nights and art exhibitions in the cavernous interior. Detox weekend brunch (€25) includes superfood salads.

Le 104   Arts Centre
(01 53 35 50 00; www.le104.fr; 5 rue Curial, 19e; noon-7pm Tue-Fri, 11am-7pm Sat & Sun; ; Riquet) Watch for circus, theatre, music, monthly balls, magic shows and an

eclectic range of other events at this former funeral parlour turned city-funded art space. Some shows are free; others require admission.

New Morning
Jazz, Blues

(Map p254; www.newmorning.com; 7 & 9 rue des Petites Écuries, 10e; MChâteau d'Eau) This highly regarded auditorium with excellent acoustics hosts big-name jazz concerts (Ravi Coltrane, Lake Street Dive) as well as a variety of blues, rock, funk, salsa, Afro-Cuban and Brazilian music. Check upcoming concerts online.

✪ Le Marais, Ménilmontant & Belleville

Cave du 38 Riv'
Jazz

(Map p254; ☑01 48 87 56 30; www.38riv.com; 38 rue de Rivoli, 4e; ☺concerts from 8.30pm; MHôtel de Ville) In the heart of Le Marais on busy de Rivoli, a tiny street frontage gives way to a fantastically atmospheric vaulted stone cellar with jazz concerts most nights; check the agenda online. Jam sessions with free admission often take place on Mondays.

Le Carreau du Temple
Cultural Centre

(Map p254; ☑01 83 81 93 30; www.carreaudu temple.eu; 2 rue Perrée, 3e; ☺box office 10am-10pm Mon-Sat; MTemple) The quarter's old covered market with gorgeous art-nouveau ironwork is now the city's most architecturally appealing cultural centre and entertainment venue. The place where silks, lace, leather and other materials were sold in the 19th century is now a vast stage for exhibitions, concerts, sports classes and theatre. Check the programme online.

La Java
World Music

(Map p254; www.la-java.fr; 105 rue du Faubourg du Temple, 11e; ☺8pm-dawn Mon-Sat; MGoncourt) Built in 1922, this is the dance hall where Édith Piaf got her first break, and it now reverberates to the sound of live salsa, rock and world music. Live concerts usually take place at 8pm or 9pm during the week. Afterwards a festive crowd gets dancing to electro, house, disco and Latino DJs.

8pm-2am Thu-Sat; MᴹPyrénées) This old-fashioned bistro and *musette* at the top of Parc de Belleville is an atmospheric venue for performances of *chansons* featuring accordions and an organ grinder three times a week. It's a lively favourite with locals, so booking ahead is advised.

❂ Bastille & Eastern Paris

Cinema

The film-lover's ultimate city, Paris has some wonderful movie houses to catch new flicks, avant-garde cinema and priceless classics.

Foreign films (including English-language films) screened in their original language with French subtitles are labelled 'VO' (*version originale*). Films labelled 'VF' (*version française*) are dubbed in French.

L'Officiel des Spectacles (www.offi.fr) list the full crop of Paris' cinematic pickings and screening times; online check out http://cinema.leparisien.fr or www.allocine.com.

First-run tickets cost around €12 for adults (€14 for 3D). Most cinemas have across-the-board discounts before noon.

Nouveau Casino Live Music
(Map p254; ☑01 43 57 57 40; www.nouveau casino.net; 109 rue Oberkampf, 11e; ⊘Tue-Sun; MᴹParmentier) This club-concert annexe of Café Charbon (p177) has made a name for itself amid the bars of Oberkampf with its live-music concerts (usually Tuesday, Thursday and Friday) and lively club nights on weekends. Electro, pop, deep house, rock – the programme is eclectic, underground and always up to the minute. Check the website for listings.

Le Vieux Belleville Live Music
(Map p254; ☑01 44 62 92 66; www.le-vieux-bel leville.com; 12 rue des Envierges, 20e; ⊘concerts

La Flèche d'Or Live Music
(☑01 44 64 01 02; 102bis rue de Bagnolet, 20e; ⊘hours vary; MᴹGambetta, Alexandre Dumas) Just over 1km northeast of place de la Nation in a former railway station on central Paris' outer edge, awesome music venue the Golden Arrow – named for the train to Calais in the 1930s – hosts both indie rock concerts and house/electro DJ nights and has a solid reputation for promoting new talent. Tickets average around €17 to €32.

La Cinémathèque Française Cinema
(www.cinematheque.fr; 51 rue de Bercy, 12e; tickets adult/child €6.50/4; ⊘noon-7pm Mon & Wed-Sun; MᴹBercy) This national institution is a temple to the 'seventh art' and always screens its foreign offerings in their original versions. Up to 10 films a day are shown, usually retrospectives (Spielberg, Altman, Eastwood) mixed in with related but more obscure films.

Le Motel Live Music
(Map p254; www.lemotel.fr; 8 passage Josset, 11e; ⊘6pm-2am Tue-Sun; MᴹLedru-Rollin) This hole-in-the-wall venue in the hot-to-boiling-point 11e has become the go-to indie bar around Bastille. It's especially well loved for its comfy sofas, inexpensive but quality drinks (craft beers on tap and indie cocktails; happy hour is from 6pm to 9pm) and excellent music, with live bands and DJs Tuesday to Saturday (plus quiz nights on Sunday).

Le Balajo Live Music
(Map p254; ☑01 47 00 07 87; www.balajo.fr; 9 rue de Lappe, 11e; ⊘hours vary; MᴹBastille) A mainstay of Parisian nightlife since 1936,

this ancient ballroom is devoted to evening salsa classes and Latino music during the week, with an R&B slant on weekends when the dance floor rocks until *aube* (dawn). But the best time to visit is for its old-fashioned *musette* (accordion music) gigs on from 2pm to 7pm Sundays and Mondays.

✪ Latin Quarter

Café Universel   Jazz, Blues
(Map p252; ☑01 43 25 74 20; www.cafeuniversel.com; 267 rue St-Jacques, 5e; ⊙9pm-2am Tue-Sat; ☎; MCensier Daubenton or RER Port Royal) Café Universel hosts a brilliant array of live concerts with everything from bebop and Latin sounds to vocal jazz sessions. Plenty of freedom is given to young producers and artists, and its convivial relaxed atmosphere attracts a mix of students and jazz lovers. Concerts are free, but tip the artists when they pass the hat around.

Le Caveau des Oubliettes   Jazz, Blues
(Map p252; ☑01 46 34 23 09; www.caveau-des-oubliettes.com; 52 rue Galande, 5e; ⊙5pm-2am Sun & Tue, to 4am Wed-Sat; MSt-Michel) From the 16th-century ground-floor pub (with a happy hour from 5pm to 9pm), descend to the 12th-century dungeon for jazz, blues and funk concerts, and jam sessions (from 10pm).

Église St-Julien le Pauvre   Classical Music
(Map p252; ☑01 42 26 00 00; www.concertinparis.com; 1 rue St-Julien le Pauvre, 5e; tickets free-€28; MSt-Michel) Piano recitals (Chopin, Liszt) are staged at least two evenings a week in one of the oldest churches in Paris. Higher-priced tickets directly face the stage. Payment is by cash only at the door.

Le Petit Journal St-Michel   Jazz, Blues
(Map p252; ☑01 43 26 28 59; http://petitjournalsaintmichel.fr; 71 bd St-Michel, 5e; admission incl 1 drink €20, with dinner €49-57; ⊙7.30pm-1am Mon-Sat; MCluny–La Sorbonne or RER

Luxembourg) Classic jazz concerts kick off at 9.15pm in the atmospheric downstairs cellar of this sophisticated jazz venue across from the Jardin du Luxembourg (p68). Everything ranging from Dixieland and vocals to big band and swing sets patrons' toes tapping. Dinner is served at 8pm (but it's the music that's the real draw).

Le Champo   Cinema
(Map p252; www.cinema-lechampo.com; 51 rue des Écoles, 5e; tickets adult/child €9/4; MCluny–La Sorbonne) This is one of the most popular of the many Latin Quarter cinemas, featuring classics and retrospectives looking at the films of such actors and directors as Alfred Hitchcock, Jacques Tati, Alain Resnais, Frank Capra, Tim Burton and Woody Allen. One of the two *salles* (cinemas) has wheelchair access.

Caveau de la Huchette   Jazz, Blues
(Map p252; ☑01 43 26 65 05; www.caveaudelahuchette.fr; 5 rue de la Huchette, 5e; Sun-Thu €13, Fri & Sat €15; ⊙9pm-2.30am Sun-Thu, to 4am Fri & Sat; MSt-Michel) Housed in a medieval *caveau* (cellar) used as a courtroom and torture chamber during the Revolution, this club is where virtually all the jazz greats (Georges Brassens, Thibault...) have played since the end of WWII. It attracts its fair share of tourists, but the atmosphere can be more electric than at the more serious jazz clubs. Sessions start at 10pm.

✪ St-Germain & Les Invalides

Chez Papa   Jazz
(Map p250; ☑01 42 86 99 63; www.papajazzclub-paris.fr; 3 rue St-Benoît, 6e; concerts €12; ⊙concerts 9.30pm-1.30am Tue-Sat; MSt-Germain des Prés) The doors of this snug St-Germain jazz club regularly stay open until dawn. Piano duets, blues, sax solos and singers regularly feature on the bill. Its restaurant, serving traditional French dishes (snails, foie gras, tartare, veal stew), opens from noon to 3.30pm and 7pm to 10.30pm Tuesday to Saturday.

ACTIVE PARIS

Picturesque parks, sporting highlights and unique local-led tours

Active Paris

Ready to unwind with the Parisians? Take a break from the concrete and check out the city's glorious parks and two vast forests, the Bois de Boulogne and Bois de Vincennes, which act as its 'green lungs'. The city also has some stunning swimming pools, both historic and new, and a rapidly expanding network of cycling lanes. As one of the world's most visited cities, Paris is well set up for visitors with a host of guided tours, from bike, boat, bus, scooter and walking tours (including some wonderful local-led options in off-the-beaten-track areas) to more unusual themed options, including photography tours, film-location tours and treasure hunts.

In This Section

Spectator Sports 198

Swimming Pools 198

Inline Skating.......................................198

Parks...199

Forests 200

Guided Tours 201

What to Watch

From late May to mid-June, the French Open heats up at the Stade Roland Garros in the Bois de Boulogne. The Tour de France races up the Champs-Élysées at the end of July every year. The main football (soccer) season runs from August through to April.

Marquinhos in action at Parc des Princes (p198)

The Best...

Outdoor Spaces

Bois de Boulogne (p201) Cycle, row, stroll the gardens, hit the amusement park or catch a steeplechase.

Bois de Vincennes (p200) Home to a zoo, the kid-packed Parc Floral and pick-up football matches.

Jardin du Luxembourg (p68) Stroll among the statues, play tennis, jog in style and entertain the kids.

Parc des Buttes Chaumont (p200) Quirky spot has a faux Greek temple, abandoned railway line and t'ai chi vibes.

Parc de la Villette (p199) Natural history museum, botanic gardens and sprinkler-dodging picnics.

Sporting Venues

Parc des Princes (p198) Home to local football team Paris St-Germain (PSG).

Stade Roland Garros (p198) Prestigious grounds of the French Open.

Hippodrome d'Auteuil (p201) Steeplechases in the Bois de Boulogne.

AURÉLIEN MEUNIER/GETTY IMAGES ©

French Open is held on clay at the Stade Roland Garros late May to mid-June. Much-needed renovations began in 2016 and will incorporate a new Court No 1 with 15,000 seats and a retractable roof, among other changes. The project is slated for completion in 2020; the tournament will continue during that time.

Sporting Information

Local teams include football team Paris St-Germain (www.psg.fr) and rugby teams Racing 92 (www.racing92.fr) and Stade Français Paris (www.stade. fr). Catch France's national rugby team, Les Bleus, at the Stade de France.

For upcoming events, click on Sports & Games (under the Going Out menu) at http://en.parisinfo.com.

Stade de France
YURI TURKOV/SHUTTERSTOCK ©

🚹 Spectator Sports

Stade de France Stadium
(🕿 08 25 05 44 05; www.stadefrance.com; St-Denis La Plaine; stadium tours adult/child €15/10; Ⓜ St-Denis-Porte de Paris) This 80,000-seat stadium was built for the 1998 FIFA World Cup, and hosts major sports and music events. Stadium tours lasting 90 minutes take you behind the scenes, providing no event is underway. Tours in English depart at 11am and 2pm from April to August, and at 2pm Tuesday to Sunday from September to March from Gate E.

Parc des Princes Spectator Sport
(www.psg.fr; 24 rue du Commandant Guilbaud, 16e; Ⓜ Porte de St-Cloud) The Parc des Princes is the home ground of Paris' top-division football (soccer) team, Paris St-Germain (PSG).

Stade Roland Garros Spectator Sport
(www.rolandgarros.com; 2 av Gordon Bennett, 16e, Bois de Boulogne; Ⓜ Porte d'Auteuil) The

🏊 Swimming Pools

Piscine Joséphine Baker Swimming
(🕿 01 56 61 96 50; www.piscine-baker.fr; quai François Mauriac, 13e; adult/child pool €6/3, sauna €10/5; ⏱ 7am-11pm Mon-Fri, 9am-8pm Sat & Sun Jun-Sep, shorter hours Oct-May; Ⓜ Quai de la Gare) Floating on the Seine, this striking swimming pool is named after the 1920s American singer. The 25m-by-10m, four-lane pool and large sun deck are especially popular in summer when the roof slides back. Also here is a children's paddling pool.

Piscine de la Butte Aux Cailles Swimming
(🕿 01 45 89 60 05; www.mairie13.paris.fr; 5 place Paul Verlaine, 13e; adult/child €3/1.70; ⏱ hours vary; Ⓜ Place d'Italie) Built in 1924, this art deco swimming pool complex takes advantage of the lovely warm artesian well water nearby. Along with a spectacular vaulted indoor pool, there are two outdoor pools. Hours fluctuate; check schedules online.

🛼 Inline Skating

Pari Roller Skating
(Map p246; http://pari-roller.com; place Raoul Dautry, 14e; ⏱ 10pm-1am Fri, arrive 9.30pm; Ⓜ Montparnasse Bienvenüe) The world's largest inline mass skate, Pari Roller regularly attracts more than 10,000 bladers. Dubbed 'Friday Night Fever', this fast-paced skate covers a different 30km-odd route each week. Most incorporate cobblestones and downhill stretches, and are geared for

experienced bladers only (for your safety and everyone else's). It takes place year-round except when wet weather makes conditions treacherous.

Like its gentler counterpart, the Marais-based **Rollers & Coquillages** (Map p254; www.rollers-coquillages.org; 37 bd Bourdon, 4e; ⊘2.30pm Sun; Ⓜ Bastille), it's accompanied by yellow-jersey-clad volunteer marshals, along with police (some on inline skates) and ambulances. Wear bright clothes to make yourself visible to drivers and other skaters.

Nomadeshop (Map p254; ☏ 01 44 54 07 44; www.nomadeshop.com; 37 bd Bourdon, 4e; half-/full-day skate rental from €5/8; ⊘11am-1.30pm & 2.30-7.30pm Tue-Fri, 10am-7pm Sat, noon-6pm Sun; Ⓜ Bastille) offers skate rental.

Parks

Parc de la Villette   Park

(https://lavillette.com; 211 av Jean Jaurès, 19e; ⊘6am-1am; Ⓜ Porte de la Villette, Porte de Pantin) Embracing 55 hectares, this vast city park is a cultural centre, kids playground and landscaped urban space at the intersection of two canals, the Ourcq and the St-Denis. Its futuristic layout includes the colossal mirror-like sphere of the Géode cinema and the bright-red cubical pavilions known as *folies*. Among its themed gardens are the Jardin du Dragon (Dragon Garden), with a giant dragon's tongue slide for kids, the Jardin des Dunes (Dunes Garden) and Jardin des Miroirs (Mirror Garden).

Promenade Plantée   Park

(La Coulée Verte René-Dumont; Map p254; cnr rue de Lyon & av Daumesnil, 12e; ⊘8am-9.30pm Mon-Fri, from 9am Sat & Sun Mar-Oct, 8am-5.30pm Mon-Fri, from 9am Sat & Sun Nov-Feb; Ⓜ Bastille, Gare de Lyon, Daumesnil) The disused 19th-century Vincennes railway viaduct was reborn as the world's first elevated park, planted with a fragrant profusion of cherry trees, maples, rose trellises, bamboo corridors and lavender. Three storeys above ground, it provides

 Swimming Etiquette

If you want to go swimming at either your hotel or in a public pool, you'll need to don a *bonnet de bain* (bathing cap) – even if you don't have any hair. You shouldn't need to buy one ahead of time as they are generally sold at most pools. Men are required to wear skin-tight trunks (Speedos); loose-fitting Bermuda shorts are not allowed.

Piscine Joséphine Baker
JULIEN HEKIMIAN/GETTY IMAGES ©

a unique aerial vantage point on the city. Staircases provide access (lifts/elevators here invariably don't work). Along the first, northwestern section, above av Daumesnil, art-gallery workshops beneath the arches form the Viaduc des Arts (p154).

Île aux Cygnes   Island

(Isle of Swans; Map p246; btwn Pont de Grenelle & Pont de Bir Hakeim, 15e; Ⓜ Javel–André Citroën, Bir Hakeim) Paris' little-known third island, the artificially created Île aux Cygnes, was formed in 1827 to protect the river port and measures just 850m by 11m. On the western side of the Pont de Grenelle is a soaring one-quarter scale Statue of Liberty replica (p96), inaugurated in 1889. Walk east along the Allée des Cygnes – the tree-lined walkway that runs the length of the island – for knock-out Eiffel Tower views.

Parc Montsouris   Park

(av Reille, 14e; ⊘8.30am-9.30pm May-Aug, shorter hours Sep-Apr; Ⓜ Porte d'Orléans or

 Boules

You'll often see groups of earnest Parisians playing *boules* (France's most popular traditional game, similar to lawn bowls) in the Jardin du Luxembourg and other parks and squares with suitably flat, shady patches of gravel. The **Arènes de Lutèce** (Map p252; 49 rue Monge, 5e; ⊙8am-8.30pm Apr-Oct, to 5.30pm Nov-Mar; ⓂPlace Monge) FREE *boulodrome* in a 2nd-century Roman amphitheatre in the Latin Quarter is a fabulous spot to absorb the scene. There are usually places to play at Paris Plages.

RER Cité-Universitaire) The name of this sprawling lakeside park – planted with horse-chestnut, yew, cedar, weeping beech and buttonwood trees – derives from *moque souris* (mice mockery) because the area was once overrun with the critters. Today it's a delightful picnic spot and has endearing playground areas, such as a concrete 'road system' where littlies can trundle matchbox cars (BYO cars). On Wednesday, Saturday and Sunday from 3pm to 6pm there are marionette shows (€4) and pony rides (€3.50).

Parc des Buttes Chaumont
Park

(Map p254; rue Manin & rue Botzaris, 19e; ⊙7am-10pm May-Sep, to 8pm Oct-Apr; ⓂButtes Chaumont, Botzaris) One of the city's largest green spaces, Buttes Chaumont's landscaped slopes hide grottoes, waterfalls, a lake and even an island

topped with a temple to Sibylle. Once a gypsum quarry and rubbish dump, it was given its present form by Baron Haussmann in time for the opening of the 1867 Exposition Universelle. The tracks of the abandoned 19th-century Petite Ceinture railway line, which once circled Paris, run through the park.

Square du Vert-Galant
Park

(Map p250; place du Pont Neuf; ⊙24hr; ⓂPont Neuf) Chestnut, yew, black walnut and weeping willow trees grace this picturesque park at the westernmost tip of the Île de la Cité, along with migratory birds including mute swans, pochard and tufted ducks, black-headed gulls and wagtails. Sitting at the islands' original level, 7m below their current height, the waterside park is reached by stairs leading down from the Pont Neuf. It's romantic at any time of day but especially in the evening watching the sun set over the river.

Forests

Bois de Vincennes
Park

(bd Poniatowski, 12e; ⓂPorte de Charenton, Porte Dorée) In the southeastern corner of Paris, Bois de Vincennes encompasses some 995 hectares. Originally royal hunting grounds, the woodland was annexed by the army following the Revolution and then donated to the city in 1860 by Napoléon III. A fabulous place to escape the endless stretches of Parisian concrete, Bois de Vincennes also contains a handful of notable sights, including a bona fide royal chateau, **Château de Vincennes** (01 48 08 31 20; www. chateau-de-vincennes.fr; av de Paris, Vincennes; guided tour adult/child €9/free; ⊙10am-6pm mid-May–mid-Sep, to 5pm mid-Sep–mid-May; ⓂChâteau de Vincennes), with massive fortifications and a moat.

Paris' largest, state-of-the-art zoo, the **Parc Zoologique de Paris** (Zoo de Vincennes; ☎08 11 22 41 22; www.parczoologiquede paris.fr; cnr av Daumesnil & rte de Ceinture du Lac Daumesnil, 12e; adult/child €22/16.50; ⊙9.30am-8.30pm May-Aug, shorter hours

Sep-Apr; Ⓜ Porte Dorée), is also here, as is the magnificent botanical park **Parc Floral de Paris** (☏01 49 57 24 84; www.vincennes. fr; Esplanade du Chateau de Vincennes or rte de la Pyramide; adult/child €5.50/2.75; ☺9.30am-8pm summer, shorter hours rest of year; 🚶; Ⓜ Château de Vincennes), with exciting playgrounds for older children. The wood also has a lovely lake, with boats to rent and ample green lawns to picnic on.

Bois de Boulogne   Park

(bd Maillot, 16e; Ⓜ Porte Maillot) On the western edge of Paris just beyond the 16e, the 845-hectare Bois de Boulogne owes its informal layout to Baron Haussmann, who was inspired by Hyde Park in London. Be warned that the Bois de Boulogne becomes a distinctly adult playground after dark, especially along the allée de Longchamp, where sex workers of all stripes cruise for clients.

In the south are two horse-racing tracks, the Hippodrome de Longchamp for flat races and the **Hippodrome d'Auteuil** (www. france-galop.com; Champ de Courses d'Auteuil, 16e, Bois de Boulogne; adult from €5, child free; Ⓜ Porte d'Auteuil) for steeplechases.

🟢 Guided Tours

Parisien d'un Jour –
Paris Greeters   Walking

(www.greeters.paris; by donation) See Paris through local eyes with these two- to three-hour city tours. Volunteers – mainly knowledgable Parisians passionate about their city – lead groups (maximum six people) to their favourite spots. Minimum two weeks' notice is needed.

Paris à Vélo, C'est Sympa!   Cycling

(Map p254; ☏01 48 87 60 01; www.parisvelosympa. com; 22 rue Alphonse Baudin, 11e; Ⓜ Richard Lenoir) Runs three guided bike tours (adult/child €35/29; three hours): a Heart of Paris tour, Unusual Paris (taking in artist studios and mansions) and the Contrast tour, combining nature and modern architecture. Tours depart from its bike rental shop (p237).

Paris Photography Tours   Tours

(☏06 17 08 54 45; www.parisphotography tours.com; 3hr day/night tours for 1-4 people €170) Customised tours by professional photographers take into account your level of experience and what you most want to capture, such as nature, architecture or street life. Tours can also incorporate lessons on how to improve your photographic skills.

Left Bank Scooters   Tours

(☏06 78 12 04 24; www.leftbankscooters.com; 3hr tours per 1st/2nd passenger from €150/50) Runs a variety of scooter tours around Paris, both day and evening, as well as trips out to Versailles and sidecar tours. Car or motorcycle licence required. Also rents scooters (50/125/300cc scooters per 24 hours €70/80/100).

Fat Tire Bike Tours   Cycling

(☏01 82 88 80 96; www.fattiretours.com; tours from €29) Offers both day and night bicycle tours of the city, both in central Paris and further afield to Versailles and Monet's Garden (p99) in Giverny.

Paris Walks   Walking

(☏01 48 09 21 40; www.paris-walks.com; 2hr tours adult/child €15/10) Long established and well respected, Paris Walks offers two-hour thematic walking tours on art, fashion, chocolate, the French Revolution and more.

Set in Paris   Walking

(Map p252; ☏09 84 42 35 79; http://setinparis. com; 3 rue Maître Albert, 5e; 2hr tours €25; ☺tours 10am & 3pm; Ⓜ Maubert-Mutualité) From its cinema-style 'box office' HQ in the Latin Quarter, Set in Paris' two-hour walking tours take you to locations throughout Paris where movies including *The Devil Wears Prada, The Bourne Identity, The Three Musketeers, The Hunchback of Notre Dame, Ratatouille, Before Sunset,* several James Bond instalments and many others were filmed. Advance reservations are recommended.

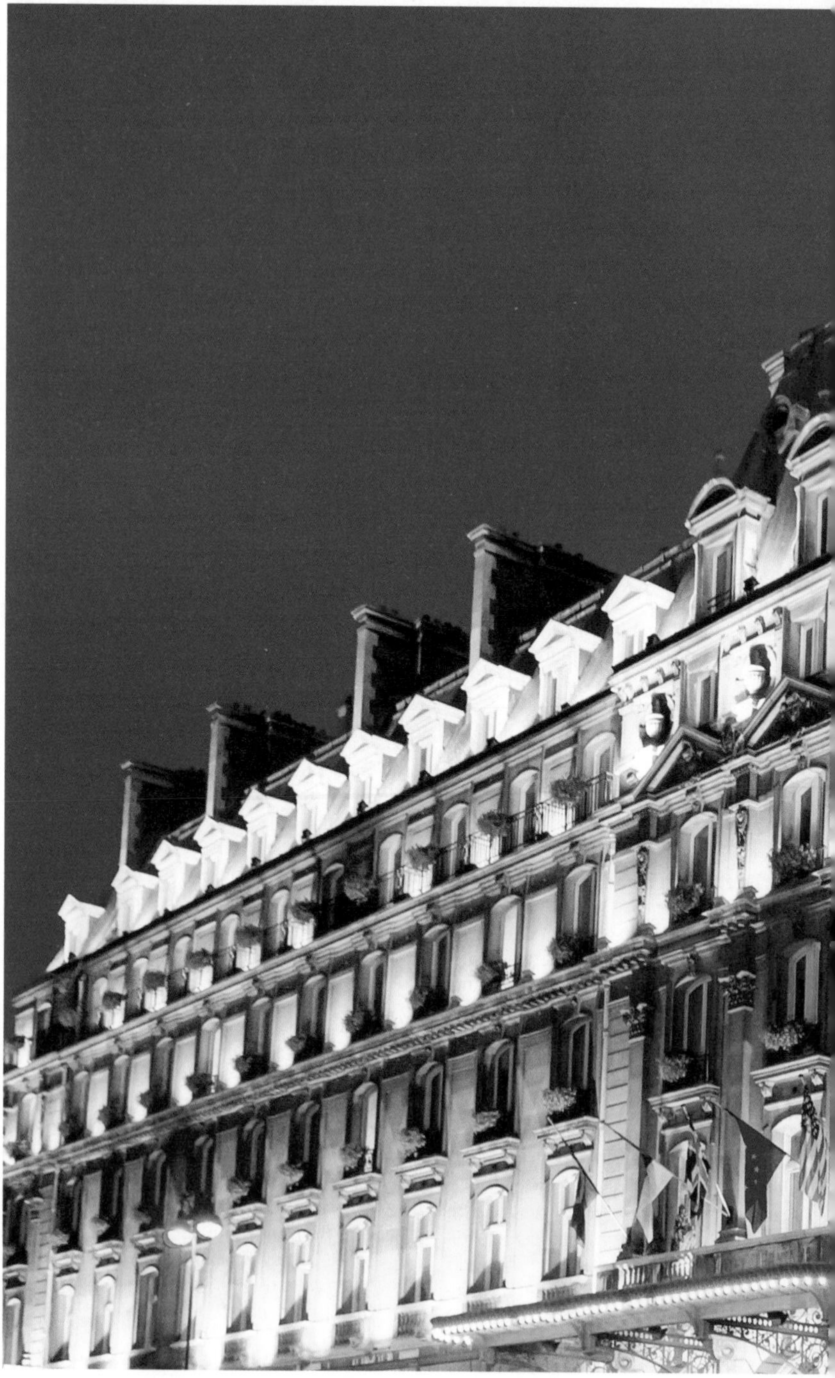

REST YOUR HEAD

Top tips for the best accommodation

Rest Your Head

As one of the world's most visited cities, Paris has a wealth of accommodation for all budgets, from a recently reinvigorated hostel scene that now includes purpose-built, state-of-the-art flashpacker pads to charming old-school hotels, intimate boutique gems, hipster hang-outs, eye-popping designer havens, sleep-drink-dine-dance lifestyle hotels, and deluxe hotels and palaces, some of which rank among the finest in the world. Be sure to reserve as far ahead as possible, especially at busy times including weekends, public and school holidays and the summer months. Apartment rentals are also very popular in Paris and give you the opportunity to live like a Parisian, shopping at the local markets and visiting neighbourhood bars. Choosing a central option with good transport links will allow you to maximise your time.

In This Section

Accommodation Types......................206

Need to Know......................................207

Where to Stay.....................................209

Prices/Tipping

A 'budget hotel' in Paris generally costs up to €130 for a double room with en suite bathroom in high season (breakfast not included). For a midrange option, plan on spending €130 to €250. Luxury options run €250 and higher.

Bellhops usually expect €1 to €2 per bag; it's not necessary to tip the concierge, cleaners or front-desk staff.

Room with a view – a hotel overlooking Palais Garnier

Reservations

Reservations are almost always essential – walk-ins are practically impossible and rack rates are unfavourable relative to online deals (usually best directly via hotels' official websites). Reserve your room as early as possible and make sure you understand the cancellation policy. Check-in is generally in the middle of the afternoon and check-out in the late morning.

Useful Websites

Lonely Planet (www.lonelyplanet.com/france/paris/hotels) Reviews of Lonely Planet's top choices.

Paris Hotel Service (www.parishotel service.com) Boutique hotel gems.

Paris Hotel (www.hotels-paris.fr) Well-organised hotel booking site with lots of user reviews.

Room Sélection (www.room-selec tion.com) Select apartment rentals centred on Le Marais.

Paris Attitude (www.parisattitude. com) Thousands of apartment rentals, professional service, reasonable fees.

Accommodation Types

Hotels

Hotels in Paris are inspected by government authorities and classified into six categories, from no star to five stars. The vast majority are two- and three-star hotels, which are generally well-equipped. All hotels must display their rates, including TVA (*taxe sur la valeur ajoutée*; valued-added tax), though you'll often get *much* cheaper prices online, especially on the hotels' own websites, which invariably offer the best deals.

Parisian hotel rooms tend to be small by international standards. Families will probably need connecting rooms, but if children are too young to stay in their own room, it's possible to make do with triples, quads or suites in some places.

Cheaper hotels may not have lifts/elevators and/or air-conditioning. Some don't accept credit cards.

Breakfast is rarely included in hotel rates; heading to a cafe often works out to be better value (and more atmospheric).

Hostels

Paris is awash with hostels, and standards are consistently improving. A wave of state-of-the-art hostels have recently opened their doors, such as the design-savvy 950-bed 'megahostel' by leading hostel chain Generator near Canal St-Martin, 10e, and, close by, two by the switched-on St Christopher's group.

The more traditional (ie institutional) hostels can have daytime lock-outs and curfews; some have a maximum three-night stay. Places that have upper age limits tend not to enforce them, except at the busiest of times. Only the official *auberges de jeunesse* (youth hostels) require guests to present Hostelling International (HI) cards or their equivalent.

CATHERINE LE NEVEZ/LONELY PLANET ©

Hotel room at Fraser Suites Le Claridge Champs-Élysées

Not all hostels have self-catering kitchens, but rates generally include a basic continental breakfast.

B&Bs & Homestays

Bed-and-breakfast (B&B) accommodation (*chambres d'hôte* in French) is on the rise.

Paris Quality Hosts (Hôtes Qualité Paris; www.hotesqualiteparis.fr), a scheme run by the city of Paris, fosters B&Bs, in part to ease the isolation of Parisians, some half of whom live alone. There's often a minimum stay of three or four nights.

Need to Know

Taxe de Séjour

The city of Paris levies a *taxe de séjour* (tourist tax) per person per night on all accommodation, running from €0.22 in budget campgrounds to €1.65 in three-star hotels to €3.30 in five-star properties. If you happen to be staying in a palace or something similarly grand the tax is €4.40 per night.

Internet Access

Wi-fi (pronounced 'wee-fee' in French) is virtually always free of charge at hotels and hostels. You may find that in some hotels, especially older ones, the higher the floor, the less reliable the wi-fi connection.

Smoking

Smoking is officially banned in all Paris hotels.

 Apartment Rentals

Families – and anyone wanting to self-cater – should consider renting a short-stay apartment. Paris has a number of excellent apartment hotels, including the international chain Apart'hotels Citadines (www.citadines.com).

For an even more authentic Parisian experience, home-sharing options are also available, whether a room in someone's apartment or the entire property. Rental agencies (eg Room Sélection, Paris Attitude) are among the organisations that list furnished residential apartments for short stays. Apartments often include facilities such as washing machines, and can be good value. The cheapest rates are usually in local neighbourhoods in outer (higher-numbered) *arrondissements*. Many older Parisian buildings don't have lifts/elevators; check the *étage* (floor). Parisian apartments are often tiny (in studios, the sofa often doubles as the only bed); confirm the size beforehand. Also establish whether prices include electricity.

Beware of direct-rental scams whereby scammers compile fake apartment advertisements at too-good-to-be-true prices from photos and descriptions on legitimate sites. Book only with reputable companies. Above all, never send money via an untraceable money transfer.

Where to Stay

Neighbourhood	Atmosphere
Eiffel Tower & Western Paris	Close to Paris' iconic tower and museums. Upmarket area with quiet residential streets. Short on budget and midrange places.
Champs-Élysées & Grands Boulevards	Luxury hotels, famous boutiques and department stores, gastronomic restaurants, great nightlife. Some areas extremely pricey. Nightlife hotspots can be noisy.
Louvre & Les Halles	Epicentral location, excellent transport links, major museums, shopping galore. Few bargains. Noise can be an issue in some areas.
Montmartre & Northern Paris	Village atmosphere. Hilly streets, some parts very touristy. Pigalle's red-light district, although well lit and safe, won't appeal to all.
Le Marais, Ménilmontant & Belleville	Buzzing nightlife, hip shopping, fantastic eating options. Lively gay and lesbian scene. Very central. Can be noisy in areas where bars and clubs are concentrated.
Bastille & Eastern Paris	Few tourists, allowing you to see the 'real' Paris up close. Excellent markets, loads of nightlife options. Some areas slightly out of the way.
The Islands	Accommodation centred on the peaceful Île St-Louis. No metro station here. Limited self-catering shops, minimal nightlife.
Latin Quarter	Energetic student area, stacks of eating and drinking options, late-opening bookshops. Rooms hardest to find during conferences and seminars (March to June and October).
St-Germain & Les Invalides	Stylish, central location, superb shopping, sophisticated dining. Budget accommodation is seriously short changed.
Montparnasse & Southern Paris	Good value, few tourists, excellent links to both major airports. Some areas out of the way and/or not well served by metro.

Pont Alexandre III with Hôtel des Invalides (p104) in the background

In Focus

Paris Today   **212**
Grand-scale plans for the city's
infrastructure and green transport
initiatives continue apace.

History   **214**
A saga of battles, bloodshed, grand
excesses, revolution, reformation,
resistance, renaissance and constant
reinvention.

Architecture   **219**
Paris' cityscape spans Roman
baths to medieval wonders, art-
nouveau splendours and stunning
contemporary additions.

Arts   **223**
The capital's museums and galleries –
and its streets, parks and metro
stations – contain a cache of artistic
treasures, while its literary, music and
film scenes are flourishing.

Paris Today

The Latin motto fluctuat nec mergitur *('tossed but not sunk') was adopted by Paris around 1358. Officialised by Baron Haussmann in 1853, it still appears on the city's coat of arms. It remains emblematic of the city's resilient spirit after Paris recovered from 2015's terrorist attacks and grand-scale plans for the city's infrastructure and greener living continue to surge ahead.*

Greater Paris

The Grand Paris (Greater Paris) redevelopment project got the green light in 2016. The scheme will eventually connect the outer suburbs beyond the bd Périphérique ring road with the city proper. This is a significant break in the physical and conceptual barrier that the *périphérique* has imposed until now, but, due to the steadily growing suburban population (10.5 million, compared to 2.2 million inside the *périphérique*), a real need to redefine Paris, on both an administrative and infrastructural scale, has arisen.

The crux of Grand Paris is a massive decentralised metro expansion, with 68 new stations and six suburban lines, with a target completion date of 2030. The principal goal is to connect the suburbs with one another, instead of relying on a central inner-city hub from which all lines radiate outwards. Ultimately, the surrounding suburbs – Vincennes,

Neuilly, Issy, St-Denis etc – will lose their autonomy and become part of a much larger Grand Paris governed by the Hôtel de Ville.

Evolving Architecture

Architectural change doesn't come easy in Paris, given the need to balance the city's heritage with demands on space. But new projects continue to gather steam. The controversial Tour Triangle, a glittering glass triangular tower designed by Jacques Herzog and Pierre de Meuron, will be the first skyscraper in Paris since Tour Montparnasse in 1973 when it is completed at Porte de Versailles in 2018. Other high-rise projects include Duo, two Jean Nouvel–designed towers (180m and 122m) in the 13e, slated for completion in 2020.

Nouvel is also among the architects working on the 74-hectare Île Seguin-Rives de Seine (www.ileseguin-rives deseine.fr) development of the former Renault plant on a Seine island in Boulogne-Billancourt, which will become a Greater Paris cultural hub.

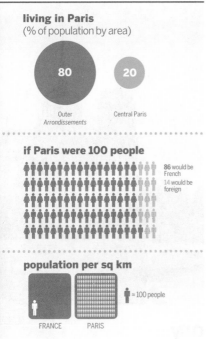

living in Paris
(% of population by area)

80 — Outer Arrondissements

20 — Central Paris

if Paris were 100 people

86 would be French
14 would be foreign

population per sq km

♦ ≈ 100 people

FRANCE   PARIS

Greener Living

Mayor of Paris Anne Hidalgo is focused on greening the city and reducing car traffic and pollution. Since taking office in 2014, Hidalgo has pedestrianised 3.3km of Right Bank expressway between the Tuileries and Bastille, closed the Champs-Élysées on the first Sunday of each month, and established an annual car-free day. In 2017, she introduced the Crit'Air Vignette (compulsory anti-pollution sticker) for all cars, motorcycles and trucks registered after 1997 (including foreign-registered vehicles) between 8am and 8pm Monday to Friday (older vehicles are banned during these hours). Ongoing projects include reducing parking spaces by 55,000 per year, instigating a city-wide maximum speed limit of 30km per hour, investing €150 million in cycling infrastructure and banning diesel cars by 2020.

Transport aside, other green initiatives include a goal of 100 hectares of green roofs, façades and vertical walls, a third of which will be devoted to urban agriculture.

Economic Advancements

In order to compete with other key European cities to attract tourism and investment, Paris established 'tourist zones' that allow Sunday trading for shops. Other forward steps include the 2017 opening of the world's biggest start-up campus, Station F (https://stationf.co), in the 13e, home to hundreds of individual start-up and creative businesses.

MATTEO COLOMBO/GETTY IMAGES ©

History

With its cobbled streets, terraced cafes and iconic landmarks, Paris evokes a sense of timelessness, yet the city has changed and evolved dramatically over the centuries. And Paris' epic history – from Roman battles to revolution and beyond – is not just consigned to museums and archives: reminders of the city's past can be glimpsed around every corner.

3rd century BC	**52 BC**	**AD 509**
Celtic Gauls called Parisii arrive in the Paris area and set up wattle-and-daub huts on the Seine.	Roman legions under Titus Labienus crush a Celtic revolt on Mons Lutetius and establish the town of Lutetia.	Clovis I becomes the first king of the Franks and declares Paris the seat of his new kingdom.

The Beginnings to the Renaissance

Paris was born in the 3rd century BC, when a tribe of Celtic Gauls known as the Parisii settled on what is now the Île de la Cité. Centuries of conflict between the Gauls and Romans ended in 52 BC, when Julius Caesar's legions crushed a Celtic revolt. Christianity was introduced in the 2nd century AD, and Roman rule ended in the 5th century with the arrival of the Germanic Franks. In 509 Frankish king Clovis I united Gaul and made Paris his seat.

France's west coast was beset in the 9th century by Scandinavian Vikings (also known as Norsemen and, later, as Normans). Three centuries later, the Normans started pushing toward Paris, which had risen rapidly in importance: construction had begun on the cathedral of Notre Dame in the 12th century, the Louvre began life as a riverside fortress around 1200, Sainte-Chapelle was consecrated in 1248 and the Sorbonne opened in 1253.

1643
'Sun King' Louis XIV ascends the throne aged five but only assumes absolute power in 1661.

14 July 1789
The French Revolution begins when a mob arms itself with stolen weapons and storms the prison at Bastille.

1793
Louis XVI is tried, convicted and executed; Marie-Antoinette's turn comes nine months later.

★ **Best Roman Legacies**

Crypte Archéologique (p49)

Musée National du Moyen Âge (p88)

Arènes de Lutèce (p200)

The Vikings' incursions heralded the Hundred Years' War between Norman England and Paris' Capetian dynasty, bringing French defeat in 1415 and English control of the capital in 1420. In 1429 the 17-year-old Jeanne d'Arc (Joan of Arc) rallied the French troops to defeat the English at Orléans. With the exception of Calais, the English were eventually expelled from France in 1453.

The Renaissance helped Paris get back on its feet in the late 15th century. Less than a century later, however, turmoil ensued as clashes between Huguenot (Protestant) and Catholic groups culminated in the St Bartholomew's Day massacre in 1572.

The Revolution to a New Republic

A five-year-old Louis XIV (later known as the Sun King) ascended the throne in 1643 and ruled until 1715, virtually emptying the national coffers with his ambitious battling and building, including the construction of his extravagant palace at Versailles. The excesses of this grandiose king and his heirs, including Louis XVI and his Vienna-born queen Marie Antoinette, eventually led to an uprising of Parisians on 14 July 1789, kick-starting the French Revolution. Within four years, the Reign of Terror was in full swing.

The unstable post-revolutionary government was consolidated in 1799 under Napoléon Bonaparte, who declared himself First Consul. In 1804 he had the Pope crown him emperor of the French, and went on to conquer most of Europe before his eventual defeat at Waterloo in present-day Belgium in 1815. He was exiled to St Helena, and died in 1821.

France struggled under a string of mostly inept rulers until a coup d'état in 1851 brought Emperor Napoléon III to power. At his behest, Baron Haussmann razed whole tracts of the city, replacing them with sculptured parks, a hygienic sewer system and – strategically – boulevards too broad for rebels to barricade. Napoléon III embroiled France in a costly war with Prussia in 1870, which ended within months with the French army's defeat and the capture of the emperor. When the masses in Paris heard the news, they took to the streets, demanding a republic.

1799	1852–70	1940
Napoléon Bonaparte overthrows the Directory and seizes control of the government in a coup d'état.	During the Second Empire of Napoléon III much of the city is redesigned or rebuilt by Baron Haussmann as the Paris we know today.	Germany launches the battle for France, and the four-year occupation of Paris under direct German rule begins.

Twentieth-Century History

Out of the conflict of WWI, in which 1.3 million French soldiers lost their lives, came increased industrialisation. This confirmed Paris' place as a major commercial, as well as artistic, centre and established its reputation among freethinking intellectuals.

This was halted by WWII and the Nazi occupation of 1940. During Paris' occupation, almost half the population evacuated, including General Charles de Gaulle, France's undersecretary of war, who fled to London and set up a government-in-exile. In a radio broadcast he appealed to French patriots to continue resisting the Germans, and established the Forces Françaises Libres (Free French Forces) to fight the Germans alongside the Allies. Following Paris' liberation, de Gaulle set up a provisional government, but resigned in 1946; he formed his own party (Rassemblement du Peuple Français) and remained in opposition until 1958, when he was brought back to power. He was succeeded as president in 1969 by Gaullist leader Georges Pompidou.

After the war, Paris regained its position as a creative nucleus and nurtured a revitalised liberalism that peaked with the student-led uprisings of May 1968 – the Sorbonne was occupied, the Latin Quarter blockaded and a general strike paralysed the country.

Under centre-right President Jacques Chirac's watch, the late 1990s saw Paris seize the international spotlight with the rumour-plagued death of Princess Diana in 1997, and France's first-ever World Cup victory in July 1998.

The New Millennium

In May 2001 Socialist Bertrand Delanoë was elected mayor, becoming widely popular for making Paris more liveable through improved infrastructure and green spaces.

Chirac's second presidential term, starting in 2002, was marred in 2005 by the deaths of two teenagers who were electrocuted while allegedly hiding from police in an electricity substation, which sparked riots that quickly spread across Paris, and then across France.

Contrary to the rigorous economic reform platform on which he'd been elected and against the backdrop of the global recession, Chirac's successor, Nicolas Sarkozy, struggled to keep the French economy buoyant. His popularity plummeted, paving the way for Socialist Francois Hollande's victory in the 2012 presidential elections.

With France still struggling to restart the economy, Hollande pledged to end austerity measures and reduce unemployment. Many economic policies proved ineffectual, though, and Hollande's popularity plunged even faster and further than Sarkozy's, resulting in a near total wipeout for French Socialists in the 2014 municipal elections. The 2014 election of Socialist Anne Hidalgo, Paris' first female mayor, meant the capital was one of the few cities to remain on the political left.

25 August 1944	1968	2005
Spearheaded by Free French units, Allied forces liberate Paris and the city escapes destruction.	Paris is rocked by student-led riots; de Gaulle is forced to resign the following year.	The suburbs surrounding Paris are wracked by rioting youths.

Hôtel des Invalides at the end of Pont Alexandre III

PREMIER PHOTO/SHUTTERSTOCK ©

★ **Best WWII-Era History**
Hôtel des Invalides (p104)
Bronze plaque, Arc de Triomphe (p42)
Bar Hemingway (p170)

Turbulent Times

The year 2015 was bookended by tragedy. On 7 January the offices of magazine *Charlie Hebdo* were attacked in response to satirical images it published of the prophet Muhammad. Eleven staff and one police officer were killed and a further 22 people injured.

Worse still, on the night of 13 November 2015, a series of coordinated terrorist attacks occurred in Paris and St-Denis – the deadliest on French soil since WWII. Explosions shook the Stade de France stadium; neighbourhood restaurants and their outdoor terraces in the 10e and 11e *arrondissements* were attacked by gunmen and suicide bombers; and gunmen fired into the audience of Le Bataclan, where American band Eagles of Death Metal were performing. Over the course of the evening, 130 people lost their lives (89 in Le Bataclan alone) and 368 were injured. Paris was in lockdown, the army was mobilised and a state of emergency declared.

Residents established memorials at the fatality sites and place de la République, which became the focal point for the city's outpouring of grief, and took to cafe terraces and other public spaces. The hashtag #jesuisenterrasse ('I am on the terrace') represented Parisians' refusal to live in fear.

The long-planned United Nations Climate Change Conference (COP21) went ahead from 30 November to 12 December 2015, during which world leaders reached an agreement to limit global warming to less than 2°C by the end of the century. Le Bataclan reopened in November 2016, and once again hosts local and international artists.

France's New President

France's most recent presidential elections took place in 2017. The traditional parties were eliminated in the first round, with Emmanuel Macron, who launched his centrist, pro-EU movement En Marche! in 2016 – now the party La République en Marche – defeating far-right Front National candidate Marine Le Pen 66.1% to 33.9% in the second-round run-off. At age 39, Macron became the youngest-ever French president.

2014
Spanish-born Anne Hidalgo becomes the first female mayor of Paris.

2015
Deadly terrorist attacks take place at the offices of *Charlie Hebdo* on 7 January, and in multiple locations on 13 November.

2017
Without the support of an established party, Emmanuel Macron makes history by being elected France's first centrist president.

Grande Arche (p45), La Défense district

Architecture

It took disease, clogged streets and Baron Georges-Eugène Haussmann to drag architectural Paris out of the Middle Ages and into the modern world – yet ever since Haussmann's radical transformation of the city in the 19th century, Paris has never looked back. Its contemporary skyline shimmers with the whole gamut of architectural styles, from Roman arenas to futuristic skyscrapers.

Gallo-Roman

Traces of Roman Paris can be seen in the residential foundations in the Crypte Archéologique in front of Notre Dame; in the Arènes de Lutèce; and in the *frigidarium* (cooling room) and other remains of Roman baths dating from around AD 200 at the Musée National du Moyen Âge.

The latter museum also contains the *Pillier des Nautes* (Boatsmen's Pillar), one of the most valuable legacies of the Gallo-Roman period. It is a 2.5m-high monument dedicated to Jupiter and was erected by the boatmen's guild during the reign of Tiberius (AD 14–37) on the Île de la Cité. The boat has become the symbol of Paris, and the city's Latin motto is *'Fluctuat Nec Mergitur'* (Tossed by Waves but Does Not Sink).

★ Best Medieval Treasures

Notre Dame (p46)

Sainte-Chapelle (p92)

Musée du Louvre (p52)

Musée National du Moyen Âge (p88)

Sainte-Chapelle

ASH PHOTOGRAPHY/GETTY IMAGES ©

Romanesque

A religious revival in the 11th century led to the construction of many *roman* (Romanesque) churches, typically with round arches, heavy walls, few (and small) windows, and a lack of ornamentation that bordered on the austere.

No remaining building in Paris is entirely Romanesque, but several have important representative elements, including Église St-Germain des Prés, the Romanesque bell tower of which, above the west entrance, has changed little since AD 1000.

Gothic

In the 14th century, the Rayonnant – or Radiant – Gothic style, named after the radiating tracery of the rose windows, developed. Interiors became even lighter thanks to broader windows and more translucent stained glass. One of the most influential Rayonnant buildings was Sainte-Chapelle, the stained glass of which forms a curtain of glazing on the 1st floor. The two transept façades of Cathédrale de Notre Dame de Paris and the vaulted Salle des Gens d'Armes (Cavalrymen's Hall) in the Conciergerie, the largest surviving medieval hall in Europe, are other fine examples of Rayonnant Gothic style.

By the 15th century, decorative extravagance led to Flamboyant Gothic, so named because the wavy stone carving made the towers appear to be blazing or flaming *(flamboyant)*. Several *hôtels particuliers* (private mansions) were built in this style, including Hôtel de Cluny, now the Musée National du Moyen Âge.

Renaissance

The Renaissance set out to realise a 'rebirth' of classical Greek and Roman culture and first affected France at the end of the 15th century, when Charles VIII began a series of invasions of Italy, returning with new ideas.

The Early Renaissance style blends a variety of classical components and decorative motifs (columns, tunnel vaults, round arches, domes etc) with the rich decoration of Flamboyant Gothic. Mannerism was introduced around 1530; in 1546 Pierre Lescot designed the richly decorated southwestern corner of the Cour Carrée at the Musée du Louvre.

The Right Bank district of Le Marais remains the best area for Renaissance reminders in Paris proper, with some fine *hôtels particuliers,* such as Hôtel Carnavalet, housing part of the Musée Carnavalet (the museum itself is closed for renovations until 2020).

Baroque

During the baroque period (tail end of the 16th to late 18th centuries), painting, sculpture and classical architecture were integrated to create structures and interiors of great subtlety, refinement and elegance. With the advent of the baroque, architecture became more pictorial, with painted church ceilings illustrating the Passion of Christ to the faithful, and palaces invoking the power and order of the state. Salomon de Brosse designed the Palais du Luxembourg in the Jardin du Luxembourg in 1615.

Neoclassicism

Neoclassical architecture emerged about 1740 and had its roots in the renewed interest in classical forms – a search for order, reason and serenity through the adoption of forms and conventions of Graeco-Roman antiquity: columns, geometric forms and traditional ornamentation.

Among the earliest examples of this style are the Petit Trianon at Versailles, designed by Jacques-Ange Gabriel for Louis XV in 1761. France's greatest neoclassical architect of the 18th century was Jacques-Germain Soufflot, creator of the Panthéon in the Latin Quarter.

Neoclassicism came into its own under Napoléon, who used it to embody the grandeur of imperial France and its capital: the Arc de Triomphe, the Arc de Triomphe du Carrousel and more. The climax to this great 19th-century movement was Palais Garnier, the city's opera house designed by Charles Garnier.

Baron Haussmann

The iconic apartment buildings that line the boulevards of central Paris, with their cream-coloured stone and curvy wrought-iron balconies, are the work of Baron Haussmann (1809–91), prefect of the Seine *département* between 1853 and 1870.

Art Nouveau

Art nouveau, which emerged in Europe and the USA in the second half of the 19th century under various names (Jugendstil, Sezessionstil, Stile Liberty), caught on quickly in Paris, and its influence lasted until about 1910. It was characterised by sinuous curves and flowing, asymmetrical forms reminiscent of creeping vines, water lilies, the patterns on insect wings and the flowering boughs of trees. Influenced by the arrival of exotic *objets d'art* from Japan, art nouveau's French name came from a Paris gallery that featured works in the 'new art' style.

It's expressed to perfection in Paris by Hector Guimard's graceful metro entrances, the Musée d'Orsay and the city's main department stores, Le Bon Marché and Galeries Lafayette.

Modern

Until 1968, French architects were still being trained almost exclusively at the conformist École de Beaux-Arts, reflected in most of the early impersonal and forgettable 'lipstick tubes' and 'upended shoebox' structures erected in the skyscraper district of La Défense and the 210m-tall Tour Montparnasse (1973).

Contemporary

France's leaders sought to immortalise themselves by erecting huge public edifices (*'grands projets'*) in Paris. Georges Pompidou commissioned the once reviled, now much-loved Centre Pompidou. His successor, Valéry Giscard d'Estaing, was instrumental in transforming the derelict Gare d'Orsay train station into the glorious Musée d'Orsay (1986). François Mitterrand surpassed all of the postwar presidents with monumental projects costing taxpayers €4.6 billion: Jean Nouvel's Institut du Monde Arabe (1987), mixing modern Arab and Western elements, IM Pei's glass-pyramid Musée du Louvre

Centre Pompidou

★ **Best Modern & Contemporary Designs**
Centre Pompidou (p74)
Musée du Quai Branly (p40)
Institut du Monde Arabe (p109)
Philharmonie de Paris (p189)
Grande Arche (p45)

entrance, and the tile-clad Opéra de Paris Bastille, designed by Uruguayan architect Carlos Ott are among those on his watch. Jacques Chirac orchestrated the magnificent Musée du Quai Branly, a glass, wood and sod structure with a 3-hectare experimental garden, also by Jean Nouvel.

Ongoing Renaissance

Some of Paris' loveliest art deco buildings have recently undergone a renaissance, such as a five-star hotel and spa Hôtel Molitor, opened in the Molitor swimming pool complex in western Paris, where the bikini made its first appearance in the 1930s. In Le Marais, thermal-baths-turned-1980s-nightclub Les Bain Douches opened as luxury hotel Les Bains after years of being abandoned. Preserving as many of the original art deco features as possible was a characteristic of both projects.

Drawing on the city's long-standing tradition of glass in its architecture, glass is a big feature of the 1970s-eyesore-turned-contemporary-stunner Forum des Halles shopping centre in the 1er – a curvaceous, curvilinear and glass-topped construction by architects Patrick Berger and Jacques Anziutti.

On the horizon, redevelopments include the overhaul of the art nouveau department store La Samaritaine, near Pont Neuf in the 1er; the Paris Rive Gauche development in the 13e, spanning 130 hectares around the Gare d'Austerlitz mainline train station; and Île Seguin-Rives de Seine, on the site of the former Renault plant centred on an island in the Seine in Boulogne-Billancourt to the city's west, which will become a cultural hub.

Impression: Soleil Levant (Impression: Sunrise) by Claude Monet

Arts

While art in Paris today means anything and everything – bold installations in the metro, monumental wall frescoes, space invader tags and other gregarious street art – the city's rich art heritage has its roots firmly embedded in the traditional genres of painting and sculpture. Then there are the literary arts, music and film in which Paris plays a starring role.

Baroque to Neoclassicism

According to philosopher Voltaire, French painting proper began with baroque painter Nicolas Poussin (1594–1665), the greatest representative of 17th-century classicism, who frequently set scenes from ancient Rome, classical mythology and the Bible in ordered landscapes bathed in golden light.

Jean-Baptiste Chardin (1699–1779) brought the humbler domesticity of the Dutch masters to French art, while in 1785, neoclassical artist Jacques Louis David (1748–1825) wooed the public with his vast portraits with clear republican messages. Jean-Auguste-Dominique Ingres (1780–1867), David's most gifted pupil in Paris, continued the neoclassical tradition.

Cimetière du Père Lachaise

★ **Best Literary Pilgrimages**

Cimetière du Père Lachaise (p78)

Shakespeare & Company (p155)

Bar Hemingway (p170)

Romanticism

One of the Louvre's most gripping paintings, *The Raft of the Medusa* by Théodore Géricault (1791–1824), hovers on the threshold of romanticism; his friend Eugène Delacroix (1798–1863), best known for his masterpiece commemorating the July Revolution of 1830, *Liberty Leading the People,* was a leader of the movement.

In sculpture, the work of Paris-born Auguste Rodin (1840–1917) overcame the conflict between neoclassicism and romanticism. One of Rodin's most gifted pupils was his lover Camille Claudel (1864–1943), whose work can be seen with Rodin's in the Musée Rodin.

Realism

The realists were all about social comment. Édouard Manet (1832–83) used realism to depict Parisian middle classes, yet he included in his pictures numerous references to the Old Masters.

One of the best sculptors of this period was François Rude (1784–1855), creator of the relief on the Arc de Triomphe and several pieces in the Musée d'Orsay. By the mid-19th century, memorial statues in public places had replaced sculpted tombs, making such statues all the rage.

Sculptor Jean-Baptiste Carpeaux (1827–75) began as a romantic, but his work in Paris – such as *The Dance* on the Palais Garnier and his fountain in the Jardin du Luxembourg – recalls the gaiety and flamboyance of the baroque era.

Impressionism

Paris' Musée d'Orsay is the crown jewel of impressionism. Initially a term of derision, 'impressionism' was taken from the title of an 1874 experimental painting, *Impression: Soleil Levant* (Impression: Sunrise) by Claude Monet (1840–1926). Monet was the leading figure of the school, and a visit to the Musée d'Orsay unveils a host of other members, among them Alfred Sisley (1839–99), Camille Pissarro (1830–1903), Pierre-Auguste Renoir (1841–1919) and Berthe Morisot (1841–95). The impressionists' main aim was to capture the effects of fleeting light, painting almost universally in the open air – and light came to dominate the content of their painting.

Edgar Degas (1834–1917) was a fellow traveller of the impressionists, but he preferred painting cafe life *(Absinthe)* and in ballet studios *(The Dance Class)* than the great outdoors – several beautiful examples hang in the Musée d'Orsay.

Henri de Toulouse-Lautrec (1864–1901) chose subjects one or two notches below: people in the bistros, brothels and music halls of Montmartre (eg *Au Moulin Rouge*). He is best known for his posters and lithographs, in which the distortion of the figures is both satirical and decorative.

Paul Cézanne (1839–1906) is celebrated for his still lifes and landscapes depicting southern France, though he spent many years in Paris after breaking with the impressionists. Paul Gauguin (1848–1903) is famed for his studies of Tahitian and Breton women. Both Cézanne and Gauguin were post-impressionists, a catch-all term for the diverse styles that flowed from impressionism.

Pointillism & Symbolism

Pointillism was a technique developed by Georges Seurat (1859–91), who applied paint in small dots or uniform brush strokes of unmixed colour to produce fine 'mosaics' of warm and cool tones. His tableaux *Une Baignade, Asnières* (Bathers at Asnières) is a perfect example.

Henri Rousseau (1844–1910) was a contemporary of the post-impressionists, but his 'naive' art was unaffected by them. His dreamlike pictures of the Paris suburbs and of jungle and desert scenes (eg *The Snake Charmer*) – again in Musée d'Orsay – have influenced art right up to this century.

Metro Art

Art adorns many of the 300-plus stations of the city's world-famous Métropolitain. Themes often relate to the *quartier* (neighbourhood) or name of the station. The following is just a sample of the most interesting stations from an artistic perspective.

Abbesses (line 12 metro entrance) The noodle-like pale-green metalwork and glass canopy of the station entrance is one of the finest examples of the work of Hector Guimard (1867–1942), the celebrated French art-nouveau architect whose signature style once graced most metro stations. For a complete list of the metro stations that retain *édicules* (shrine-like entranceways) designed by Guimard, see www.parisin connu.com.

Bastille (line 5 platform) A 180-sq-metre ceramic fresco features scenes taken from newspaper engravings published during the Revolution, with illustrations of the destruction of the infamous prison.

Chaussée d'Antin-Lafayette (line 7 platform) Large allegorical painting on the vaulted ceiling recalls the Marquis de Lafayette (1757–1834) and his role as general in the American Revolution.

Cluny—La Sorbonne (line 10 platform) A large ceramic mosaic replicates the signatures of intellectuals, artists and scientists from the Latin Quarter through history, including Molière (1622–73), Rabelais (c 1483–1553) and Robespierre (1758–96).

Concorde (line 12 platform) What look like children's building blocks in white-and-blue ceramic on the walls of the station are 45,000 tiles that spell out the text of the *Déclaration des Droits de l'Homme et du Citoyen* (Declaration of the Rights of Man and of the Citizen), the document setting forth the principles of the French Revolution.

Palais Royal—Musée du Louvre (line 1 metro entrance) The zany entrance on place du Palais by Jean-Michel Othoniel (b 1964) is composed of two crown-shaped cupolas (one representing the day, the other night) consisting of 800 red, blue, amber and violet glass balls threaded on an aluminium structure.

Le Grand Rex

XAVIER RICHER/GETTY IMAGES ©

★ **Best Cinematic Trips**

Forum des Images (p189)

Cinémathèque Française (p192)

Le Grand Rex (p188)

Art Ludique-Le Musée (p109)

Twentieth-Century Art

Twentieth-century French painting styles included fauvism, named after the slur of a critic who compared the exhibitors at the 1905 Salon d'Automne (Autumn Salon) in Paris with *fauves* (wild animals) because of their wild brush strokes and radical use of intensely bright colours. Among these 'beastly' painters was Henri Matisse (1869–1954).

Cubism was launched in 1907 with *Les Demoiselles d'Avignon* by Spanish prodigy Pablo Picasso (1881–1973). Cubism, as developed by Picasso, Georges Braque (1882–1963) and Juan Gris (1887–1927), deconstructed the subject into a system of intersecting planes and presented various aspects simultaneously.

Marcel Duchamp (1887–1968) captured the rebellious, iconoclastic spirit of Dadaism – a Swiss-born literary and artistic movement of revolt – in his *Mona Lisa,* complete with moustache and goatee. In 1922 German Dadaist Max Ernst (1891–1976) moved to Paris and worked on surrealism, a Dada offshoot that flourished between the wars. The most influential of this style in Paris was Spanish-born artist Salvador Dalí (1904–89), who arrived in the French capital in 1929 and painted some of his most seminal works while residing here. To see his work, visit the Dalí Espace Montmartre.

Contemporary Art

Street art is the current buzzword in the capital. In 2013 the world's largest collective street-art exhibition, La Tour Paris 13 (www.tourparis13.fr), opened in a derelict apartment block in the 13e *arrondissement*. Its 36 apartments on 13 floors were covered from head to toe with works by 100 international artists. The blockbuster exhibition ran for just one month, after which the tower was demolished in 2014. For more on street art, see p112.

Another high-profile installation featured more than 4000 portraits by French photographer JR, which covered the floor and walls of the Panthéon while it underwent renovation.

The Centre Pompidou is Paris' premier showcase of modern and contemporary art, while smaller traditional and edgy new gallery spaces across the city exhibit works by up-and-coming artists.

Literary Arts

Flicking through a street directory reveals just how much Paris honours its literary history, with listings including places Colette and Victor Hugo, avs Marcel Proust and Émile Zola, and rue Balzac. The city has nurtured countless French authors over the centuries, who, together with expat writers from Dickens onwards – including the Lost Generation's Hemingway, Fitzgerald and Joyce – have sealed Paris' literary reputation.

Contemporary French writers include Jean Echenoz, Erik Orsenna, Christine Angot (dubbed '*la reine de l'autofiction*', 'the queen of autobiography') and prize-winning Paris-based comedian/dramatist Nelly Alard, who had her second novel *Moment d'un couple* (Moment of a Couple) published in 2013; it was translated into English as Couple Mechanics in 2016.

Delving into the mood and politics of the capital's notable ethnic population is Faïza Guène (b 1985), a French literary sensation who writes in an 'urban slang' style.

Ex–French border guard turned author Romain Puértolas (b 1975) had an instant best-selling hit with his surreal, partly Paris-set 2013 novel *L'Extraordinaire Voyage du Fakir Qui Était Resté Coincé Dans une Armoire Ikea* (The Extraordinary Journey of the Fakir Who Got Trapped in an Ikea Wardrobe), which won the Grand Prix Jules Verne in 2014. It was followed in 2015 by *La Petite Fille Qui Avait Avalé un Nuage Grand Comme la Tour Eiffel* (The Little Girl Who Swallowed a Cloud as Big as the Eiffel Tower) and the zany farce *Re-vive l'Empereur* (Re-live the Emperor), imagining the contemporary return of Napoléon Bonaparte.

Chansons

The *chanson française,* a tradition dating from troubadours in the Middle Ages, was eclipsed by the music halls of the early 20th century, but was revived in the 1930s by Édith Piaf (1915–63) and Charles Trenet (1913–2001), followed by 'France's Frank Sinatra', Charles Aznavour (b 1924). In the 1950s Left Bank cabarets nurtured singers such as Léo Ferré (1916–63), Georges Brassens (1921–81), Claude Nougaro (1929–2004), Jacques Brel (1929–78), Barbara (1930–97) and the very sexy, very Paris-ian Serge Gainsbourg (1928–91).

The genre was revived once more in the new millennium as *la nouvelle chanson française* by performers such as Vincent Delerm (b 1976), Bénabar (b 1969), Jeanne Cherhal (b 1978), Camille (b 1978), and Zaz (Isabelle Geffroy; b 1980), who mixes jazz, soul, acoustic and traditional *chansons*.

Music

From organ recitals and classical concerts in Gothic architectural splendour to a legendary jazz scene, stirring *chansons,* groundbreaking electronica, award-winning world music and some of the world's best rap, music is embedded deep in the Parisian soul – this is a city where talented musicians have to audition even to perform in the metro.

Jazz

Jazz hit Paris in the 1920s with Josephine Baker, an African American cabaret dancer. In 1934 a chance meeting between Parisian jazz violinist Stéphane Grappelli (1908–97) and three-fingered Roma guitarist Django Reinhardt (1910–53) in a Montparnasse nightclub led to the formation of the Hot Club of France quintet. Claude Luter and his Dixieland band were hip in the 1950s. Today there are jazz clubs throughout the city, both hallowed and new.

Pop

French pop has come a long way since the yéyé (imitative rock) days of the 1960s as sung by Johnny Hallyday. Nosfell is one of France's most creative and intense musicians, who sings in his own invented language called 'le klokobetz'. His third album, *Massif Armour* (2014), opens and closes in 'le klokobetz' but otherwise woos listeners with powerful French love lyrics.

In 2011 Sylvie Hoarau and Aurélie Saada formed the indie folk duo Brigitte; their debut album *Et vous, tu m'aimes?* went platinum in France. Their 2014 album *A bouche que veux-tu* also achieved widespread success.

Internationally successful modern pop stars include singer-songwriters Christine and the Queens (aka Héloïse Letissier; b 1988), who released her first album *Chaleur Humaine* in 2014, and Jain (Jeanne Galice; b 1992), whose debut album, *Zanaka*, was released in 2015.

Electronica

Paris' electronic dance music is renowned; internationally successful bands such as Daft Punk and Justice head up the scene.

David Guetta, Laurent Garnier, Martin Solveig and Bob Sinclair (aka Christophe Le Friant, originally nicknamed 'Chris the French Kiss') are top Parisian electronica producers and DJs who travel the international circuit. Breakbot (Thibaut Berland; b 1981) released his first album in 2012 and gained a rapid following for his remixes. His 2016-released album *Still Waters* includes the track Star Tripper, included in Disney's Star Wars–themed music album *Star Wars Headspace*.

Film

Paris is one of the world's most cinematic cities. The world's first paying-public film screening was held in Paris' Grand Café on blvd des Capucines, 9e, in December 1895 by the Lumière brothers, inventors of 'moving pictures'. Since that time, the French capital has produced a bevy of blockbuster film-makers and stars and is the filming location of countless box-office hits by both home-grown and foreign directors. Fabulous experiences for film buffs range from exploring behind the scenes at an art-deco cinema to catching a classic retrospective in one of the Latin Quarter's many cinemas, or following in the footsteps of iconic screen heroine Amélie Poulain through the streets of Montmartre.

French cinema hasn't looked back since 2012 when *The Artist* (2011), a silent B&W romantic comedy set in 1920s Hollywood, won seven BAFTAs and five Oscars to become the most awarded film in French cinema history, including a Best Director award for Parisian Michel Hazanavicius (b 1967), and Best Actor for Jean Dujardin (b 1972), who started with one-man shows in Paris' bars and cabarets and whose later roles have included a WWII French soldier in George Clooney's *The Monuments Men* (2014).

France's leading lady is Parisian Marion Cotillard (b 1975), the first French woman since 1959 to win an Oscar, for her role as Édith Piaf in Olivier Dahan's *La Môme* (*La Vie en Rose;* 2007). The versatile actress went on to play an amputee in art film *De Rouille et d'Os* (Rust and Bone; 2012) by Parisian director Jacques Audiard (b 1952). In *Deux Jours, Une Nuit* (Two Days, One Night; 2014), screened at the 2014 Cannes International Film Festival, Cotillard plays an employee in a solar-panel factory who learns she will lose her job if her co-workers don't each sacrifice €1000 bonuses offered to them. Her latest role is in 2017's *Rock'n Roll* as the parter of Guillaume Canet (her real-life partner), who plays an actor told by his young co-star that he's no longer 'Rock'n' Roll' enough to sell films any more.

For a comprehensive overview of French films, including upcoming films, visit www.filmsdefrance.com.

Cyclists passing *bouquinistes* (used-book sellers; p156) that line the Seine

Survival Guide

DIRECTORY A–Z   230

Climate................................230
Discount Cards................230
Electricity............................230
Emergency.......................230
Gay & Lesbian
Travellers 230
Health................................231
Insurance 231
Internet Access................231

Money 231
Opening Hours..................231
Public Holidays 232
Safe Travel........................232
Telephone 232
Time 232
Toilets...............................232
Tourist Information...........232
Travellers with
Disabilities 233
Visas.................................233

TRANSPORT   233

Arriving in Paris 233
Getting Around 235

LANGUAGE   238

Directory A–Z

Discount Cards

Almost all museums and monuments in Paris have discounted tickets *(tarif réduit)* for students and seniors (generally over 60 years), provided they have valid ID. Children often get in for free; the cut-off age for a child is anywhere between six and 18 years.

EU citizens under 26 years get in for free at national monuments and museums.

Paris Museum Pass (www.parismuseumpass.com; 2/4/6 days €48/62/74) gets you into 50-odd venues in and around Paris; a huge advantage is that pass holders usually enter larger sights at a different en-trance meaning you bypass (or substantially reduce) ridiculously long ticket queues.

The handy **Paris Passlib'** (www.parisinfo.com; 2/3/5 days €109/129/155), sold on its website and at the **Paris Convention & Visitors Bureau** (Office du Tourisme et des Congrès de Paris; 25 rue des Pyramides, 1er; ⊙9am-7pm May-Oct, 10am-7pm Nov-Apr; MPyramides), covers unlimited public transport in zones 1 to 3, admission to some 50 museums in the Paris region (aka a Paris Museum Pass), a one-hour boat cruise along the Seine, and a one-day hop-on hop-off open-top bus sightseeing service around central Paris' key sights with **L'Open Tour** (☑01 42 66 56 56; www.paris.opentour.com). There's an optional €15 supplement for a skip-the-line ticket to levels one and two of the Eiffel Tower, or €21.50 for all three Eiffel Tower platforms.

Electricity

**Type E
230V/50Hz**

Emergency

Ambulance (SAMU)	☑15
Fire	☑18
Police	☑17
EU-wide emergency	☑112

Gay & Lesbian Travellers

The city known as 'gay Paree' lives up to its name. While Le Marais is the mainstay of gay and lesbian nightlife, you'll find venues throughout the city attracting a mixed crowd.

Climate

Paris

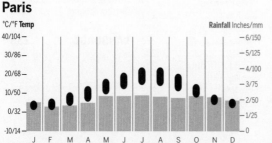

°C/°F **Temp**   Rainfall Inches/mm

40/104 —   — 6/150
30/86 —   — 5/125
20/68 —   — 4/100
10/50 —   — 3/75
0/32 —   — 2/50
-10/14 —   — 1/25
                                   — 0

J F M A M J J A S O N D

Book Your Stay Online

For more accommodation reviews by Lonely Planet authors, check out http://hotels.lonelyplanet.com/paris. You'll find independent reviews, as well as recommendations on the best places to stay. Best of all, you can book online.

The single best source of information for gay and lesbian travellers in Paris is the **Centre Gai et Lesbien de Paris Île de France** (☑01 43 57 21 47; www.centrelgbtparis.org; 63 rue Beaubourg, 3e; ☺centre & bar 3.30-8pm Mon-Fri, 1-7pm Sat, library 2-8pm Mon, Tue & Wed, 5-7pm Fri & Sat; Ⓜ Rambuteau), which has details of hotlines, helplines, gay and gay-friendly medical services and politically oriented activist associations, and a sociable bar.

Health

Hospitals

Paris has some 50 hospitals including the epicentral **Hôpital Hôtel Dieu** (☑01 42 34 88 19; www.aphp.fr; 1 place du Parvis Notre Dame, 4e; Ⓜ Cité), one of the city's main government-run public hospitals; after 8pm use the emergency entrance on rue de la Cité.

Pharmacies

Pharmacies (chemists) are marked by a large illuminated green cross outside. At least one in each neighbourhood is open for extended hours; see www.parisinfo.com for listings.

Insurance

Comprehensive travel insurance to cover theft, loss and medical problems is highly recommended. Worldwide travel insurance is available at www.lonelyplanet.com/travel-insurance. You can buy, extend and claim online anytime – even if you're already on the road.

Internet Access

❂ Wi-fi (pronounced 'wee-fee' in France) is available in most Paris hotels, usually at no extra cost, and in some museums.

❂ Free wi-fi is available in more than 300 public places. For complete details and a map of hotspots, see www.paris.fr/wifi.

❂ Expect to pay around €4 per hour for online access in internet cafes; Milk (www.milklub.com) has a central branch near Les Halles.

Money

❂ ATMs (*distributeur automatique de billets* in French) are widespread.

❂ Visa and MasterCard are accepted in most hotels, shops and restaurants; fewer accept American Express. France uses cards with an embedded microchip and PIN – few places accept swipe-and-signature. Ask your bank for advice before you leave.

Opening Hours

The following are *approximate* standard opening hours. Hours can vary by season. Many businesses close in August for summer holidays.
Banks 9am to 1pm and 2pm to 5pm Monday to Friday, some Saturday morning
Bars & cafes 7am to 2am

Practicalities

Smoking Smoking is illegal in indoor public spaces, including restaurants and bars (hence the crowds of smokers in doorways and on pavement terraces outside).
Weights & Measures France uses the metric system.

Museums 10am to 6pm, closed Monday or Tuesday

Post offices 8am to 7pm Monday to Friday, and until noon Saturday

Restaurants Noon to 2pm and 7.30pm to 10.30pm

Shops 10am to 7pm Monday to Saturday (plus Sunday in tourist zones), occasionally close in the early afternoon for lunch and sometimes all day Monday

Public Holidays

In France a *jour férié* (public holiday) is celebrated strictly on the day on which it falls – if it's a Saturday or Sunday, no provision is made for an extra day off.

The following holidays are observed in Paris:

New Year's Day (Jour de l'An) 1 January

Easter Sunday & Monday (Pâques & Lundi de Pâques) Late March/April

May Day (Fête du Travail) 1 May

Victory in Europe Day (Victoire 1945) 8 May

Ascension Thursday (L'Ascension) May (celebrated on the 40th day after Easter)

Whit Monday (Lundi de Pentecôte) Mid-May to mid-June (seventh Monday after Easter)

Bastille Day/National Day (Fête Nationale) 14 July

Assumption Day (L'Assomption) 15 August

All Saints' Day (La Toussaint) 1 November

Armistice Day/Remembrance Day (Le Onze Novembre) 11 November

Christmas (Noël) 25 December

Safe Travel

In general, Paris is a safe city and random street assaults are rare. The city is mostly well lit and there's no reason not to use the metro until it stops running. Many women do travel on the metro alone, late at night, in most areas.

Pickpocketing is typically the biggest concern. *Always* be alert and take precautions: don't carry more money than you need, and keep your credit cards, passport and other documents in a concealed pouch, a hotel safe or a safe-deposit box.

Telephone

Check with your provider about roaming costs before you leave home, or ensure your phone's unlocked to use a French SIM card (available cheaply in Paris).

○ There are no area codes in France – you always dial the 10-digit number.

○ France's country code is 🗹33 and the international access code is 🗹00.

Time

○ France is on Central European Time, one hour ahead of GMT.

○ Daylight-saving time (two hours ahead of GMT) runs from the last Sunday in March to the last Sunday in October.

Toilets

○ Public toilets in Paris are signposted *toilettes* or *WC*. The self-cleaning cylindrical toilets on Parisian pavements are open 24 hours, are reasonably clean and are free of charge. Look for the words *libre* ('available'; green-coloured) or *occupé* ('occupied'; red-coloured).

○ Cafe owners do not appreciate you using their facilities if you are not a paying customer (a coffee can be a good buy). Other good bets are major department stores and big hotels.

Tourist Information

Paris Convention & Visitors Bureau (Office du Tourisme et des Congrès de Paris; www. parisinfo.com; 25 rue des Pyramides, 1er; ⊙9am-7pm May-Oct, 10am-7pm Nov-Apr; ⓂPyramides) The main branch is 500m northwest of the Louvre. It sells tickets for tours and several attractions, plus museum and transport passes. Also books accommodation.

Travellers with Disabilities

○ For information about which venues in Paris are accessible to people with disabilities, check Accès Culture (www.accesculture.org).

○ Download Lonely Planet's free *Accessible Travel* guide from http://lptravel.to/ AccessibleTravel.

Visas

○ Generally no restrictions for EU citizens. Usually not required for most other nationalities for stays of up to 90 days.

○ Check www.france.diplo matie.fr for the latest visa regulations and the closest French embassy to your current residence.

Transport

Arriving in Paris

Practically every major airline flies through one of Paris' three airports, and most European train and bus routes cross Paris.

Climate Change & Travel

Every form of transport that relies on carbon-based fuel generates CO_2, the main cause of human-induced climate change. Modern travel is dependent on aeroplanes, which might use less fuel per kilometre per person than most cars but travel much greater distances. The altitude at which aircraft emit gases (including CO_2) and particles also contributes to their climate change impact. Many websites offer 'carbon calculators' that allow people to estimate the carbon emissions generated by their journey and, for those who wish to do so, to offset the impact of the greenhouse gases emitted with contributions to portfolios of climate-friendly initiatives throughout the world. Lonely Planet offsets the carbon footprint of all staff and author travel.

Flights, tours and rail tickets can be booked online at www.lonelyplanet.com.

Charles de Gaulle Airport

Most international airlines fly to **Aéroport de Charles de Gaulle** (CDG; ☑01 70 36 39 50; www.parisaeroport.fr), 28km northeast of central Paris. In French the airport is commonly called 'Roissy'.

Bus

There are six main bus lines.
Le Bus Direct line 2 (€17; one hour; every 30 minutes, 5.45am to 11pm) Links the airport with the Arc de Triomphe via the Eiffel Tower and Trocadéro. Children under four years travel free.
Le Bus Direct line 4 (€17; 50 to 80 minutes; every 30 minutes, 6am to 10.30pm from the airport, 5.30am to 10.30pm from Montparnasse) Links the airport with Gare Montparnasse (80 minutes) in southern Paris via Gare de Lyon (50 minutes) in eastern Paris. Under fours travel free.

Noctilien bus 140 & 143 (€8 or four metro tickets; line 140 1¼ hours, line 143 two hours; hourly, 12.30am-5.30am) Part of the RATP night service, Noctilien has two buses that go to CDG: bus 140 from Gare de l'Est, and 143 from Gare de l'Est and Gare du Nord.
RATP bus 350 (€6; 70 minutes; every 30 minutes, 5.30am to 11pm) Links the airport with Gare de l'Est in northern Paris.
RATP bus 351 (€6; 70 minutes; every 30 minutes, 5.30am to 11pm) Links the airport with place de la Nation in eastern Paris.
Roissybus (€11.50; one hour; from CDG every 15 minutes, 5.30am to 10pm and every 30 minutes, 10pm to 11pm; from Paris every 15 minutes, 5.15am to 10pm and every 30 minutes, 10pm to 12.30am) Links the airport with the Opéra.

Taxi

○ A taxi to the city centre takes 40 minutes. Fares are standardised to a flat rate: €50 to the Right Bank and €55 to the Left Bank.

Tourist Transport Passes

The Mobilis and Paris Visite passes are valid on the metro, RER, SNCF's suburban lines, buses, night buses, trams and Montmartre funicular railway. No photo is needed, but write your card number on the ticket.

Passes are sold at metro and RER stations, SNCF offices in Paris, and the airports. Children aged four to 11 years pay roughly half price.

○ The **Mobilis** card allows unlimited travel for one day and costs €7.30 (two zones) to €17.30 (five zones).

○ **Paris Visite** allows unlimited travel as well as discounted entry to certain museums and other discounts and bonuses. The 'Paris+Suburbs+Airports' pass includes transport to/from the airports and costs €24.50/37.25/52.20/63.90 for one/two/three/five days. The cheaper 'Paris Centre' pass, valid for zones 1 to 3, costs €11.65/18.95/25.85/37.25.

The fare increases by 15% between 5pm and 10am and on Sundays.

○ Only take taxis at a clearly marked rank. Never follow anyone who approaches you at the airport and claims to be a driver.

Train

CDG is served by the RER B line (€10, approximately 50 minutes, every 10 to 20 minutes), which connects with the Gare du Nord, Châtelet–Les Halles and St-Michel–Notre Dame stations in the city centre. Trains run from 5am to 11pm; there are fewer trains on weekends.

Orly Airport

Aéroport d'Orly (ORY; ☑01 70 36 39 50; www.parisaeroport. fr) is 19km south of central Paris but, despite being closer than CDG, it is not as frequently used by interna-

tional airlines, and public transport options aren't quite as straightforward.

Orly's south and west terminals are currently being unified into one large terminal suitable for bigger planes such as A380s; completion is due in 2018.

Bus

Two bus lines serve Orly:
Le Bus Direct line 1 (€12; one hour, every 20 minutes, 5.50am to 11.30pm from Orly, 4.50am to 10.30pm from the Arc de Triomphe) Runs to/from the Arc de Triomphe (one hour) via Gare Montparnasse (40 minutes), La Motte-Picquet and Trocadéro. Under fours travel free.

Orlybus (€8, 30 minutes, every 15 minutes, 6am to 12.30pm from Orly, 5.35am to midnight from Paris) Runs to/from the metro station Denfert Rochereau in southern Paris, making several stops en route.

Taxi

A taxi to the city centre takes roughly 30 minutes. Standardised flat-rate fares mean a taxi costs €30 to the Left Bank and €35 to the Right Bank. The fare increases by 15% between 5pm and 10am and on Sundays.

Train

There is currently no direct train to/from Orly; you'll need to change halfway. Note that while it is possible to take a shuttle to the RER C line, this service is quite long and not recommended.
RER B (€12.05, 35 minutes, every four to 12 minutes) This line connects Orly with the St-Michel–Notre Dame, Châtelet–Les Halles and Gare du Nord stations in the city centre. In order to get from Orly to the RER station (Antony), you must first take the Orlyval automatic train. The service runs from 6am to 11pm (less frequently on weekends). You only need one ticket to take the two trains.

Tram

Tramway T7 (€1.90, every six minutes, 40 minutes, 5.30am to 12.30am) This tramway links Orly with Villejuif-Louis Aragon metro station in southern Paris; buy tickets from the machine at the tram stop as no tickets are sold on board.

Beauvais Airport

Aéroport de Beauvais (BVA; ☑08 92 68 20 66; www. aeroportbeauvais.com) is 75km north of Paris and is served by a few low-cost flights.

Before you snap up that bargain, consider if the post-arrival journey is worth it.

Shuttle (€17, 1¼ hours) The Beauvais shuttle bus links the airport with metro station Porte de Maillot. See the airport website for details and tickets.

Gare du Nord

Gare du Nord (rue de Dunkerque, 10e; Ⓜ Gare du Nord), located in northern Paris, is the terminus for northbound domestic trains as well as several international services:

Eurostar (www.eurostar.com) Links to St-Pancras International, London. Voyages take 2¼ hours.

Thalys (www.thalys.com) Serves Brussels, Amsterdam and Cologne.

Other Mainline Train Stations

Paris has five other stations for long-distance trains, each with its own metro station: Gare d'Austerlitz, Gare de l'Est, Gare de Lyon, Gare Montparnasse and Gare St-Lazare; the station used depends on the direction from Paris.

Contact Voyages SNCF (www.voyages-sncf.com) for connections throughout France and continental Europe.

Gare Routiére Internationale de Paris-Galliéni

Eurolines (www.eurolines.fr) connects all major European capitals to Paris' eastern **Gare Routiére Internationale de Paris-Galliéni** (✐ 08

92 89 90 91; 28 av du Général de Gaulle, Bagnolet; Ⓜ Galliéni). Major new European bus company Flixbus (www.flixbus.com) and the Beauvais airport shuttle both use western **Parking Pershing** (16-24 bd Pershing, 17e; Ⓜ Porte Maillot).

Getting Around

Paris' metro and RER trains, trams, buses and night buses are run by RATP (www.ratp.fr), which has an online journey planner. Free transport maps are available at metro ticket windows and can be downloaded from the website.

Train

Paris' underground network consists of two separate but linked systems: the metro and the Réseau Express Régional (RER) suburban train line. The metro has 14 numbered lines; the RER has five main lines (but you'll probably only need to use A, B and C). When buying tickets consider how many zones your journey will cover; there are five concentric transportation zones rippling out from Paris (5 being the furthest); if you travel from Charles de Gaulle airport to Paris, for instance, you will have to buy a zone 1–5 ticket.

Metro

○ Metro lines are identified by both their number (eg ligne 1; line 1) and their colour, listed on official metro signs and maps.

○ Signs in metro and RER stations indicate the way to the correct platform for your line. The *direction* signs on each platform indicate the

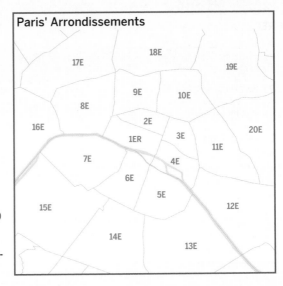

Paris' Arrondissements

17E
18E
19E
9E
8E
10E
16E
2E
1ER
3E
20E
11E
7E
4E
6E
5E
12E
15E
14E
13E

terminus. On lines that split into several branches (such as lines 7 and 13), the terminus of each train is indicated on the cars and on signs on each platform giving the number of minutes until the next and subsequent train.

○ Signs marked *correspondance* (transfer) show how to reach connecting trains. At stations with many intersecting lines, like Châtelet and Montparnasse Bienvenüe, walking from one platform to the next can take a very long time.

○ Different station exits are indicated by white-on-blue *sortie* (exit) signs. You can get your bearings by checking the *plan du quartier* (neighbourhood maps) posted at exits.

○ Each line has its own schedule, but trains usually start at 5.30am, with the last train beginning its run between 12.35am and 1.15am (2.15am on Friday and Saturday).

RER

○ The RER is faster than the metro, but the stops are much further apart.

○ If you're going out to the suburbs, make sure your ticket is for the correct zone.

Tickets & Fares

○ The same RATP tickets are valid on the metro, the RER (for travel within the city limits), buses, trams and the Montmartre funicular.

○ A ticket – white in colour and called *Le Ticket t+* – costs €1.90 (half price for children aged four to nine

years) if bought individually and €14.50 for adults for a *carnet* (book) of 10.

○ Tickets are sold at all metro stations. Ticket windows accept most credit cards; however automated machines do not accept credit cards without embedded chips (and even then, not all foreign chip-embedded cards).

○ One ticket lets you travel between any two metro stations (no return journeys) for a period of 1½ hours, no matter how many transfers are required. You can also use it on the RER for travel within zone 1, which encompasses all of central Paris.

○ Transfers from the metro to bus or vice versa are not possible.

Bicycle

Vélib'

The **Vélib'** (☑01 30 79 79 30; www.velib.paris.fr; day/ week subscription €1.70/8, bike hire up to 30/60/90/120min free/€1/2/4) bike share scheme has over 23,000 bikes for getting around the city. There are some 1800 stations city-wide, each with anywhere from 20 to 70 bike stands, all accessible around the clock.

○ To get a bike, you first need to purchase a one-/seven-day subscription, either at the terminals found at docking stations or online.

○ Terminals require a chip-and-PIN credit card (not all foreign chip-embedded cards may work). Alternatively, you can pre-purchase a subscription online.

○ After you authorise a deposit (€150) to pay for the bike should it go missing, you'll receive an ID number and PIN code.

○ Bikes are rented in 30-minute intervals. If you return a bike before a half-hour is up and then take a new one, you will not be charged.

○ If the station you want to return your bike to is full, log in to the terminal to get 15 minutes for free to find another station.

○ Bikes are geared to cyclists aged 14 and over, and are fitted with gears, an anti-theft lock with key, reflective strips and front/rear lights. Bring your own helmet (they are not required by law).

○ **Cityscoot** (www.cityscoot. eu; per min/100 min €0.28/25; ⏰7am-11pm) is a share scheme for electric scooters. Any driver's licence (including a foreign-issued licence) is valid for those born before 1 January 1988; anyone born after that date requires a current French or EU driver's licence.

Rentals

Most rental places will require a deposit (usually €150). Take ID and bank card/credit card.
Freescoot (☑01 44 07 06 72; www.freescoot.com; 63 quai de la Tournelle, 5e; 50/125cc scooters per 24hr from €55/65, bicycle/electric bike rental per 24hr from €20/40; ⏰9am-1pm & 2-7pm mid-Apr–mid-Sep, closed Sun & Wed mid-Sep–mid-Apr; Ⓜ Maubert-Mutualité)

Gepetto et Vélos (☏01 43 54 19 95; www.gepetto-velos.com; 59 rue du Cardinal Lemoine, 5e; bike rental per day from €16, child seat €5; ⏲9am-2pm & 3-7pm Tue-Sat year-round, plus 10am-2pm & 3-7pm Sun mid-Apr–mid-Sep; Ⓜ Cardinal Lemoine)

Paris à Vélo, C'est Sympa (☏01 48 87 60 01; www.parisvelosympa.com; 22 rue Alphonse Baudin, 11e; half-day/full day/24hr bike from €12/15/20, electric bike €20/30/40; ⏲9.30am-1pm & 2-6pm Mon-Fri, 9am-7pm Sat & Sun Apr-Oct, shorter hours Nov-Mar; Ⓜ Richard Lenoir)

Boat

Glassed-in trimarans that dock every 20 to 25 minutes at small piers along the Seine are run by **Batobus** (www.batobus.com; adult/child 1-day pass €17/8, 2-day pass €19/10; ⏲10am-9.30pm Apr-Aug, to 7pm Sep-Mar). Buy tickets online, at ferry stops or tourist offices. You can also buy a Pass+ that includes **L'Open Tour** (www.paris.opentour.com) buses, to be used on consecutive days. A two-day pass per adult/child costs €46/21; a three day-pass is €50/21.

Bus

Buses can be a scenic way to get around but they're slower and less intuitive to figure out than the metro.

Local Buses

Paris' bus system runs from 5.30am to 8.30pm Monday to Saturday; after that, certain evening-service lines continue until between midnight and 12.30am. Services are reduced on Sunday and public holidays, when buses run from 7am to 8.30pm.

Night Buses

⦿ The RATP runs 47 night bus lines known as Noctilien, which depart hourly from 12.30am to 5.30am. Look for navy-blue N or Noctilien signs at bus stops.

⦿ Noctilien services are included on your Mobilis or Paris Visite pass for the zones in which you're travelling. Otherwise you pay a certain number of standard €1.90 metro/bus tickets, depending on the length of journey.

Tickets & Fares

⦿ Normal bus rides embracing one or two bus zones cost one metro ticket; longer rides require two or even three tickets. Transfers to other buses are allowed on the same ticket as long as the change takes place 1½ hours between the first and last validation. This does not apply to Noctilien services.

⦿ Whatever kind of single-journey ticket you have, you must validate it in the ticket machine near the driver. If you don't have a ticket, the driver can sell you one for €2 (correct change required). If you have a Mobilis or Paris Visite pass, flash it at the driver when you board.

Taxi

⦿ The *prise en charge* (flagfall) is €3.83. Within the city limits, it costs €1.06 per kilometre for travel between 10am and 5pm Monday to Saturday (*Tarif A;* white light on taxi roof and meter).

⦿ At night (5pm to 10am), on Sunday from 7am to midnight, and in the inner suburbs the rate is €1.29 per kilometre (*Tarif B;* orange light).

⦿ Travel in the city limits and inner suburbs on Sunday night (midnight to 7am Monday) and in the outer suburbs is at *Tarif C,* €1.56 per kilometre (blue light).

⦿ The minimum taxi fare for a short trip is €7.

⦿ There's a €4 surcharge for taking a fourth passenger, but drivers sometimes refuse for insurance reasons. The first piece of baggage is free; additional pieces over 5kg cost €1 extra.

⦿ Flagging down a taxi in Paris can be difficult; it's best to find an official taxi stand.

⦿ To order a taxi, call or reserve online with **Taxis G7** (☏01 41 27 66 99, 3607; www.taxisg7.fr), **Taxis Bleus** (☏08 91 70 10 10, 3609; https://taxis-bleus.com) or **Alpha Taxis** (☏01 45 85 85 85; www.alpha-taxis-paris.fr).

Car & Motorcycle

Driving in Paris is defined by the triple hassle of navigation, heavy traffic and limited parking. Petrol stations are also difficult to locate and access. It doesn't make sense to use a car to get around, but if you're heading out of the city on an excursion, then your own wheels can certainly be useful. If you plan on hiring a car, it's best to do so online and in advance.

Language

The sounds used in spoken French can almost all be found in English. There are a couple of exceptions: nasal vowels (represented in our pronunciation guides by 'o' or 'u' followed by an almost inaudible nasal consonant sound 'm', 'n' or 'ng'), the 'funny' *u* sound ('ew' in our guides) and the deep-in-the-throat *r*. Bearing these few points in mind and reading our pronunciation guides below as if they were English, you'll be understood just fine. The markers (m) and (f) indicate the forms for male and female speakers respectively.

To enhance your trip with a phrasebook, visit **lonelyplanet.com**. Lonely Planet iPhone phrasebooks are available through the Apple App store.

Basics

Hello.
Bonjour. — bon·zhoor

Goodbye.
Au revoir. — o·rer·vwa

How are you?
Comment allez-vous? — ko·mon ta·lay·voo

I'm fine, thanks.
Bien, merci. — byun mair·see

Please.
S'il vous plaît. — seel voo play

Thank you.
Merci. — mair·see

Excuse me.
Excusez-moi. — ek·skew·zay·mwa

Sorry.
Pardon. — par·don

Yes./No.
Oui./Non. — wee/non

I don't understand.
Je ne comprends pas. — zher ner kom·pron pa

Do you speak English?
Parlez-vous anglais? — par·lay·voo ong·glay

Shopping

I'd like to buy ...
Je voudrais acheter ... — zher voo·dray ash·tay ...

I'm just looking.
Je regarde. — zher rer·gard

How much is it?
C'est combien? — say kom·byun

It's too expensive.
C'est trop cher. — say tro shair

Can you lower the price?
Vous pouvez baisser le prix? — voo poo·vay bay·say ler pree

Eating & Drinking

..., please.
..., s'il vous plaît. — ... seel voo play

A coffee	*un café*	un ka·fay
A table for two	*une table pour deux*	ewn ta·bler poor der
Two beers	*deux bières*	der bee·yair

I'm a vegetarian.
Je suis végétarien/végétarienne. (m/f) — zher swee vay·zhay·ta·ryun/ vay·zhay·ta·ryen

Cheers!
Santé! — son·tay

That was delicious!
C'était délicieux! — say·tay day·lee·syer

The bill, please.
L'addition, s'il vous plaît. — la·dee·syon seel voo play

Emergencies

Help!
Au secours! — o skoor

Call the police!
Appelez la police! — a·play la po·lees

Call a doctor!
Appelez un médecin! — a·play un mayd·sun

I'm sick.
Je suis malade. — zher swee ma·lad

I'm lost.
Je suis perdu/perdue. (m/f) — zhe swee pair·dew

Where are the toilets?
Où sont les toilettes? — oo son lay twa·let

Transport & Directions

Where's ...?
Où est ...? — oo ay ...

What's the address?
Quelle est l'adresse? — kel ay la·dres

I want to go to ...
Je voudrais aller à ... — zher voo·dray a·lay a ...

Behind the Scenes

Writer Thanks

Merci mille fois first and foremost to Julian and to the innumerable Parisians who provided insights, inspiration and great times. Huge thanks too to Destination Editor Daniel Fahey, Managing Destination Editor Jennifer Carey and everyone at Lonely Planet. As ever, a heartfelt *merci encore* to my parents, brother, *belle-sœur* and *neveu* for sustaining my lifelong love of Paris.

Acknowledgements

Climate map data adapted from Peel MC, Finlayson BL & McMahon TA (2007) 'Updated World Map of the Köppen-Geiger Climate Classification', *Hydrology and Earth System Sciences*, 11, 1633–44.

Illustrations pp50–1, pp56–7 and pp86–7 by Javier Zarracina.

This Book

This guidebook was researched, written and curated by Catherine Le Nevez. The previous edition was researched by Catherine Le Nevez, Christopher Pitts and Nicola Williams.

Destination Editor Daniel Fahey

Product Editors Carolyn Boicos, Kate Mathews

Book Designer Mazzy Prinsep

Senior Cartographer Mark Griffiths

Assisting Editors Michelle Bennett, Katie Connolly, Joel Cotterell, Andrea Dobbin, Kathryn Rowan

Assisting Book Designers Meri Blazevski, Fergal Condon

Cover Researcher Wibowo Rusli

Thanks to Victoria Harrison, Liz Heynes, Katherine Marsh, Isabel Robles, Eize Siegersma, Tony Wheeler

Send Us Your Feedback

We love to hear from travellers – your comments keep us on our toes and help make our books better. Our well-travelled team reads every word on what you loved or loathed about this book. Although we cannot reply individually to postal submissions, we always guarantee that your feedback goes straight to the appropriate authors, in time for the next edition. Each person who sends us information is thanked in the next edition, the most useful submissions are rewarded with a selection of digital PDF chapters.

Visit lonelyplanet.com/contact to submit your updates and suggestions or to ask for help. Our award-winning website also features inspirational travel stories, news and discussions.

Note: We may edit, reproduce and incorporate your comments in Lonely Planet products such as guidebooks, websites and digital products, so let us know if you don't want your comments reproduced or your name acknowledged. For a copy of our privacy policy visit lonelyplanet.com/privacy.

Index

59 Rivoli 77

A

accommodation 19, 203-9, **209**
activities 4-17, 195-201, *see also individual activities*
air travel 233-5
ambulance 230
apartment rentals 207
Arc de Triomphe 42-5
Arc de Triomphe du Carrousel 91
architecture 213, 219-22
area codes 232
Arènes de Lutèce 200
arrondissements 19, **235**
Art 42 113
art galleries, *see individual galleries*
Art Ludique-Le Musée 109
art nouveau 29
arts 29, 30, 112-13, 223-8
Atelier Brancusi 76
ATMs 231

B

Bastille **254-5**
drinking 179-80
entertainment 192-3
food 132-4
nightlife 179-80
shopping 153-4
Bastille Day 12
bathrooms 232
beer 10, 174

Belleville **254-5**
drinking 176-9
entertainment 191-2
food 130-2
nightlife 176-9
shopping 151-3
bicycle travel, *see* cycling
bistros 120
boat travel 72-3, 237
Bois de Boulogne 201
Bois de Vincennes 200-1
books 226-7
boules 200
bouquinistes 156
breweries 174
budgeting 18, 31, 118, 165, 204, 207, 230, 234
bus travel 237
business hours 145, 164, 231-2
buskers 189

C

Canal St-Martin 152
car travel 237
Carrousel du Louvre 55
Catacombes, Les 94-5
cell phones 232
Centre Pompidou 74-7
Champs-Élysées **246-7**
drinking 168-70
entertainment 188
food 123, 125
nightlife 168-70
shopping 148-9
chansons 227
Château de Versailles 84-7, **86-7**
Château de Vincennes 200
cheese 137
chemists 231
children, travel with 32-3, 146
Christmas markets 16
Cimetière du Montparnasse 95

Cimetière du Père Lachaise 78-81, **80-1**
Cinéaqua 32
cinema 192, 228
festivals 8, 13
Cirque d'Hiver Bouglione 15
Cité de l'Architecture et du Patrimoine 40
Cité des Sciences 32
climate 19
Clos Montmartre 61
clubbing 30, 166, 178, *see also* drinking & nightlife
cocktails 6, 172
coffee 165, 167, 175
Conciergerie 93
cooking courses 96-7
costs 18, 31, 118, 165, 204, 207, 230, 234
courses 96-7
covered passages 110-11, **110-11**
credit cards 231
cruises 72-3
culture 223-8
currency 18
cycling 236-7
tours 201

D

dangers 232
disabilities, travellers with 233
discount cards 230
Docks en Seine 109
drinking & nightlife 163-83, **165**, *see also individual neighbourhoods*
costs 165
language 165
opening hours 164
tipping 165
wine-tasting courses 97
driving 237

E

eastern Paris **254-5**
  drinking 179-80
  entertainment 192-3
  food 132-4
  nightlife 179-80
  shopping 153-4
economy 213
Église de la Madeleine 100-1
Église du Dôme 104
Église St-Eustache 76-7
Église St-Germain des Prés 105
Église St-Louis des Invalides
  104
Eiffel Tower 36-9
Eiffel Tower area **246-7**
  drinking 168
  entertainment 188
  food 122-3
  nightlife 168
  sights 40-1
electricity 230
emergencies 230, 238
entertainment 185-93, see also
  individual neighbourhoods
  tickets 186, 188
environmental issues 213
Espace Dalí 61
etiquette 130
events 4-17, 31, see also
  individual events

F

family travel, see children, travel
  with
fashion shows 31
ferry travel 237
festivals 4-17, 31, see also
  individual festivals
Fête des Tuileries 13
films 192, 228
  festivals 8, 13
fire services 230
flea markets 157

Fontaine des Médici 71
food 28, 117-41, **119**, see also
  individual neighbourhoods
  bakeries 121
  bistros 120
  budgeting 118
  cheese 137
  children, travel with 32-3
  chocolate 150
  cooking courses 96-7
  etiquette 130
  festivals 10, 14
  language 119, 132, 238
  macarons 124
  markets 82-3
  meal types 127
  neobistros 120
  shopping 147
  tipping 118
  tours 96-7, 123
  traditional French 120
  wine-bar dining 120
football 198
forests 200-1
Forum des Halles 77
free attractions 31
French language 238
French Open 10
French Revolution 216

G

Galerie de Minéralogie et de
  Géologie 107
Galerie des Enfants 107-8
Galerie Itinerrance 113
Galeries d'Anatomie Comparée
  et de Paléontologie 107
Galeries du Panthéon
  Bouddhique 41
Galeries Lafayette 148
gardens, see individual gardens
Gare du Nord 235
gay travellers 230-1
graffiti 112-13, 226

Grand Paris (Greater Paris)
  redevelopment project 212-13
Grande Galerie de l'Évolution
  107
Grands Boulevards
  drinking 168-70
  entertainment 188
  food 123, 125
  nightlife 168-70
  shopping 148-9

H

Haussmann, Baron 221
health 231
hip-hop music 30
history 214-18
holidays 232
Hôtel des Invalides 104-5
Hôtel Matignon 67

I

ice skating 16
Île aux Cygnes 199
Île de la Cité, see Islands, the
inline skating 198-9
Institut du Monde Arabe 109
Institut Français de la Mode 109
insurance 231
internet access 207, 231
internet resources 18
  accommodation 205
  nightlife 178
Islands, the **250**
  drinking 180
  food 134-5
  nightlife 180
  shopping 154-5
itineraries 20-7

J

Jardin d'Acclimatation 32
Jardin des Plantes 106-9
Jardin des Tuileries 90-1

Jardin du Carrousel 91
Jardin du Luxembourg 68-71
Jardin du Palais Royal 101
jazz music 11, 14, 187, 227
Jeu de Paume 90-1

L

language 238
  drinking & nightlife 165
  food 119, 132
  shopping 144
Latin Quarter **252**
  drinking 180-1
  entertainment 193
  food 136-8
  nightlife 180-1
  shopping 155-6
Le Cordon Bleu 96
Le Grand Musée du Parfum 91
Le Marais **254-5**
  drinking 176-9
  entertainment 191-2
  food 130-2
  nightlife 176-9
  shopping 151-3
Les Catacombes 94-5
Les Halles **250**
  drinking 170-1, 173
  entertainment 188-9
  food 125-7
  nightlife 170-1, 173
  shopping 149, 151
Les Invalides **246-7**
  drinking 181-3
  entertainment 193
  food 138-41
  nightlife 181-3
  shopping 156-61
lesbian travellers 230-1
literature 31, 226-7
Louvre 52-7, **56-7**

Louvre area **250**
  drinking 170-1, 173
  entertainment 188-9
  food 125-7
  nightlife 170-1, 173
  shopping 149, 151

M

macarons 124
Macron, Emmanuel 218
Maison et Jardins de Claude Monet 98-9
Marché Bastille 82-3
Marché Beauvau 83
Marché Biologique des Batignolles 83
Marché d'Aligre 83
Marché des Enfants Rouges 115
Marché Edgar Quinet 83
Marché Raspail 83
markets 16, 82-3, 157, *see also individual markets*
measures 231
medical services 231
Ménagerie du Jardin des Plantes 108
Ménilmontant **254-5**
  drinking 176-9
  entertainment 191-2
  food 130-2
  nightlife 176-9
  shopping 151-3
metro travel 235-6
metro-station art 225
mobile phones 232
Mona Lisa 55
money 18, 230, 231, 234
Montmartre **249**
  drinking 173-5
  entertainment 189-91
  food 127-30
  nightlife 173-5
  shopping 151

Montparnasse **246-7**
  drinking 183
  food 141
  nightlife 183
Mosquée de Paris 108-9
motorcycle travel 237
Moulin Blute Fin 61
Moulin Radet 61
Moulin Rouge 190
Musée d'Art et d'Histoire du Judaïsme 115
Musée de la Marine 40
Musée de la Sculpture en Plein Air 109
Musée de l'Armée 104
Musée de l'Homme 40
Musée de l'Orangerie 90
Musée de Montmartre 61
Musée des Plans-Reliefs 105
Musée d'Orsay 62-5
Musée du Luxembourg 71
Musée du Quai Branly 40
Musée Guimet des Arts Asiatiques 41
Musée Marmottan Monet 99
Musée Maxim's 91
Musée National d'Art Moderne 75
Musée National du Moyen Âge 88-9
Musée National Picasso 114-15
Musée Rodin 66-7
Muséum National d'Histoire Naturelle 107-8
museums 31, *see also individual museums*
music 31, 227-8
  festivals 8, 11, 13, 14, 15, 16

N

nightclubs 30, 166, 178, *see also* drinking & nightlife
nightlife, *see* drinking & nightlife

northern Paris
  drinking 173-5
  entertainment 189-91
  food 127-30
  nightlife 173-5
  shopping 151
Notre Dame 46-51, **50-1**
Nuit Blanche 15

O

opening hours 145, 164, 231-2

P

painting 223-6
Palais de Chaillot 40
Palais de Justice 93
Palais de Tokyo 41
Palais du Luxembourg 71
Palais Garnier 100-1
Palais Royal 101
Panthéon 89
Parc de la Villette 199
Parc des Buttes Chaumont 200
Parc des Princes 198
Parc du Champ de Mars 40
Parc Floral de Paris 201
Parc Montsouris 199-200
Parc Zoologique de Paris 200-1
Paris Cocktail Week 6
Paris Plages 12
parks 199-200, *see also individual parks*
Passage du Perron 101
passages couverts 110-11, **110-11**
Pavillon de l'Arsenal 115
Père Lachaise cemetery 78-81, **80-1**
perfume 30, 91, 150
Petit, Philippe 40
pharmacies 231
photography 28
Picasso, Pablo 114-15
place de la Madeleine 149
Place du Tertre 60-1

place Igor Stravinsky 77
planning
  budgeting 18, 31, 118, 165, 204, 207, 230, 234
  calendar of events 4-17
  children, travel with 32-3
  itineraries 20-7
  repeat visitors 30
Point Zéro des Routes de France 49
police 230
politics 217, 218
pollution 213
population 212-13
Promenade Plantée 199
public holidays 232
puppetry 71
Pyramide Inversée 55

R

river cruises 72-3
Rock en Seine 13

S

Sacré-Cœur 58-61
safety 232
Sainte-Chapelle 92-3
Salle des Gens d'Armes 93
Seine 72-3, 102-3, **102-3**
senior travellers 230
Shakespeare & Company 155
shopping 30, 143-61, **145**, *see also individual neighbourhoods*
  accessories 146
  bouquinistes 156
  children, shops for 146
  concept stores 147
  fashion 146
  food 147
  language 144, 238
  markets 16, 157, 82-3
  opening hours 145
  sales 145

souvenirs 150
vintage fashion 161
Sidecar cocktail 172
skating 198-9
smoking 207, 231
soccer 198
southern Paris 141, 183
souvenirs 150
sports 195-201, *see also individual sports*
Square du Vert-Galant 200
Stade de France 198
Stade Roland Garros 198
Statue of Liberty 96
St-Germain **246-7**
  drinking 181-3
  entertainment 193
  food 138-41
  nightlife 181-3
  shopping 156-61
street art 30, 112-13, 226
swimming 198, 199

T

Taste of Paris 10
taxis 237
tearooms 167, 175
telephone services 232
tennis 198
terrorist attacks 218
Théâtre du Luxembourg 71
theft 232
time 232
tipping 118, 165, 204
toilets 232
Tomb of the Unknown Soldier 44
Tombeau de Napoléon 1er 105
Tour de France 12
tourist information 232
tours
  cycling 201
  food 96-7, 123
  river cruises 72-3

tours *continued*
  walking 80-1, 102-3, 110-11, 201, **80-1**, **102-3**, **110-11**
  wine 97
train travel 235-6
travel passes 234
travel to/from Paris 233-5
travel within Paris 19, 235-7

V

Versailles 84-7, **86-7**
visas 233

W

walking tours 80-1, 102-3, 110-11, 201, **80-1**, **102-3**, **110-11**
Wall for Peace Memorial 40
weather 19
websites, *see* internet resources
weights 231
western Paris **246-7**
  drinking 168
  entertainment 188
  food 122-3

  nightlife 168
  sights 40-1
wi-fi 207, 231
wine 169
  tasting courses 97
wine bars 120, 166
WWII 217

River boat passing Notre Dame (p46)

MATT MUNRO/LONELY PLANET ©

Paris Maps

Champs-Élysées, St-Germain, Les Invalides & Montparnasse 246

Montmartre 249

Les Halles & Île de la Cité 250

Latin Quarter 252

Le Marais, Bastille & Eastern Paris 254

Champs-Élysées, St-Germain, Les Invalides & Montparnasse

Palais Garnier

Jardin des Tuileries

Musée d'Orsay

Musée Rodin

Hôtel des Invalides

Arc de Triomphe

Eiffel Tower

FAUBOURG ST-GERMAIN

See Les Halles & Île de la
Cité Map (p250)

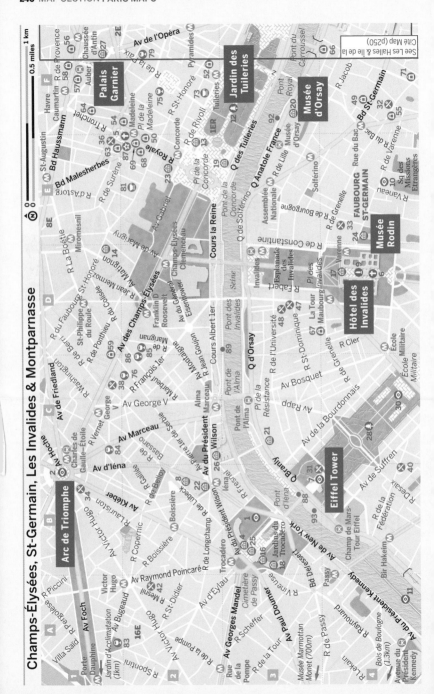

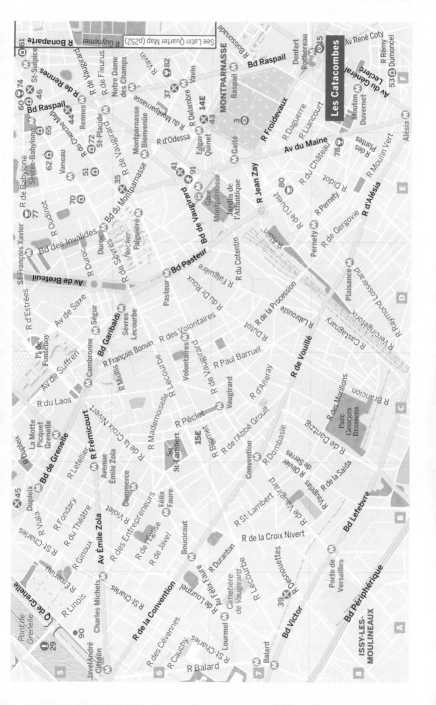

Les Catacombes

MONTPARNASSE

14E

15E

ISSY-LES-MOULINEAUX

Champs-Élysées, St-Germain, Les Invalides & Montparnasse

◎ Sights

1 Aquarium de Paris Cinéaqua B3
2 Arc de Triomphe B1
3 Cimetière du Montparnasse F7
4 Cité de l'Architecture et du
   Patrimoine B3
5 Église de la Madeleine E2
6 Église du Dôme D4
7 Eiffel Tower..B3
   Galerie des Galeries.........................(see 56)
8 Galeries du Panthéon
   Bouddhique B2
9 Hôtel des Invalides D4
10 Hôtel Matignon...E4
11 Île aux Cygnes A4
12 Jardin des Tuileries F3
13 Jeu de Paume E2
14 Le Grand Musée du Parfum D1
15 Les Catacombes...F8
16 Musée de la Marine....................................B3
17 Musée de l'Armée.......................................D4
18 Musée de l'Homme.....................................B3
19 Musée de l'Orangerie E3
20 Musée d'Orsay F3
21 Musée du Quai Branly C3
22 Musée Guimet des Arts
   Asiatiques..B2
23 Musée Maxim's E2
24 Musée Rodin...E4
25 Palais de Chaillot..B3
26 Palais de Tokyo C2
27 Palais Garnier..F1
28 Parc du Champ de Mars C4
29 Statue of Liberty Replica A5
30 Wall for Peace Memorial..........................C4

✗ Eating

31 58 Tour Eiffel B3
32 À la Petite Chaise.......................................F4
33 Besnier E4
34 Bustronome B1
35 Chez Dumonet E6
36 Crabe Royal E1
37 La Rotonde Montparnasse........................F6
38 Ladurée C1
   Lafayette Gourmet ....(see 57)
39 Le Beurre Noisette A7
40 Le Casse Noix...B4
41 Le Ciel de Paris...E6
   Le Jules Verne ....(see 31)
42 Le Petit Rétro..A2
43 Marché Edgar Quinet.................................F6
44 Marché Raspail...F5
45 Poilâne..B5
46 Poilâne...F5
47 Restaurant David Toutain.........................D3
   Restaurant Musée
   d'Orsay ....(see 20)
   Steak Point ....(see 57)
48 Tomy & Co D3

◎ Shopping

49 Alexandra Sojfer...F4
50 Boutique Maille E2
51 Chercheminippes..E5
52 Colette F2
53 Comptoir des Catacombes......................F8
54 Fauchon..F2
55 Fermob..F4
56 Galeries Lafayette..................................... F1
57 Galeries Lafayette – Home &
   Gourmet F1
58 Galeries Lafayette – Men's Store F1
   Galeries Lafayette Fashion
   Show ....(see 56)
59 Guerlain...D1
60 Hermès...F5
61 JB Guanti F5
62 La Grande Épicerie de Paris E5
63 La Maison de la Truffe E1
64 La Maison du Miel F1
65 Le Bon Marché F5
66 Magasin Sennelier......................................F4
67 Mayaro...D3
68 Patrick Roger E2
69 Place de la Madeleine E2
70 Quatrehomme E5
71 Sabbia Rosa F4
72 Smallable Concept Store..........................E5

◎ Drinking & Nightlife

73 Angelina...F2
74 Au Sauvignon...F5
75 Bar Hemingway F2
76 Blaine C2
77 Coutume...E5
78 Félicie E8
79 Harry's New York Bar F2
80 Hexagone Café E7
81 Honor E2
82 La Quincave F6
83 St James Paris...A1
84 Upper Crèmerie..C1
85 Wine by One..D2
   Yoyo ....(see 26)
86 Zig Zag Club C2

◎ Entertainment

87 Kiosque Théâtre Madeleine E2
   Palais Garnier.....................................(see 27)
   Palais Garnier Box Office ....(see 27)
   Théâtre National de Chaillot..............(see 4)

◎ Activities, Courses & Tours

88 Bateaux Parisiens B3
89 Bateaux-Mouches.......................................D3
90 Le Cordon Bleu A5
91 Pari Roller E6
92 Paris Canal Croisières...............................F3
93 Vedettes de Paris B3

Montmartre

N 0 ——— 250 m
0 ——— 0.1 miles

La REcyclerie
(1km)

Basilique du
Sacré-Cœur

MONTMARTRE

PIGALLE

⊚ Sights
1 Basilique du Sacré-Cœur	C2
2 Brasserie la Goutte d'Or	D2
3 Clos Montmartre	B1
4 Espace Dalí	B2
5 Moulin Blute Fin	A1
6 Moulin Radet	B1
7 Musée de Montmartre	B1
8 Place du Tertre	B2

⊗ Eating
9 Le Bistrot de la Galette	B2
10 Le Miroir	B2
11 Le Pantruche	B3
12 L'Été en Pente Douce	C2
13 Mesdemoiselles Madeleines	B3

⊙ Shopping
14 Belle du Jour	B2
15 Pigalle	B3
16 Spree	B2

⊙ Drinking & Nightlife
17 Au P'tit Douai	A2
18 Café des Deux Moulins	A2
19 La Fourmi	B3
La Machine du Moulin Rouge	(see 24)
20 Le Progrès	B2
21 Le Très Particulier	A1
22 Lulu White	B3

⊙ Entertainment
23 Le Divan du Monde	B3
24 Moulin Rouge	A2

Les Halles & Île de la Cité

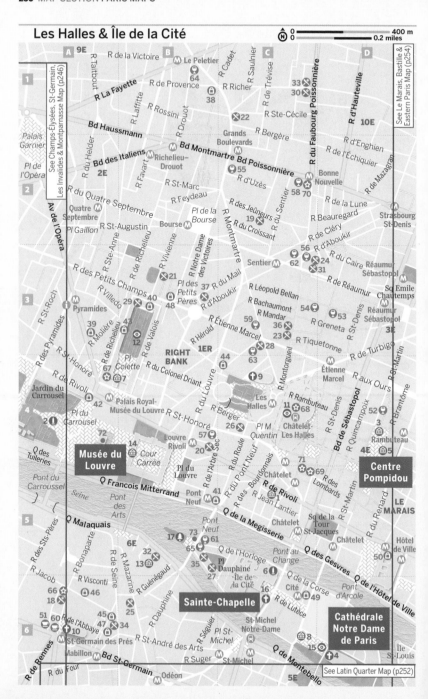

See Champs-Élysées, St-Germain, Les Invalides & Montparnasse Map (p246)

See Le Marais, Bastille & Eastern Paris Map (p254)

See Latin Quarter Map (p252)

Les Halles & Île de la Cité

◉ Sights

1	59 Rivoli	C5
2	Arc de Triomphe du Carrousel	A4
3	Atelier Brancusi	D4
4	Cathédrale Notre Dame de Paris	D6
5	Centre Pompidou	D4
6	Conciergerie	C5
7	Conseil d'État	A4
8	Crypte Archéologique	C6
9	Église St-Eustache	C4
10	Église St-Germain des Prés	A6
11	Forum des Halles	C4
12	Jardin du Palais Royal	B3
13	Monnaie de Paris	B5
14	Musée du Louvre	B4
15	Point Zéro des Routes de France	D6
16	Sainte-Chapelle	C6
17	Square du Vert-Galant	B5

⊗ Eating

18	Au Pied de Fouet	A6
19	Bambou	C2
20	Chez La Vieille	B4
21	Da Roco	B3
22	Floquifil	C1
23	Fou de Pâtisserie	C3
	Freddy's	(see 34)
24	Frenchie	C3
	Frenchie Bar à Vins	(see 24)
	Frenchie to Go	(see 24)
25	Goût de Brioche	B6
26	La Tour de Montlhéry – Chez Denise	C4
27	Le Caveau du Palais	B5
28	Le Cochon à l'Oreille	C3
29	Le Grand Véfour	B3
30	L'Office	C1
31	Miss Kale	C3
32	Restaurant Guy Savoy	B5
33	Richer	C1
34	Semilla	A6
35	Sequana	B5
36	Stohrer	C3
37	Tradi	B3

ⓐ Shopping

38	À la Mère de Famille	B1
39	Antoine	A3
40	Boîtes à Musique Anna Joliet	B3
41	Bouquinistes	B5
42	Carrousel du Louvre	A4
43	Didier Ludot	B3
44	E Dehillerin	C4
45	Finger in the Nose	A6
46	Gab & Jo	A6
47	La Dernière Goutte	A6
	Le Chocolat Alain Ducasse	(see 51)
48	Legrand Filles & Fils	B3
49	Marché aux Fleurs Reine Elizabeth II	C6
	Marché aux Oiseaux	(see 49)
50	Paris Rendez-Vous	D5

⊚ Drinking & Nightlife

51	Café de Flore	A6
52	Café La Fusée	D4
53	Club Rayé	D3
54	Experimental Cocktail Club	C3
55	Frog & Underground	C2
56	Hoppy Corner	C3
	Le Bar du Caveau	(see 27)
57	Le Garde Robe	B4
58	Le Rex Club	C2
59	Le Tambour	C3
60	Les Deux Magots	A6
61	Les Jardins du Pont-Neuf	B5
62	Lockwood	C3
63	Ô Chateau	C3
64	PanPan	B1
65	Taverne Henri IV	B5

⊛ Entertainment

66	Chez Papa	A6
67	Comédie Française	A4
	Forum des Images	(see 11)
68	La Place	C4
69	Le Baiser Salé	C5
70	Le Grand Rex	C2
71	Sunset & Sunside	C5

⊕ Activities, Courses & Tours

72	Louvre Guided Tours	A4
73	Vedettes du Pont Neuf	B5

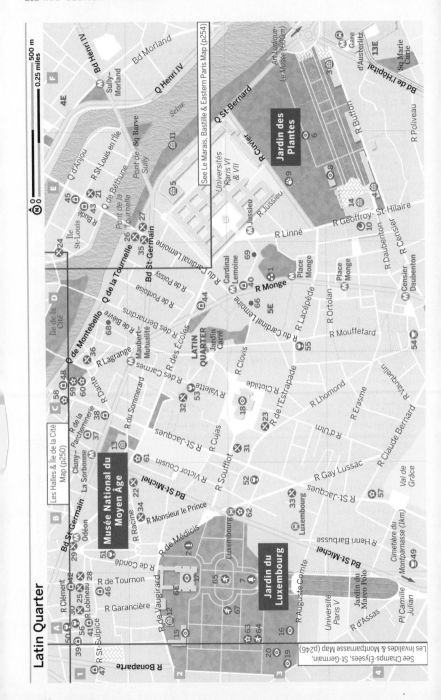

Latin Quarter

See Le Marais, Bastille & Eastern Paris Map (p254)

Les Halles & Île de la Cité Map (p250)

Musée National du Moyen Âge

Jardin des Plantes

Jardin du Luxembourg

LATIN QUARTER

See Champs-Élysées, St-Germain, Les Invalides & Montparnasse Map (p246)

500 m
0.25 miles

Latin Quarter

◎ Sights

1 Arènes de Lutèce...D3
2 Fontaine des Médici....................................B2
3 Galerie d'Anatomie Comparée et
   de Paléontologie......................................F4
4 Galerie de Minéralogie et de
   Géologie..E4
   Galerie des Enfants........................(see 14)
   Grande Galerie de l'Évolution..........(see 14)
5 Institut du Monde Arabe............................E2
6 Jardin des Plantes.....................................E3
7 Jardin du Luxembourg...............................A3
8 Les Grandes Serres...................................E4
9 Ménagerie du Jardin des Plantes.............E3
10 Mosquée de Paris.....................................E4
11 Musée de la Sculpture en Plein
   Air..E2
12 Musée du Luxembourg.............................A2
13 Musée National du Moyen Âge.................C1
14 Muséum National d'Histoire
   Naturelle...E4
15 Orangery...A2
16 Orchards...A3
17 Palais du Luxembourg..............................A2
18 Panthéon...C3
19 Pavillon Davioud......................................A3
20 Rucher du Luxembourg............................A3

⊗ Eating
   Bar à Vins AT.....................................(see 35)
21 Berthillon...E1
22 Bouillon Racine..B2
23 Café de la Nouvelle Mairie........................C3
24 Café Saint Régis.......................................D1
25 Gérard Mulot..A1
26 La Rôtisserie..E2
27 La Tour d'Argent.......................................E2
28 L'Amaryllis de Gérard Mulot.....................A1
   L'Avant Comptoir.............................(see 29)
29 L'Avant Comptoir de la Mer......................B1
30 L'Avant Comptoir du Marché.....................A1
31 Le Comptoir du Panthéon.........................C3
   Le Comptoir du Relais.......................(see 29)
32 Le Coupe-Chou...C2
33 Les Papilles...B3
   Mosquée de Paris.............................(see 10)
34 Polidor..B2
35 Restaurant AT..E2

   Shakespeare & Company Café.......(see 48)
36 Sola...C1

ⓐ Shopping
37 Abbey Bookshop.......................................C1
38 Album..C1
39 Au Plat d'Étain...A1
40 Bières Cultes...D3
41 Catherine B..A1
42 Cire Trudon..A1
43 Clair de Rêve..E1
44 Le Bonbon au Palais................................D2
   Les Comptoirs de La Tour
   d'Argent..(see 27)
45 L'Îles aux Images.....................................E1
46 Marie Mercié..A1
47 Pierre Hermé..A1
48 Shakespeare & Company..........................C1

◉ Drinking & Nightlife
49 Caffé Juno...B4
50 Frog & Princess..A1
51 Le 10...B1
52 Le Crocodile...B3
53 Le Pub St-Hilaire......................................C2
54 Le Verre à Pied..D4
55 Little Bastards...D3
   Mosquée de Paris.............................(see 10)
56 Tiger Bar...A1

⊕ Entertainment
57 Café Universel..B4
58 Caveau de la Huchette..............................C1
59 Église St-Julien le Pauvre.........................C1
60 Le Caveau des Oubliettes.........................C1
61 Le Champo...C2
62 Le Petit Journal St-Michel.........................B3
63 Théâtre du Luxembourg............................A3

◉ Activities, Courses & Tours
64 Children's Playgrounds.............................A3
65 Grand Bassin Toy Sailboats......................A2
   Hammam de la Mosquée de
   Paris..(see 10)
66 Le Foodist...D3
67 Pony Rides...A2
68 Set in Paris..D1
69 Wine Tasting in Paris................................D3

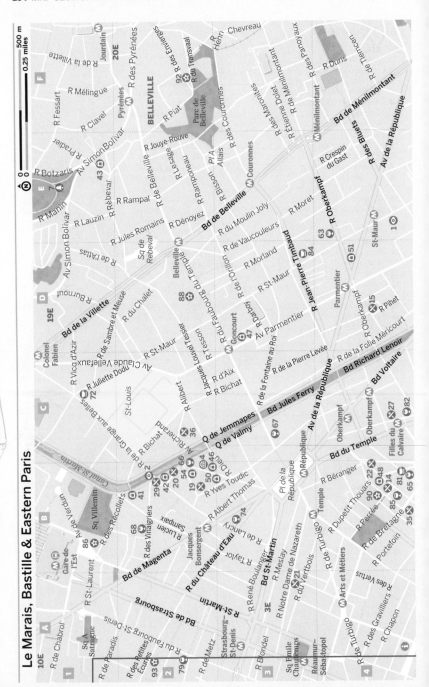

Le Marais, Bastille & Eastern Paris

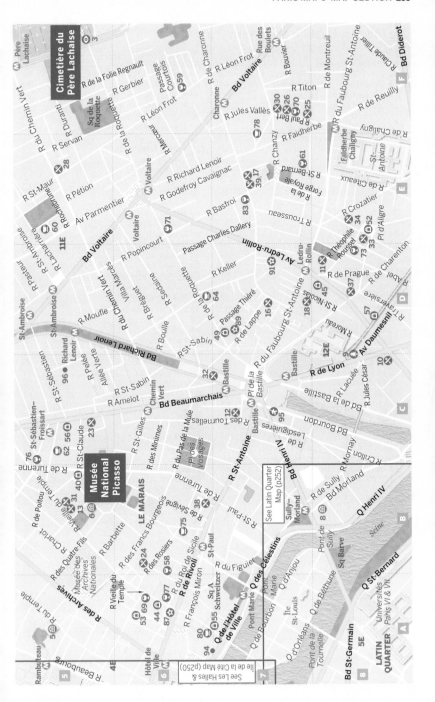

Le Marais, Bastille & Eastern Paris

◉ Sights
1 Brasserie BapBap E4
2 Canal St-Martin B2
3 Cimetière du Père Lachaise F5
4 Espace Beaurepaire B2
5 Musée d'Art et d'Histoire du
    Judaïsme A5
6 Musée National Picasso B5
7 Parc des Buttes Chaumont E1
8 Pavillon de l'Arsenal B8
9 Promenade Plantée C8

✦ Eating
10 À la Biche au Bois C8
11 Blé Sucré D8
12 Brasserie Bofinger C7
13 Breizh Café B5
14 Café Pinson B4
15 Chambelland D4
16 Chez Paul D7
17 Clamato E7
18 Dersou D7
19 Du Pain et des Idées B2
20 Fric-Frac B2
21 Istr A3
22 Jacques Genin B4
   La Cantine de Merci .... (see 56)
23 La Maison Plisson C5
24 L'As du Fallafel B6
25 Le 6 Paul Bert F7
26 Le Bistrot Paul Bert F7
27 Le Clown Bar C4
28 Le Servan E5
29 Le Verre Volé B2
30 L'Écailler du Bistrot F7
31 L'Epicerie du Breizh Café B5
32 Marché Bastille C7
33 Marché Beauvau E8
34 Marché d'Aligre E8
35 Marché des Enfants Rouges B4
36 Matière à C2
37 Passerini D8
38 Rainettes B6
39 Septime E7

⊕ Shopping
40 Andrea Crews B5
41 Antoine et Lili B2
42 Artazart B2
43 Belleville Brûlerie E1
44 Edwart A6
45 Fermob D8
46 Frivoli B2
47 Fromagerie Goncourt D3
48 La Boutique Extraordinaire B4
49 La Manufacture de Chocolat D7

50 Liza Korn B2
51 Made by Moi D4
52 Marché aux Puces d'Aligre E8
53 Mariage Frères A6
54 Medecine Douce B2
55 Mélodies Graphiques A7
56 Merci C5
57 Viaduc des Arts D8

◉ Drinking & Nightlife
58 3w Kafé B6
59 A La Française F6
60 Beans on Fire E5
61 Bluebird E7
62 Boot Café C5
63 Café Charbon E4
64 Café des Anges D6
65 Candelaria B4
66 Chez Prune B2
67 Gibus Club C3
68 Gravity Bar B2
69 La Belle Hortense A6
70 La Cave Paul Bert F7
71 La Fée Verte E6
72 La Fontaine de Belleville C1
73 Le Baron Rouge D8
74 Le Coq B3
75 Le Loir dans La Théière B6
76 Le Mary Céleste C5
77 Le Pick-Clops A6
78 Le Pure Café F7
79 Le Syndicat A2
80 L'Ebouillanté A6
81 Ob-La-Di B4
82 PasDeLoup C4
83 Septime La Cave E7
84 The Hood D3
85 Wild & the Moon B4

◉ Entertainment
86 Café A B1
87 Cave du 38 Riv' A6
88 La Java D2
89 Le Balajo D7
90 Le Carreau du Temple B4
91 Le Motel D7
92 Le Vieux Belleville F2
93 New Morning A2
   Nouveau Casino .... (see 63)

◉ Activities, Courses & Tours
94 La Cuisine Paris A6
95 Nomadeshop C7
96 Paris à Vélo, C'est Sympa! C5
   Rollers & Coquillages .... (see 95)

Symbols & Map Key

Look for these symbols to quickly identify listings:

◉ Sights

⊗ Eating

❸ Activities

⊖ Drinking

❺ Courses

✪ Entertainment

◉ Tours

🔒 Shopping

✪ Festivals & Events

ℹ Information & Transport

These symbols and abbreviations give vital information for each listing:

🌱 Sustainable or green recommendation

FREE No payment required

☏ Telephone number

☺ Opening hours

P Parking

☺ Nonsmoking

❄ Air-conditioning

@ Internet access

📶 Wi-fi access

🏊 Swimming pool

🚌 Bus

⛴ Ferry

🚊 Tram

🚃 Train

📖 English-language menu

🥗 Vegetarian selection

👪 Family-friendly

Find your best experiences with these Great For... icons.

🖼 Art & Culture

📖 History

🏖 Beaches

💬 Local Life

💳 Budget

🐦 Nature & Wildlife

☕ Cafe/Coffee

📷 Photo Op

🚲 Cycling

🔭 Scenery

↱ Detour

🛍 Shopping

🍸 Drinking

📼 Entertainment

🚕 Short Trip

✨ Events

🏀 Sport

👨‍👩‍👧 Family Travel

🚶 Walking

🍽 Food & Drink

❄ Winter Travel

Sights

🏖 Beach
🐦 Bird Sanctuary
☸ Buddhist
🏰 Castle/Palace
✝ Christian
☯ Confucian
🕉 Hindu
☪ Islamic
🕉 Jain
✡ Jewish
🗿 Monument
🏛 Museum/Gallery/ Historic Building
🏚 Ruin
⛩ Shinto
🪯 Sikh
☯ Taoist
🍷 Winery/Vineyard
🦁 Zoo/Wildlife Sanctuary
◉ Other Sight

Points of Interest

🏄 Bodysurfing
🏕 Camping
☕ Cafe
🛶 Canoeing/Kayaking
● Course/Tour
🤿 Diving
🍸 Drinking & Nightlife
🍴 Eating
🎭 Entertainment
♨ Sento Hot Baths/ Onsen
🛍 Shopping
🎿 Skiing
🛏 Sleeping
🤿 Snorkelling
🏄 Surfing
🏊 Swimming/Pool
🚶 Walking
🏄 Windsurfing
❸ Other Activity

Information

🏦 Bank
🏛 Embassy/Consulate
➕ Hospital/Medical
@ Internet
👮 Police
✉ Post Office
☎ Telephone
🚻 Toilet
ℹ Tourist Information
● Other Information

Geographic

🏖 Beach
⊶ Gate
🛖 Hut/Shelter
🗼 Lighthouse
🔭 Lookout
▲ Mountain/Volcano
🌴 Oasis
🛝 Park
)(Pass
🧺 Picnic Area
💧 Waterfall

Transport

✈ Airport
Ⓑ BART station
⊗ Border crossing
Ⓣ Boston T station
🚌 Bus
↔🚡↔ Cable car/Funicular
─🚴─ Cycling
─⛴─ Ferry
Ⓜ Metro/MRT station
═🚝═ Monorail
P Parking
⛽ Petrol station
Ⓢ Subway/S-Bahn/ Skytrain station
🚕 Taxi
↔🚉↔ Train station/Railway
╍╍╍ Tram
⊖ Tube Station
Ⓤ Underground/ U-Bahn station
● Other Transport

Our Story

A beat-up old car, a few dollars in the pocket and a sense of adventure. In 1972 that's all Tony and Maureen Wheeler needed for the trip of a lifetime – across Europe and Asia overland to Australia. It took several months, and at the end – broke but inspired – they sat at their kitchen table writing and stapling together their first travel guide, Across Asia on the Cheap. Within a week they'd sold 1500 copies. Lonely Planet was born.

Today, Lonely Planet has offices in Franklin, London, Melbourne, Oakland, Dublin, Beijing, and Delhi, with more than 600 staff and writers. We share Tony's belief that 'a great guidebook should do three things: inform, educate and amuse'.

Our Writer

Catherine Le Nevez

Catherine's wanderlust kicked in when she road-tripped across Europe from her Parisian base aged four. She's been hitting the road at every opportunity since, travelling to around 60 countries and completing her Doctorate of Creative Arts in Writing, Masters in Professional Writing, and postgrad qualifications in Editing and Publishing along the way. Over the past dozen-plus years she's written scores of Lonely Planet guides and articles covering Paris, France, Europe and far beyond. Her work has also appeared in numerous online and print publications. Topping Catherine's list of travel tips is to travel without any expectations.

STAY IN TOUCH LONELYPLANET.COM/CONTACT

AUSTRALIA The Malt Store, Level 3, 551 Swanston St, Carlton, Victoria 3053
📞 03 8379 8000,
fax 03 8379 8111

IRELAND Unit E, Digital Court. The Digital Hub, Rainsford St, Dublin 8, Ireland

USA 124 Linden Street, Oakland, CA 94607
📞 510 250 6400,
toll free 800 275 8555,
fax 510 893 8572

UK 240 Blackfriars Road, London SE1 8NW
📞 020 3771 5100,
fax 020 3771 5101

 twitter.com/lonelyplanet

 facebook.com/lonelyplanet

 instagram.com/lonelyplanet

 youtube.com/lonelyplanet

 lonelyplanet.com/newsletter